If Americans *Really* Understood the Income Tax

IF AMERICANS *REALLY* UNDERSTOOD THE INCOME TAX

Uncovering Our Most Expensive Ignorance

John O. Fox

Westview
PRESS

A Member of the Perseus Books Group

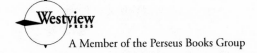

Copyright © 2004 by John O. Fox

Published in the United States of America by Westview Press, A Member of the Perseus Books Group, 5500 Central Avenue, Boulder, Colorado 80301–2877, and in the United Kingdom by Westview Press, 12 Hid's Copse Road, Cumnor Hill, Oxford OX2 9JJ.

Find us on the world wide web at www.westviewpress.com

Westview Press books are available at special discounts for bulk purchases in the United States by corporations, institutions, and other organizations. For more information, please contact the Special Markets Department at the Perseus Books Group, 11 Cambridge Center, Cambridge, MA 02142, or call (617) 252–5298, (800) 255-1514 or email specialmarkets@perseusbooks.com.

A Cataloging-in-Publication data record for this book is available from the Library of Congress.

ISBN 0-8133-4238-4

The paper used in this publication meets the requirements of the American National Standard for Permanence of Paper for Printed Library Materials Z39.48–1984.

10 9 8 7 6 5 4 3

To Gretchen, with all my love

Contents

Tables and Figures

Tables

Figures

Foreword

John Fox's superb new book is timely and essential reading as a new President and Congress deliberate which tax laws are in the country's best interest for this century.

When I served on President Kennedy's Tax Task Force and, later, as his Commissioner of the Internal Revenue Service, I became convinced that America's tax system needed major surgery. Multimillion-dollar loopholes for certain industries and classes of individuals, combined with onerously high tax rates for the great mass of taxpayers, were endangering public confidence in the entire federal tax structure. After returning to private practice, I urged Americans to send an outpouring of letters to members of Congress to end its ongoing destructive policy of legislating special tax privileges.

That outpouring never occurred. While tax rates have fallen considerably, too many of the underlying laws have become increasingly complex and worse—much worse. Because of this trend, I think it vitally important to the health and strength of this nation that people across the land read Fox's book. They will learn why Congress must greatly simplify the laws, eliminating all but the most compelling tax-relief provisions, and simultaneously reduce tax rates for everyone. They will be surprised to discover, as Fox ably demonstrates in an entire chapter devoted to the subject, that reforms along these lines in fact advance the fundamental beliefs of both conservatives and liberals alike.

Two myths sustain most relief or so-called incentive provisions—that they make the laws "fairer" or "promote economic growth." No one has written more persuasively than Fox why this rarely is true and why most taxpayers would be best served by a far simpler, broad-based, lower rate system guided by a single principle: People with equal dollar ability to pay taxes should pay the same amount, and people with greater dollar ability to pay should pay more. According to this principle, two married couples, each with two children and the same income, generally would expect to pay the same taxes, regardless of who their employers might be, the sources of their income, or how they spend that income. Yet Fox enumerates well over 100 special laws that allow one such couple to pay less, and often far less. In fact, nothing in our tax laws assures that if the Joneses have considerably more income than the Smiths, the Joneses will pay considerably more. Indeed, they may pay less.

With great clarity, Fox explains why simpler, more equitable laws would actually be more conducive to economic growth. They also would stunningly demonstrate to the nation Congress's willingness to focus and act more pointedly on the basis of principle rather than politics, which surely would earn our greater trust and enhance more accurate reporting on tax returns.

In sum, Fox argues convincingly that reforming the tax laws does not require adopting a flat tax or a consumption tax, but that it does require Congress to (1) eliminate or restrict most special deductions, exclusions, and deferrals, and thereby curb excessive manipulations of the tax laws to promote discrete social and economic objectives, (2) retain only essential tax credits, making them more selective and efficient, (3) lower all progressive rates across the board, and (4) cease sidestepping budgetary constraints through tax code "backdoor financing."

In this highly readable and straightforward book, Fox gives the public at-large—and tax experts as well—valuable tools to better understand the competing forces at work in legislating tax policy. With these tools at hand, ordinary citizens, by exercising their collective voices, might well be heard by Congress and the White House alike.

Mortimer M. Caplin
Former U.S. Commissioner of Internal Revenue (1961–1964)
Senior Member, Caplin & Drysdale, Washington, D.C.
Professor Emeritus, University of Virginia School of Law

Preface

Democracy is a difficult kind of government. It requires the highest quali-
ties of self-discipline, restraint, a willingness to make commitments and
sacrifices for the general interest, and also it requires knowledge.
                                                            —John F. Kennedy

The individual income tax, the principal source of federal revenue for the last
half of the twentieth century and long viewed as worthy of public support,
has become something of a monster: unimaginably complicated, frequently
unfair, and an excessive drag on the economy. Widespread agreement exists
at almost every level of our society that changes should be made. Indeed, a
central issue for our nation is whether to abandon the federal individual income tax and replace it with a consumption tax, such as a so-called flat tax.
Missing from public discourse, however, and desperately needed if we are to
make informed judgments about the future direction of tax policy, is a clear
explanation of what has gone wrong and what reforms of the income tax
could be made.

I have written this book to help Americans understand the issues and the
alternatives. For example, the choice between an income tax and a flat tax is
not over the size of government revenues; Congress always can modify the
income tax to produce the same amount of revenue that it would want from
a flat tax. Nor is the choice between a simple flat tax, which can allow tax returns to fit on a postcard, and our current income tax, which often requires a
tax return of many pages and attachments. The income tax can be enormously simplified. Flat tax proposals typically eliminate itemized deductions
such as for home-mortgage interest, state and local income taxes, property
taxes, and charitable contributions; and they disallow deductions by employers for the payment of fringe benefits such as employees' health insurance
premiums. The income tax could be reformed in these ways and also could
be rid of many other special provisions that hugely complicate the tax laws.
Yes, income tax returns could be greatly simplified and shortened; many
could fit on a postcard. Were Congress inclined this way, it also could substantially lower progressive tax rates for everyone without sacrificing tax rev-

enue; alternatively, Congress could adopt a single, flat rate for the income tax if the public preferred.

Those who wish to replace the income tax with a flat tax argue that Congress never would have the courage to make the income tax relatively simple. They may be right. If so, we would be naive to believe that the same Congress would enact a pure, simple flat tax. To the contrary, Congress would be subjected to enormous political pressures—from the real estate industry, charitable organizations, the health-insurance industry, and countless other organizations as well as millions of individual taxpayers—to create special exceptions. As explained in Chapter 13, hopes for a simple alternative to the income tax quickly could vanish, along with hopes for a low, flat tax rate.

Whereas this book explores at great length different viewpoints about tax policy and the alternatives, it also reflects my point of view. I favor overhauling the income tax, not discarding it, with provisions for a reasonable transition to new rules. I believe that if the public insisted, Congress could reform the income tax, consistent with basic principles of both conservatives and liberals, to make the tax reasonably fair, far simpler, and far more supportive of economic growth. The reforms would allow Congress to lower all tax rates substantially without sacrificing tax revenues. Unlike principal flat tax proposals, however, I would not eliminate all taxes on capital gains, dividends, interest, and other passive income; such blanket exemptions would overly reward the rich and are unnecessary to sustain economic growth. The reforms I propose would make it far more likely that households with equal abilities to pay would pay equally and that households with greater abilities to pay would pay appropriately more.

I also recognize that the public, and Congress, may not be prepared for the overhaul that I believe would work best. Throughout this book, readers will learn about partial measures that would advance goals of a fairer, simpler, and economically sounder system.

My recommendations follow from the observation, shared by so many Americans, that Congress's decisions over many decades to offer vast patchworks of rewards for using our income as Congress deems worthy, and of penalties if we do not, too often have failed to advance tax justice or promote a stronger economy. Indeed, Congress has ignored the root explanation for the public's contempt for our income tax laws: The laws lack any overriding, sensible principles that most taxpayers can recognize and accept. Consequently, income tax laws encourage us to believe that Congress does little more than play a game of political favorites, a game that Americans increasingly distrust.

With good reason. Although we pay what is called an income tax, one special rule after another, favoring one taxpayer over another, carves out so many holes in the system that as critics have noted, the system looks like Swiss cheese. Inevitably, such a system taxes Americans very inconsistently.

Depending on the source of our income, how we receive it, and how we spend it, we may be taxed on much more or much less than our neighbor, even if our income and household size are comparable.

Collectively, these special provisions heavily affect tax rates. When so much income is protected from tax, Congress must impose much higher tax rates on the remaining income in order to raise a given amount of revenue. If Congress greatly simplified the laws—if income tax laws more closely produced a *genuine tax on income*—far more income would become taxable. Then, Congress could greatly lower tax rates across the board yet collect the same amount of revenue as under the current system. These observations confront us with the central policy question: Is the complexity of the tax laws worth the price? We can answer this question only if we rigorously identify what complexity buys and at what cost.

The answers, as this book discusses, are profoundly disturbing. Although necessary at times to promote fairness or to resolve difficult technical problems, complexity in the income tax laws typically cannot be justified on either ground. Equally disturbing is our government's twofold historic reluctance to identify and publicize who among us benefits most from the special tax laws and to quantify the revenue, economic, and social outcomes. As a result, few people, including politicians, understand the consequences of the tax choices made by Congress. Most astonishing, few tax lawyers or accountants do.

My own ignorance did not dawn on me until the early 1980s. I had been in the private practice of law in Washington, D.C., since 1964, specializing in tax matters. I had worked hard to master the nuts and bolts of my trade, although the laws were growing exponentially and were making all practitioners uneasy about their expertise. Eventually, I discovered how little I understood about the role played by tax laws in our society. Worse, I never had thought about it much.

Apparently neither had my teachers, at least not in preparing their curriculums. In my college courses in U.S. history and political science, taxation was mentioned only anecdotally. In the law school where I received my basic law degree and took many courses in taxation, and in a second law school where I received a master's degree in taxation, we were armed with detailed knowledge of tax laws that would allow us to minimize our clients' tax payments. But I cannot recall a single class in which a professor discussed whether the provisions were good for the economy, which taxpayers benefited from various provisions of the Internal Revenue Code and by how much, whether they were deserving, what behavior was encouraged or discouraged by the tax laws and what behavior they produced, the revenue loss to the government from special tax provisions, or how much tax rates might be reduced for all taxpayers if these provisions were eliminated. We learned the relevance of one set of laws to another within the code but not their relevance to the society governed by the code. Never did we pause to imagine an ideal tax system. Yet the professors were distinguished, the schools highly regarded. With some notable exceptions, teaching taxation remains only marginally changed today.

Other tax lawyers with whom I practiced had similar experiences. We talked a great deal about how to interpret the laws and what our clients could or could not do under them. But although we took to railing against the growing and unnecessary complexity of the laws, we ignored their broader significance. We did not recognize what these laws told us about the kind of nation we were or were becoming. As I now look back, such inattention seems odd because we frequently debated other government policies.

My ignorance turned into a challenge. Over the past 20 years, I have attempted to educate myself about tax policy. Eventually, I began to educate others. After my family and I moved from Washington, D.C., to Massachusetts in 1984, I realized that college students should have the opportunity that I never had: to study comprehensively the role of taxation in our society and, in particular, to study the role played by the government's preeminent tax, the federal individual income tax.

Students should understand why, if we tax income, so much income is *un*-taxed. What good does Congress achieve by favoring one form of income over another, one form of savings over another, one form of personal expenditure over another? What harm results? Congress has littered the tax laws with behavioral incentives and relief provisions to achieve discrete social or economic objectives it deems worthy; but what do these special laws achieve—for whom and at what cost? What are the consequences for the poor, the middle class, and the rich and for the economy as a whole? Who is overtaxed? Undertaxed? Can progressive rates be justified, or should Congress adopt a single, flat rate applicable to all taxable income? How should we go about making these judgments?

Once familiar with tax concepts and data, students can recognize political rhetoric that dissembles rather than informs. They can begin to judge, as perhaps never before, what is fair and sensible independent of their or their families' income levels. Then they can test their own values against those of the tax system. By the end of such a course, they should be capable of making informed judgments about how our government could do better.

Courses in U.S. history, political science, sociology, American studies, women's studies, and minority studies rarely mention tax policy because the teachers are untrained and probably unaware of its relevance. Undergraduate economics students tend only briefly to consider tax policy, typically in a course on public finance. To me, viewing the subject as at best tangential to a college curriculum ignores that tax policies and their consequences cut across all of these disciplines, as they cut across all of American life. Mt.

Holyoke College agreed. Since 1985, I have been teaching a course there called Taxation and the Values of Democracy.

The idea of writing a book about the individual income tax emerged when I could not find a suitable one for students who were unfamiliar with the laws and policy considerations. But quickly I realized that I should write for a far broader audience, for a public at odds with the existing income tax yet uncertain about the alternatives. Thus I have written with the enormous diversity of Americans in mind. This audience ranges from the childless to parents, from the young to the elderly, from ordinary workers to CEOs. It includes, of course, law school students of taxation, who would find technical sections of the Internal Revenue Code and interpretations of them far more meaningful when evaluated in light of their social, economic, and revenue implications. I have written for teachers in various disciplines who never considered tax policy seriously but who now want balanced and systematic guidance in order to teach its relevance to their own areas of interest. And I have written for graduate students of public policy and public policy think-tank analysts who need to evaluate federal income tax policies.

My premise is that the income tax provides a lens through which we can see our nation as it actually is, distinct from what it purports or wishes to be. How we tax ourselves establishes and reflects many of our nation's values. Income taxation must be fair if our nation is to be fair. While immensely complicated, fairness at a minimum means that our tax burdens must correlate strongly with our ability to bear them. At the same time, the system must make economic sense if our nation is to be economically healthy. Finally, income tax laws, for the most part, must be understood and trusted if they are to endure effectively. By failing to satisfy all of these standards, our tax system predictably fuels widespread cynicism about our government.

Although conservatives and liberals disagree about many aspects of tax policy, I am confident that Congress could restructure the system on principles of fairness, simplicity, and economic growth that reflect far better the shared principles of conservatives and liberals. Our best bet for achieving these goals is a system that taxes income more consistently and at lower rates—a system, as I will demonstrate, that reflects more accurately the common values of our society regardless of political affiliation. Americans are entitled to demand as much.

Whether Americans will make such demands depends, in the first place, on whether our nation engages in genuine debate about tax issues in a format that informs the public. This book gives Americans the information and tools that will enable them to participate actively in that debate. I have been warned, however, that a book of this kind will interest few who are not already versed in tax policy. No matter how clearly presented, the issues, so the warning goes, are too complicated for most people to understand. Responding to similar arguments years ago, the distinguished tax lawyer and writer Louis Eisenstein suspected that the real difficulty "is that they might understand too well."[1] I am betting that Eisenstein had it right.

John O. Fox

Note

[1] *A note to readers:* To avoid the awkward reference to he/she or him/her when using the third person pronoun, I have alternated between the masculine and the feminine from chapter to chapter. I also assure you that the names of taxpayers, except such obvious names as William Gates or Donald Trump, are fictitious. Any similarity between the names used and any actual taxpayers is purely conicidental.

Acknowledgments

With the publication of my book, I have at last the opportunity to thank publicly friends, family members, and experts who have generously supported this project. Robert Repetto persuaded me over dinners in Washington to write the book; his keen mind and sophisticated understanding of economics were invaluable from beginning to end. Ellen Westbrook was an ideal editor. She taught me a great deal about writing and the technical requirements of the manuscript, provided energy and encouragement, and, without any background in tax policy or economics, asked substantive questions that only someone with her intellectual gifts could have understood needed answering. Jon Bakija, coauthor with Joel Slemrod of the excellent book *Taxing Ourselves*, commented on the entire manuscript, offering keen insights into the thinking of economists. Through the years Ed Sunderland, self-designated cheerleader, generously gave of his time to prepare tables and figures and to critique chapters and my latest ideas.

Early on, help and encouragement came from many sources: John McNulty wrote a lengthy evaluation and commendation of early chapters; Doug Amy, Gina Despres, Charles Galvin, James Repetti, Arthur Schlesinger Jr., and Philip Selznick offered useful suggestions. Walter Nicholson always made himself available to explain economic concepts, review chapters, and refine data. A number of economists reviewed particular chapters or assisted with technical matters: Gerald Auten, Leonard Berman, Daniel Feenberg, William Even, Jane Gravelle, and Robert McIntyre. Chris Pyle counseled wisely on whatever I brought before him. George Idelson and David Schimmel tested my ideas and made useful suggestions for broadening the book's audience. Eileen Keegan skillfully improved the presentation of all tables and figures and organized the entire reference list.

Many others commented on particular chapters or otherwise advanced the project, among them Daniel Beller, Nan Burroughs, Russell Christopher, Joseph Gebhardt, Martin Gilens, George Goodwin, Nina Grabill, Bradley Hensley, Oliver and Lisa Houck, Will Johnston, Robert Kaiser, John Korbel, Matthew Leighton, Nicholas Lemann, Susan Lemkin, William Levit Jr., Fred McGinness, Lewis Mainzer, Frank Mankiewicz, Bill Maynes, Rebecca Mutch, Susan Nicholson, Patricia O'Brien, Joost Polak, Peter Purdy, Pete Reider, Claire Renkin, Sam Roberson, David and Ruth Scott, Paul Serotkin, Peter Sherman, Robert Stewart, Mary Sunderland, and Robert Trezevant.

I will repeat here the usual disclaimer: I take full responsibility for the entire manuscript; any errors are my own.

Over fifty people responded to my request for a possible title for the book. Some titles were very funny; all were helpful. Several of these people deserve special mention: Reuben and Phyllis Aaronson, Robert Kaiser, Sandy Ain, Berry Silverman, Jonathan and Beth Winickoff.

At Westview, I am particularly grateful to Leo Wiegman, executive editor, whose confidence in the book led to its publication and who advised in countless ways, always with good humor. Diane Hess meticulously edited the manuscript for Westview, Kay Mariea oversaw the entire production, and Meegan Finnegan handled the marketing of the book.

I am grateful to Professor Adrian Kragen, whose courses at Boalt Hall inspired me to specialize in tax matters; to Albert Arent and Earl Colson, excellent lawyers and teachers, with whom I practiced early in my career; to my students at Mt. Holyoke College, whose questions and observations have advanced my own thinking; and to my father, whose high professional standards have inspired my work as a lawyer, teacher, and writer.

Though I recognize the obstacles to achieving the comprehensive reforms advocated in these pages, my decision to write this book was influenced in part by my belief that Americans usually make the right choices when the choices are fully explained to them. This belief is rooted in the teachings of my mother, who often reminded me that we are capable of bringing out either the best or the worst in people and whose life was devoted to bringing out the best.

The affection of my sister, Myra, and my children, Joseph and Margaret, helped me weather the difficult times.

Finally, I have been sustained throughout by Gretchen's love and humor, which she counsels should not be misconstrued to mean that she favors my writing another book.

J. O. F.

Acronyms

ACCF	American Council for Capital Formation
AGI	adjusted gross income
AMT	alternative minimum tax
CBO	Congressional Budget Office
EBRI	Employee Benefit Research Institute
EITC	earned-income tax credit
ERISA	Employment Retirement Security Act of 1974
ERTA	Economic Recovery Tax Act of 1981
FICA	Federal Insurance Contributions Act
GDP	gross domestic product
HUD	Department of Housing and Urban Development
IRA	individual retirement account
IRS	Internal Revenue Service
ITC	investment tax credit
JCT	Joint Committee on Taxation
NFIB	National Federation of Independent Business
NTL	normal income tax law
OECD	Organization for Economic Cooperation and Development
OMB	Office of Management and Budget
OTA	Office of Tax Analysis
PAC	political action committee
SEP	simplified employee pension
SSA	Social Security Administration
SSI	Supplemental Security Income
VAT	value-added tax

1

Introduction

I honor the human race. When it faces life head-on, it can almost remake itself.

—Eleanor Roosevelt

Overall Tax Trends and Comparison * Blaming the Income Tax * Concerns About the Income Tax Itself * Some Facts About Upper- and Lower-Income Taxpayers * What Is Missing from This Analysis? * The Relationship Between Untaxed Income and Tax Rates * Winners and Losers * The Economic Debate * Corporate Income Taxes * The Politics of Taxation * This Book

---

This book explains why Congress should restore the income tax to a relatively simple tax on income at low, moderately progressive rates. Were Congress to enact bold reforms, tax rates could range from 10 percent (or less) for the majority of taxpayers to under 30 percent for top taxpayers yet raise the same revenues as are raised today through much higher tax rates.

By distorting the income tax beyond recognition from one that could consistently tax people primarily by the level of their income, different congresses over the years have forced the income tax to become something it need not and could not successfully be. As our nation begins the twenty-first century, we would be best served if Congress rediscovered the advantages of a genuine tax on income. One advantage would be to achieve a highly favorable political compromise. As explained in Chapter 6, taxing income consistently and at moderately progressive tax rates would advance simultaneously the principles of conservatives and liberals far better than does the current system.

In its treatment of the income tax in the 1990s alone, Congress was like an alcoholic on a binge. Staggering in every direction, Congress vastly complicated the all-too-complicated laws, exposing some income to tax while protecting comparable income from tax. It also opened a wide and disturbing chasm between the top tax rates on income from labor and on income from **capital gains**.[1] For example, in 1993, Congress raised the top tax rate on ordinary income by 28 percent (from a rate of 31 percent to 39.6 percent), and it expanded the income tax on Social Security benefits for middle- and upper-income taxpayers. In 1997, Congress cut the top tax rate on capital gains for the highest-income taxpayers by 28 percent (from a rate of 28 percent to 20 percent, and eventually to 18 percent) and added countless special relief rules favoring one set of taxpayers over another.

We should not be surprised, therefore, to find ourselves in the midst of a brewing tax revolution. Many members of Congress, nearly all of whom voted for the 1997 legislation, along with other politicians, economists, and ordinary citizens, claim we should no longer tolerate the income tax. They favor junking it altogether, citing its inequities, complexities, and excessive drag on the nation's economy.

Their challenge cannot be ignored. It requires answers to two fundamental questions. First, can the income tax be made reasonably fair, simple, and economically efficient? Second, are its flaws worth repairing, or would it be preferable to adopt a very different tax system?

I am convinced that the flaws can be repaired. This book addresses how. I also believe the flaws are worth repairing: No alternative tax system would be preferable to a reasonably fair, simple, and economically efficient income tax. The task is difficult, of course. So, too, has been balancing the budget. Yet the 1997 balanced-budget accord, although imperfect, is fresh evidence that Congress and the White House remain capable of a collaborative discipline that cynics previously insisted was impossible in the absence of a constitutional amendment.

> *If the cynics are correct, we should expect Congress to treat any tax system, including any flat tax, as it has the income tax— as a political football.*

Nevertheless, we have good reason to doubt whether Congress, even if members were to agree in principle on the necessary reforms to the income tax, would have the political will to enact sufficient numbers of them. Convictions that no foreseeable Congress can rise to the challenge reflect a basic cynicism that extends beyond what one may think about Congress or what members of Congress may think about themselves. Ultimately, the cynicism is about American voters who, we are to assume, are incapable of electing representatives to do the right thing. Such cynicism can easily be characterized as realism. If, however, the cynics are correct, we should expect Congress to treat any alternative tax system as it has the income tax—as a political football.

Members of Congress who would replace the income tax commonly favor a form of **consumption tax** that would tax income we consume rather than save or invest. Advocates believe such a system—which effectively would tax individuals on their income from labor but not from dividends, interest, capital gains, and other forms of savings and investment—would be fairer and simpler and would stimulate greater economic growth. In my view, elaborated throughout this book, our annual income is the most reliable indicator of our ability to pay taxes, and allocating tax burdens by our annual ability to pay should be the cornerstone of a fair tax policy. In sum, our nation would be served best by a system that defines income comprehensively—that includes income from savings and investments as well as from wages—but taxes income at far lower tax rates than today's rates.

The income tax is just as capable as a consumption tax of accommodating smaller (or larger) government.

Whichever system you prefer, the choice between income or consumption as the basis for taxation is separate from the political judgment about the proper size and reach of the federal government. Consumption tax advocates commonly, and passionately, oppose big government. Passions aside, the income tax is just as capable as any consumption tax of accommodating smaller (or larger) government. In short, the degree of federalism in this country reflected in tax policy turns not upon whether Congress relies on an income tax or a consumption tax but on how the particular tax is crafted.

Passions on the subject of taxation always have been an American staple. Our nation, after all, was born from revolt against oppressive taxation by Great Britain. The income tax itself emerged from an insurgency, seeded in the late nineteenth century, against tariffs that unfairly favored certain domestic industries over others. Worse, according to social reformers, tariffs operated regressively; they drove up costs of food and other items basic in daily life, absorbing a higher percentage of the incomes of ordinary families than of wealthier ones.

Feelings about the introduction of an income tax also ran deep, as they had throughout its original incarnation as an emergency measure during the Civil War. Then, the *New York Times* praised it as "probably one of the most equitable and bearable taxes that can be imposed."[2] In contrast, Justin Morrill of Vermont, a reluctant supporter of the tax as a member of the House Ways and Means Committee, vehemently opposed efforts to impose progressive tax rates. They "punish men because they are rich," he warned, "seizing the property of men for the crime of having too much."[3] Indeed, the Sixteenth Amendment, which laid the foundation for the modern income tax, remains a historical curiosity: In 1909, a U.S. Senate dominated by millionaires voted unanimously for it.

Enacted in 1913 after three-quarters of the states had finally ratified the amendment earlier that year, the income tax was lambasted by the *St. Louis Globe-Democrat* as "wrong in principle and un-American in spirit."[4] Yet it was welcomed by none other than the *Wall Street Journal*, which noted that the "change from indirect to direct taxation is a mark of economic progress."[5] No one, however, was more sanguine about the new tax than the House Ways and Means Committee, which proclaimed that "all good citizens . . . will willingly and cheerfully support and sustain this, the fairest and cheapest of all taxes."[6]

We have come a long way. If such cheerfulness ever existed, it is gone. Our will is being tested as never before. People do not quarrel in principle with Franklin Roosevelt that "taxes . . . are the dues that we pay for the privileges of membership in an organized society."[7] Instead, we have become increasingly doubtful about what such membership buys.

History teaches that the more we trust the government to defend or expand on our privileges, the more willing we are to pay these dues, including high levels of income taxes. World War II was an extreme case in point. Four months after Pearl Harbor, the National Association of Manufacturers, normally opposed to high income taxes, urged that "all income over and above that needed to keep our business structure alive should be taxed to the limit—leaving only enough for survival."[8] Huge taxes on businesses and individuals followed; individual rates rose as high as 94 percent. "Not a single war millionaire," declared President Roosevelt, "will be created in the country as a result of the war disaster."[9]

Even years after the war, concerns about the unprecedented federal debt attributable to the war and about the dangers of inflation kept top rates in the range of 90 percent. Yet protests against these rates remained remarkably muted. The income tax continued to be viewed popularly as a fair tax, just as most Americans trusted government to do right by them in general.

If we do not trust Congress's behavior in general, we cannot be expected to embrace the tax system by which it conducts its affairs.

This relationship between our attitude toward the income tax and our trust in the government that oversees it is not surprising. Taxes are the lifeblood of government, the principal means by which private funds are redistributed for public use. If we do not trust Congress's behavior in general, we cannot be expected to embrace the tax system by which it conducts its affairs, whatever that system might be. If Congress can, however, fashion a fair and sound tax system, we are more likely to trust it to conduct the other affairs of government responsibly.

Entirely predictable, then, was the parallel between growing hostility toward the federal income tax over recent decades and the public's changing attitude toward the federal government. In 1964, 77 percent of those surveyed said they trusted the federal government "to do what is right" just about always or most of the time. By 1992, the figure had plummeted to about 20 percent, where it remains today.[10]

Overall Tax Trends and Comparisons

Apart from believing that their taxes are not well spent, many people feel that the combined taxes exacted from them by federal, state, and local governments are excessive. These feelings can be expected when wages have been flat or declining, making each tax dollar more precious, as has been the case for so many workers over the past decades. Taxpayers may be surprised to learn, however, that personal and corporate taxes paid to all levels of government in this country, as a percentage of our **gross domestic product** (GDP), have changed little over the past 25 years, oscillating around 30 percent, about where they are today.

Judged by the ratio of their taxes to GDP, Americans fare better than people living in the vast majority of other industrialized societies. For example, citizens of the 24 nations that belong to the Organization for Economic Cooperation and Development (OECD), which includes industrialized nations in North America, Europe, and the Pacific, pay on average 25 percent more taxes in relation to their GDP than do we. The tax burden imposed on citizens of our principal economic competitor, Japan, is about the same as ours.[11]

Blaming the Income Tax

Even assuming, for sake of discussion, that taxes overall are too high in the United States, is the individual income tax primarily to blame? As seen in Table 1.1, income tax revenues in 1997 were 9.2 percent of GDP, higher than the 8.0 percent average from 1960 through 1979 and the 8.4 percent average for the 1980s and 1990s. Higher revenues in 1997 arose, however, in the context of an unusually strong economy and a low unemployment rate, both of which significantly increased the amount of income that could be taxed. Furthermore, concerns about historic rises in federal taxes as a percentage of GDP should begin with social insurance taxes. Only 3 percent of GDP some 40 years ago, they equaled 8 percent of GDP by 1997. Perhaps most striking, social insurance taxes claim (and have claimed for many years) a higher percentage of the income of the great majority of taxpayers than do federal income taxes. Federal individual income tax revenues also are less than state and local tax revenues. According to all of these measures, the federal individual income tax seems less of a villain than it is made out to be.

Concerns About the Income Tax Itself

Even though Americans pay lower taxes than citizens in many other industrialized countries, they have come to view the federal individual income tax as the unfairest tax of all.[12] One explanation is the dreaded annual tax return, whose very existence violates Jean-Baptiste Colbert's first principle of taxa-

TABLE 1.1 Government Tax Revenues, 1997

	$ (in billions)	% of Tax Revenues	% of GDP
Total federal tax revenues	1,720	100.0	21.2
Personal income taxes	746	43.4	9.2
Social insurance taxes	647	37.6	8.0
Corporate income taxes	210	12.2	2.6
Excise taxes and custom duties	79	4.6	1.0
Estate and gift taxes	21	1.2	0.3
Miscellaneous	17	1.0	0.2
Total state and local taxes	869	100.0	10.7
Total federal, state, and local taxes	2,589	100.0	31.9

SOURCE: Joel Slemrod and Jon Bakija, *Taxing Ourselves,* 2nd ed. (Cambridge: MIT, 2000), 18, table 2.1.

tion. As finance minister to Louis XIV, Colbert advised that "the art of taxation consists of so plucking the goose as to achieve a maximum of feathers with the minimum of hissing."[13]

Hissing diminishes with a tax's diminishing visibility, as when buried in the sales price of consumer goods. It is very evident when the individual tax return absorbs about 27 hours of the average taxpayer's time, or over 3 billion hours for all individual returns, excessive by any standard. In addition, about half of us, fearful of erring because of inordinately complicated rules or fearful of missing tax savings opportunities, incur the expense of an expert to prepare our returns.[14]

Our distress with the burdens of tax returns revolves around our sense that too little of the complexity advances our own values or interests.

If Congress greatly simplified the tax system by taxing income more consistently, our returns would take far less time to prepare and we would have far less need to hire experts to prepare them. To the extent that we support some complexity to ensure a fairer or otherwise workable system, we would be more willing to accept the inconvenience and added costs of more complicated tax returns. It follows that our distress with the burdens of tax returns revolves around our sense that too little of the complexity advances our own values or interests.

This conviction itself is complicated, stemming as it does from various perspectives. Many believe that the system exacts excessive amounts from lower-income households. Members of the middle class often feel that they pay too much, and lower- and middle-income taxpayers together overwhelmingly feel that the rich pay too little.[15] One Gallup Poll, for example, revealed that only 6 percent of people between 32 and 49 years of age believed that "if they pay more taxes, they can count on the government to make the wealthy pay their share."[16] Yet those who accuse the income tax system of being most unfair often are the wealthy themselves, who insist it is they who pay too much.

Some Facts About Upper- and Lower-Income Taxpayers

Largely because the federal government fails to take seriously its responsibility to enlighten Americans about their respective tax burdens, our perceptions of the subject are influenced heavily by rumor and anecdotal evidence. We also overly depend on conversations with members of our particular income class. Myths abound. This is not new. Joseph Minarik noted in a 1978 poll "the prevailing opinion . . . that more than half of the very wealthy paid no tax at all, when in fact only about 0.6 percent paid no tax."[17]

The public also has a distorted idea of how their earnings compare with the earnings of others. For example, many taxpayers believe that earning $100,000 is commonplace today. Yet according to statistics published by the Internal Revenue Service, only 5.9 percent of all tax returns in 1997 reported that much or more total income (see Table 1.2, column B), referred to as **adjusted gross income**, or **AGI**. Despite the number of high-profile athletes, entertainers, and corporate executives with prodigious incomes, only one-tenth of 1 percent of all returns in 1997 claimed $1 million or more of adjusted gross income.

Had everyone paid taxes in proportion to the income (or AGI) on their returns for 1997, the bottom 94 percent of all taxpayers would have paid more, not less.

Moreover, most of these taxpayers not only pay taxes but also pay proportionately more taxes than their respective share of adjusted gross income. In 1997, people with $1 million or more of AGI (row 10, column A) paid *16.7 percent* of all taxes (column G) from *8.5 percent* of all AGI (column C). In other words, their taxes were nearly double their percentage of all AGI. By contrast, taxpayers with under $100,000 of AGI paid on average a smaller percentage of all taxes than their share of all AGI (compare all of column G with all of column C). Taxpayers with $40,000 to $50,000 of AGI, for example, reported 8.8 percent of all AGI but paid only 6.4 percent of all taxes. Had everyone paid taxes in proportion to their AGI, the bottom 94 percent of taxpayers would have paid more, not less. Note too that taxpayers with $100,000 or more of AGI paid 55 percent of all taxes.

TABLE 1.2   Federal Individual Income Tax Data by Income Class, 1997

(A) Taxpayers Grouped by Income[a] ($)	(B) % of All Returns	(C) % of All Income	(D) % of All Taxable Income	(E) Tax as % of Income[b]	(F) Tax as % of Taxable Income[b]	(G) % of All Taxes
(1) 0–9,999	23.1	2.8	.5	1.8	14.8	.3
(2) 10,000–19,999	20.1	7.3	3.5	4.4	13.2	2.2
(3) 20,000–29,999	14.7	8.9	6.9	7.6	14.4	4.6
(4) 30,000–39,999	10.7	9.1	8.2	9.6	15.4	5.9
(5) 40,000–49,999	8.0	8.8	8.5	10.7	16.2	6.4
(6) 50,000–74,999	12.4	18.6	19.0	11.9	17.1	15.1
(7) 75,000–99,999	5.3	11.1	11.9	14.4	19.8	11.0
(8) 100,000–199,999	4.4	14.2	16.1	17.8	23.0	17.3
(9) 200,000–999,999	1.4	11.7	14.7	26.0	30.0	20.6
(10) 1,000,000 –	.1	8.5	11.2	28.8	32.0	16.7

[a]*Income* as used here refers to adjusted gross income, or AGI, which is the gross income reported on all tax returns minus adjustments, as explained in Chapter 4.
[b]Columns E and F indicate, respectively, the average tax paid on AGI and on taxable income.
SOURCE: Internal Revenue Service, *Statistics of Income—1997: Individual Income Tax Returns* (Washington, D.C.: IRS, 2000).

As I soon will discuss, these statistics tell less than the full story, in part because they do not reveal enormous variations within income groups, and in part because enormous amounts of income are excluded from AGI.

Let us turn for the moment to what was extracted from the middle class, and whether it was excessive. To know, we must first define *middle*. Conditions for and perceptions of this status have changed over the years. A sense of pride and well-being, once the hallmark of middle-class life, has been displaced in many cases by financial doubts and anxieties.

The top 5.9 percent of taxpayers (those with $100,000 or more of AGI) paid 55 percent of all taxes.

Middle-class members on the whole used to be secure in their jobs, enjoy reasonable pay and benefits at work and prospects for increases, and be hopeful about their and their children's future. Today, waves of corporate downsizing and movements of corporate operations abroad have left a rising number of the middle class worried about whether they will be able to retain their jobs, if they have not already been laid off. With only modest improvement in their earnings over the years, many are frustrated and embarrassed by concerns they will not be able to pay bills for their children's college education. Many, if not most, face the likelihood they will not have saved enough to maintain their standard of living when they retire even if their Social Security and Medicare benefits are not cut. In sum, feeling trapped in a world unexpectedly dominated by financial uncertainties and insecurities, people once solidly middle class frequently see the income tax as a bad investment that digs them deeper into debt.

To judge whether the middle class is overtaxed, however, we must define its members by their relationship to others, not by a misery index. In 1997, the **median tax return**—where the bottom half of all returns ends and the top half begins—reported about $23,000 of adjusted gross income. This figure suggests the modesty of most taxpayers' incomes. Let us now consider Doug and Ruth Schott of Telluride, Colorado. The Schotts had two dependent children and $55,000 of AGI in 1997, nearly 2.5 times the income on the median return. If the Schotts had claimed only the minimum available deductions, they would have owed $5,625 in federal income taxes, *or 10.2 percent* of their AGI. But the Schotts itemized their deductions, which brought their income taxes well below 9 percent of their AGI; if we take into account their tax-exempt fringe benefits at work, their actual tax burden as a percentage of all of their income was even less.

Suppose that we extend the boundaries of the middle class to all taxpayers with $50,000 to $75,000 of AGI in 1997 (rows 1 to 6, column A of Table 1.2), which excludes at the top only the highest 11.2 percent of all returns. Their income taxes averaged only 14.4 percent of their AGI.

Perhaps most surprising, a median-income family of four with two children, according to estimates of the Congressional Budget Office, will have paid the lowest percentage of its income in income taxes in 1999 than it has paid in over three decades.[18]

What Is Missing from This Analysis?

These statistics suggest that the vast majority of taxpayers might be disposed favorably toward our income tax system, at least in its distribution of tax burdens. But the statistics do not account for inaccurate, often fraudulent, returns. Most important, they ignore large distinctions among taxpayers in the amount of income they legally exclude from their returns and in the amount of personal deductions they legally claim.

For 1992, the most recent year for which we have published statistics, the Internal Revenue Service estimated that individuals illegally failed to pay $91 to $94 billion in individual income taxes; the figure was about $23 billion in 1973. This **tax gap**, as the IRS calls it, mainly was caused by people failing to report income, sometimes unintentionally, often willfully; to a lesser extent, the tax gap resulted from overstatements of deductions. When this gap is combined with unpaid corporate income taxes, the total tax gap in 1992 may have been as high as $127 billion;[19] it probably approaches $200 billion today. The figure is at once daunting and frightening. A growing number of people whom the government previously has counted on to report income honestly now believe that it is legitimate, or worth the gamble, to pay by their own rules. The odds of getting away with a dishonest return are high: The percentage of audited individual tax returns has fallen below 1 percent, reflecting sharp cutbacks in the IRS's operating budget and the number of auditors.

> *Nearly half of all individual income each year legally is untaxed.*

The illegal annual tax gap is dwarfed, however, by a legal tax gap. Collectively, nearly *half* of all individual income each year is *legally untaxed*, as explained in Chapter 5. For 1997, this meant that over $2.8 trillion of income—a staggering *$2,800,000,000,000*—legally escaped taxation.

Much of the $2.8 trillion was not even required to be reported on our tax returns. This legal avoidance of taxes on our income follows from myriad programs within the tax laws that offer tax relief or that attempt to micromanage our lives or the economy by advancing one social or economic goal after another. I am not referring here to drug or gambling money or unreported tip income or unreported cash payments to home-improvement workers. Instead, I have in mind above-board income such as tax-free employer-paid premiums for health insurance, disability income insurance, and life insurance; tax-free employer reimbursements for out-of-pocket medical expenses, educational expenses, child-care expenses, general education expenses, and commuting expenses; the tax-free accumulation of income within life insurance policies, employer pension plans, and individual retirement accounts (**IRAs**); tax-free interest on state and local bonds; tax-free scholarships; and tax-free gains on sales of family residences.

We have been trained not to think of these payments as income, although they are income in economic terms. Indeed, you might rejoice initially at the news that so much income escapes our returns. Your feelings might change, however, once you realize that most taxpayers in any one year share little of the tax savings involved. For them, the income reported on their tax returns more closely approximates their actual income. By contrast, a minority of taxpayers enjoys a great deal of legally untaxed income. These taxpayers save a great deal as a result, making their real tax picture very different from the statistical averages in Table 1.2.

The balance of the untaxed $2.8 trillion of income was attributable to **personal deductions**. These are distinguished from deductions for the costs of producing income, such as expenses of employment or of running a business, which are necessary to measure income accurately. Personal deductions are related to personal lifestyles and situations. For the great majority of taxpayers, personal deductions consist of **personal exemptions** for each member of their household plus a **standard deduction**, both adjusted annually for inflation. These deductions—totaling $7,050 for single filers and $18,200 for a couple with two children in 1997—pale in comparison to personal deductions of high-income taxpayers.

High-income taxpayers cannot claim personal exemptions because Congress reduces and ultimately eliminates these exemptions as taxpayers' incomes rise above certain levels. But these households more than make up for this loss through **itemized deductions.** Only itemizers may deduct mortgage-interest payments on one or two homes, real estate taxes on any number of homes, state and local income taxes, charitable contri-

> *In 1997, itemized deductions averaged $293,000 for itemizers with $1 million or more of AGI.*

butions, out-of-pocket medical expenses, uninsured losses from storm damage, and a grab bag of other personal expenses. In 1997, these deductions averaged $293,000 for itemizers with $1 million or more of AGI.

We also know that taxpayers with the highest reported incomes have, on average, the highest incomes that are not legally required to be reported. Consequently, they often pay a much smaller percentage of their income in taxes than indicated by the figures so far discussed. Opportunities to exclude or defer income from taxation and to claim itemized deductions extend, however, far beyond the rich. Indeed, behind the over 120 million tax returns filed each year are millions of different stories. These show that people with the same household size and income (as measured by economists) often pay very different amounts of taxes. They also show that Neighbor A, who has the same household size but considerably more income than Neighbor B, often pays less in taxes than Neighbor B.

To summarize, income exclusions and personal deductions, which greatly complicate federal income tax laws, can alter greatly our tax liabilities. Whether they should exist, in what amounts, and for whom inevitably become core issues for federal income tax policy.

The Relationship Between Untaxed Income and Tax Rates

Evaluating the extensive opportunities to exclude income and to deduct personal expenses exposes the critical interplay between **taxable income**—the income that is in fact taxed—and *tax rates.* Each tax rate sets the percentage of our taxable income that is payable to the federal government. Progressive tax rates, which rise as taxable income exceeds certain thresholds, range today from a low of 15 percent on a basic level of taxable income to as high as 39.6 percent on very high levels of taxable income. They operate on the principle that as our incomes increase relative to that of others, it is fair that we sacrifice an increasing percentage of it.

Just the opposite principle is at work with laws that allow us to exclude income and claim itemized deductions. The higher the potential tax rate on our income, the greater the tax savings from each untaxed dollar of income. For example, each $1,000 excluded from our income saves us $150 if it would have been taxed at the 15 percent bracket; we save $396 if it would have been taxed at the 39.6 percent bracket. In short, income exclusions and personal deductions undermine the effectiveness of progressive tax rates: They reward most those people who have the most income.

> *Income exclusions and personal deductions undermine the effectiveness of progressive tax rates: They reward most those people who have the most income.*

Rewarding them this way does not necessarily mean that the net result is unfair or unwise. You might believe that a given progressive tax-rate structure makes sense only if these counterbalancing laws exist and that without them, the top rates should be much lower. In fact, you might favor not taxing income from savings and investments at all. You also might object to progressive rates to start with, believing that the same flat rate should apply to all taxable income. Whatever you believe, the link between tax rates and the rules determining taxable income is undeniable. Tax rates can produce tax revenue only from income within their reach. Having placed so much income beyond the government's reach, Congress adopts much higher tax rates than would otherwise be necessary to raise a given amount of tax revenue.

Adversaries on the question of how high tax rates ought to run often minimize the crucial nexus between taxable income and tax rates. One message for people who favor imposing high rates on the rich is that high rates produce no tax revenue on untaxed income; and as rates rise, the rich, who are talented at arranging for their income to be untaxed, become more motivated to pursue such arrangements. Conversely, people who favor lowering tax rates on the rich must recognize that much of the income of the rich already escapes taxation altogether. Is not a zero tax rate on that income too low? Both camps would do well to consider a middle ground in which more income of the rich is subject to tax but at lower tax rates.

Winners and Losers

The maze of complex laws that allows so much income to be excluded or deferred from tax and that grants so many personal deductions spans the spectrum of life in this country. It shapes our behavior and destinies. It defines national priorities. Taking advantage of these laws has become a national pastime, producing winners and losers. Winning can involve sophisticated tax planning or sheer luck. Losing can result from ignorance, the inability to plan, or bad luck.

Winners find employment with companies that allocate as much of their compensation as possible to tax-free fringe benefits that pay their personal expenses. Their employers contribute handsomely to one or more tax-exempt retirement plans for their benefit. Winners convert ordinary income into capital gains by receiving a portion of their salary through special stock options to acquire their employer's stock. They receive tax-exempt scholarships to college or graduate school that pay for tuition, books, and supplies. They receive tax-exempt wages for working abroad. They minimize the tax on their investments by acquiring bonds whose interest is tax exempt, by acquiring an expensive home and later selling it for a large profit without paying any tax on their gain, by accumulating large cash values tax free within life insurance policies and then using the cash (also free of tax) to pay their insurance premiums, and by deferring the tax on their gains in the stock market or in real estate. Winners inherit highly appreciated property and never pay an income tax on the appreciation or an estate tax on their inheritance. They deduct the interest on large mortgages for two splendid homes. They live in a state that relies on income taxes that they may deduct rather than on sales taxes that they cannot. And winners deduct all of their charitable contributions, even if a tiny percentage of their income.

Losers in this national tax game are workers who have no fringe benefits, do not participate in tax-exempt retirement plans at their jobs, and never receive options to acquire their employer's stock. They receive no tax relief for their rent, yet their incomes on average are far less than homeowners' incomes. Losers are single people who are officially poor by government standards but are required to pay income taxes. They are mothers who receive neither child-care assistance at work nor any relief for their child-care costs under the tax laws. Losers include students who must earn their college tuition without any, or with only a modest, tax break. Losers invest in taxable savings accounts and have to realize their capital gains to pay their bills. Losers are among the 70 percent of taxpayers who cannot deduct their charitable gifts, even when these gifts are a relatively large percentage of their income.

In these and myriad other ways, our government expresses its values, values voters need to understand and address. Too often these values are not in the best interests of most Americans. Thus emerges the pivotal question: Would our country be strengthened if, after making sure that no one is taxed on in-

> *Would our country be strengthened if, after making sure that no one is taxed on income needed to pay for basic necessities, Congress limited income tax relief to the few cases that present a highly compelling social, economic, or administrative need?*

come needed to pay for basic necessities, Congress limited tax relief to the relatively few cases that present a highly compelling social, economic, or administrative need? Such a simpler system would make it more likely that people with similar incomes and household sizes would be taxed similarly. Then, too, with so much more income subject to tax, Congress could, without sacrificing tax revenues, reduce tax rates across the board, to *10 percent or less* for most taxpayers and *below 30 percent* for the top taxpayers, as discussed in later chapters.

This last point is crucial. The reforms considered in these pages are not intended to increase or decrease the government's revenue. They are intended solely to create a better model for raising whatever revenue needs to be raised. In other words, they are **revenue neutral**. They would be equally applicable regardless of the size of the federal government.

The Economic Debate

So far, we have focused on issues of fairness and social policy. To most economists, the formulation of tax policy begins with concerns about the impact of tax laws on the economy. Which laws, they ask, allow for the strongest economic growth while raising sufficient revenue to pay for government programs? With economic growth should come more new businesses and business innovation, more jobs at higher pay, and larger returns on investments. In short, a tax system that maximizes long-term economic growth potentially can help everyone.

Questions about the relationship between taxes and the economy achieved such prominence in the 1980s and early 1990s because of growing concerns about our nation's modest economic growth rate. Two standard measures of our economy reveal this decline: **gross domestic product** (GDP) and our **labor productivity**—the amount produced in the private business sector from an hour of labor. The more goods and services we produce for each hour we work, the more the economy grows. Unfortunately, the average annual growth rates of our GDP and productivity, adjusted for inflation, had been in free fall since the 1960s, though both growth rates have been recovering smartly in recent years.

Most disturbing has been the decline in the rate of our **national saving**, which now is less than half the 1950s rate. National saving is the sum of government and private saving. The annual budget at last has begun to produce a surplus. But a string of federal deficits since 1970, particularly dramatic in the 1980s and early 1990s, skyrocketed the government's debt. Over the same period, the private sector saved a smaller percentage of its disposable income. Economists generally agree that controlling federal deficits and increasing the private saving rate are critical to long-term economic growth and stability.

To what extent is the low rate of national saving attributable to the tax laws? Most economists probably would agree with Michael Boskin, once chair of President Bush's Council of Economic Advisors, that "the tax code is . . . one of the culprits."[20] How culpable is a matter of opinion. We know that arbitrary and conflicting rules of the tax laws, and the higher tax rates that necessarily follow, distort and discourage private economic behavior in ways that excessively constrain economic growth. By picking out certain forms of income, savings, investment, and expenditures for more favorable tax treatment, the income tax laws teach us to allocate our resources in a manner that often yields the *best after-tax result* for us individually but not the *optimum pretax return* that would strengthen the nation's economy. We may reject Investment A that will yield a higher return than Investment B be-

> *Arbitrary and conflicting rules of the tax laws and the higher tax rates that necessarily follow excessively constrain economic growth.*

cause, after taxes, Investment B leaves us with more income. One classic example of **economic distortion**, probably to the surprise of many readers, is the overinvestment in expensive family homes induced by income tax laws. As discussed in Chapter 10, this overinvestment makes money less available and more expensive for investments in new companies, new technologies, and other options that likely would improve economic growth.

The more incentives Congress creates that pit our self-interest against the national interest, the more dysfunctional tax laws become. These incentives become most alluring, and harmful, when combined with high tax rates. Then, tax-favored behavior saves even more taxes. By contrast, tax laws would distort our economic behavior far less if they taxed income far more consistently and at much lower tax rates. Such a tax environment would encourage us to maximize our pretax rate of return, that is, to allocate our resources qualitatively in the most economically productive ways.

How much particular tax rates distort these qualitative decisions is the subject of considerable uncertainty among economists. Economists also hotly debate to what extent lowering rates would increase the quantity of our savings, investment, and labor. All of these issues are highly relevant to concerns about federal revenues. If lowering rates did not sufficiently increase the quantity of income subject to tax, federal revenues would decline. Thus the solitary strategy of lowering tax rates is a risky business unless the goal is to reduce tax revenues.

In the 1970s, when tax rates ran as high as 70 percent, people called supply-siders discounted the risk. Far fewer supply-siders would discount the risk now that the top rate has fallen to 39.6 percent. Still, some believe that the qualitative improvement in the way we save and invest, and the quantitative increase in our savings, investment, and labor, all induced by the lower rates, would be sufficient to generate enough additional income for lower rates to pay for themselves, at least over time. The great weight of the economic literature, however, supports another view: Lowering tax rates across the board from today's levels would reduce tax revenue unless Congress either adopted reforms that subject more income to tax or reduced budget expenditures. If rate reductions were large and Congress failed to take these accompanying steps, the government's revenue loss likely would be large.

Even if rate reductions reduced tax revenues, they might stimulate economic growth. No consistent historic correlation appears, however, between the level of the highest tax rates and economic growth rates. For example, the U.S. private business sector's average annual rate of growth in productivity was three times greater from 1951 through 1963 than from 1987 through 1995; yet the top marginal tax rates on individuals averaged 91 percent in the former period and 34 percent in the latter (see Figure 9.1).[21] The economy might have grown even faster from 1951 through 1963 had the top tax rates been lower, but we cannot argue reliably that high progressive tax rates preclude strong economic growth.

> *Notwithstanding claims of supply-siders, no consistent historic correlation appears between the level of the highest tax rates and economic growth rates.*

Nor is the evidence convincing that the economies of countries with a high ratio of taxes to GDP consistently grow more slowly than the economies of countries with a lower ratio. For example, from 1970 through 1990, the experience of members of the OECD was mixed. Economies of some lower-taxed countries, such as Japan and Portugal, grew rapidly; but the economies of some higher-taxed countries, such as Norway, Finland, and Austria, fared far better than the economies of some countries with considerably lower taxes, such as the United States, Australia, and New Zealand.[22]

This is not to say that high rates do not deter economic growth. Indeed, the thesis of this book is that the tax system would promote a stronger economy if Congress lowered tax rates across the board as part of comprehensive reforms that eliminated most special provisions that protect income from tax.

> *The tax system would promote a stronger economy if Congress lowered tax rates across the board and eliminated most of the special provisions protecting income from tax.*

Congress, however, should cautiously implement new laws, allowing for smooth transitions from the old system to avoid shocking the economy or treating taxpayers unfairly. It also should be conservative in its tax estimates in order to be reasonably confident the reforms will be revenue neutral. The lower tax rates should be tied to the additional income Congress estimates will be exposed to tax rather than on assumptions about how the new system will stimulate the economy. If and as the economy responds favorably and produces even more income, Congress can lower rates further.

Corporate Income Taxes

Like individuals, corporations formed for profit are subject to extensive and complex federal income tax laws. These laws deserve their own book. For the most part, they are beyond the scope of this one. They will be considered in Chapter 12 on capital gains and in Chapter 13 on the **flat tax**.

The Politics of Taxation

The individual income tax is in such disrepair because it has been viewed only partly as a method to raise revenue. Presidents and congresses have used it to implement broad social policies to stimulate economic growth and to serve special interests. As Sheldon Pollock, a law school professor, has written, "The incoherence and complexity of the tax code can be attributed to . . . a 'pluralist' tax-policy making process that accommodates nearly every organized economic interest at once."[23] Empowered by the Constitution and the institutions of government and enticed by elective politics, presidents and congresses have refused to set reasonable boundaries on what they wish to achieve from federal income tax policy. Unlike federal monetary policy, which is governed by the independent Federal Reserve Board, federal income tax policy is nothing short of a feeding ground for unlimited political manipulation.

Federal income tax policy is nothing short of a feeding ground for unlimited political manipulation.

The politics of taxation—the negotiations, horse-trading, and posturing between presidents and congresses and within Congress; the power of committee chairs; the roles of lobbyists, public and private interest groups, including political action groups (PACs) and grassroots groups, legal and economic experts, the media; and much more—has been richly chronicled in many fine books.[24] Although I will review the structure and consequences of the legislative process, I will leave to other writers the explanations and stories of the intricate political maneuverings behind tax policy.

This Book

I will examine, in a manner understandable to readers untrained in economics, the impact of tax policies on individual economic behavior and on our nation's economic growth. Throughout, I will consider which tax policies would be fairest across the spectrum of taxpayers. In doing so, I will explain and test the values of the tax system chosen by Congress. This book also will give you the opportunity to compare our current tax system with a simpler one that raises the same amount of revenue for the government while taxing people more consistently on their income at much lower rates. With this information, you will be able to sort out what you value and what you do not, and what direction you believe Congress should take.

Chapters 2 through 4 introduce you to the basic language, concepts, and issues of income taxation. Chapter 5 then explains how Congress calculates the enormous revenue losses from special provisions of the tax laws; the chapter also indicates the adverse impact of these special provisions on tax rates and identifies which taxpayers receive the tax savings from these special provisions. Chapter 6 argues that eliminating most of these special provisions would make the income tax laws far more compatible with the basic beliefs of both conservatives and liberals; it also suggests how much lower tax rates could be within each income class if the special provisions were eliminated. Chapter 7 offers a methodology for examining the official government values expressed through the tax system and reviews many concrete examples of these values. Chapter 8 explores the debate about whether progressive rates or a single, flat rate is fairer, and Chapter 9 explores conflicting views of economists about the impact of tax rates on economic behavior. Chapters 10 through 12 examine three of the most controversial subjects regarding tax policy: the favorable treatment of homeownership and employer-based retirement plans for employees and the special treatment of capital gains. Chapter 13 compares two alternatives: a flat tax and a reformed income tax. Chapter 14 summarizes my observations and recommendations.

Because of limitations on the length of this book, inevitably I have been selective about what issues to cover and what to cover extensively. If I have performed my job well, you will understand the process for judging most issues of federal income tax policy. At a minimum, you should be equipped to ask the right questions of anyone running for federal office about each special provision of the tax laws:

- What is the goal of the special provision?
- Who ought to benefit primarily from it?
- Does the special provision focus well on that goal?
- What revenue loss to the federal government is anticipated because of the special provision?
- Does the goal justify that revenue loss and the likely need to raise tax rates to recover the revenue?
- How much will the special provision alter the price of the activity being subsidized? For example, how much more will houses cost because of the mortgage-interest deduction on loans to purchase houses? And will the net tax savings from the deduction more than offset such increased prices?
- To what extent does the special provision justify other special provisions? In other words, how does Congress answer the question

posed by constituents: If you are going to extend relief there, why not here?

Finally, the administrative issues:

- How difficult is the special provision to understand?
- What will it cost taxpayers in time and money to claim correctly?
- What is the government's cost for overseeing it?

Were it not for political pressures, few special provisions likely could survive this scrutiny. Regrettably, few are subjected to such scrutiny, at least for public viewing.

2

What in the World Is Income?

In form, the tax is upon the value of a privilege, and income is nothing but the measure.

—Benjamin N. Cardozo, former justice of the Supreme Court

Income as Economic Gain * Income Strictly Defined—The Haig-Simons Concept Identifying Income * Measurement Problems * Ambiguities About Consumption * Income, the Tax Base, and Tax Rates

---

Since the arrival of the income tax in 1913, the relationship between Americans and their government has never been the same. Four years earlier, Congress had imposed a 1 percent corporate income tax that required corporations annually to account to the federal government for their income. But in 1913, an entire society was required to adjust to the notion that an individual's annual income, formerly a private matter for most, would be tracked by the federal government and exposed to whatever claim Congress decided to make on it.[1]

Congress's ability to secure the public's continued support for the income tax depended on how it answered a series of new, singularly important questions. First, what was income and how was it to be measured? The answers, partly abstract, partly practical, never have been simple. Crucial and more difficult decisions had to be made about which income was to be counted and when, which income was to be ignored, and what deductions would be allowed for personal circumstances or expenses. The answers would determine who would pay and who would not. For those who would pay, Congress had to set tax rates.

> *The ultimate responsibility for tax policy always has resided with voters who elect members of Congress.*

20

Would there be a single rate, or would rates rise as taxable income rose? If so, where should rates begin and end?

If reasoned well, the answers would solve budgetary needs through careful balancing of competing social, economic, and administrative goals. Congress also had to attend to issues of federalism. In all events, the public expected Congress to distribute tax burdens fairly.

These questions and their answers have filled volumes of texts that explain tax laws. They also have preoccupied generations of economists, lawyers, accountants, lobbyists, and special-interest groups. Congress provides its own answers, but the ultimate responsibility for tax policy always has resided with voters who elect members of Congress. Ultimately, then, the American public needs to address these questions in order to elect officials who will advance tax policies that it believes are sound.

The public's first step is to settle on a definition of income itself. What is it, and how should it be measured? Only by answering these questions can we identify what the government *potentially can tax* as distinguished from what it *chooses to tax*. Without these answers, we lack a sound basis to evaluate Congress's judgments. Similarly, to know whether to be happy or angry about how we and others fare under the federal income tax, we must be able to identify what income we have and which portion of it is taxed compared with the income of others. For these reasons, economist David Bradford has written, "The key to understanding the income tax, and to improving it, is a clear grasp of the meaning of income."[2] Relatively few people have that grasp. Regrettably, neither our government nor our schools ever have taken this problem seriously.

> "The key to understanding the income tax, and to improving it, is a clear grasp of the meaning of income."
> (David Bradford)

This chapter does. Although technical at times, it offers the essential building blocks for you to gain a firm grasp of the meaning of income and a broader sense of how our tax laws depart from it. I expect that over the following chapters, you increasingly will recognize the importance of Bradford's observation.

Income as Economic Gain

Gross Income and Net Income

Economists generally view income as an *increase in our capacity or power to spend, save, or invest*.[3] In its various permutations, this increased capacity or power represents our *economic gain*. Wages are the most common example. The more we earn, the more our gain, which increases our capacity or power to spend, save, or invest.

Because income represents gain, costs to produce it must be accounted for to measure it accurately. In other words, **gross income**—the amount received for services or sales—may differ from **net income**—what remains after subtracting the costs of producing gross income. When economists speak of income, they have in mind net income.

For most of us, wages or salaries represent both our gross income and our net income from work because we do not incur any special costs to produce

When economists speak of income, they have in mind net income.

them. But some workers deserve to compute their net income after subtracting certain costs of their jobs or businesses, for example, the worker who pays union dues as a condition of membership in her union at work; the commission salesperson who pays for her automobile costs when driving from customer to customer each day; and the independent accountant who hires staff, pays rent and liability insurance, and acquires equipment and supplies to prepare financial reports and tax returns. Only then will such workers know whether, and by how much, their capacity or power to spend, save, or invest has increased.

Not all costs in the production of income are treated identically. Business costs such as wages, rent, and insurance premiums are deducted in full each year because they have value only for that year. Deducting this year the entire cost of an asset to be used for more than a year, such as a $50,000 computer, would understate this year's income and overstate future income. Instead, the cost of the asset is spread, or *depreciated*, over its anticipated useful life, with a portion deducted each year. These adjustments are called **depreciation deductions**.

Consumption

Economists divide expenditures into two categories—those considered costs of producing income, which must be accounted for when measuring income, and those irrelevant to the costs of producing income. Economists

Consumption diminishes our spendable income but is ignored in calculating how much income we have in the first place.

deem the latter personal expenditures, referred to as **consumption expenses**, or, for short, "consumption."

Consumption diminishes our spendable income but is ignored in calculating how much income we have in the first place. The importance of this distinction cannot be overstated. The tax laws would overstate someone's income if it taxed her gross income without taking into account costs of producing it. After subtracting these costs, policymakers must decide, as a separate matter, whether any of her consumption should be taken into account to make the tax laws fair, advance social policies, or stimulate economic behavior. For example, because taxes should not drive people into poverty, legislators must decide what amount of income a taxpayer is entitled to consume to cover basic living needs, such as food, clothing, and shelter, before she should owe any income tax.

Debates over what allowances are appropriate for consumption—what I refer to as the second task in tax policy (after discovering how much income we have in the first place)—always have been fierce and will be explored in the remaining chapters. In this chapter we will consider distinctions between costs of producing income and consumption as well as the often difficult task of characterizing costs as one or the other.

Income Strictly Defined—
The Haig-Simons Concept

Background

Early on, people's sources of income were far more limited than they are today. Typically, our grandparents were paid by check or cash for their work. Sometimes they received goods or services in return. In a company town, they might have gained credit at the company store, where they bought their groceries and other household items. Some people might have sold their house, farm, or business for a profit. Some had interest from savings accounts or gains from investing in the stock market, although the amounts usually were small.

As time passed, investment opportunities became increasingly sophisticated, as were the forms of compensation. Some employers offered rank-and-file as well as key employees a growing menu of indirect (or "fringe") benefits at work. Employers might pay their employees' health- and accident-insurance premiums or might give employees special deals on the company's products and services, such as free flights for airline employees on their days off. Growing numbers of employers began to fund retirement plans for employees. Key employees received options to buy their employer's stock under very favorable terms.

In these cases and all their permutations, Congress had to decide whether the employer offerings fell within the definition of income and, if so, whether they should be taxed. Invariably, Congress's deliberations were subject to relentless efforts of well-orchestrated special-interest groups and lobbyists who advocated their constituents' claims for special dispensation from the tax laws.

The Haig-Simons Formula

Although few members of Congress would recognize it, a formula widely accepted by economists has long applied to define and measure income. Often our income tax laws reflect it; often they do not. The formula, popularly referred to as **Haig-Simons**, was developed in the 1920s and 1930s by Professors Robert Haig and Henry Simons.[4] At first, you will find some of the formula's terminology a bit daunting. You also are likely to discover that its teachings conflict with habits that you (and most people) have developed for thinking about what is or is not income. But with some patience, Haig-Simons will become familiar, manageable, and instructive.

> *Haig-Simons provides a blueprint for something close to a tax on all income.*

Haig-Simons provides a blueprint for something close to a tax on all income. At times, it can be very impractical or simply unacceptable. Nevertheless, it enables you to recognize income in all its permutations, regardless of what the tax laws say. Indeed, Haig-Simons enables you to appreciate how much income that could be taxed escapes taxation each year because of one tax provision or another. Armed with this information, you then can evaluate Congress's judgments about what constitutes taxable income.

We start with the principle that income represents economic gain over a given period of time, such as a calendar year. If you have both gains and losses, you must net them to calculate whether you are ahead or behind, that is, whether you have income overall.

> *Our income—our economic gain—equals the increase in our net worth plus what we consume.*

As defined by Haig-Simons, our income—our economic gain—over a specified period of time equals the sum of (a) *the increase in our net worth* plus (b) *what we consume*. Yes, that is quite a formula. If you take it one step at a time, however, you will see how capable you are of working with it. Let us assume the period for determining our income is a calendar year, which is what nearly all of us use for income tax purposes. And remember: Income represents economic gain; our economic gain is determined before our personal expenditures; and for that reason, we must add back what we consume to the increase in our net worth to determine our starting point—our income.

Increase in Net Worth

Your **net worth**, or wealth, equals the total value of your assets minus your debts and liabilities. Your assets are things that you own, such as your house, household furnishings, clothing, jewelry, artwork, stocks, bonds, and automobiles. Their value, as used in the formula, means their fair market value—what you could sell them for to the public. Your debts include what you owe on your mortgage and credit cards. Your liabilities include what you owe to the person whose car you have damaged.

Someone who is poor—who might own nothing but also owe nothing—has the same net worth as someone who owns $1 million of assets but also owes $1 million. Each has a net worth of zero. If you have assets worth $1 million and you owe $600,000, your net worth is $400,000. Let us now consider a change in your net worth during the year.

For the purpose of simplicity, we will assume that your net worth as of January 1, 2000, was zero because you owned nothing and owed nothing. If by December 31, 2000, your net worth increased to $70,000, then the change in your net worth—the first step of Haig-Simons—was $70,000. The same would be true if you began the year with a net worth of $400,000 and ended with a net worth of $470,000. You saved $70,000. You are $70,000 wealthier.

Consumption Expenses

Our consumption reduces our net worth but not the calculation of our income. For that reason, the amount of our consumption must be added to the change in our net worth, as if we had consumed nothing for the year. Also, because income means economic gain, expenses incurred to produce gross income must be subtracted from gross income to determine what we have gained. If these expenses exceed our gross income, we have no income; instead, we have a loss.

For Janet Freider, a freelance photographer in San Francisco, Haig-Simons means that to calculate her income for the year, she must subtract her business expenses from the payments she receives for her work. These expenses include rent for her photography studio and the cost of film to photograph her subjects. The rent she pays for her personal apartment and the cost of film she buys to take pictures purely for pleasure are consumption expenses and are not subtracted from her gross income to measure what has come in—her income—for the year.

Returning to our example, if, by the end of 2000, you consumed $30,000 while saving $70,000, you must add *$30,000* to *$70,000* as the second step of Haig-Simons. This makes sense because if you began the year with a zero net worth, you must have had $100,000 of economic gain to have saved $70,000 and spent $30,000. Stated otherwise, had you not consumed $30,000, your net worth would have increased by $100,000 (step 1), your consumption would have been zero (step 2), and your income still would have been $100,000.

Money you borrow is never income. If you borrowed $10,000 during the year, your net worth would not change: Your new asset of $10,000 would have been offset by your new debt of $10,000. (This observation is independent of the interest you pay for the loan and how you invest the loan proceeds.) Also, repaying the $10,000 would not alter your income because it does not alter your net worth: Your assets would decline by $10,000; so, too, would your debts.

Nor does your income change when you consume your savings. If you begin the year with a net worth of $50,000, all in a savings account, spend it on a once-in-a-lifetime trip around the world, and end the year with a zero net worth, your income is zero: The change in your net worth (a decline of $50,000) plus your $50,000 of consumption equals zero.

> *A consistent definition of income must initiate our efforts to make rational and wise decisions about the kind of income tax laws we want.*

Of course, tax policy extends far beyond defining income. But most policy experts agree that a consistent definition of income must initiate our efforts to make rational and wise decisions about the kind of income tax laws we want. As explained by economist Richard Musgrave, "While the . . . [Haig-Simons] concept does not answer all problems (and what policy rule ever does?), it points to the solution of most specific issues of income definition; and though the concept has to be qualified in application by considerations of administrative feasibility, and equity must give way at times to other policy objectives, construction of a fair income tax is well-nigh impossible without the guidance of a basic income concept."[5]

Now that income in the Haig-Simons or economic sense has been explained, we will examine some of its important implications. This exercise is not to decide tax policy. It is to demonstrate the maximum amount of income that, in theory, we could be required to report on our tax returns, although I will note certain practical problems that arise by applying Haig-Simons. In subsequent chapters, I will address the questions that flow from this discussion: Which income as defined by Haig-Simons should be reported, and what adjustments to it should be made in order to advance a fair, simple, and economically sensible tax system?

Identifying Income

We commonly think of income as the cash we earn directly, such as from work, savings, and investments. Under Haig-Simons, income can be any form of economic gain, including in-kind receipts of services or property.

An architect, for example, is deemed to receive $10,000 of fee income for designing a building regardless of whether the client pays her $10,000 in cash, performs $10,000 of repairs on her home, or gives her $10,000 in land. If you pay less than full value for personal goods and services provided by your employer, such as for meals, lodging, dependent care, or athletic facilities, the amount of each bargain is income to you. For example, if you spend a week for free at your employer's beach house on the island of St.

Thomas as your reward for achieving the highest sales volume in your office this year, and if the house normally rents for $5,000 per week, you have $5,000 of income under Haig-Simons, just as if you had received a $5,000 bonus and paid it for your personal use of the house.

Indirect Compensation and Saving

Income may be received indirectly as well as directly. Imagine if, for tax purposes, your reportable income from work was limited to your wages. A friendly employer could agree to pay for your housing, food, clothing, transportation, health care, schooling, entertainment, and vacations, leaving little to be paid as wages. Some people work for friendly employers.

Haig-Simons does not reward you for finding a friendly employer. It counts indirect compensation at work as much as direct compensation, refusing to distinguish between employees who pay for their personal expenses from the wages they receive (direct compensation) and employees who have employers pay these expenses (indirect compensation). For example, whether your employer pays your $3,000 health-insurance premium or pays you the $3,000 and you pay the premium, you have realized $3,000 of income under Haig-Simons.

> *Haig-Simons does not reward you for finding a friendly employer.*

Sources of Income and Intentions of Payer

In determining any increase in your net worth, Haig-Simons ignores the source or intention of those providing it. Your receipt of previously untaxed Social Security benefits or interest on a state bond is no different from receiving wages or interest on your savings account. Each increases your capacity to consume. The same is true when you receive a gift or an inheritance. By demarcating gifts and inheritances as income, Haig-Simons eliminates the need for separate gift- and estate-tax laws.

Appreciation

When our Coca-Cola stock appreciates or depreciates in value, we are taxed on the gain or may deduct the loss under our tax laws only when we *realize* the gain or loss, which typically occurs when we sell the stock. In the interim, although the stock may greatly increase in value each year, the appreciation is not considered income on our tax return. Also, when we eventually sell the stock for a profit, we are not charged interest by the government on the tax we were able to defer even if the appreciation was twentyfold over 20 years.

Under Haig-Simons, the increased value of our Coca-Cola stock for the year constitutes income even if we retain the stock. In other words, income includes the mere appreciation of our stock. Similarly, a decline in value for the year represents a loss. For example, if your $50,000 of Coca-Cola stock that you bought on July 15, 2000, increased in value to $65,000 by December 31, 2000, your capacity or power to consume increased by $15,000 (ignoring inflation and brokerage fees). Whether you elect to exercise that power is irrelevant under Haig-Simons, which would characterize the $15,000 as income in 2000. If you then sold the stock in 2001 for $65,000, you would not have any further income because your $15,000 gain already has been taxed. The sale merely altered the form of your asset—from stock to cash. If your stock depreciated by $15,000 during 2000, Haig-Simons would recognize the loss even if you continued to own the stock.

> *Under Haig-Simons, income includes the appreciation of our stock during the year even if we retain the stock.*

The economic value of deferring the taxes on our appreciating investments, interest free, can be enormous. Imagine how much better off you would be if you could defer the taxes, interest free, on your wages. Assume that the taxes were $20,000 each year and you invested them in a tax-exempt account at 8 percent interest for 20 years. By then, you would have accumulated $988,000: $400,000 of deferred taxes plus $588,000 of interest. Let us assume that the entire $988,000 then is distributed to you, at which time you must pay the $400,000 tax. What about the $588,000? The IRS would be entitled only to the tax you owe on it, which at most would be 39.6 percent today; you would keep the balance, leaving you well over $300,000 ahead.

> *A system that does not tax people annually on the appreciation of their assets expands the wealth gap between the rich and all others unless the rich are taxed heavily in other ways.*

Now you can understand why, conceptually, the right to defer the tax on the annual appreciation of our assets (ignoring inflation), whether we hold the assets personally or in an individual retirement account, is economically equivalent under Haig-Simons to an interest-free loan from the government of the amount of the tax. People with the largest tax deferrals receive the largest interest-free loans. Typically, these people are the richest among us. They have more assets that appreciate and are best able to defer indefinitely gains on their most highly appreciated assets. Consequently, a system that does not tax people annually on the appreciation of their assets inevitably expands the wealth gap between the rich and all others unless the rich are taxed heavily in other ways.

We also know that the appreciation of our assets often has ongoing tangible economic value. For example, if your stock appreciates by $20,000, you can pledge it to a bank and borrow more than when you bought the stock. If the appreciation were $2 million, its tangible economic value would be even more noticeable. Highly sophisticated transactions also occur, typically the province of multimillionaires working in conjunction with investment bankers, that allow them to convert the appreciation of their assets into cash without technically "realizing" the gain. In 1995, according to the *New York Times*, three such transactions, if they had been taxed, would have produced as much as $190 million of capital gains taxes.[6]

Imputed Income

A rigorous application of Haig-Simons requires the recognition of imputed income. The concept, although recognized in tax laws of some other countries, will seem entirely foreign to you. It always has been foreign to our tax laws.

Imputed income is the theoretical net value to you from your use of property that you own or from performing services for yourself that have economic value. For example, if you use the lawn mower you own to cut your lawn, you are viewed under Haig-Simons as if you were renting the mower to yourself, just as you might rent it to others; and you would recognize imputed income if the fair rental value of the lawn mower exceeds the cost to you of owning and maintaining it. The same calculation would be made for your personal use of your residence and family car. Likewise, when the vegetables you grow are worth more than the out-of-pocket costs you incur in growing them, the difference is imputed income.

Our government actually recognizes imputed income in measuring national income. Imputed income also has received a great deal of attention in economic literature over the years. Nonetheless, it never will and, in my view, never should be part of our tax laws. If Congress ever tried, it would witness the mother of all tax revolts. Still, readers need to be familiar with imputed interest to evaluate other tax issues addressed in later chapters.

Measurement Problems

Just as identifying income is the essential first step for thinking about income tax policy, measuring it accurately must be the second. In fact, when measurement is too difficult, the income must be ignored, at least for the time being. Some measurement issues can be very challenging. Here are a few important ones.

Taxing Appreciation

Measuring the annual appreciation of an asset is simple if the asset is traded in a public market, such as the New York Stock Exchange, where stock values are quoted daily. But most assets not traded on an exchange are difficult to value until they are sold. For example, no one knows the ongoing value of millions of family businesses scattered throughout this country, and no single, acceptable method exists to appraise them. Any attempt to appraise them annually would vary from business to business and appraiser to appraiser. Even if an acceptable method existed, taxing the annual appreciation might force owners to sell their businesses to pay the tax, which would be unacceptable.

As a compromise, we might tax the appreciation only of publicly traded assets while postponing the tax on other assets until they are sold or exchanged; but singling out owners of publicly traded assets for taxation in this way would be unfair to them. It also would distort economic markets and thereby diminish economic growth: People would shy away from publicly traded assets in favor of others that might promise less real economic growth but yield a better return once taxes were taken into account.

For these reasons, unrealized appreciation is a prime example of an increase in net worth that, as a practical matter, should not be treated as income. Even so, we will want to keep in mind the advantage of the tax deferral when we consider other issues about the proper treatment of capital gains.

Inflation

Inflation is a two-edged sword in taxation. Ignoring it under the tax laws can hurt us, such as by overstating our capital gains, or help us, such as by overstating our mortgage-interest deductions. Haig-Simons takes inflation into account in all tax calculations. Our income tax laws make inflation adjustments for personal exemptions, standard deductions, tax tables, and other limited purposes. But the laws always have ignored inflation when calculating income and itemized deductions.

Ignoring inflation can hurt us, such as by overstating our capital gains, or help us, such as by overstating our mortgage-interest deductions.

Inflation refers to the increase in the cost of the same goods and services from year to year. If the ABC stock you bought one year ago for $100 per share now is worth $103 but inflation since the time of your purchase has been 3 percent, you have a **nominal capital gain**—the economic gain disregarding inflation—of $3. But since the $3 nominal gain is attributable entirely to inflation, you are no better off than you were the year before: This year it takes $103 to buy what $100 bought last year. If you sold the stock for $103, you would not have income under Haig-Simons because you would have no economic gain; under our tax laws, you would report $3 of income. Similarly, if you earned 5 percent on your savings account for a year in which inflation was 3 percent, your income under Haig-Simons would be 2 percent; under our laws, you would report the full 5 percent as income.

Before condemning the tax laws as entirely heartless, you might consider how they help you repay debts. If you owe Citibank $100,000 on your home mortgage in a year when inflation is 3 percent, Citibank needs $3,000 from you by the end of the year in order for its $100,000 loan to be worth at the end of the year what it was worth at the beginning of the year. If you pay 10 percent interest during the year, your interest deduction, and Citibank's income, would be limited to 7 percent under Haig-Simons; the remaining 3 percent would be deemed a restoration of principal. Under our system, your deduction and Citibank's income is the full 10 percent, which helps you but hurts Citibank.

Although **inflation adjustments** throughout the tax laws make theoretical sense, they would pose substantial administrative problems because of the vast number of calculations that taxpayers would have to make and the IRS would have to oversee. Only, however, by removing inflation in all cases would Congress consistently apply Haig-Simons to our income tax laws and treat all taxpayers equitably. As discussed in Chapter 12 on capital gains, eliminating inflation solely from capital gains taxation would discriminate unfairly in favor of certain taxpayers.

In-Kind Benefits

Haig-Simons counts **in-kind benefits** as income whether for employees (such as the free use of their employer's beach house) or for the poor. Many in-kind benefits, however, such as food stamps for the poor, may have less value to recipients than the objective value assigned to them. For example, under Haig-Simons, someone who receives $3,000 of food stamps presumably would be charged with having received $3,000 of income, although she may have valued far more receiving $3,000 in cash, which she could have allocated as she liked between food and other needs.

Employees might make an analogous case about some of their fringe benefits. If, however, tax laws were reformed to tax in-kind benefits, employees could negotiate with their employers to receive cash instead. People receiving food stamps are unlikely to be offered a cash option.

Ambiguities About Consumption

Categorizing Expenses as Costs of Producing Income or Consumption

I noted previously that Haig-Simons identifies two categorizes of expenditures. The first relates to the production of income. In order to measure income accurately, that is, to identify economic gain (or loss), we must subtract these expenditures from gross income. The second category, consumption, is unrelated to the production of income and does not enter into the calculation of our economic gain. Categorizing an expenditure correctly can be problematic.

For example, because no one can work without food, clothing, and a place to live, one might argue that a basic allowance should be made for these costs when measuring income. Alternatively, we might agree with economists' typical view that ordinary living costs are too indirect to be considered costs of producing income; some closer connection to the actual production of income must be involved. By this reasoning, the overnight charge for a motel room when we are working out of town for the day would be a cost of producing income, but our regular rent would not. A doctor's cost to purchase a white robe that she must wear at work would be relevant, whereas the cost of regular clothing she wears under the robe, which can be worn for general use, would not; that would be a consumption item. Our tax laws actually make judgments along these lines.

What about the costs of commuting to work? Although obviously related to work, these costs are associated closely with the personal (consumption) decision about where to live. You might choose to live downtown, within walking distance of work, because you like the city or despise commuting; or you might live in distant suburbs because housing may be cheaper and the public schools better. From this perspective, shared by our tax laws, commuting expenses look more like consumption than like the costs of producing income.

Certain expenditures, although clearly not costs of producing income, may not fall entirely into the consumption category either, at least according to some interpretations of Haig-Simons. Charitable gifts are prime examples.

Charitable Gifts

Strictly interpreted, Haig-Simons ignores whether our consumption expenditures are for ourselves or others. Some commentators maintain that consumption under Haig-Simons ought not to include expenditures that are selfless. For example, New York billionaire George Soros might make a charitable gift to a U.S. foundation that he has created to assist Hungarians and others in their efforts to become citizens of the United States, or he might give to a homeless shelter in Iowa. One could argue that if Mr. Soros has $100 million of income but gives $10 million to these charities, his income is $90 million, the same as someone who has $90 million of income and makes no charitable gifts.

> Some commentators maintain that consumption ought not to include expenditures that are selfless.

Mr. Soros's situation would be murkier if the homeless shelter were near his home. Then, he would benefit at least indirectly by promoting his community's health and safety. He would benefit directly from gifts that supported the local ballet company whose performances he regularly attends.

Other commentators reject such refinements. They assume that each charitable gift gives the donor personal satisfaction—what economists refer to as a "warm glow"—equal to the value of the gift, even if the gift provides her with no economic gain; otherwise, the donor presumably would not have made the gift. Viewed this way, a charitable gift is no different from the purchase of a yacht; it is simply another form of consumption.

Remember that the conundrum here is only over the measurement of income. Even if charitable gifts are consumption, some adjustment for them still may be appropriate to promote charitable giving.

Income, the Tax Base, and Tax Rates

I began this chapter by observing that to think critically about income tax policy, readers need to understand the term *income* as used by economists. You now have taken that step; you will refine your understanding in succeeding chapters. Despite some practical problems when applying Haig-Simons, we will apply this definition of income subsequently because it is the most stable one upon which economists can agree.

> *Each time you choose to sympathize with an individual's plight or to advance some particular social or economic goal, you narrow the tax base and nearly always force yourself to impose higher tax rates to meet the revenue goal.*

Ahead of you lies the remainder of your task: to consider which income should be counted on each year's tax return, which income should be deferred to a later year, and which income should not be counted at all. You also must decide which consumption should affect our tax liabilities.

All of these judgments are critically important to your choice of tax rates or a single rate. In fact, you will find yourself, believe it or not, engaged in the construction of the nation's individual income **tax base**—the total taxable income that must be reported on all individual income tax returns. Each time you choose to sympathize with an individual's plight or to advance some particular social or economic goal by protecting income from tax, you narrow the tax base and nearly always force yourself to impose higher rates to meet the revenue goal. Each time you resist such inclinations, you have secured a broader tax base and can select lower rates to meet the identical revenue goal. In most cases, you also will have kept the tax laws simpler.

3

Our Income Tax System:

Accomplishing Too Little While Attempting Too Much

The spirit of a people, its cultural level, its social structure, the deeds its policy may prepare—all this and more is written in its fiscal history. . . . He who knows how to listen to its message here discerns the thunder of world history more clearly than anywhere else.

—Joseph Schumpeter, leading early-twentieth-century economist

Background * The Tax Legislative Process * Conflicting Themes of Tax Policy * Our Income Tax Odyssey: 1913 to the Present * Where Are We Now? * Do We Have What We Asked For?

World War I catapulted the United States into the forefront of military powers and the income tax into the forefront of federal taxes. The war's massive revenue demands far exceeded what could be produced by tariffs, **excise taxes**, the sale or leasing of public lands and natural resources, and loans. Ever since, Congress has depended on the vast revenue-producing capacity of the income tax to subsidize our nation's efforts in war and peace. This chapter reviews highlights of the income tax's odyssey to its present state. In the course of this review, I will examine the basic process in Congress for enacting tax legislation and will identify overarching themes responsible for the complexity and inconsistencies in tax policy rampant throughout our system.

Background

Individual and corporate income taxes now generate about 91 percent of all federal revenue for our national defense, interest on our national debt, and all foreign and domestic programs other than those paid from special government trust funds, such as Social Security and Medicare. Each income tax, however, does not contribute equally. Each did so, more or less, early on; but since 1944, the individual income tax always has contributed more revenue than the corporate income tax. Today, it produces more than four times as much (see Table 1.1).

In short, for over 50 years, the individual income tax has been the preeminent federal tax to support social and economic programs paid from the general budget. These programs range from housing to education, from job training to safety in the workplace, from natural resource development to environmental protection, from public health to basic scientific research, from community development to the exploration of space, from welfare for the poor to assistance for the most advantaged. Through all of its manifestations, both in taking from us and giving back, the individual income tax has become the dominant expression, and symbol, of the federal government.

Through all its manifestations, both in taking from us and giving back, the individual income tax has become the dominant expression, and symbol, of the federal government.

What is at stake here has changed greatly over time. The sheer contrast in size of federal government budgets and income tax revenues between 1913 and now is almost unimaginable. In 1913, when the U.S. population already had reached 100 million, the federal budget amounted to only $1 billion (equivalent to about $17 billion today). The entire public debt accumulated since 1789 barely exceeded $1 billion. The first income tax raised $28 million. The Internal Revenue Service, then called the Bureau of Internal Revenue, employed 4,000 people.

Two world wars, the Great Depression, the ambitions of a welfare state, the liberal programs of Lyndon Johnson's Great Society, and post–World War II obligations as the world's most powerful country transformed a modest central government—once reluctant to intervene in private social or economic decisions and international affairs—into a goliath. With our population only 260 percent that of 1913, income tax collections (adjusted for inflation) exceed 1913 collections by about 2,000 percent. The federal budget approaches $1.9 trillion. The government's total debt exceeds $5.5 trillion. The IRS employs 110,000 people. Similarly, the individual income tax was transformed from a simple system into the vast, complex one we know today. How did this happen?

The Tax Legislative Process

Division of Power

Despite the government's metamorphosis since 1913, the basic structure for raising and collecting taxes that exists today always was in place. Each president attempts to impress upon Congress his own tax agenda, counseling and cajoling members as he sees fit; but according to the U.S. Constitution, he has power only to approve or veto a bill enacted by Congress. From the beginning, the right to initiate tax legislation under the Constitution has resided with the branch of government expected to be the guardian of the ordinary people, the House of Representatives: "All Bills for raising Revenue shall originate in the House of Representatives" (Article I, Section 7). This means that no matter what the president or the Senate may demand, even the most insignificant bill cannot work its way through Congress unless the House has acted first.

> *From the beginning, the right to initiate tax legislation under the Constitution has resided with the House of Representatives.*

The Senate, in turn, always has been entitled to accept, modify, or reject whatever tax bill the House of Representatives might adopt. Once the House opens the door to new tax legislation, the Senate may, if it wishes, attempt to blow the hinges off, so to speak, by exercising its virtually unlimited constitutional power "to propose or concur with Amendments" (Article I, Section 7). As an example, the Tax Equity and Fiscal Responsibility Act of 1982, comprehensive legislation principally developed by the Senate and ultimately approved by the House, began with a House bill that proposed minor changes in the tax laws.

According to House rules, bills begin (as in 1913) within the powerful Ways and Means Committee, where roughly two-thirds of the members are drawn from the party in control of the House. To go anywhere, a bill must gain majority support of the committee; otherwise, the House cannot even consider it. Whether the committee will consider a bill is at the discretion of its chair, who traditionally is the senior member drawn from the majority party. His influence over tax legislation always has made him one of the country's most powerful political leaders. This political fact also has important local implications because the district the chair represents usually is assured an ample share of federal funds and projects. The Second District of Arkansas, which includes Little Rock, had the best run. Wilbur Mills, its representative from 1939 to 1977 and a member of Ways and Means for 32 years, was its chair for 16 years, from 1958 to 1974, the longest continuous tenure of a chair in the history of the committee.

The committee conducts public hearings on bills it considers worthy, at which government officials, interested groups and individuals, and independent experts are invited to testify. If passed by the committee and the House, the bill travels to the Senate's Committee on Finance, the counterpart to Ways and Means, where representation is in proportion to party strength. Like the chair of Ways and Means, the Finance Committee's chair, traditionally the senior member of the majority party, exercises great power over tax legislation. As Jeffrey Birnbaum and Alan Murray recall in *Showdown at Gucci Gulch*, the Tax Reform Act of 1986 became viable only after the "remarkable conversion" to real tax reform by the committee's chair, Robert Packwood.[1]

After conducting its hearings, the Finance Committee decides, by majority vote, whether the Senate will consider the bill. Unlike in the House, where the floor debate usually is limited and few amendments are possible, the debate on the Senate floor is wide open. Any amendment is possible.

If the Senate rejects the bill, it might be dropped or sent back to the Finance Committee for reconsideration. In the rare case of the Senate approving the House bill as originally proposed, the bill then is sent to the president for approval. When the Senate adopts a modified bill, a conference committee from the House and the Senate attempts to work out the differences. If it does, the compromise is submitted to the House, where the process begins anew. Once again, the House must initiate.

Role of Government Experts

Economists, lawyers, accountants, actuaries, and others within as well as outside of government always have informed the deliberations of Congress over tax policy—while often being pressured, coached, and monitored by the White House and Treasury Department. Early on, government expertise on tax policy was informal and confined largely to a relative handful of people. Today, the White House, the Treasury Department, and Congress have their own highly organized and substantial groups of experts who evaluate tax proposals and estimate their anticipated revenue consequences.

Attached to the White House are the Office of Management and Budget, the Council of Economic Advisors, and the National Economic Council, all headed by political appointees. Within the Treasury Department resides the expertise of the Internal Revenue Service, whose commissioner is appointed by the president. The major role of the IRS, however, is not policy analysis but tax collection and enforcement. Primarily specialized offices, such as the Office of Tax Analysis, whose professional civil servants are employed from one administration to another, perform policy analysis at the Treasury Department. In addition to experts serving on the Ways and Means and Finance Committees and on some of the members' individual staffs, Congress turns to the considerable expertise of its Congressional Budget Office, Joint

Committee on Taxation, and Congressional Research Service, whose staffs are expected to be nonpartisan.

The work of all these organizations is prodigious and impressive, frequently generating findings that politicians who solicited them do not want to hear. Yet the sheer number and size of their efforts and those of experts outside of government, often conflicting because of different assumptions and methodology, undermine their collective value. Political partisanship in the quality and tenor of economic analysis by economists outside of government also has become more commonplace. This partisanship may have something to do with the growing public prominence of economists, which has not always served the profession or the nation well.

Conflicting Themes of Tax Policy

Collecting Taxes Versus Advancing Social and Economic Agendas

We know politicians are aware that promising lower taxes can pay off handsomely at the ballot box. Political pandering aside, Congress's need to collect income taxes often conflicts with its desire to advance social and economic agendas that promote housing, health care, education, retirement, and much more. Advancing these agendas through the tax system means taxing certain income less. In fact, the great paradox in the evolution of income tax policy is that Congress became as concerned with protecting income from tax as with taxing income.

These concerns extended far beyond guarding people from tax on an amount of income necessary to enjoy a basic standard of living. Even by the 1920s, politicians began to gravitate toward policies that exploited the potential of the income tax to ease our hardships and encourage constructive habits at home, at work, and in our communities. Momentum accelerated late in World War II and the decades that followed to view the income tax laws as an opportunity to engage on a grand scale in individual and organizational behavior modification. As if managing nursery plants, Congress sprinkled income exclusions and deductions throughout the garden of tax laws to help ensure that each of us grew in the right direction.

> *The great paradox in the evolution of income tax policy is that Congress became as concerned with protecting income from tax as with taxing income.*

By so manipulating the tax laws, Congress has tried to mold a nation. Federal income tax policy became a matter of balancing—balancing the advantages of revenue collection based on consistent principles of taxation against the advantages of selective tax relief and incentives.

True and False Egalitarian Policies

The art form of American government in the twentieth century was to fit egalitarian principles within the structure of our capitalistic system. No one denies that unfettered capitalism, with its free-market outcomes, allows for extremes of wealth and poverty. Egalitarianism in this country, at least its mainstream version, attempts to moderate these extremes while assuring those who are successful in the world of work and investments that they will receive just rewards for their efforts.

The income tax has figured prominently in the egalitarian arsenal by taxing people with high incomes proportionally more than people with low incomes (see Table 1.2). In most cases a much smaller percentage of the adjusted gross income (AGI) of low-income earners than of higher-income earners is exposed to tax. In 1997, for example, a married couple with $13,000 of AGI could deduct $12,700 through personal exemptions and a standard deduction. Thus only $300, or about 3 percent, of the couple's AGI was subject to tax. By comparison, a married couple with $130,000 of AGI and $65,000 of deductions remained taxable on 50 percent of its AGI. It follows that even with a single, flat tax rate, the typical high-income taxpayer would pay proportionally more of his AGI in taxes than would low-income taxpayers.

Tax rates, however, always have been progressive, rising as taxable income exceeds different levels. Consequently, when we look at average tax rates paid on taxable income, we see that people with the highest taxable income also typically pay the highest average tax rate. For example, most people today pay only the bottom, 15 percent rate; by contrast, the 15 percent rate applies to only a small portion of the taxable income of taxpayers with over $1 million of income, whose average tax rate in 1997 on their taxable income was 32 percent (see Table 1.2).

People with the highest taxable income typically pay the highest average tax rate.

To understand our relative tax burdens, however, we must know the portion of our *income* (as distinguished from *taxable income*) that we each pay. This inquiry leads to a major theme of this book: Congress undermines the effectiveness of progressive tax rates by allowing so much income of middle- and upper-income taxpayers, beyond a basic amount to cover household needs, to escape status as taxable income.

Income exclusions and deductions achieve a seductively misleading egalitarian coloration because potentially they are or someday may be accessible to everyone. Such access gives the impression that all of us are equal in the eyes of the tax law. But Congress knows better. Inviting everyone to the tax starting line in no sense produces equal results. People with the largest incomes invariably come out best for two reasons: On average, they have the largest exclusions and deductions; and their tax savings from each $1 excluded or deducted from income is greatest.

Consider an employee's right to exclude contributions to a pension plan for his benefit. The initial income tax savings from each $1 of exclusion is 15 cents if he is taxed on that $1 at a 15 percent tax rate; it is 39.6 cents, or 2.6 times as much, if he is taxed at the 39.6 percent rate. Consequently, if the contribution is $30,000 for an executive in the 39.6 percent marginal tax bracket and is $3,000 (one-tenth as much) for a clerk in the 15 percent marginal tax bracket, the executive's income tax savings of *$11,888* (39.6% x $30,000) is not 10 times greater than the *$450* (15% x $3,000) saved by the clerk; it is *26 times greater.*

> *Progressive tax rates are egalitarian; special income exclusions and deductions are anti-egalitarian.*

In sum, progressive tax rates are egalitarian; special income exclusions and deductions, as drafted by Congress, are anti-egalitarian. They operate regressively: The great bulk of the tax savings from special social and economic programs in the tax laws redound to the benefit of more able taxpayers. These special income exclusions and deductions primarily explain the gap each year between economic income and taxable income. They also explain why our tax liability may have little to do with our ability to pay.

The actual tax gap between income and taxable income is astonishing. As mentioned in the preface, *the federal government taxes today little more than half of all individual income.* Consequently, although tax rates range from 15 percent to 39.6 percent, individual income tax collections only slightly exceed 10 percent of all individual income, leaving us with nearly 90 percent to pay other taxes and expenses and to save. Of course, many people pay more, and some much more, than 10 percent of their income in federal income taxes. Because their opportunities to avoid taxes are vast, those with the highest incomes have as a group the largest discrepancies in tax burdens. In fact, tax inequities abound *among* the rich: Some pay a great deal in taxes; others pay relatively little.

> *Individual income tax collections amount to little more than 10 percent of all individual income.*

The elimination of so much income from tax follows from the cumulative effect of Congress's manipulation of the tax laws over the years. A number of fine books have been devoted entirely to the evolution of the income tax.[2] My own summary follows.

Our Income Tax Odyssey: 1913 to the Present

The enormous gap between income and taxable income, and the higher tax rates that followed, might never have existed had the federal government evolved incrementally. International and national convulsions beyond the government's control led Congress down a very different path.

Woodrow Wilson: 1913–1920

Woodrow Wilson campaigned for president in 1912 on the egalitarian theme of advancing equality of opportunity for the average American. One target for change was the government's reliance on regressive tariffs for much of its revenue. The Sixteenth Amendment, effective February 1913, gave Congress a new option. The amendment became necessary after the Supreme Court's controversial decision in 1895 in *Pollock v. Farmers' Loan and Trust Company,* which declared the 1894 income tax law unconstitutional. The Court's decision turned on its finding that a tax on rent from real estate was a direct tax subject to Article I, Section 2, of the Constitution, which requires that all direct taxes, along with representation in the House of Representatives, be apportioned among the states in accordance with the census.[3] For example, a state with 10 percent of the population would have to pay 10 percent of income taxes on rental income even if its people received only 5 percent of such income.

> *The 1913 income tax was designed to be a class tax: Only the richest would pay it.*

The Sixteenth Amendment gave Congress virtually unlimited power "to lay and collect taxes on incomes, from whatever source derived, without apportionment among the several States, and without regard to any census or enumeration." The income tax law that followed, as part of the Underwood-Simmons Tariff Act of October 1913, was quintessentially egalitarian. It reduced tariffs, added an income tax, and made sure that the income tax would be collected exclusively from those most financially able.

Congress had designed a class tax: Only the richest would pay it. At a time when yearly per capita income averaged $333, Congress granted taxpayers an exemption of $4,000 (equivalent to about $68,000 today) if married, $3,000 if not. These exemptions left no more than 2 percent of the population with income subject to tax.

Apart from these significant exemptions, Congress's 1913 definition of taxable income was truer to the principles of a broad-based tax than any other version of the income tax since. Most income was counted; the principal exclusions were for life insurance proceeds and for interest on state and federal obligations. Few personal deductions were available; the most prominent were for all interest and tax payments, including all federal taxes. Even so, the income tax initially amounted more to an inconvenience than a hardship for the rich because tax rates ranged only from 1 percent to 7 percent. Still, to dissenters like Henry Cabot Lodge, a millionaire senator from Massachusetts, its large personal exemptions and progressive rates amounted to "the pillage of a class."[4]

Whatever it was, the income tax clearly was more than an inconvenience after the onset of World War I. Skyrocketing war budgets prompted skyrocketing tax rates to pay them. Individual rates reached 67 percent by 1917 and 77 percent by 1918, producing revenue that exceeded all other federal tax collections. Even then, no more than 20 percent of the population filed returns, and less than 8 percent owed taxes.

Very high tax rates on high incomes came at a price, for the system and the economy. Early evidence appeared from an unexpected quarter. Wealthy individuals accustomed to giving large sums to colleges and universities curtailed their contributions because, after taxes, they had much less to give. College and university presidents promptly descended on Capitol Hill to advocate that individuals be entitled to deduct their charitable gifts in order not to be taxed on income they gave away. Congress agreed. In 1917, all charitable gifts became deductible.

> *Republicans would change the focus of tax policy from redistribution to the dynamic interplay between taxes and the economy.*

High tax rates, however, had much broader implications. Because they claimed most of the top income of wealthy individuals, the wealthy increasingly invested their funds in tax-exempt bonds or in other ways minimized their taxes, often forsaking highly taxed but sound economic investments that yielded greater pretax returns. This strategy became the special concern of Republicans who occupied the White House from 1921 through 1932. They would change the focus of tax policy from redistribution to the dynamic interplay between taxes and the economy.

Andrew Mellon: 1921–1932

The new Republican leadership insisted that lower tax rates, plus incentives for businesses and individuals to save and invest, would strengthen the economy and ultimately produce more income tax revenue than a single-minded policy of redistribution. Less could be more. Not unexpectedly, the most influential spokesman for the new policy had a large stake in it.

Andrew Mellon, a brilliant financier worth an estimated $600 to $800 million, was one of the nation's richest citizens when, in 1921, he became secretary of the Treasury. He would hold that office for all presidents of the 1920s—Warren Harding, Calvin Coolidge, and Herbert Hoover—dominating federal fiscal policy as no Treasury secretary had since Alexander Hamilton.

Mellon did not oppose the income tax: "The principle that a man should pay tax in accordance with his 'ability to pay' is sound," he would write.[5] Some tax historians even maintain that many of the wealthiest families viewed the income tax as an essential instrument of the status quo, helping to preserve capitalism against radical attacks of socialists and others. Mellon warned, however, that attempts to soak the rich could sink a nation. "The history of taxation," he said,

> shows that taxes which are inherently excessive are not paid. The high rates inevitably put pressure upon the taxpayer to withdraw his capital from productive business and invest it in tax-exempt securities or to find other lawful methods of avoiding the realization of taxable income. The result is that the sources of taxation are drying up; wealth is failing to carry its share of the tax burden; and capital is being diverted into channels which yield neither revenue to the Government nor profit to the people."[6]

According to Mellon, ordinary workers along with their advocates must recognize that overly burdensome taxes on the rich serve no one's best interest. Any policy, such as high tax rates, "that endangers or retards the country's normal development also jeopardizes to that extent the prosperity of each individual taxpayer."[7]

Following Mellon's lead, Congress in the 1920s sent the top individual tax rate plunging as low as 24 percent. To encourage investments in marketable assets and the sale of profitable ones, Congress enacted the first special tax rate—a maximum of 12.5 percent—on long-term capital gains, covering gains on stocks, bonds, and other investments. For the first time, too, the tax laws enhanced employer-sponsored retirement plan savings: Employers could deduct their contributions to the plans, and neither the contributions nor the income from them were taxable to participants until withdrawn.

Congress also granted advantages to certain forms of transactions and investments, three of which were very significant.

- Stockholders of an acquired corporation could swap their appreciated stock tax free for stock in the acquiring corporation, a law that made acquisitions less expensive and accelerated the consolidation of corporate America.
- Owners of real estate could swap, tax free, their appreciated real estate for other real estate, which facilitated the consolidation of large real estate holdings among wealthy investors.
- Oil and gas drillers and investors received highly favorable tax deductions.

Between 1921 and the beginning of the Great Depression in 1929, the economy grew impressively at nearly a 4 percent compound rate. To what extent this growth was attributable to new tax policies is unclear. A post–World War I economic boom could be expected. Congress also had drastically reduced government expenditures, producing budget surpluses that left much more income to be invested and spent by the private sector.

Benefits from the stronger economy, however, barely trickled down to ordinary workers. Between 1920 and 1929, according to one leading study, real **disposable income**, while rising 97 percent for the top 1 percent of all individuals, rose only 6 percent for the bottom 93 percent.[8]

The Great Depression

Sparked by the stock market collapse in October 1929, the Great Depression was less selective. It brought down nearly everyone. It also led to such persistent and rising budget deficits that President Hoover and Congress eventually ended their romance with low rates. In 1932, hoping to collect more taxes from the nation's wealthiest citizens, Congress, at Hoover's urging, sent the top individual rate zooming from 25 percent to 63 percent, the largest single rate increase in federal income tax history.

A few years later, Franklin Roosevelt persuaded Congress to move rates even higher. His New Deal offer of a safety net for the needy and the unemployed and of assistance to businesses in distress required the federal government to assume responsibilities far beyond any assumed before. All of this assistance cost money. What would not be borrowed would come mainly from the income tax, once again dominated by redistributive goals. Congress imposed major new taxes on corporations and boosted the top individual tax rate to 79 percent by 1936 and to 81 percent by 1940. Yet the economy continued to struggle. The income tax remained a class tax; only 3 percent of the population had taxable returns in 1936, only 9 percent by 1940. The incidence of taxable returns has never again been so low.

World War II to 1960:
Roosevelt, Truman, and Eisenhower

Once again, a world war would transform the political and fiscal landscape. In the case of the individual income tax, the transformation was permanent. The costs of World War II made New Deal budgets look puny. In 1940, when the pre–World War II New Deal budget was largest, the federal government spent only $9 billion, equivalent to $109 billion in 1999 dollars. In 1945, the government spent $98 billion, equivalent to $940 billion in 1999 dollars.

Congress boosted the top individual tax rate during the war as high as *94 percent* on taxable income above $200,000. Moreover, it no longer could afford to limit the income tax to the most successful citizens. Our nation's survival was at stake. Everyone who could pay would be expected to do so. "The gold is in the foothills, not in the mountains," the saying went.[9] Drastic reductions in the personal exemption and the deduction for dependents exposed most of the middle class to taxation. The income tax became a mass tax. By 1945, with each personal exemption and dependent deduction worth only $500, at least some income tax was owed by 74 percent of all households.

Not surprisingly, the sudden expansion of the tax system to the middle class put pressure on Congress to carve out new exceptions to the tax base. Small personal exemptions and dependent deductions failed to protect sufficient income from tax to cover the average worker's bills. He also gained negligible relief from personal deductions for interest, state and local taxes, medical expenses, and charitable contributions because his payments in this regard were small at best. Consequently, in 1944,

> *The sudden expansion of the tax system to the middle class created pressure on Congress to carve out new exceptions to the tax base.*

Congress offered taxpayers a standard deduction as an alternative to itemized personal deductions. The standard deduction was available without proof of expenditures. It also was modest, amounting to the lesser of 10 percent of a taxpayer's adjusted gross income or $1,000. If your AGI equaled $10,000 or more, your standard deduction was $1,000. If your AGI equaled $2,000, you could deduct $200.

Because of government wage freezes, World War II ignited the movement toward fringe benefits, which were ignored by the freeze. They also were ignored by Congress and the IRS, which informally treated them as if they were tax-free gifts. As years passed, fringe benefits for workers would decorate the tax code like ornaments on a family Christmas tree, each sparkling evidence of a caring government. Each shrank the tax base. Each reduced tax collections.

The government borrowed heavily to get through the war. Public debt rose from $45 billion in 1940 to $238 billion in 1945. This debt, plus the danger of inflation from a surge of consumer demand after the war, persuaded Truman, a Democrat, and Eisenhower, a Republican, to maintain very high income tax rates on corporations and individuals. In 1960, the year Kennedy was elected president and the last year of Eisenhower's presidency, the top individual rate was 91 percent.

Kennedy to Clinton

Except during the 1920s, concerns about the economic impact of progressive tax rates had always formed the tail of tax-rate policy. The dog was a particular vision of tax justice, prompted usually by war or depression and represented by steeply progressive rates on the top income of upper-income taxpayers. Kennedy changed our thinking.

Worried about a stagnating economy, Kennedy warned Congress in January 1963 that the "most urgent task facing our Nation at home today is to end the tragic waste of unemployment and unused resources—to step up the growth and vigor of our national economy—to increase job and investment opportunities—to improve our productivity." Advancing themes reminiscent of Andrew Mellon and later echoed by Ronald Reagan, Kennedy blamed much of our economic woes on the income tax. Designed for a war economy and later to restrain inflation, "our present income tax rate structure," he said, "now holds back consumer demand, initiative, and investment. . . . It has become increasingly clear . . . that the largest single barrier to full employment of our manpower and resources and to a higher rate of economic growth is the unrealistically heavy drag of Federal income taxes on private purchasing power, initiative and incentive. Our economy is check-reined today by a war-born tax system at a time when it is far more in need of the spur than the bit."[10]

Kennedy's message must be read in context; it often has been quoted out of context by flat tax enthusiasts who attempt to identify him with their cause. By advocating a reduction of the top rate from 91 percent to 65 percent, Kennedy affirmed a belief in progressive rates; his goal was to tame, not eliminate, their redistributive objectives. His rhetoric about tax rates, however, set the tone for tax policy that prevailed until Clinton's presidency, and it prompted a "new economics." Blending conservative ideas of the 1920s about taxation and liberal ideas of the 1930s about government spending, the government would restore economic growth in general and create jobs in particular through an aggressive fiscal policy of creative public expenditures, lower tax rates, and stimulative tax abatements. Simultaneously, the income tax laws would continue to nurture our personal lives in countless ways.

Kennedy's message often has been quoted out of context by flat tax enthusiasts who attempt to identify him with their cause.

Beginning with Lyndon Johnson and accelerating with Ronald Reagan, top tax rates began a precipitous fall. By 1988, the last year of Reagan's presidency, the top rate for corporations had become 34 percent (from 52 percent when Kennedy was elected and 46 percent when Reagan was first elected); and the top individual rate for the wealthiest taxpayers, which had been 70 percent in 1981, stood at only 28 percent, nearly returning to the level of the 1920s. The top rate rose slightly under George Bush to 31 percent and then to 39.6 percent under Clinton, who attempted to straddle the tax-rate pendulum while reinvigorating a policy of manipulating the tax laws to shape economic and social outcomes.

Notable efforts have been made at times to broaden the tax base, including proposals by Kennedy himself and the significant reforms of 1986. Yet, over the past 50 years the proportion of our income that is protected from tax other than by personal exemptions and the standard deduction has grown greatly. Individual income taxes as a percentage of GDP remained relatively stable over this period largely because the value of personal exemptions plummeted as a percentage of per capita income. Thus, as Eugene Steuerle observes in *The Tax Decade,* an increasing percentage of the income

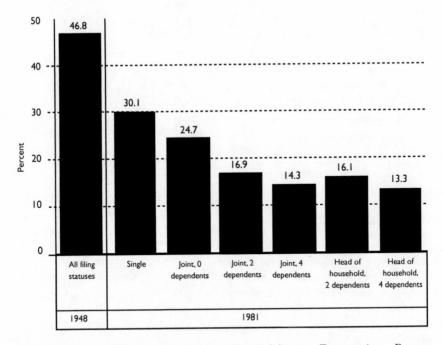

FIGURE 3.1   Tax-Exempt Threshold per Family Member, Expressed as a Percentage of Per Capita Personal Income, by Filing Status, 1948 and 1981
SOURCE: C. Eugene Steuerle, *The Tax Decade* (Washington, D.C.: Urban Institute Press, 1992), 20, figure 2.2.

of low- and moderate-income taxpayers, who rely heavily on personal exemptions to exempt them from tax, became taxable.[11] For example, tax-exempt levels of AGI in 1948 were close to one-half of per capita personal income; by 1981, only 17 percent of the AGI of a married couple with two children was exempt from tax[12] (see Figure 3.1). In short, the tax base expanded at the lower end of the income spectrum while it shrank for many middle- and upper-income taxpayers in part because of new tax protections enacted in recent decades but mainly because they maximized legitimate tax-avoidance opportunities long in place.

What was or was not taxed had become a guidebook of government values that bore upon nearly every aspect of people's lives. This observation is equally true today. The tax system, as Schumpeter's quotation introducing this chapter suggests, reveals more about this country than anything else. We learn which choices to make about our job; our compensation package; our insurance; our retirement planning; our decision to change jobs, work overseas, or retire; our investments and whether to sell them or retain them for life. We learn whether to buy or rent our family home and, if we buy our home, how expensive it should be, how much to finance, and, later on, whether to sell it; whether to marry, divorce, remarry; whether to have children and how many; whether to pay alimony or child support if we are divorced; whether and how to be charitable; whether and how to make gifts to a spouse, children, grandchildren, or others. The list goes on and on.

> *What was or was not taxed had become a guidebook of government values that bore upon nearly every aspect of people's lives.*

Growing gaps in the tax base from income exclusions, deferrals, and deductions were accompanied by mounting government deficits. Like Americans individually, the government became accustomed to living on credit, a habit Alexander Hamilton warned us about 200 years ago: "To extinguish a debt which exists, and to avoid the contracting more, are ideas always favored by public feeling and opinion; but to pay taxes for the one or the other purpose, which are the only means of avoiding the evil, is always more or less unpopular. These contradictions are in human nature."[13] From 1960 through 1997, our government paid its bills only once—in 1969. After 1981, annual federal deficits commonly exceeded $200 billion. In 1992, George Bush's last year in office, the deficit reached nearly $300 billion.

Budget deficits not only have shrunk dramatically since then; we have now entered a period of budget surpluses, which may last for many years. Still, as *Washington Post* columnist David Broder wrote in 1998, Congress has yet to address "the $14 trillion of unfunded obligations for the retirement and health-care benefits of the baby-boomer generation, now just 10 years away from starting to impose its unprecedented burdens on its children and grandchildren."[14] Furthermore, the idea of each year systematically retiring a significant portion of the government's acknowledged debt remains, as Hamilton warned, controversial. True, if the economy grows each year and the federal debt does not increase, the debt becomes a smaller percentage of the gross domestic product; the same would be true for the interest paid by the government on its loans, provided that interest rates do not rise. Nonetheless, because interest payments now rival defense as the largest single category of general budget expenditures and nearly equal all discretionary outlays of the government exclusive of defense, they continue to stake a high and preferential claim on federal resources.

Where Are We Now?

Our income tax system today is as equally devoted to protecting income from tax as it is to taxing income. An enormous amount of income never is required to be reported. In many other cases, the tax on income is deferred interest free. Often, the deferral can be forever. A significant amount of income that must appear on our tax returns is reduced by personal deductions unrelated to the costs of producing it.

This chasm between income in economic terms and taxable income is dramatic. One might imagine two interconnected but distinct rooms in the architecture of the income tax system, the Taxall Room and the Tax Haven Room. Together they hold all of our income each year. Trapped in the Taxall Room is all taxable income, which is divided into two bundles, one for us to keep and one to send to the government. The government obtains its share through a system of progressive tax rates that rise as taxable income gets higher.

For example, in 1999, single people owed the government 15 percent on their first $25,750 of taxable income; 28 percent on their taxable income between $25,751 and $62,450; 31 percent on their next taxable income up to $130,250; 36 percent on their taxable income between $130,251 and $283,150; and 39.6 percent on anything above. Thus tax burdens in the Taxall Room not only increase as taxable income increases; the government's share increases on each additional dollar of taxable income that falls within higher-rate brackets.

By contrast, the Tax Haven Room is a refuge for all untaxed income. Here, the tax rate is zero. The tax savings on income that enters the Tax Haven Room are greatest for people with the most income in the room, people who would otherwise be taxed on that income at the highest tax rate.

Because the tax laws currently allow massive amounts of income to be siphoned away from taxable income, the two rooms today are of about equal size. In 1997, individuals had about $6.27 trillion of income (see Table 3.2), exclusive of the sizable income illegally hidden from the Internal Revenue Service. Yet programs within the tax system eliminated 46 percent, or $2.86 trillion, from the potential tax base. Progressive tax rates could apply only against the remaining 54 percent, or $3.41 trillion. The $727 billion they generated produced an effective yield of only 11.6 percent of the $6.27 trillion of income. Had the tax base been much broader, all tax rates, including the bottom 15 percent, could have been much lower and yet could have raised the same amount of tax revenue.

These observations underscore the critical relationship between the size of the tax base and the level of tax rates. To raise a given amount of revenue, broad tax bases—consisting of a high percentage of all income—are paired with low tax rates, and narrow tax bases are paired with high tax rates. Assume, for example, that you and your neighbor each earn $50,000, that the government needs to raise $20,000 of taxes from your combined $100,000 of income, and, for simplicity, that only one tax rate is chosen. If each of you can reduce your income by $10,000, leaving $80,000 of taxable income, the tax rate must be 25 percent, and each of you pays $10,000. If each of you can reduce your income to $25,000, narrowing

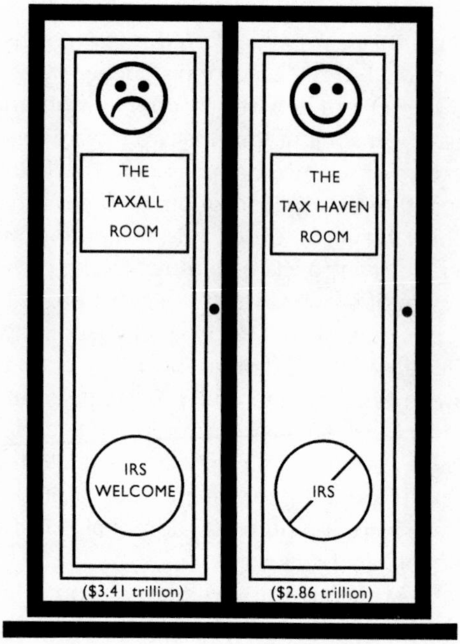

FIGURE 3.2   Individual Taxable Income and Untaxed Income, 1997
SOURCE: Internal Revenue Service, *Statistics of Income—1997: Individual Income Tax Returns* (Washington, D.C.: IRS, 2000); and author's computations. See Appendix B of Chapter 5 for computation of untaxed income.

your combined tax base to $50,000, the tax rate must be 40 percent; each of you again pays $10,000.

Notice, however, what happens if $40,000 of your income but only $10,000 of your neighbor's is taxable. The tax base remains $50,000; the tax rate again must be 40 percent to yield $20,000 of taxes; but you will pay $16,000, whereas your neighbor will pay only $4,000 (see Table 3.1).

In other words, you must pay a much higher tax rate and much more in taxes than would be necessary if your neighbor did not receive tax breaks that reduced his taxable income below yours. Of course, no one actually is taxed on all of his income, but the unequal taxation of equals abounds under our laws because of the panoply of special exclusions and deductions.

Do We Have What We Asked For?

Some commentators maintain that Americans get the tax system they ask for. Political scientists Carolyn Webber and Aaron Wildavsky argued shortly before the Tax Reform Act of 1986 that however widespread the criticism of the income tax might be, "the tax process is . . . an accurate reflection of public opinion." The public's investment in the existing tax code was so great and "uncertainty about the effects of alternatives so substantial," Webber and Wildavsky believed, that "even if the tax code in its entirety were not supported by a single individual, the odds are against radical change."[15] The

TABLE 3.1. Comparison of Tax Consequences for People with Same Income but Different Tax Bases

	Income	Tax Base	Tax Rate	Tax
You	$50,000	$40,000	40%	$16,000
Neighbor	$50,000	$10,000	40%	$4,000
Total	$100,000	$50,000	40%	$20,000

SOURCE: Author's calculations.

Tax Reform Act of 1986 quickly proved them wrong. By eliminating or limiting many of the provisions of the tax laws that protected income from tax, and by sharply reducing tax rates, it offered convincing evidence that with effective leadership, radical change could take place.

The question remains whether Americans would prefer a system that raises the same amount of tax revenue but applies the base-broadening principles of the 1986 act far more completely and lowers tax rates across the board. The alternative I have in mind would vastly reduce the federal government's role in micromanaging our lives through the income tax. The new system would retain only the most essential provisions that protect income from tax and would substantially reduce tax rates for all taxpayers. The top rate could fall below 30 percent; the bottom rate could be 10 percent or less.

Despite their apparent contempt for the existing system, Americans might opt for it, or for incremental reforms of it, over a system that is untried. By insisting, however, that the tax process reflects public opinion, Webber and Wildavsky overlooked two crucial facts: The public never has been adequately informed about the choices, and as a consequence, Congress never has heard its real opinion. If the full picture were before them, most Americans might conclude, as I have, that Congress's misguided insistence on asking the income tax system to do so much has been a formula for achieving too little.

4

The Cruellest Month

April is the cruellest month
—T. S. Eliot, "The Waste Land"

The Gepettos and the Antons *
Taxing People Fairly and Efficiently

Eliot's grim sobriquet for April, written in 1922, opens his controversial poem of despair over the pervasive spiritual drought he observed in the world. For very different reasons, Americans today would say that Eliot got April exactly right. April ushers in tax season, noted for the nasty convergence of rising blood pressure and declining wealth.

To prepare readers for this season, prior chapters focused on broad policy issues. You encountered economists' comprehensive definition of income as an increase in one's capacity or power to spend, save, or invest. You followed the navigation of tax legislation through Congress. You saw chronicled the titanic struggle between the countervailing forces of progressive tax rates applied to taxable income and provisions that erode the economic definition of income and thereby allow so much income to be subject to a zero tax rate. You learned of the resulting likelihood that people with equal abilities to pay taxes will carry greatly unequal tax burdens. The consequences of this struggle were measured in statistics that compared trillions of dollars of taxable income to trillions more of untaxed income, numbers of staggering importance but so large that we have difficulty putting them in context.

These cosmic numbers are the sum total of over 100 million individual taxpayer experiences each year. The context, then, is both grand and molecular. Now it is time to move from our telescope trained on the tax galaxies to a microscope that explores the tax fates of individual occupants. What do all the laws mean for the secretary, the bank clerk, the coal miner, writers, editors, computer programmers, stockbrokers, teachers, doctors, lawyers, corporate executives, and the rest of society? Except for the Michael Jordans and Henry Kravises of the world, our individual tax numbers are statistically insignificant, not even a blip on the national income accounts. But to us individually, the numbers are major.

April brings this individual liability home. It propels us to our own bottom line. Rhetoric about income exclusions and deductions move from the abstract to the concrete. We encounter tax justice, or injustice, firsthand. For most people, their income tax liability affects the lifestyle they enjoy.

In a general sense, every person's tasks are alike. We (or someone else) total our gross income that must be reported on our tax returns. We calculate our deductions, compute the tax, determine if we have any credits to offset the tax, and subtract the taxes we have paid. We then will know whether we are debtors or creditors—whether we owe or are owed.

On most returns, gross income consists only of earned income, such as salary and wages, plus a smattering of interest and dividends. Few of the elderly, however, will have earned income. Instead, they will report Social Security payments, although in most cases these will be tax exempt. A minority of the elderly receive pensions or annuities. In a typical year, about 10 percent of taxpayers have income from their own business or profession; 9 percent have capital gains; 8 percent receive unemployment compensation; 5 percent receive net rental income; 3 percent have income from partnerships or closely held corporations; and less than 1 percent receive alimony or income from farming, estates, or trusts. (For the 15 categories of gross income enumerated on the standard tax return, see the 1999 return of President and Mrs. Clinton, which is reproduced in part as an appendix to this chapter.)[1]

Over 40 percent of all taxpayers file returns on simplified forms—form 1040EZ or 1040A. To do so they must have limited types of income, claim a standard deduction, and satisfy other requirements. Everyone else files the Big Bertha of tax returns, the full-blown form 1040. Appropriately intimidated by thousands of formidable words of instructions in the standard IRS booklet, the majority of 1040 filers (along with many people who file the 1040EZ or 1040A) hire a professional to prepare their returns. At least in this way, they might assume that their returns are prepared correctly and that they claim whatever tax-saving advantages may be available. A degree of skepticism is justified even here. Professional tax return preparation is part skill, part art. For example, *Money* magazine asked 45 professional tax preparers to compute the tax liability of a hypothetical taxpayer for the year 1996. It received 45 different answers.[2]

All of us suspect, however, that even when our tax liabilities are determined correctly, the range of results can be astonishing among people with similar amounts of income. Rob Delk, CPA, knows this all too well. Rob engaged in tax planning and tax return preparation for nearly every kind of taxpayer for over 30 years in Oxnard, California. No one plied his trade better or had a better reputation. But Rob became fed up with the system and the practice.

There were too many laws to keep straight, too many forms to file, too many returns running five to six inches thick. Tax season, a tolerable three-month period of mostly seven-day workweeks when he began accounting,

> *Even when our tax liabilities are determined correctly, the range of results can be astonishing among people with similar amounts of income.*

had expanded to the better part of five hectic months. His clients were loyal. Many considered themselves friends. Yet too many of the high-income earners, the ones whose returns required the most work, had taken to grumbling about their misfortunes—what Rob described as "always feeling sorry for themselves"—when, in Rob's view, they should have been thankful for their remarkable good luck. The grumblers focused only on the portion of their taxable income that the government took rather than on the much larger portion of their income that they kept, much of which was excluded from their returns. Rob knew they were not blaming him, but their disappointment weighed heavily.

Not all of his wealthy clients were like that. Most expressed their gratitude for his work, as did many other clients. The latter included people who could not take advantage of significant tax savings opportunities yet still wanted Rob to prepare their returns. But the accounting profession he once loved had lost its appeal. At the end of tax season in 1998, he retired.

Rob left with his stories, many humorous, others poignant. Some stories, he believes, need to be told in order for the public to understand how arbitrary the tax results can be. Here are two of his last (with names and a few details changed to obscure identities) that he thought "tell a lot about our system." They are about the Gepettos and the Antons.

The Gepettos and the Antons

Beverly and Leonard Gepetto, in their mid-50s, live in a stately, neocolonial house located in an exclusive, gated community on the outskirts of Oxnard. Married late in life and unable to have children of their own, they eventually adopted two girls, both of whom attend a private high school. Jan and Rick Anton, in their late 30s, were high school sweethearts who married while sophomores at Occidental College in Los Angeles when Jan became pregnant with the first of their two daughters. They rent a modest, three-bedroom split-level house one block from the public high school that their daughters attend.

In 1997, the Gepettos had $200,000 of **economic income**; the Antons had just under $67,000. But after all exclusions and deductions, it was the Antons who had the most taxable income and who paid the most taxes. The Gepettos' tax liability was so low not from cheating but from playing fair and square. That is, they played according to rules established by Congress.

The Gepettos

Beverly arrived at Rob's office one morning in April 1998 to review her and Leonard's 1997 joint tax return. Outgoing and athletic, Beverly is a successful obstetrician-gynecologist who practices through her corporation, Beverly Gepetto, M.D., P.A. Leonard quit his job over a year before as a staff reporter for the *Los Angeles Times* to write his first novel, based on a grisly obituary he once wrote. Leonard's parents pay the tuition for their daughters' schooling and expect to pay for most of the girls' college expenses.

The Gepettos' tax return recorded *$109,540* of *gross* income, most of which was wages paid to Beverly by her corporation (see Table 4.1). Leonard had no income from his writing but incurred costs for research and writing that were deductible as a business loss. These costs covered supplies, depreciation of his office in their house, a share of their house's utility and insurance costs allocable to his office, and half the operating and maintenance costs of his car, which half the time he used in connection with his work.

What was remarkable about their return was the *$91,000* of missing income, all properly excluded: *$6,000 of tax-exempt interest* on Los Angeles County bonds and *$85,000* of *employee benefits* from Beverly's corporation. Of these benefits, $30,000 was permanently tax exempt: $9,000 for a family health insurance policy with Blue Cross/Blue Shield; $5,500 for a disability income insurance policy that would pay Beverly $50,000 per year if she were disabled; and $15,500 to pay out-of-pocket medical expenses for family psychological counseling and their daughters' orthodontia.

> *What was remarkable about the Gepettos' return was the $91,000 of missing income.*

Beverly's largest employee benefit by far was her corporation's giant contribution of $50,000 to its new pension plan, called a "defined benefit plan" (explained in Chapter 11), to fund her retirement. Neither the contribution nor the $5,000 of earnings on it for the year was taxable currently to her. Comparable contributions will be made for many years, which should build the fund (along with its earnings) to over $1 million when Beverly is 65. The funds eventually will be taxable to her as she receives distributions over her retirement years, but her right to defer the tax, interest free, increases the ultimate value of her pension enormously.

The Gepettos' gross income also turned out to be their *adjusted gross income,* or AGI. AGI is defined as gross income minus certain *adjustments.* For most taxpayers, AGI is synonymous with gross income; only about 15 percent of all taxpayers claim any adjustments. The adjustments include alimony payments, employee moving expenses, deductible contributions to individual retirement accounts or to self-employment retirement plans, and half of all Social Security taxes paid by the self-employed. The Gepettos claimed none.

TABLE 4.1   The Gepettos' Gross Income, 1997

Source	Amount ($)
Wages	106,500
Dividends	1,250
Net capital gains	9,935
Business loss	(8,145)
Total gross income	109,540

SOURCE: Author's calculations.

They had plenty of other ways to reduce their AGI. Because family size affects the ability of households to pay taxes, taxpayers may claim a deduction—called a *personal exemption*—for themselves and for qualifying dependents, typically minor children. In 1997, the deduction amounted to $2,650 per person, or $10,600 for the four Gepettos. What mattered most to the Gepettos, however, were the savings they realized from *$58,200 of itemized deductions.* Itemized deductions include out-of-pocket medical expenses, interest on home mortgages, state and local income and personal property taxes, real estate taxes on personal homes, casualty and fire losses, and miscellaneous expenses.

The Gepettos' itemized deductions fell into three categories: $48,000 of interest payments on three loans secured by mortgages on their two residences; $9,200 for California income taxes and Oxnard real estate taxes; and $1,000 for charitable contributions to their church and to a construction fund for the theater-arts building at their daughters' school. One of the

TABLE 4.2   The Gepettos' AGI, Itemized Deductions, and Taxable Income, 1997

		Amount ($)
Adjusted gross income (AGI)		109,540
Deductions		
Itemized deductions		
Mortgage interest	(48,000)	
State and local taxes	(9,200)	
Charitable contributions	(1,000)	
Personal exemptions	(10,600)	
		(68,800)
Taxable income		40,740

SOURCE: Author's calculations.

TABLE 4.3 Computation of the Gepettos' 1997 Economic Income Less Personal
Exemptions and a Standard Deduction

		Amount ($)
Economic income		
AGI as reported	109,540	
Fringe benefits	85,000	
Bond interest	6,000	
		200,540
Deductions		
Personal exemptions	(10,600)	
Standard deduction	(6,900)	(17,500)
Taxable income		183,040

SOURCE: Author's calculations.

loans helped them buy their Oxnard house. A second helped them buy their
ski condominium in Lake Tahoe. A third loan, called a **home equity loan** to
distinguish it from loans used to buy, build,
or improve a family residence, was used to
buy their new Jeep Cherokee and to pay off
credit-card debts. These personal deductions
shrank their AGI to a mere *$40,740* of tax-
able income (see Table 4.2).

> *Under Haig-Simons, the Gepettos would have had over $200,000 of income, not $109,540.*

Their taxable income was a far cry from
their economic income—the increase in their wealth for the year. Had their
income been computed under Haig-Simons, Beverly would have had
$191,500 of income from her job: $106,500 of salary plus her $85,000 of
employee benefits because they added to her "power to spend, save, or invest."[2] For the same reason, the Gepettos' $6,000 interest on their L.A.
County bond would have been taxable. Finally, as in the case of over 70 percent of all taxpayers, if the Gepettos had been limited to a standard deduction, they would have deducted $6,900, not $58,200. Consequently, their
AGI would have exceeded $200,000, and their taxable income would have
exceeded $183,040 (see Table 4.3).

As it was, their *taxable income* of *$40,740* fell entirely within the 15 per-
cent rate bracket, which for joint returns in 1997 applied to up to $41,200
(see Table 4.4).[3] Their tax of $6,111 (15 percent x $40,740) represented a
mere 3 percent of their *$200,540* of real income. Beverly knew Rob had
guided her well over the years. She thanked him for a final time.

TABLE 4.4 Tax Rate Schedule for Married Filing Jointly, 1997

Tax Rate (%)	Taxable Income ($)
15.0	0–41,200
28.0	41,201–99,600
31.0	99,601–151,750
36.0	151,751–271,050
39.6	271,051–

SOURCE: Internal Revenue Code.

The Antons

Later in the day came Jan's turn. Rob always was struck by the way the Antons combined upbeat personalities with frilless lives. Both work long hours for EcoTravel, a small company that publishes travel books about scenic areas of the northwest United States and Canada. Jan edits and Rick markets the publications. Their only fringe benefit was $4,800 paid by EcoTravel to a health-maintenance organization for their family health insurance.

Despite Rob's urging, the Antons have resisted buying a house, believing that the risk of earthquakes makes homeownership a poor investment. They also fear becoming house poor—having too little money left over for other needs. Instead, they have saved most of their discretionary income for their girls' anticipated college expenses. Both girls are superb students and have ambitions, encouraged by Jan and Rick, to attend a fine eastern college, where the costs will be high even if the girls receive scholarships. The Antons also help support Rick's mother, a widow who receives small pension and Social Security payments.

The Antons' tax profile was simple. They had $66,700 of gross income—$59,000 of salaries from EcoTravel plus $7,700 of taxable interest and dividends. Each claimed the maximum $2,000 deduction for contributions to individual retirement accounts. After their personal exemptions and standard deduction, they were left with $45,200 of taxable income (see Table 4.5).

The Antons claimed a standard deduction because it was more than they could itemize.

Most striking was the Antons' inability to benefit from itemizing; yet they incurred housing, medical, and interest expenses, paid California income taxes, made charitable contributions, and paid Rob's fee for preparing their 1996 tax returns. Why did they fare so badly?

To begin with, no deduction ever has existed for home rental payments. Next, the deduction for out-of-pocket medical expenses was unavailable because the amount spent by the Antons, which included expensive orthodontia for one of their daughters, fell short of 7.5 percent of their AGI; only

TABLE 4.5 The Antons' Gross Income, AGI, Adjustments, Deductions, and Taxable Income , 1997

		Amount ($)
Gross income		66,700
Adjustments (IRAs)		(4,000)
AGI		62,700
Deductions		
Personal exemptions	(10,600)	
Standard deduction	(6,900)	
		(17,500)
Taxable income		45,200

SOURCE: Author's calculations.

out-of-pocket medical expenses in excess of that amount may be deducted. The Antons' personal interest expenses could not be deducted because to be deductible, the debt on which the interest was paid had to be secured by a mortgage on a personal residence they owned. They owned none. Finally, Rob's $750 accounting fee, which fell under the category "miscellaneous expenses," was not deductible because only miscellaneous expenses in excess of 2 percent of a taxpayer's AGI are deductible; and Rob's fee, as their only miscellaneous expense, fell far short of the 2 percent.

Only two categories of itemized deductions were available to the Antons: their California income taxes ($1,822) and their charitable contributions ($1,955). Together, these fell far short of the $6,900 standard deduction.

The Antons ended up paying *$7,300* of federal income taxes. This exceeded by nearly $1,200 the Gepettos' payment not only because the Antons had nearly $4,500 more taxable income but because $4,000 was subject to the 28 percent tax rate (see Tables 4.4 and 4.6).[5]

The Antons' Questions for the Gepettos

The Gepettos and Antons have never met. Imagine, however, that Rob brought Beverly and Jan together in his office that April morning and that Beverly, feeling she had nothing to hide, disclosed to Jan her entire tax story. Jan might have wondered why a government heavily in debt and steeped in the rhetoric of hard choices would tax the Gepettos so lightly. Like you, she may have had many specific questions for Congress. Here are a few.

- Why should the government subsidize a generous family health insurance policy for the Gepettos that costs $9,000, when a basic pol-

TABLE 4.6 Tax Computation on the Antons' $45,200 of Taxable Income

Tax Rates	Tax
15% on first $41,200	$6,180
28% on next $ 4,000	$1,120
Total tax	$7,300

SOURCE: Author's calculations.

icy, like the one provided by the Antons' employer, was available for less than $5,000?
- Why should 100 percent of the Gepettos' out-of-pocket medical expenses paid by Beverly's corporation be excluded from their income when the Antons could not deduct out-of-pocket medical expenses that fell short of 7.5 percent of their AGI?
- Why should the government shield from current taxation annual contributions as high as $50,000 to a retirement plan for Beverly and the earnings on the plan that together will produce a retirement fund for Beverly in excess of $1 million?
- Why should the Gepettos be entitled to deduct all of their interest payments, including interest on loans used to buy a car and pay off credit-card debts, simply because they own their house, when the Antons cannot deduct any personal interest payments?
- Why should the Gepettos be entitled to deduct all of their charitable contributions, which are a tiny percentage of their AGI, when the Antons receive no tax benefit for their charitable contributions, which represent a much higher percentage of their AGI?

Taxing People Fairly and Efficiently

We will address these questions in the chapters ahead. All suggest that our tax system fails to allocate tax burdens fairly or on a sound economic basis. No one would doubt that the Gepettos' economic income gave them far greater ability to pay income taxes than the Antons'. This ability to pay, based on our economic income and the size of our household, ought to be the cornerstone of a fair tax policy. Members of Congress may claim they agree, but Congress behaves otherwise. It favors having the Antons pay more taxes than the Gepettos in order to accommodate a range of substantial personal expenses, savings, and investments by the Gepettos.

This is not to say that the Gepettos' tax story is typical, even among physicians with the same practice income. Although physicians commonly benefit from sizable pension-plan contributions and generous health-care packages, the pension payments for Beverly and the medical reimbursements for her family were unusually large. The Gepettos' mortgage-interest payments also were large, although many taxpayers claim much larger ones. Turning to the Antons, we know that most people with their income own a home and claim itemized deductions. By comparing these two returns, however, we begin to appreciate how difficult the task becomes to craft a fair, simple, and economically sound income tax once Congress decides to adjust our tax burdens depending in such large part on how we receive, spend, and invest our income.

> *Our ability to pay, based on our economic income and the size of our household, ought to form the cornerstone of a fair tax policy.*

Rob has countless other stories—about teachers, post office workers, artists, architects, city planners, small-business owners, factory managers, owners of companies that recently have "gone public," and retirees—that illustrate how often our ability to pay taxes may have little to do with what taxes we owe. If, one by one, we counted economic income and evaluated tax outcomes, readers would be struck by the widely disparate results that follow from Congress's piecemeal policy tampering.

Predictable cases involve upper-income households that have access to sophisticated tax planners like Rob and have the resources to maximize their tax savings. We need only recall headline stories about corporate executives whose companies granted them options to buy huge quantities of company stock. Since these employees do not have to exercise the stock options for years, they can watch the stock rise dramatically in value, then buy it for the old price and not be taxed on their millions of dollars of gain until they decide to sell.

Many other less obvious cases involve taxpayers with unremarkable incomes who enjoy enormous tax advantages often because of the good fortune of having the right employer. Consider university professors, not often identified by themselves or outsiders as victorious in the tax game. (These comments apply equally to college professors.) First, most universities offer professors a salary-reduction plan (technically called a "cafeteria plan"), under which they can choose to reduce their salary in exchange for having the university pay various personal expenses. For example, payments might be made for health insurance premiums if not otherwise paid by the university, out-of-pocket medical expenses for the professor and her family, and up to $5,000 of child-care expenses, all tax free. Less than half of all employees in this country participate in an employer-sponsored retirement plan, but virtually every university offers a tax-exempt retirement plan that, in addition to the university's own contributions, allows tax-free salary reductions for contributions designated by its professors.

Professors and their families typically receive tax-free use of the university's athletic facility, replete with exercise and weight rooms; tennis, squash, and racquetball courts; and swimming pool. Professors pay favorable prices when they eat at the campus cafeteria, when they buy computers through their university, and when they rent houses or apartments from universities.

Universities often lend money to professors to buy a house at interest rates at the bottom of the market. All occur without tax consequences.

Best of all, the university may allow the spouse or children of a professor to enroll in its undergraduate degree-granting program free of charge, waiving all tuition and fees. Alternatively, it may pay all or a portion of the tuition and fees for their attendance at another college or university, once again without tax consequences. No one outside the academic community is entitled to comparable tax treatment.

> *As long as our tax system recognizes large gaps between economic and taxable income, the taxes owed by people with equal abilities to pay often will be in disequilibrium.*

The cumulative income value of these perks can approach or exceed a professor's actual salary. Most of these tax-free benefits must be offered to other employees of the university on a nondiscriminatory basis. But readers employed outside the academic community who receive few perks at work may conclude that Congress has chosen unwisely to allow so much of our tax liability to turn upon who our employer happens to be.

As long as our tax system continues to recognize such large gaps between economic income and taxable income, the taxes owed by people with equal abilities to pay taxes often will be in disequilibrium. People with considerably greater abilities to pay may end up owing less in taxes than people with considerably less ability to pay. Whether these results can be justified depends on the offsetting advantages.

What, then, are the social and economic arguments for each departure? How well do they stand up? In light of mounting attacks on the income tax, these questions require nothing short of examining the entire treasure trove of income exclusions, deductions, and credits. Remarkably, for nearly a quarter of a century, Congress has had in place one of the essential tools for doing so—its own hypothetical model of a broad-base income tax, to which we now turn. If Congress ever took the model seriously, April might someday seem less cruel.

F O R M	1040	Department of the Treasury – Internal Revenue Service **U.S. Individual Income Tax Return**	1999	(99)	IRS Use Only – Do not write or staple in this space.

For the year Jan. 1 – Dec. 31, 1999, or other tax year beginning _____, 1999, ending _____   OMB No. 1545-0074

Label (See Instructions on page 18.) Use the IRS label. Otherwise, please print or type.	L A B E L H E R E	Your first name and initial **William J.** Last name **Clinton**		Your social security number
		If a joint return, spouse's first name and initial **Hillary Rodham** Last name **Clinton**		Spouse's social security number
		Home address (number and street). If you have a P.O. box, see page 18. **1600 Pennsylvania Avenue, N.W.**	Apt. no.	▲ **IMPORTANT!** ▲ You must enter your SSN(s) above.
		City, town or post office, state, and ZIP code. If you have a foreign address, see page 18. **Washington, DC 20500**		

Presidential Election Campaign (See page 18.)

		Yes	No	Note: Checking "Yes" will not change your tax or reduce your refund.
Do you want $3 to go to this fund?		X		
If a joint return, does your spouse want $3 to go to this fund?		X		

Filing Status

Check only one box.

1		Single
2	X	Married filing joint return (even if only one had income)
3		Married filing separate return. Enter spouse's soc. sec. no. above & full name here ▶
4		Head of household (with qualifying person). (See page 18.) If the qualifying person is a child but not your dependent, enter this child's name here ▶
5		Qualifying widow(er) with dependent child (year spouse died ▶ 19___). (See page 18.)

Exemptions

6a	☒	**Yourself.** If your parent (or someone else) can claim you as a dependent on his or her tax return, do not check box 6a.		No. of boxes checked on 6a and 6b **2**
b	☒	**Spouse**		

c **Dependents:**

(1) First name Last name	(2) Dependent's social security number	(3) Dependent's relationship to you	(4) Chk if qualifying child for child tax credit (see page 19)	
Chelsea V. Clinton		Daughter		● lived with you **1**
				● did not live with you due to divorce or separation (see page 19)
				Dependents on 6c not entered above

If more than six dependents, see page 19.

d	Total number of exemptions claimed		Add numbers entered on lines above ▶ **3**

Income

Attach Copy B of your Forms W-2 and W-2G here. Also attach Form 1099-R if tax was withheld.

If you did not get a W-2, see page 20.

Enclose, but do not attach any payment. Also, please use Form 1040-V.

7	Wages, salaries, tips, etc. Attach Form(s) W-2	7	200,000
8a	Taxable interest. Attach Schedule B if required	8a	6,008
b	Tax–exempt interest. DO NOT include on line 8a.	8b	9,917		
9	Ordinary dividends. Attach Schedule B if required	9	11,396
10	Taxable refunds, credits, or offsets of state and local income taxes (see page 21)	10	
11	Alimony received	11	
12	Business income or (loss). Attach Schedule C or C-EZ	12	20,214
13	Capital gain or (loss). Attach Schedule D if required. If not required, check here ▶ ☐	13	179,849
14	Other gains or (losses). Attach Form 4797	14	
15a	Total IRA distributions	15a		b Taxable amount (see pg 22)	15b	
16a	Total pensions and annuities	16a		b Taxable amount (see pg 22)	16b	
17	Rental real estate, royalties, partnerships, S corporations, trusts, etc. Attach Schedule E	17	
18	Farm income or (loss). Attach Schedule F	18	
19	Unemployment compensation	19	
20a	Social security benefits	20a		b Taxable amount (see pg 24)	20b	
21	Other income.	21	
22	Add the amounts in the far right column for lines 7 through 21. This is your **total income** ... ▶	22	417,467

Adjusted Gross Income

23	IRA deduction (see page 26)	23	
24	Student loan interest deduction (see page 26)	24	
25	Medical savings account deduction. Attach Form 8853....	25	
26	Moving expenses. Attach Form 3903	26	
27	One-half of self-employment tax. Attach Schedule SE......	27	1,428
28	Self-employed health insurance deduction (see page 28) ...	28	
29	Keogh and self-employed SEP and SIMPLE plans........	29	
30	Penalty on early withdrawal of savings	30	
31a	Alimony paid. b Recipient's SSN ▶ _____	31a	
32	Add lines 23 through 31a	32	1,428
33	Subtract line 32 from line 22. This is your **adjusted gross income** .... ▶	33	416,039

KFA For Disclosure, Privacy Act, and Paperwork Reduction Act Notice, see page 54.   Form **1040** (199

64

Tax and Credits	34 Amount from line 33 (adjusted gross income)	34	416,039

Tax and Credits

34 Amount from line 33 (adjusted gross income) **34** 416,039

35 a Check if: ☐ You were 65 or older, ☐ Blind; ☐ Spouse was 65 or older, ☐ Blind
   Add the number of boxes checked above and enter the total here ......► 35a

Standard Deduction for Most People

Single:
$4,300

Head of household:
$6,350

Married filing jointly or Qualifying widow(er):
$7,200

Married filing separately:
$3,600

b If you are married filing separately and your spouse itemizes deductions or you were
   a dual-status alien, see page 30 and check here ....► 35b ☐

36 Enter your itemized deductions from Schedule A, line 28, OR standard deduction
   shown on the left. But see page 30 to find your standard deduction if you checked
   any box on line 35a or 35b or if someone can claim you as a dependent **36** 81,358

37 Subtract line 36 from line 34 .... **37** 334,681

38 If line 34 is $94,975 or less, multiply $2,750 by the total number of exemptions claimed on line 6d.
   If line 34 is over $94,975, see the worksheet on page 31 for the amount to enter. **38** 0

39 Taxable income. Subtract line 38 from line 37.
   If line 38 is more than line 37, enter -0- **39** 334,681

40 Tax (see page 31). Check if any tax is from a ☐ Form(s) 8814 b ☐ Form 4972 ......► **40** 84,305

41 Credit for child and dependent care expenses. Att. Form 2441 ... **41**

42 Credit for the elderly or the disabled. Attach Schedule R **42**

43 Child tax credit (see page 33)................... **43**

44 Education credits. Attach Form 8863 .... **44**

45 Adoption credit. Attach Form 8839 .... **45**

46 Foreign tax credit. Attach Form 1116 if required **46**

47 Other. Check if from a ☐ Form 3800 b ☐ Form 8396
   c ☐ Form 8801 d ☐ Form (specify) **47**

48 Add lines 41 through 47. These are your total credits..... **48**

49 Subtract line 48 from line 40. If line 48 is more than line 40, enter -0- ......► **49** 84,305

Other Taxes

50 Self-employment tax. Att. Sch. SE **50** 2,856

51 Alternative minimum tax. Attach Form 6251 .... **51** 4,943

52 Social security and Medicare tax on tip income not reported to employer. Attach Form 4137 .... **52**

53 Tax on IRAs, other retirement plans, and MSAs. Attach Form 5329 if required........ **53**

54 Advance earned income credit payments from Form(s) W-2 ..... **54**

55 Household employment taxes. Attach Schedule H **55**

56 Add lines 49 through 55. This is your total tax ....► **56** 92,104

Payments

57 Federal income tax withheld from Forms W-2 and 1099 .... **57** 50,782

58 1999 estimated tax payments and amount applied from 1998 return . **58** 43,600

59 a Earned income credit. Att. Sch. EIC if you have a qualifying child.
   b Nontaxable earned income: amt. ►
   and type ► **59a**

60 Additional child tax credit. Attach Form 8812 .... **60**

61 Amount paid with request for extension to file (see page 48) **61**

62 Excess social security and RRTA tax withheld (see page 48) **62**

63 Other payments. Check if from a ☐ Form 2439 b ☐ Form 4136 .. **63**

64 Add lines 57, 58, 59a, and 60 through 63. These are your total payments ......► **64** 94,382

Refund

Have it directly deposited! See page 48 and fill in 65b, 65c, and 65d.

65 If line 64 is more than line 56, subtract line 56 from line 64. This is the amount you OVERPAID **65** 2,278

66a Amount of line 65 you want REFUNDED TO YOU.............► **66a**

b Routing number ►c Type: ☐ Checking ☐ Savings

d Account number

67 Amount of line 65 you want APPLIED TO 2000 ESTIMATED TAX ► **67** 2,278

Amount You Owe

68 If line 56 is more than line 64, subtract line 64 from line 56. This is the AMOUNT YOU OWE.
   For details on how to pay, see page 49 ....► **68**

69 Estimated tax penalty. Also include on line 68 .... **69**

Sign Here

Under penalties of perjury, I declare that I have examined this return and accompanying schedules and statements, and to the best of my knowledge and belief, they are true, correct, and complete. Declaration of preparer (other than taxpayer) is based on all information of which preparer has any knowledge

Joint return?
See page 18
Keep a copy for your records

Your signature ▶ _William J. Clinton_ Date 4-10-00 Your occupation U.S. President Daytime telephone number (optional)

Spouse's signature. If a joint return, BOTH must sign ▶ _Hillary Rodham Clinton_ Date 4-10-00 Spouse's occupation Attorney

Paid Preparer's Use Only

Preparer's signature ▶ _Robert L. Jones_ CPA Date 4/10/00 Check if self-employed ☐ Preparer's SSN or PTIN

Firm's name (or yours if self-employed) and address HARITON, MANCUSO & JONES, P.C. EIN
11140 ROCKVILLE PIKE
ROCKVILLE, MD ZIP code 20852

Form 1040 (19

SCHEDULES A&B
(Form 1040)

Schedule A – Itemized Deductions

OMB No 1545-0074

1999

Department of the Treasury
Internal Revenue Service   (99)

▶ Attach to Form 1040.   ▶ See Instructions for Schedules A and B (Form 1040).

Attachment
Sequence No. **07**

Name(s) shown on Form 1040

William J. and Hillary Rodham Clinton

Your social security number

Medical and Dental Expenses		Caution: Do not include expenses reimbursed or paid by others		
	1	Medical and dental expenses (see page A-1) **1**		
	2	Enter amount from Form 1040, line 34 . . . | **2** |		
	3	Multiply line 2 above by 7.5% (.075) **3**		
	4	Subtract line 3 from line 1. If line 3 is more than line 1, enter –0–	**4**	0
Taxes You Paid (See page A-2)	5	State and local income taxes **5**		18,850
	6	Real estate taxes (see page A-2) **6**		13,081
	7	Personal property taxes **7**		
	8	Other taxes. List type and amount ▶		
		8		
	9	Add lines 5 through 8.	**9**	31,931
Interest You Paid (See page A-3)	10	Home mortgage interest and points reported on Form 1098 . . . . **10**		10,714
	11	Home mortgage interest not reported on Form 1098. If paid to the person from whom you bought the home, see page A-3 & show that person's name, ID no. & address ▶		
Note: Personal interest is not deductible		**11**		
	12	Points not reported on Form 1098. See page A-3 . . . . **12**		
	13	Investment interest. Attach Form 4952, if required. (See page A-4) **13**		
	14	Add lines 10 through 13.	**14**	10,714
Gifts to Charity If you made a gift and got a benefit for it, see page A-5.	15	Gifts by cash or check. If any gift of $250 or more, see pg. A-4 . . . . **15**		39,200
	16	Other than by cash or check. If any gift of $250 or more, see page A-4. You **MUST** attach Form 8283 if over $500 . . . . **16**		
	17	Carryover from prior year **17**		
	18	Add lines 15 through 17.	**18**	39,200
Casualty and Theft Losses	19	Casualty or theft loss(es) Attach Form 4684. (See page A-5.)	**19**	0
Job Expenses and Most Other Miscellaneous Deductions (See page A-5 for expenses to deduct here.)	20	Unreimbursed employee expenses – job travel, union dues, job education, etc. You **MUST** attach Form 2106 or 2106–EZ if required (See page A-5) ▶		
		20		
	21	Tax preparation fees. **21**		
	22	Other expenses – investment, safe deposit box, etc. List type and amount ▶ Pell Rudman Trust Co. ____ 10,892 Tax Prep. & Acctng. Serv. ____ 5,625		
		22	16,517	
	23	Add lines 20 through 22 . . . . **23**	16,517	
	24	Enter amount from Form 1040, line 34 . . . . **24** | 416,039		
	25	Multiply line 24 above by 2% (.02) **25**	8,321	
	26	Subtract line 25 from line 23. If line 25 is more than line 23, enter –0–.	**26**	8,196
Other Miscellaneous Deductions	27	Other – from list on page A-6. List type and amount ▶		
		27		0
Total Itemized Deductions	28	Is Form 1040, line 34, over $126,600 (over $63,300 if married filing separately)? ☐ **No.** Your deduction is not limited Add the amounts in the far right column for lines 4 through 27. Also, enter this amount on Form 1040, line 36. ☒ **Yes.** Your deduction may be limited. See page A-6 for the amount to enter.	Reduction –8,683 } . . . . ▶ **28**	81,358

KFA **For Paperwork Reduction Act Notice, see Form 1040 Instructions.**

Schedule A (Form 1040) 1999

66

Schedules A&B (Form 1040) 1999
Name(s) shown on Form 1040. Do not enter name and social security number if shown on other side.
OMB No. 1545-0074   Page 2
Your social security number

William J. and Hillary Rodham Clinton

Schedule B – Interest and Ordinary Dividends

Attachment
Sequence No. 08

Part I
Interest

(See page B-1 and the instructions for Form 1040, line 8a)

Note: If you had over $400 in taxable interest, you must also complete Part III.

	Amount
1 List name of payer. If any interest is from a seller-financed mortgage and the buyer used the property as a personal residence, see page B-1 and list this interest first. Also, show that buyer's social security number and address ▶	
1st Union National Bank Trustee	2,350
Bank of America CD	1,241
Bank of America Checking	237
Deposit on N.Y. Residence	233
Mercantile Bank of Arkansas	300
Pell Rudman Trust Company, N.A.	1,522
Riggs Bank N.A.	125

Note: If you received a Form 1099-INT, Form 1099-OID, or substitute statement from a brokerage firm, list the firm's name as the payer and enter the total interest shown on that form

2 Add the amounts on line 1.	2	6,008
3 Excludable interest on series EE and I U.S. savings bonds issued after 1989 from Form 8815, line 14. You MUST attach Form 8815	3	
4 Subtract line 3 from line 2. Enter the result here and on Form 1040, line 8a ▶	4	6,008

Part II
Ordinary Dividends

(See page B-1 and the instructions for Form 1040, line 9)

Note: If you had over $400 in ordinary dividends, you must also complete Part III.

	Amount
5 List name of payer. Include only ordinary dividends. If you received any capital gain distributions, see the instructions for Form 1040, line 13. ▶	
1st Union National Bank Trustee	9,650
Pell Rudman Trust Company, N.A.	1,746

Note: If you received a Form 1099-DIV or substitute statement from a brokerage firm, list the firm's name as the payer and enter the ordinary dividends shown on that form

6 Add the amounts on line 5. Enter the total here and on Form 1040, line 9 ▶	6	11,396

Part III
Foreign Accounts and Trusts

(See page B-2.)

You must complete this part if you (a) had over $400 of interest or ordinary dividends; (b) had a foreign account; or (c) received a distribution from, or were a grantor of, or a transferor to, a foreign trust.

		Yes	No
7a At any time during 1999, did you have an interest in or a signature or other authority over a financial account in a foreign country, such as a bank account, securities account, or other financial account? See page B-2 for exceptions and filing requirements for Form TD F 90-22.1			X
b If "Yes," enter the name of foreign country ▶			
8 During 1999, did you receive a distribution from, or were you the grantor of, or transferor to, a foreign trust? If "Yes," you may have to file Form 3520. See page B-2			X

SCHEDULE C-EZ
(Form 1040)

Department of the Treasury
Internal Revenue Service   (99)

Net Profit From Business

(Sole Proprietorship)

▶ Partnerships, joint ventures, etc., must file Form 1065 or 1065-B

▶ Attach to Form 1040 or Form 1041.   ▶ See instructions on back.

OMB No. 1545-0074

1999

Attachment
Sequence No. 09A

Name of proprietor

Hillary Rodham Clinton

Social security number (SSN)

Part I   General Information

| You May Use Schedule C-EZ Instead of Schedule C Only If You: | ▶ | • Had business expenses of $2,500 or less
• Use the cash method of accounting
• Did not have an inventory at any time during the year.
• Did not have a net loss from your business.
• Had only one business as a sole proprietor. | **And You:** | ▶ | • Had no employees during the year.
• Are not required to file Form 4562, Depreciation and Amortization, for this business See the instructions for Schedule C, line 13, on page C-3 to find out if you must file
• Do not deduct expenses for business use of your home
• Do not have prior year unallowed passive activity losses from this business. |

A Principal business or profession, including product or service

Author

B Enter code from pages
C-8 & 9 ▶   711510

C Business name. If no separate business name, leave blank

D Employer ID no. (EIN), if any

E Business address (including suite or room no.). Address not required if same as on Form 1040, page 1

City, town or post office, state, and ZIP code

Part II   Figure Your Net Profit

1	Gross receipts. Caution: If this income was reported to you on Form W-2 and the "Statutory employee" box on that form was checked, see **Statutory Employees** in the instructions for Schedule C, line 1, on page C-2 and check here . . . . ▶ ☐	**1**		20,214
2	Total expenses. If more than $2,500, you must use Schedule C. See instructions	**2**		
3	Net profit. Subtract line 2 from line 1. If less than zero, you must use Schedule C. Enter on **Form 1040, line 12,** and ALSO on **Schedule SE, line 2.** (Statutory employees do not report this amount on Schedule SE, line 2. Estates and trusts, enter on Form 1041, line 3.)	**3**		20,214

Part III   Information on Your Vehicle. Complete this part ONLY if you are claiming car or truck expenses on line 2.

4 When did you place your vehicle in service for business purposes? (month, day, year) ▶ _____ .

5 Of the total number of miles you drove your vehicle during 1999, enter the number of miles you used your vehicle for:

a Business _____ **b** Commuting _____ **c** Other _____

6 Do you (or your spouse) have another vehicle available for personal use? . . . . ☐ Yes ☐ No

7 Was your vehicle available for use during off-duty hours? . . . . ☐ Yes ☐ No

8 a Do you have evidence to support your deduction? . . . . ☐ Yes ☐ No

b If "Yes," is the evidence written? . . . . ☐ Yes ☐ No

For Paperwork Reduction Act Notice, see Form 1040 instructions.

Schedule C-EZ (Form 1040) 1999

KFA

68

SCHEDULE D
(Form 1040)

Department of the Treasury
Internal Revenue Service (99)

Capital Gains and Losses

▶ Attach to Form 1040.　　▶ See Instructions for Schedule D (Form 1040).

▶ Use Schedule D-1 for more space to list transactions for lines 1 and 8.

OMB No. 1545-0074

1999

Attachment
Sequence No. 12

Name(s) shown on Form 1040

William J. and Hillary Rodham Clinton

Your social security number

Part I　Short-Term Capital Gains and Losses – Assets Held One Year or Less

(a) Description of property (Example, 100 sh XYZ Co)	(b) Date acquired (Mo., day, yr)	(c) Date sold (Mo., day, yr)	(d) Sales price (see page D-5)	(e) Cost or other basis (see page D-5)	(f) GAIN or (LOSS) Subtract (e) from (d)	

2 Enter your short-term totals, if any, from Schedule D-1, line 2 .... | **2** | | | | |

3 Total short-term sales price amounts. Add column (d) of lines 1 and 2 .... | **3** | | | | |

4 Short-term gain from Form 6252 and short-term gain or (loss) from Forms 4684, 6781, and 8824 .... | | | | **4** | |

Pell Rudman Trust Company, N.A.
5 Net short-term gain or (loss) from partnerships, S corporations, estates, and trusts from Schedule(s) K-1 | **5** | 57,755 |

6 Short-term capital loss carryover Enter the amount, if any, from line 8 of your 1998 Capital Loss Carryover Worksheet ....| **6** (|) |

7 Net short-term capital gain or (loss). Combine lines 1 through 6 in column (f) .... ▶ | **7** | 57,755 |

Part II　Long-Term Capital Gains and Losses – Assets Held More Than One Year

(a) Description of property (Example, 100 sh XYZ Co)	(b) Date acquired (Mo., day, yr)	(c) Date sold (Mo., day, yr)	(d) Sales price (see page D-5)	(e) Cost or other basis (see page D-5)	(f) GAIN or (LOSS) Subtract (e) from (d)	(g) 28% RATE GAIN or (LOSS) *(see instr. below)

9 Enter your long-term totals, if any, from Schedule D-1, line 9 .... | **9** | | | | |

10 Total long-term sales price amounts. Add column (d) of lines 8 and 9 .... | **10** | | | | |

11 Gain from Form 4797, Part I; long-term gain from Forms 2439 and 6252; and long-term gain or (loss) from Forms 4684, 6781, and 8824 . ... | **11** | |

Pell Rudman Trust Company, N.A.
12 Net long-term gain or (loss) from partnerships, S corporations, estates, and trusts from Schedule(s) K-1 . | **12** | 122,094 |

13 Capital gain distributions. See page D-1 .... | **13** | |

14 Long-term capital loss carryover. Enter in both columns (f) and (g) the amount, if any, from line 13 of your 1998 Capital Loss Carryover Worksheet .... | **14** (|)(|

15 Combine lines 8 through 14 in column (g). .. .. | **15** | |

16 Net long-term capital gain or (loss). Combine lines 8 through 14 in column (f) .... ▶ | **16** | 122,094 |

Next: Go to Part III on the back.

* 28% Rate Gain or Loss includes all "collectibles gains and losses" (as defined on page D-5) and up to 50% of the eligible gain on qualified small business stock (see page D-4).

For Paperwork Reduction Act Notice, see Form 1040 instructions.

Schedule D (Form 1040) 1999

KFA

5

The Untold Story:
Congress's Own Calculation of Its Revenue Losses from Special Provisions of the Tax Laws

[T]he tax code is the single greatest source of lobbying activity in Washington.
—Dick Armey
U.S. House of Representatives

Background: The Disadvantages of Special Tax-Saving
Provisions * Avoiding Scrutiny by Not Knowing * Accounting
for Tax Preferences and Tax Expenditures * The Normal
Income Tax Law * Comparison of Results Under Our Tax
Law and the NTL * The Concept of Tax Expenditures * The
Controversy over the Concept of Tax Expenditures *
Counting Tax Expenditures * A Snapshot of the Estimates:
2000–2004 * How Much Income Is Missing? * Who Receives
the Tax Savings? * Thinking About Tax Expenditures

Background: The Disadvantages of Special Tax-Saving Provisions

The central challenge for individual income tax policy is to define the tax base. What income should be taxable? What personal deductions should be allowed? Congress's answers establish how much of our income will be taxed. These answers vary among us, as we saw with the Gepettos and the Antons. Simply put, though my dollar of income buys as much as yours and each of us has one less dollar for each dollar we spend, even when our total dollars and household size are equal, federal income tax laws often sharply distinguish between your dollar and mine. Why should we be judged so unequally?

Why also are the dollars of people who have so many often favored over the dollars of people who have relatively few? Why, for example, are the Donald Trumps of the world entitled to pyramid gigantic real estate holdings tax free through an exchange of one parcel of land or building for another, time after time, whereas an elderly couple must pay tax on their modest gain when they sell their family farm for cash? Why does Congress allow the William Simons of the world to postpone, perhaps forever, paying millions of dollars of tax on their sale of a corporation's stock to its employee stock option plan as long as they invest the proceeds in the U.S. stock market, whereas an ordinary family must pay taxes on its gain when it sells its business to another family in town and invests the proceeds in the U.S. stock market?

> *Laws protecting income from tax rather than exposing income to tax are most responsible for unfair results under the income tax laws.*

These distinctions exist because a majority of Congress believes, or behaves as if it believes, that such distinctions are in the nation's best interest. Like the Energizer battery, distinctions of one kind or another go on, and on, and on, revealing a massive and largely unjustifiable congressional game of picking tax favorites—favorite income, favorite expenses, favorite taxpayers. Counterintuitive as it may seem, laws protecting income from tax rather than exposing income to tax are most responsible for inequities under the income tax laws—results that prevent equals from being taxed equally. When fully analyzed, these laws too rarely hold up before the simple question, "Why me and not you?"

Attacking these special provisions is so difficult because so many seem to be worthy on first blush. Discovering the full story requires digging deeply because typically it is obscured by decades of misleading assurances by politicians that the special provisions exist primarily for the ordinary taxpayer. Exclusive of the tax savings from personal exemptions and standard deductions, the ordinary taxpayer is but a minor beneficiary of the collective tax savings from all of these special provisions. Uncovering the identity of major beneficiaries exposes deeply troubling questions about tax justice.

> *Most people pay more in taxes, not less, because of the cumulative impact of special provisions that protect income from tax.*

Written by Congress, the story of that justice is about Congress's values. For the first 55 years of the income tax, Congress refused even to acknowledge publicly how much income escaped taxation. Readers initially might think, "Thank God, less of our income is taxed!" Why would we want Congress to spend our hard-earned tax dollars thinking of ways to tax what presently is untaxed? Although there are broad economic reasons for doing so, let us begin with how the current tax system affects individual taxpayers. Most people pay more in taxes, not less, because of the cumulative impact of special provisions that protect income from tax. This result follows because of the unfavorable relationship between their tax savings, if any, from the special provisions and the higher tax rates they must pay on their income that is taxed.

Like wealth in this country, tax savings from these special provisions are highly concentrated. The top tenth of all taxpayers reaps about 50 percent of the savings; the bottom half, only about 5 percent. Yet these special provisions affect everyone because Congress must set tax rates on the remaining income at levels that will produce the desired revenue. These tax rates, including the bottom rate, must be considerably higher than if considerably more income were taxed.

> *The top tenth of all taxpayers reaps about 50 percent of the tax savings from special tax provisions; the bottom half, only about 5 percent.*

Assuming, as we will see, that most special provisions do not stimulate economic growth and that many constrain it, the mathematical equation looks roughly like this: The less some people pay because of the special provisions, the more other people pay. Probably we do not mind if we receive a fair share of the tax savings from special provisions, though even then we may suffer if the economic distortions that are an outgrowth of the special provisions lower our overall income. But if our tax savings from the special provisions are modest, our personal tax bill likely is higher than if special provisions were eliminated and tax rates were reduced proportionately for everyone. The massive complexity of laws driven by special provisions also increases our cost of compliance and the revenue government needs to pay for its demanding oversight responsibilities.

> *If our tax savings from the special provisions are modest, our personal tax bill likely is higher than if special provisions were eliminated and tax rates were reduced proportionately for everyone.*

For all of these reasons, we need to explore reforms that would produce a comprehensive definition of income that would yield a broad tax base while allowing for much lower tax rates. We will call this a **broad-base low-rate system.**

Avoiding Scrutiny by Not Knowing

After the early days of the income tax, Congress progressively lost interest in a broad-base low-rate system. It also lacked interest in informing the public about the tax revenue the government lost from each of the special provisions Congress enacted. Not until 1974 was it required to do so. The political advantages of the old way were obvious.

Take, for example, the home-mortgage interest deduction. By not publicizing who received the tax savings, Congress could indulge more easily the excesses of the deduction, which allowed the wealthiest homeowners—who could be among the largest political contributors—to deduct millions of dollars of interest each year. Nondisclosure also helped Congress perpetuate the popular myth that the deduction primarily served the ordinary homeowner, though higher-income homeowners always reaped the great majority of the tax savings. Nondisclosure obscured the excesses of special provisions that deferred taxes on pension-plan accumulations, and it perpetuated the myth that the provisions primarily benefited ordinary workers.

> *Congress's failure to publish relevant data about special provisions meant that it was unwilling to be candid about its judgments.*

Congress may have believed that these and numerous other outcomes from special provisions were the quid pro quo for progressive tax rates; but Congress's failure to publish revenue and distributional data about special provisions meant that it was unwilling to be candid about its judgments. A less generous view is that Congress chose not to be accountable. Fortunately, in 1974, Congress mandated that some data be made public.

Accounting for Tax Preferences and Tax Expenditures

Much credit for the mandate belongs to Stanley Surrey, a prominent tax expert from Harvard Law School and a Treasury Department official. In the 1960s, Surrey publicly challenged Congress to change its habits. Along with other tax specialists, Surrey insisted that not accounting for the government's revenue losses from special provisions that protected income from tax was inexcusable as a matter of budget and tax policy. He also believed that once an annual accounting took place, Congress eventually might realize that eliminating or sharply modifying most special provisions would produce a fairer, simpler, and more economically sound tax system.

Surrey's cause then, like mine now, was to fix the system itself, not to generate more tax revenue. Under revenue-neutral reforms, the broader tax base would be accompanied by lower tax rates to produce the same tax revenues as before. If, however, the more consistent treatment of income and lower tax rates also enhanced economic growth, as should be true, individual incomes would increase, as would tax revenue. Congress then could reduce rates even further.

Surrey and his brigade of reformers finally prevailed. Information published informally beginning in 1968 became mandated by the Budget Act of 1974. Ever since, members of Congress and the public have had access to estimates of the additional income tax revenue that theoretically could be collected if Congress eliminated most special provisions of the tax laws that protect income from tax. The special provisions are referred to as **tax preferences,** and the revenue losses they produce are referred to as **tax expenditures,** terms used frequently throughout this book.

> *Since 1974, Congress must identify each special provision, or tax preference, and must estimate its revenue cost, or tax expenditure, to the government.*

Congress assigned the task of cataloging tax preferences and calculating tax expenditures to its own nonpartisan Joint Committee on Taxation, which publishes the figures annually in a 25-page document titled *Estimates of Federal Tax Expenditures* (the Estimates). The president's Office of Management and Budget (OMB) also prepares its own, comparable figures. Both documents identify each tax preference and list the tax expenditure from it for the current year and succeeding four years. For example, the Joint Committee estimates that the home-mortgage interest deduction will cost the government (and save certain taxpayers) $55 billion in 2000 and $301 billion from 2000 through 2004.[1]

The 1974 act does not require Congress, and Congress does not require the Joint Committee, to tabulate how the tax savings from tax preferences are distributed among different income groups. Fortunately, at the end of each year's Estimates, the Joint Committee volunteers distribution tables for nine tax expenditures—itemized deductions for medical expenses, home-mortgage interest, real estate taxes, state and local income and personal property taxes, and charitable contributions; **tax credits** for children, child care, and earned income; and the exemption of most Social Security and railroad retirement benefits. In each case the tax savings are divided among nine income groups, beginning with taxpayers having up to $10,000 of income and ending with taxpayers who have $200,000 or more of income. These tables reveal how important similar tables would be for all tax expenditures.

Consider the child-care tax credit. Tax credits offset our actual tax liability dollar for dollar: A $1 credit reduces our tax liability by $1. The child care credit helps working parents pay child-care costs they incur for up to two children, who usually must be under the age of 13. For taxpayers with $10,000 or less of adjusted gross income, the maximum credit is $720 for one child and $1,440 for two or more children. The credit gradually declines to $480 for one child ($960 for two or more children) as a taxpayer's AGI moves from $10,000 to $28,000. Thereafter, the decline stops: Taxpayers with $28,001 or $280,001 are eligible for the same $480/$960 maximum credit.

TABLE 5.1 Distribution by Income Class of $2.2 Billion Tax Savings from Child-Care Credit, 1999

(A) Taxpayers Grouped by Income*	(B) Tax Savings ($ millions)	(C) % of Tax Savings
(1) 0–9,999	—	—
(2) 10,000–19,999	87	—
(3) 20,000–29,999	328	14.9
(4) 30,000–39,999	297	13.5
(5) 40,000–49,999	304	13.8
(6) 50,000–74,999	531	24.1
(7) 75,000–99,999	350	15.9
(8) 100,000–199,999	252	11.5
(9) 200,000–	52	—

*As used by the Joint Committee, "income" means the total of AGI plus tax-exempt interest, employee contributions for health plans and life insurance, the employer's share of FICA tax, nontaxable Social Security benefits, and several other items.

SOURCE: Joint Committee on Taxation, *Estimate of Federal Tax Expenditures For Fiscal Years 2000–2004* (Washington, D.C.: GPO, 1999), JCS-13-99, 29, table 3.

The credit saved taxpayers approximately $2.2 billion of taxes in 1999 (see Table 5.1). While it nominally has most value for very low-income parents, parents with under $10,000 of income received virtually none of the tax savings because the credit is available only to parents who owe taxes, and these parents do not owe taxes. Parents with $100,000 or more of income received $304 million of the tax savings.

Armed with this information, we are better equipped to explore a series of questions. Should Congress assist working parents with their child-care expenses? If so, does the existing tax credit deliver sufficient assistance to the population that deserves federal aid? Alternatively, should the subsidy be *refundable?* If it were refundable, any excess of the credit over the taxes actually owed would be paid by check to the parents, which would help low-income parents most. Should any of the credit benefit high-income households?

Regrettably, little of such questioning, when it does occur, reaches the public; and with the notable exception of congressional debates preceding the 1986 Reform Act, the Estimates have affected tax policy only marginally. Once legislated, even the least justifiable tax preferences have proven difficult to uproot. Still, the obscurity of the Estimates remains striking. Except among tax-policy mavens, their very existence has been one of Washington's best kept public secrets. Few people, including tax lawyers and accountants, know about them. Few members of Congress mention them. Major newspapers might briefly refer to them from time to time. Not a single newspaper has given them what they deserve—the attention of a cadre of experts who at least once a year explain and debate the new data in a format that would intrigue and inform readers. The story never makes the nightly news.

It should! The potential for fundamental tax reform suggested by the Estimates is startling. From 2000 through 2004, individual income tax expenditures enumerated by the Joint Committee, added together, are estimated at $2.965 trillion, approximately twice the likely national defense budget for those years. They recently have been growing at about 6 percent per year, far faster than our economy. Tax expenditures for corporations, also significant, will be far less than for individuals, costing the government an estimated $389 billion over the same five-year period.

> *From 2000 through 2004, individual income tax expenditures may cost the government $2.965 trillion, over twice the likely national defense budget for those years.*

Tax expenditures are not, however, by definition or implication, necessarily bad policy. They may or may not make the laws fairer or promote sound social or economic behavior. But on this we can agree: An understanding of the nuts and bolts of tax preferences and expenditures is essential to rational decision-making by Congress and the public.

Let us turn to the nuts and bolts now. What are tax preferences, and how are tax expenditures measured? The answers turn on the Joint Committee's definition of a hypothetical **normal income tax law (NTL).** Readers will find the normal income tax law familiar. It has a broad tax base that draws heavily on Haig-Simons.

The Normal Income Tax Law

Our starting point is the 1974 Budget Act. It mandated that Congress catalog "those revenue losses attributable to provisions of the Federal tax laws which allow a special exclusion, exemption or deduction from gross income or which provide a special credit, a preferential rate or a deferral of liability." Notice the words *special, preferential,* and *deferral.* They are key, yet the act does not define them. That was left to the Joint Committee.

Some definitions are easier than others. If you have income this year but no tax liability on it until a later year, your tax liability has been *deferred.* For example, your tax-deductible contribution of $2,000 to an individual retirement account defers the tax on $2,000 of income.

Defining a *preferential* rate can be more complicated. Today's maximum 20 percent rate on capital gains, compared with the maximum rate of 39.6 percent on ordinary income, is an obvious candidate.[2] Some experts believe that any rate below the highest rate on ordinary income is preferential. But the NTL considers progressive rates normal, including the alternative minimum tax.

Most controversial is the meaning of *special*. Along with the other terms, it eventually would be defined by reference to the Joint Committee's normal income tax law (the NTL). This law is the Joint Committee's idea of what our income tax laws would look like without tax preferences. With few exceptions, the NTL eliminates every provision that the Joint Committee deems special, preferential, or a deferral of liability. Remember, the NTL is neither an actual law nor a law recommended by the Joint Committee. It is solely a model of a possible tax law.

> *The normal income tax law (NTL) is the Joint Committee's idea of what our income tax laws would look like without tax preferences.*

Surrey would have been pleased with the Joint Committee's work. The NTL consists of a very broad tax base that counts as income nearly all our economic gain during the course of a year. For example, contrary to our laws, employee fringe benefits are not excluded; interest on state and local bonds is not exempt; and income accumulated each year in employer pension plans and individual retirement accounts is not deferred.

On the other hand, although gifts and inheritances clearly increase a recipient's "power or capacity to consume," the NTL does not count them as income because they are subject to federal gift- and estate-tax laws. The Joint Committee also has made practical judgments that depart from Haig-Simons for administrative reasons. For example, the NTL taxes gains from investments only when realized, such as when they are sold or exchanged, because measuring unrealized gains often would be difficult. The NTL ignores imputed income, such as the net rental value of the house we own and live in, also because of the difficulty of calculating the income. Perhaps most controversial, the NTL does not make adjustments for inflation when measuring income or deductions, again because of administrative difficulties that a fully inflation-adjusted system would create. Each of these exceptions to Haig-Simons actually corresponds with our own tax laws.

On the deduction side, the NTL recognizes that income is to be reduced by all costs necessary to produce it. These include costs you incur as the owner of a business or as an employee in your work. Otherwise, the NTL allows only two personal adjustments—personal exemptions and standard deductions—because, according to the Joint Committee, they "approximate the level of income below which it would be difficult for an individual or a family to obtain minimal amounts of food, clothing, and shelter."[3] No one is entitled to itemized deductions or to tax credits.

To summarize, with relatively few exceptions that the Joint Committee deems practical, the NTL follows the principles of a broad-base income tax as defined by Haig-Simons.

Comparison of Results Under Our Tax Law and the NTL

The remarkable differences between the potential tax results under the Joint Committee's NTL and the actual tax results under our system can be appreciated by comparing what hypothetically could have happened if the NTL had been in place in 1997 (the most recent year for which we have complete data on individual income tax returns). This comparison assumes that taxpayers would not have altered their economic behavior had the NTL been in place; estimating any change in economic behavior would be too speculative for these purposes.

As seen in Table 5.2, on $3.43 trillion of actual taxable income, taxpayers owed $727 billion of taxes.[4] This

> *In 1997, taxpayers paid an average tax rate on their taxable income of* 21.3 percent. *Under the NTL, the average tax rate would have been* 14.7 percent.

meant that taxpayers paid an average tax rate on their taxable income of *21.3 percent* (21.3 x $3.43 trillion = $727 billion). By comparison, taxable income under the NTL was $4.93 trillion, or $1.5 trillion more than under our tax laws. With so much more income to tax, the NTL could have raised the same $727 billion of taxes with an average tax rate of only *14.7 percent.*

The Concept of Tax Expenditures

Calling a law that prevents the government from collecting income taxes a tax expenditure probably strikes readers as anomalous. After all, an expenditure means something spent. The term tax expenditure makes sense, however, when viewed as a departure from a comprehensive income tax. "Special income tax provisions are referred to as tax expenditures because they are considered analogous to direct outlay programs," explains the Joint Committee, "and the two can be considered as alternative means of accomplishing similar budget policy objectives."[5] In other words, Congress subsidizes all sorts of programs either by writing checks or by creating special provisions in the tax laws that reduce government receipts. Either way, the government has less money.

For example, Congress helps homeowners afford their real estate taxes by allowing them an itemized deduction for the taxes they pay. To simplify the tax laws, Congress could eliminate the deduction. Let us assume, however, that Congress believes that the subsidy makes sense. Congress then could authorize the Department of Housing and Urban Development (HUD) to issue checks to itemizers that, after taxes, would equal their tax savings had the deduction not been eliminated. Either way—through the tax deduction or HUD's check—the government would have less money and these homeowners more.

TABLE 5.2 Comparison of Actual Tax Returns and Returns Under Hypothetical Normal Income Tax Law (NTL) to Raise $727 Billion of Tax Revenue, 1997 (rows 1–3 in $trillions)

	(A) Actual Returns	(B) NTL	(C) Difference
(1) Adjusted gross income (AGI)	4.97	6.27	+1.30
(2) Less personal deductions	1.54	1.34	-0.21
(3) Taxable income	3.43	4.93	+1.50
(4) Average tax rate	21.20	14.70	-6.50

SOURCE: The amount of AGI under the NTL is from the author's estimates; no one has published the complete data. For an explanation of the author's calculations, see Appendix 5.B.

Tax expenditures operate a lot like budget **entitlement programs**. As the Joint Committee explains: "Tax expenditures are most similar to those direct spending programs that have no spending limits and that are available as entitlements to those who meet the statutory criteria established for the programs."[6] Most of us who benefit from tax expenditures have come to expect the benefits each year; yet without a visible government check in hand, we typically do not see ourselves as part of a government transfer program. Thus tax expenditures are a dangerous way for the government to do business and makes tampering with them a dangerous act by those seeking election.

> *Most of us who benefit from tax expenditures have come to expect the tax benefits each year; yet because no government check is involved, we are not inclined to believe that we are part of a government transfer program.*

Whether visible or not, tax expenditures are government programs. Like direct government grants, they promote certain kinds of activities, influence certain individual behavior, or ameliorate certain hardships. All save money for the beneficiaries. As the Congressional Budget Office explained in its presentation of President Bush's 1992 budget: "The cost of [a taxpayer's] medical care is reduced both by direct Government expenditures for the Medicare and Medicaid programs and by the exclusion from individual taxpayer income of the medical insurance premiums that employers pay for their employees."[7]

Consider the income tax exclusion of most Social Security retirement benefits, one of the largest and least understood of all tax expenditures. Recipients commonly believe that because Social Security taxes are withheld from their wages and are subject to federal income tax, the retirement benefits themselves have already been taxed. A typical retiree's lifetime wage withholdings, however, represent today only about 15 percent of the retirement benefits that he and his beneficiaries will receive; the remaining 85 percent never has been taxed. But unlike untaxed pension-plan benefits, 100 percent of which must be counted as income as we receive them, previously untaxed Social Security retirement benefits do not automatically count as income. In fact, about two-thirds of Social Security

> *Today's typical retiree has paid income taxes on about only 15 percent of the Social Security retirement benefits that he and his beneficiaries will receive.*

retirement recipients currently do not owe an income tax on any of their retirement benefits.[8] The tax exemption, expected to cost the government a massive $132 billion for the years 2000 through 2004, is a form of government welfare, yet most recipients would not qualify for welfare under standards imposed by other federal programs.

Whether Social Security retirement benefits are taxable is determined in most cases by the following formula: Recipients add (a) their AGI,[9] (b) their tax-exempt bond interest, and (c) half of their Social Security benefits. For married couples, if the total does not exceed $32,000, their entire benefits are tax free; the same is true for all other taxpayers if the total does not exceed $25,000.

Consider David and Betty Harrell, a retired couple in Baltimore. In 1999, they had $24,000 of AGI, no tax-exempt bond interest, and $15,000 of Social Security retirement benefits. All $15,000 from Social Security was tax exempt after applying the previous formula: Their AGI ($24,000) plus half of their Social Security retirement benefits ($7,500) equaled $31,500, which was less than $32,000. Had 85 percent of the $15,000 been subject to tax at the Harrells' 15 percent tax bracket, they would have paid $1,913 in taxes and kept the remaining $13,087 of benefits.

Congress's judgment to subsidize the Harrells' retirement is to be compared with dramatically tougher eligibility standards applied under the Supplemental Security Income (SSI) program, the principal federal income subsidy for the elderly poor. Frank and Mary O'Brien, a retired elderly couple who also live in Baltimore, were ineligible in 1999 to receive SSI benefits because their $9,500 of income from Social Security and pensions exceeded the SSI threshold of $9,252. By any standard of need, the government should favor the O'Briens over the Harrells, who have about four times more income. As a balance sheet matter, the government could as easily have given the O'Briens $1 of SSI benefits as it could forgo collecting $1 of income taxes on the Harrells' Social Security benefits.

As a general principle, welfare standards for the elderly ought to be identical for tax laws and direct outlay programs. Indeed, every tax expenditure ought to be subject to rigorous evaluation. After all, approximately $545 billion of individual income tax expenditures for 2000 collectively represent by far the government's largest discretionary domestic programs if defense expenditures are ignored. The president's proposed budget for 2000 for nondefense **discretionary spending programs** —for agriculture, commerce, education, energy, health and human services, housing and urban development, environmental protection, transportation, law enforcement, and much more—was $320 billion, or 59 percent of all individual income tax expenditures. This gap between the two is projected to grow substantially in the years ahead. In sum, the heart of the government's discretionary social and economic programs exists in its income tax laws. We owe it to ourselves to see that these laws are exposed to no less critical review than any direct program of government subsidies.

The Controversy over the Concept of Tax Expenditures

Although most experts agree that the basic tenets of Haig-Simons ought to guide any effort to construct a normal income tax model, they disagree about details. As an example, law professor William Andrews has suggested that charitable contributions and payments for state and local taxes should be deemed "refinements" of Haig-Simons rather than "departures" from it.[10] Others go so far as to argue that disagreements about details should preclude establishing a model of a comprehensive income tax. These experts favor examining each tax issue on its merits without reference to a particular concept of income.

The most prominent early advocate of this ad hoc approach to tax policy was the distinguished law professor Boris Bittker. Writing in the 1960s in a series of debates with Joseph Pechman, Richard Musgrave, and Charles Galvin, all distinguished tax economists, Bittker objected to calling tax preferences "exceptions" to a model tax system constructed primarily from the teachings of Haig-Simons. Finding "distressing vagueness" in terms like tax preferences, he argued that the exceptions to a broad-base income tax were so numerous and so inconsistently advanced by different experts that any exception became fair game.[11]

Pechman maintained that only two conditions warranted any departure from a broad-base tax structure: "First, the departure must promote a major national objective and . . . the tax mechanism [must be] the most efficient method of achieving it; or, second, it is impractical to tax the particular item."[12] Musgrave believed that Bittker's "counsel of despair is unjustified and damaging to income tax reform."[13] Galvin noted the obvious: "Bittker's suggestion of ad hoc settlements will get us nowhere. We have had a surfeit of patchwork and piecemeal effort."[14]

We still do. Fortunately, through the NTL, we at least have the government's model of a broad-base income tax and an estimate of the tax revenue theoretically lost from exceptions to it. At a minimum, the NTL offers a worthy starting point for framing a real national debate about which income tax policies serve our society best.

Counting Tax Expenditures

Each tax expenditure equals the tax revenue that the government theoretically loses because of the related tax preference. For these calculations, the Joint Committee assumes that all other provisions of the tax laws remain unchanged. When, for example, it calculates the revenue loss (the tax expenditure) from the deduction for real estate taxes on personal houses (the tax preference), it assumes that Congress has not modified or eliminated any other tax preferences.

> *Estimates of tax expenditures are theoretical; the actual figures could be higher or lower than estimated.*

The revenue loss is theoretical because the Joint Committee does not know, or estimate, how taxpayer behavior might change if one or more tax preferences were eliminated. It also does not know, or estimate, whether the elimination of a tax preference would have any particular economic impact. Yet the Joint Committee knows that taxpayers may behave differently and the economy could be affected. If so, the actual impact on tax revenues from the elimination of a tax preference could be higher or lower than estimated.

For example, without the deduction for real estate taxes on personal houses, people might buy less expensive houses, borrow less to buy them, and pay less interest because of the smaller loans. The lower interest payments in turn would reduce the tax expenditure for mortgage-interest deductions. Houses also might decline in value, which could hurt the economy. Some of the money that previously would have been invested in expensive houses might, however, be invested in start-up companies and other enterprises that could strengthen the economy.

As this discussion suggests, anticipating the ancillary consequences of eliminating one or more tax expenditures is too speculative for the Joint Committee to undertake in its preparation of the Estimates. Trying to anticipate the consequences, however, would be highly relevant to any consideration of tax reforms.

A Snapshot of the Estimates: 2000–2004

Totaling each tax expenditure can approximate only roughly the sum of all tax expenditures. Nonetheless, the numbers are too daunting to ignore: The figure reaches $548 billion for 2000 and, as mentioned earlier, nearly $3 trillion for 2000 through 2004. A list of most tax expenditures—over 100 exist for individual taxpayers alone—appears in Appendix 5.A to give readers a picture of the variety and magnitude of taxes that the government theoretically could collect were the NTL in place. Table 5.3 lists the 20 largest tax expenditures.

Some tax preference terminology will seem foreign. It may also be surprising that, as Table 5.3 indicates, nearly two-thirds of all tax expenditures arise from exclusions from gross income; most of these are related to employment. Itemized deductions play a significant but much smaller role than you might expect.

How Much Income Is Missing?

Regrettably, neither the Joint Committee nor the Treasury Department publishes figures that explain how it arrives at its tax expenditure estimates. Consequently, we have no way of knowing, for any particular tax expenditure, how much income they assume is protected by tax, how that income is spread among income groups, or the average tax rate that would be applied against that income within each income group. Yet we know that the Joint Committee and the Treasury Department must make such calculations, at least in some fashion, to produce their estimates; and we know too that these calculations would then indicate the total income protected from tax by all tax expenditures. Some information is available from the *Statistics of Income* data published annually by the IRS with respect to our individual tax returns. For most of the information, however, we must rely on our own best estimates, aided by a few limited studies by other organizations.

By my rough calculation, the nearly $3 trillion of tax expenditures from 2000 through 2004 result from tax preferences that protect approximately $16.8 trillion of income from tax. That is, in addition to the income protected by personal exemptions and standard deductions, a staggering $16.8 trillion of certain people's income might not be taxed during these five years because of special exclusions, exemptions, deferrals, deductions, or credits; a preferential tax rate; and deferrals of tax liabilities adopted by Congress.[15]

Who Receives the Tax Savings?

I have also estimated the allocation of total tax expenditures among income groups. Stripped of rhetoric, tax expenditures offer little to the poorest taxpayers and progressively more to progressively successful taxpayers. As seen in Table 5.4, in 1997 the top 5.9 percent of all taxpayers (with $100,000 or more of AGI) received 37.7 percent of the tax savings from tax preferences (add rows 8 and 9 of column D); the bottom 43.2 percent of all taxpayers (with under $20,000 of AGI) received only 8.2 percent. Average tax savings per tax return were equally skewed. For people with over $200,000 of AGI, the average tax savings was $47,508, nearly 20 times the average tax savings of people with $30,000 to $40,000 of AGI.

TABLE 5.3 The 20 Largest Tax Expenditures in the Federal Individual Income Tax
for Fiscal Years 2000–2004 (in $billions)

		2000	*2000–2004*
(1)	Exclusion: net pension plan and Keogh plan contributions and earnings	81.0	442.1
(2)	Exclusion: employer contributions for medical insurance premiums and medical care	58.0	324.1
(3)	Deduction: interest for owner-occupied homes	55.2	301.4
(4)	Reduced rates: tax on long-term capital gains	36.0	194.6
(5)	Deduction: nonbusiness state and local income and personal property taxes	35.5	190.0
(6)	Deduction: charitable contributions	28.0	162.9
(7)	Exclusion: untaxed Medicare benefits	24.9	146.0
(8)	Exclusion: untaxed Social Security benefits	24.4	131.9
(9)	Exclusion: basis adjustment on capital gains at death (the "step-up")	23.7	136.1
(10)	Exclusion: investment income on life insurance and annuity contracts	22.9	121.8
(11)	Deduction: real estate taxes on owner-occupied homes	18.9	101.3
(12)	Credit: children under age 17	17.1	84.5
(13)	Exclusion: interest on public-purpose state and local bonds	13.3	71.4
(14)	Exclusion: capital gains on sale of family residence	12.9	65.1
(15)	Deduction and exclusion: for IRA contributions and accumulations	12.2	70.7
(16)	Exclusion: employee benefits under employer's cafeteria plan	6.9	39.6
(17)	Deduction: accelerated depreciation of business equipment	6.8	31.1
(18)	Exclusion: miscellaneous employee fringe benefits	6.5	36.7
(19)	Tax credit: tuition for postsecondary education	5.4	27.5
(20)	Exclusion: workers' compensation benefits	5.0	27.6

SOURCE: Joint Committee on Taxation, *Estimates of Federal Tax Expenditures for Fiscal Years 2000–2004* (Washington, D.C.: GPO, 1999), JCS-13-99, 15–24.

TABLE 5.4 Tax Expenditures Distributed Among Taxpayers, 1997

(A) Taxpayers Grouped by AGI ($)	(B) % of All Returns	(C) Total Tax Expenditures (in $billions)	(D) % of All Tax Expenditures	(E) $ of Tax Expenditures per Return
(1) 0–9,999	23.1	13.6	3.2	482
(2) 10,000–19,999	20.1	21.3	5.0	869
(3) 20,000–29,999	14.7	32.2	7.6	1,789
(4) 30,000–39,999	10.6	33.3	7.9	2,569
(5) 40,000–49,999	8.0	35.2	8.3	3,597
(6) 50,000–74,999	12.4	75.4	17.7	4,967
(7) 75,000–99,999	5.3	53.9	12.6	8,350
(8) 100,000–199,999	4.4	75.2	17.6	13,983
(9) 200,000–	1.5	85.8	20.1	47,508

SOURCE: Author's calculations. See Appendix B of this chapter.

Thinking About Tax Expenditures

Most of the larger tax expenditures are examined closely in this book. The legitimacy of even the smallest tax expenditures, however, must be at issue in any debate about income tax policy. In the context of our current $1.9 trillion federal budget, we can lose sight of their importance. Each year Congress vigorously debates funding programs such as the Peace Corps, the Export-Import Bank, occupational safety and health, low-rent public housing loans, and the National Endowment for the Arts, each of which receives less (and some far less) than $1 billion.

A staggering $16.8 trillion of certain people's income might not be taxed from 2000 through 2004 because of tax preferences.

Equal attention should be given annually to tax expenditures that cost the government less than $1 billion, such as the exclusion for the value of employer-provided meals and lodging, the exclusion for earnings of individual retirement accounts used for higher education, and the exclusions for employer-paid long-term-care insurance premiums. Is there a compelling need for the tax relief? Is the relief distributed fairly? Are the economic consequences desirable? What are the administrative implications?

As we struggle with these questions, something intriguing emerges about tax reform: the prospect of liberals and conservatives finding extensive common ground by pursuing a broad-base low-rate system, one in which your dollar and mine would be judged far more equally.

Appendix 5.A
Major Tax Expenditures in the Federal Individual Income Tax
for Fiscal Years 2000–2004 (revenue loss in billions of dollars)

	2000	2000–2004
*Exclusions and Deferrals from Gross Income*ᵃ		
<u>Related to Current Employment</u>		
a. Net exclusions of retirement plan contributions and earnings:		
(i) Pension plans	76.0	416.0
(ii) Individual retirement accounts (IRAs)	12.2	70.7
(iii) Self-employment (Keogh) plans	5.0	26.1
b. Exclusion of other employer-provided benefits (nonmilitary):		
(i) Contributions for medical insurance premiums and medical care	58.0	324.1
(ii) Benefits under cafeteria plans	6.9	39.5
(iii) Miscellaneous fringe benefits	6.5	36.7
(iv) Workers' compensation disability and survivors' benefits	5.0	27.6
(v) Workers' compensation medical benefits	4.5	24.6
(vi) Employer-paid transportation expenses to and from work	3.6	18.4
(vii) Premiums on group life insurance	2.0	11.0
(viii) Medical care, etc., for military dependents, retirees, and others	1.6	8.0
(ix) Voluntary employees' beneficiary associations (VEBAs)	1.4	7.9
(x) Employee meals and lodging (other than military)	.8	4.2
(xi) Employer-provided child care	.4	2.4
(xii) Housing allowances for ministers	.4	2.0
(xiii) Employer-provided education assistance	.3	.8
(xiv) Employee stock ownership plans (ESOPs)	.2	1.1
(xv) Premiums on accident and disability insurance	.2	1.0
(xvi) Adoption credit and employee adoption benefit exclusion	.2	.8
(xvii) Employee awards	.1	.7
(xviii) Special benefits for disabled coal miners	.1	.4
(xix) Military disability benefits	.1	.4
c. Exclusion of income earned abroad by U.S. citizens	2.4	14.1

d. Exclusion of benefits and allowances to armed
    forces personnel   <u>2.0</u>   <u>9.9</u>

    Subtotal   [189.9]   [1,048.4]

Related to Postemployment
a. Exclusion of untaxed Social Security benefits   24.4   131.9
b. Exclusion of untaxed Medicare benefits   24.9   89.7
c. Exclusion of veterans' disability, pension,
    and GI benefits   <u>2.3</u>   <u>12.6</u>

    Subtotal   [51.6]   [234.2]

Capital Gains
a. Step-up of tax basis of capital gains at death   23.7   136.1
b. Exclusion of capital gains on home sales   12.9   65.1
c. Carryover of tax basis on gifts   2.3   12.6
d. Deferral of gain on like-kind exchanges   .4   7.8
e. Deferral of gain on nondealer installment sale   <u>.3</u>   <u>2.5</u>

    Subtotal   [39.6]   [224.1]

Exclusion of Interest on State and Local Bonds
a. Public-purpose bonds   13.5   71.8
b. Private-purpose bonds   <u>3.2</u>   <u>20.8</u>

    Subtotal   [16.7]   [92.6]

Miscellaneous
a. Exclusion of investment income of life
    insurance and annuity contracts   22.9   121.8
b. Exclusion of scholarship and fellowship income   1.1   6.5
c. Cash public-assistance benefits   .7   3.7
d. Foster care payments   .5   2.7
e. From imputed-interest rule   .2   1.2
f. Tax on earnings of qualified state tuition programs .1   .7
g. Other   <u>—</u>   <u>.5</u>

    Subtotal   [25.5]   [137.1]

Deductions

Itemized Deductions
a. Interest for owner-occupied homes   55.2   301.4
b. Taxes:
    (i) Nonbusiness state and local
         income and personal property   35.5   190.0

(ii) Real estate—owner-occupied homes	18.9	101.3
c. Charitable contributions	28.0	162.9
d. Medical expenses (in excess of 7.5% of AGI)	4.4	25.4
e. Casualty and theft losses	.2	1.3
Subtotal	[142.2]	[782.3]

Business Deductions

a. Depreciation in excess of alternative depreciation system:		
(i) Equipment	6.8	13.1
(ii) Rental housing	1.5	9.2
(iii) Buildings other than rental housing	.7	8.3
b. Expensing of depreciable business property	.5	3.1
c. Excess of percentage over cost depletion— all fuel and nonfuel minerals	.4	5.5
d. Amortization of business start-up costs	.3	1.8
e. Expensing of costs of raising dairy and breeding cattle	.2	.9
f. Empowerment-zone tax incentives	.1	1.2
g. Cash accounting for agriculture and other businesses	.1	.6
h. Other	—	.4
Subtotal	[10.6]	[62.1]

Miscellaneous

a. Reduced rates on long-term capital gains	36.0	194.6
b. Additional standard deduction for blind and elderly	2.0	10.8
c. Health insurance and long-term care premiums for self-employed	1.2	9.3
d. Parental personal exemption for students 19–23	.7	3.9
e. Interest on student loans	.3	1.8
Subtotal	[40.2]	[220.4]

Total Deductions	[193.0]	[1,064.8]

Tax Credits

a. Children under 17	17.1	84.5
b. Tuition for postsecondary education	5.4	27.5
c. Earned income[b]	4.0	21.1
d. Low-income housing	2.5	13.1
e. Child and dependent care expenses	2.2	11.1
f. Employer-paid FICA taxes on tips	.2	1.8

g.	Production of nonconventional fuel	.2	1.4
h.	Rehabilitation of historic structures	.1	2.3
i.	Electricity production for wind, etc.	.1	.4
j.	Disabled-access expenditures	.1	.4
k.	Work opportunity	.1	.4

Total Credits   [32.0]   [164.0]

Total Individual Tax Expenditures for 2000: $ 548.3 billion

Total Individual Tax Expenditures for 2000–2004: $2,965.2 billion

SOURCE: Joint Committee on Taxation, *Estimates of Federal Tax Expenditures for Fiscal Years 2000–2004,* JCS-13-99 (Washington, D.C.: GPO, 1999), 15–24. table 1.
bThe figures in the table show the effect of the earned-income credit on receipts. The increase in outlays is $25.8 billion in 2000 and $134.5 billion for the years 2000 to 2004.

Appendix 5.B

No government or other publication allocates all or even most significant tax expenditures within income classes, tells us how much income is protected by each significant tax preference, or allocates such income among income classes. The government's failure here represents a massive disservice to the public, to policy analysts, and to our elected representatives. Without such data we are deprived of crucial information needed to evaluate the enormous role played by tax preferences in American life.

I have done my best to begin to fill this void; I hope that my efforts are only the beginning of many others. Inevitably, my data are heavily flawed; yet until more sophisticated models prove me wrong, I believe that they roughly approximate the actual figures.

Calculations for Table 5.2

My calculations of the income that would be counted in 1997 under the Joint Committee's NTL began with AGI reported on all returns for 1997. I then added the income that would be excluded or deferred from tax (the "missing income") because of the tax expenditures enumerated by the Joint Committee. To arrive at these missing income figures, I (a) allocated each of these tax expenditures among income classes (as explained further with respect to Table 5.4), (b) totaled these tax expenditures for each income class, (c) assumed an average marginal tax rate applicable within each income class that would have yielded the tax expenditures, (d) divided the total tax expenditures within each income class by the applicable tax rate to arrive at the missing income within each income class, and (e) totaled the missing income for each income class. To reduce NTL income to NTL taxable income, I then calculated the total personal exemptions and standard deductions within each income class, which required estimating the number of exemptions and size of the standard deduction for singles, married filing jointly, married filing separately, heads of households, and surviving spouses.

Calculations for Table 5.4

I began with the Joint Committee's allocation of nine tax expenditures within income classes. I then turned to an allocation of tax expenditures within income classes for employer-based pension plans for 1993 prepared by the Employee Benefit Research Institute of Washington, D.C. (EBRI), and for employer-paid health insurance premiums for 1994 prepared by the Congressional Budget Office (CBO); in each case, I adjusted the figures to approximate their values in 1997. For all other significant tax expenditures, I used tax return data or relied on analogies to other data. For example, I allocated tax expenditures for other employee fringe benefits on the same basis that CBO allocated tax expenditures for health insurance premiums. Tax-exempt interest could be allocated from tax return data, and I assumed that a similar allocation occurred for the tax-free buildup of cash value within life insurance policies. I also assumed that the tax expenditure for the step-up in basis of inherited assets would approximate the allocation of long-term capital gains, which is available from tax return data. And so it went.

Even the Joint Committee, EBRI, and CBO data created complications because they each used different definitions of income (all enhancements of AGI) for dividing taxpayers among income classes, whereas tax return data is based on AGI. Also, some data grouped taxpayers by households rather than tax returns. We need and deserve something better.

6

Common Ground:
Fitting Reforms for Conservatives and Liberals Alike

Truth has already ceased to be itself if polemically said.
—Ralph Waldo Emerson

The American Creed * Standing Together: The Shared
Values of Tax Policy * An Old Idea Whose Time Has
Come

If voters could overhear a forthright conversation among leading conservative and liberal thinkers about federal income tax policy, they would be surprised to discover far more unity between the two camps than polemicists on
either side care to admit. I refer here to a conversation among conservatives
and liberals uncluttered by elective politics. Of course, if given the choice,
many conservatives favor scrapping the income tax for a consumption tax
that would minimize or eliminate the taxation of income from savings and
investment. But for purposes of this conversation, we are to assume that the
income tax will be retained by Congress; and our conservative and liberal
thinkers are charged with the task of developing a single income tax policy
that most closely approximates each of their distinctive ideologies.

Both groups favor fundamental changes in the income tax laws to achieve a
fairer, simpler, and economically sounder system. Although their deep philo-
sophical differences lead to very different articulations of these goals, their
joint strategies would be to eliminate or curtail most tax preferences and to
lower all tax rates. As Eugene Steuerle, an economist who served in the Trea-

sury Department under four presidents and is widely respected for his nonpartisan views, has written, "A progressive and broad-based tax structure is in many ways both a liberal and a conservative policy . . . especially when compared to other financing alternatives."[1] It also offers the best antidote to what Thomas Edsall refers to in *The New Politics of Inequality* as the "inherent contradiction between equity [fairness], efficiency, redistribution and investment . . . in developing economic policy in advanced capitalist democracies."[2]

Why does a broad-base low-rate system offer the common ground on which to craft tax reform? Generalizations are risky because they never can reflect the diversity of views within conservative or liberal camps. But you can judge for yourself whether the following statements about conservatives and liberals hold up well. Certainly if conservatives and liberals can agree on how to proceed, moderates should have little difficulty joining in.

The American Creed

This country combines a political system that promises equal rights and opportunity for all and an economic system that guarantees unequal incomes. Both exist within what the historian Samuel Huntington refers to as the American creed, a set of core political values consisting of "liberty, equality, individualism, and democracy," all subject to the rule of law under the Constitution.[3] Sharp divisions arise over priorities; each element, however, of the American creed belongs to the orthodoxy of conservatives and liberals.

> *Principles of liberty, equality, individualism, and democracy belong to the orthodoxy of both conservatives and liberals.*

Conservatives

Conservatives have consistently stressed liberty and individualism. Liberty, or liberalism, here refers to the classical, eighteenth-century model, the essence of which was freedom from government control. Individualism, as the natural companion of liberty, is, in Huntington's words, "the right of each person to act in accordance with his own conscience and to control his own destiny free of external restraint, except insofar as such restraint is necessary to ensure comparable rights to others."[4] Conservatives believe in minimizing the intrusion of government in our private lives. Governmental laws are justified only when the objective cannot or is not likely to be adequately achieved without them and when they are compellingly in the public interest.

In economics, conservatives continue to draw heavily on the antimercantilist teachings of the eighteenth-century Scottish economist Adam Smith. Smith wrote in *The Wealth of Nations* that an entrepreneur intending to advance only his own self-interest is guided by an *invisible hand* that promotes the public interest "more effectually than when he really intends to promote it." When left to his own devices, Smith argued, the entrepreneur would create more wealth for everyone, including the laborer, than when directed by the good intentions of statesmen who have the "folly and presumption" to believe they know better.[5] Conservatives today recognize that society cannot rely entirely on a self-regulating economy. Nevertheless, they strongly favor limiting the influence of government on the economic marketplace. In their view, the invisible hand of competition usually remains the best hope for maximizing private and public welfare.

Conservatives, as well as liberals, recognize that any income tax interferes with the economic marketplace by depriving taxpayers of income that they might use differently from uses selected by the government. Income taxes can discourage work, savings, and investment by reducing the rewards from engaging in these activities. Income taxes also can skew how we use our income, often away from the most economically productive use. A principal goal of conservatives, therefore, is to minimize the adverse influences of the income tax on our economic behavior. While insisting that the income tax be fair, conservatives are more reluctant than liberals to sacrifice economic goals for the sake of attempting to achieve a fairer system. Indeed, in their view, the less efficient the system becomes, the less likely it will serve the broad, long-term interests of all members of society.

> *Tax preferences collectively undermine the invisible hand in which conservatives have such faith.*

These observations explain why conservatives, given an opportunity to rewrite the income tax laws, would be particularly sensitive to the economic inefficiencies of most tax preferences. In the more than 100 ways that tax preferences relieve us from tax because of the type of income we have or the way we receive or spend it, tax preferences represent a massive intrusion by the federal government into our market choices. Higher tax rates, necessitated by the resulting tax expenditures, test our resolve to work, save, and invest; they discourage entrepreneurship; and they magnify the rewards from tax-favored (as distinguished from the most economically rewarding) activities. In sum, tax preferences undermine the invisible hand in which conservatives have such faith.

For these reasons, a broad-base lower-rate system would be doubly attractive to conservatives. Barber Conable, the leading Republican income tax authority in the House of Representatives in the 1970s and early 1980s, noted its advantages over a decade ago. "Most economists agree," he observed, "that the goal for tax legislators should be to broaden the tax base gradually by eliminating preferences. . . . A broad tax base means marginal tax rates can be kept low so that taxes affect economic decision making as little as possible."[6]

A major point of disagreement between conservatives and liberals concerns the need for a special, low tax rate on capital gains. Conservatives favor taxing capital gains lightly (or not at all) in order to stimulate investment and entrepreneurship, to lower the cost of capital to businesses, to reduce the double tax on corporate earnings, and to encourage taxpayers to sell rather than hold on to their investments when they believe that a sale makes economic sense. Liberals believe that a favorable capital gains rate unfairly benefits the richest taxpayers. They also question the economic payoff. (All of these issues are addressed in Chapter 12.) Lowering rates across the board would lessen the need for a special tax rate on capital gains. But even if a compromise worked out between liberals and conservatives included a favorable tax rate on capital gains, the much lower tax rates on ordinary income likely would make the spread between the top capital gains rate and the top rate on ordinary income far less than the nearly 20-point spread today, which would please conservatives and liberals.

A broad-base low-rate system would reduce conservative ardor for a special, low tax rate on capital gains.

Finally, conservatives favor taxing all income (except capital gains) at the same flat rate or at only moderately progressive tax rates. They believe that high progressive tax rates unfairly penalize success. Conservatives argue that our tax laws should encourage the accumulation of new **wealth**—new successes. Much of this new wealth is from earned income, which is more difficult to shelter from tax than is the return on old wealth, most of which exists as untaxed capital appreciation. Lowering tax rates on earned income would reduce the tax advantage of old wealth. Furthermore, high tax rates, in the minds of conservatives, are counterproductive. By excessively encouraging upper-income taxpayers to minimize their taxable income, high rates excessively constrain economic growth and might even reduce rather than increase tax revenue.

A system that taxes most income in excess of the amount households need to meet basic living expenses would respond to all of these concerns among conservatives. Rates would be both lower and flatter than today. If our conservatives and liberals desired, the new broad-base low-rate format could raise the same revenue and retain the same distribution of tax burdens within income classes as the existing system. Each group would have more income exposed to tax, but the tax rates on its income would be lower.

The new format could raise the same revenue and retain the same distribution of tax burdens within income classes as the existing system.

Compare Tables 6.1 and 6.2. Table 6.1 shows the actual distribution of tax burdens in 1997 by income classes, beginning with taxpayers whose adjusted gross income (AGI) is less than $10,000 (row 1). Consider taxpayers with $50,000 to $75,000 of AGI in 1997 (row 6). On average, their average tax rate amounted to *17.1 percent* of their *taxable* income (column E), and they paid *15.1 percent* of *all individual income taxes* (column F).

Now turn to Table 6.2, which distributes income and taxes as if the NTL had applied, assuming taxpayers did not modify their economic behavior. All taxpayers would have found their AGI greatly expanded under the NTL (compare the C columns of Tables 6.1 and 6.2). Nevertheless, they would have paid the same percentage of all taxes (compare F columns of both tables). Thus taxpayers with $50,000 to $75,000 of AGI still would have paid *15.1 percent* of *all taxes* (column F), but they would have done it by paying an average tax rate of only *12.0 percent* on their *taxable income* (column E).

In fact, in the Table 6.2 example, only the top 1 percent of taxpayers (with AGI of $200,000 or more) would have paid an average tax rate above 14.2 percent on their taxable income. The expanded amount of taxable income under the NTL makes the lower rate possible. The lower rate in turn enables taxpayers to make decisions about working, saving, investing, and starting a new company with far less attention to the tax consequences.

Of course, not all people within each income class would experience the new system similarly. Those who benefit greatly from tax preferences would be expected to pay considerably more, whereas those who benefit little from tax preferences would be expected to pay considerably less. Everyone else would pay about the same. Our conservatives could reconcile themselves to these consequences, but they would express concerns to their liberal friends that a broad-base tax might eventually become a means to shift much higher tax burdens to higher-income taxpayers. Such concerns are understandable. If Congress minimized the role of tax preferences, a great deal more income of higher-income taxpayers would become exposed to tax. Then, the opportunity to soak the rich might lead Congress to jack up their tax rates.

> *Conservatives would express concerns that a broad-base tax might eventually become a means for shifting much higher tax burdens to higher-income taxpayers.*

James Madison had the taxing power of Congress in mind when, shortly after the Constitutional Convention, he acknowledged the supreme danger of majority rule: "To secure the public good, and private rights, against the danger of such a faction," he wrote in November 1787, "and at the same time to preserve the spirit and the form of popular government, is then the great object to which our inquiries are directed."[7] No constitutional barrier exists today to bar a majority of lower- and middle-income representatives in Congress from voting to return top rates on upper-income taxpayers to the high levels known less than two decades ago. The expanded tax base also could entice Congress to raise rates across the board to pay for new, expensive federal programs that conservatives would oppose on principle.

TABLE 6.1 Tax Payments of $727 Billion Under Existing Tax Law, 1997

(A) Taxpayers Grouped by AGI ($)	(B) % of All Returns	(C) % of AGI	(D) Tax as % o f AGI	(E) Tax as % of Taxable Income	(F) % of All Taxes
(1) 0–9,999	23.1	2.8	1.8	14.8	.3
(2) 10,000–19,999	20.1	7.3	4.4	13.2	2.2
(3) 20,000–29,999	14.7	8.9	7.6	14.4	4.6
(4) 30,000–39,999	10.6	9.1	9.6	15.4	5.9
(5) 40,000–49,999	8.0	8.8	10.7	16.2	6.4
(6) 50,000–74,999	12.4	18.6	11.9	17.1	15.1
(7) 75,000–99,999	5.3	11.1	14.4	19.8	11.0
(8) 100,000–199,999	4.4	14.2	17.8	23.0	17.3
(9) 200,000–	1.5	20.2	26.9	30.8	37.3

SOURCE: Internal Revenue Service, *Statistics of Income–1997: Individual Income Tax Returns* (Washington, D.C.: IRS 2000).

TABLE 6.2 Tax Payments of $727 Billion Under Hypothetical Normal Income Tax Law (NTL), 1997

(A) Taxpayers Grouped by AGI ($)	(B) % of All Returns	(C) Total Expanded AGI (in $billions)	(D) Tax as % of Expanded AGI	(E) Tax as % of Taxable Income	(F) % of All Taxes
(1) 0–9,999	23.1	264	1.0	4.8	.3
(2) 10,000–19,999	20.1	506	3.1	6.1	2.2
(3) 20,000–29,999	14.7	611	5.5	8.0	4.6
(4) 30,000–39,999	10.7	590	7.3	9.8	5.9
(5) 40,000–49,999	8.0	548	8.5	11.0	6.4
(6) 50,000–74,999	12.4	1,121	9.8	12.0	15.1
(7) 75,000–99,999	5.3	653	12.3	14.2	11.0
(8) 100,000–199,999	4.4	829	15.2	16.9	17.3
(9) 200,000–	1.5	1,146	23.8	24.9	37.3

NOTE: Taxpayers are grouped by their AGI as reported on their 1997 tax returns, holding their tax payments constant.
SOURCE: Author's calculations. See Appendix B of Chapter 5 for calculation of expanded AGI under NTL.

Perhaps any vote to adopt a broad-base low-rate system would have to be accompanied by a law that, except in the event of a national emergency, requires the vote of a supermajority of each branch of Congress, such as 60 percent, before rates could be increased. Some conservatives believe that only a constitutional amendment to that effect would suffice. But a constitutional amendment would be incapable of addressing adequately the circumstances that might justify Congress to act, and it would invite endless litigation.

Furthermore, no such amendment or other congressional legal restraint was proposed during the last significant presidential initiative to achieve a comprehensive income tax. The president then was Ronald Reagan. Reagan called on the Treasury Department in 1984 to devise a "historic reform [of the income tax] for fairness, simplicity and incentives for growth. I am asking Secretary Don Regan for a plan for action to simplify the entire tax code so all taxpayers, big and small, are treated fairly."[8] The result, a monumental report (called Treasury I) by the Treasury Department, declared that the key to such a system "is to define real taxable income comprehensively, to exempt families with poverty-level incomes from tax, and to subject taxable income to a rate structure that, while mildly progressive, avoids rates so high that they stifle incentives and prevent economic growth. In short, the income tax should be broad-based, simple, and fair."[9] These conservative principles remain sound today.

Finally, some leading economists believe that a nation's reliance on a progressive income tax constrains rather than enhances the size of its central government. Eugene Steuerle, a principal architect of Treasury I, notes that nations that have abandoned communism or socialism have commonly introduced a progressive income tax or assigned it greater importance coincident with establishing market economies. "Whatever the definition of progressivity," Steuerle has written, "it is clear that expansion of government expenditures often requires that increases in tax rates move *down* the income distribution" (italics added), where the bulk of the population resides.[10]

Liberals

For liberals, as that term has come to be used this century, the brightest lights of the American creed are equality and democracy. At a minimum, equality ensures not only equal legal and political rights but also equal opportunity to succeed in our society. A democratically elected government must guarantee these rights in principle and vigilantly help ordinary and less able Americans exercise them. As the liberal philosopher John Rawls has argued, "To provide genuine equality of opportunity, society must give more attention to those with fewer native assets and to those born into the less favorable social positions."[11]

It follows that a government constitutionally charged to "promote the general Welfare" must buffer these Americans from the unrestrained effects of the marketplace. Otherwise, in the view of liberals, a purely market-driven economy will leave them behind while excessively rewarding people who have a special talent to make money or who begin life with the advantage of inherited wealth. Arthur Okun, a principal economic adviser to Lyndon Johnson, put it this way: "The market needs a place, and the market needs to be kept in its place."[12]

> *"To provide genuine equality of opportunity, society must give more attention to those with fewer native assets and to those born into the less favorable social positions." (John Rawls)*

Consistent with these principles, liberals conclude that taxes should be markedly redistributive—from the most able to the less able members of society. A fair tax system, in their view, treads lightly on typical Americans and claims progressively more real economic income of people who become progressively more successful. Thus liberals would want to ensure that expanding the definition of income did not result in taxing the poor or increasing the taxes on the ordinary household. Conservatives appear to agree. All major flat tax proposals in recent years exempt from tax a basic amount of income that exceeds the basic amount protected under existing laws.

Liberals also would be pleased with the lower tax rates that could be applied to lower- and middle-income households under a broad-base system. In the normal income tax law (NTL) model set forth in Table 6.2, people who filed the *bottom 69 percent of all tax returns* (those in 1997 with less than $50,000 of AGI) were able to maintain their identical share of the overall tax burden while paying a rate less than *10 percent on their taxable income*; and people who filed the bottom 89 percent of all tax returns (with less than $75,000 of AGI) paid a rate of no more than 12 percent on their taxable income.

Predictably, liberals differ sharply with conservatives when addressing the higher end of the income scale, where liberals want the rates to be much higher than do conservatives. Nevertheless, conservatives would urge liberals to recognize that high tax rates on the taxable income of upper-income taxpayers are underproductive because they always are accompanied by large numbers of tax preferences and inspire upper-income taxpayers to explore opportunities to avoid taxation. In 1977, for example, when tax rates ranged from 14 to 70 percent, returns reporting the top 5 percent of income paid

> *Conservatives would urge liberals to recognize that high tax rates on the taxable income of upper-income taxpayers are underproductive.*

an average tax of only 20 percent.[13] A broad-base low-rate system offers far greater assurance that all upper-income taxpayers would be taxed on their real, economic income. As mentioned earlier, the system can be designed so that they collectively pay at least as much as they would under the existing system, with those who benefit most today from tax expenditures paying more, and those who benefit relatively little paying less.

A broad-base low-rate system would have an analogous impact on middle-income taxpayers, among whom tax expenditures also are arbitrarily distributed. It is true that the typical middle-income taxpayer benefits far less from tax expenditures than does the typical upper-income taxpayer. In 1997, the typical taxpayer whose AGI ranged from $50,000 to $75,000 saved nearly $5,000 from tax expenditures, whereas the typical taxpayer whose AGI ranged from $100,000 to $200,000 saved nearly $14,000 (see column E of Table 5.4). Nevertheless, within the $50,000 to $75,000 group, some taxpayers saved very little from tax expenditures; others saved a lot. Thus if Congress adopted a broad-base low-rate system, middle-income taxpayers who have had large fringe benefits, mortgage-interest deductions, and other ways to shelter significant amounts of income from tax, would be expected to pay more than in the past; typical middle-income taxpayers would pay about the same; and those who have sheltered modest levels of income would pay less. Liberals should not object.

> *The liberal agenda focuses tax relief on those who need it most, which would be consistent with the conservative view of government.*

Liberals, like conservatives, would be pleased that the broad-base low-rate system would advance the opportunity of ordinary Americans to improve their circumstances by retaining such a large percentage of the profits from their hard work and innovation. Horatio Alger dreams of rags to riches cross all political boundaries. Still, liberals would not want to abandon tax preferences that temper special hardships. The liberal agenda thus focuses tax relief on those who need it most, which would be consistent with the conservative view that government should intervene in our private lives only where absolutely necessary.

These principles would spare taxpayers their ordinary share of tax burdens only when the cause was highly compelling. Goals of liberty would be tempered by humanity, goals of equality by rationality.[14] As Michael Walzer has argued, "Liberty and equality are the two chief virtues of social institutions, and they stand best when they stand together."[15]

Standing Together:
The Shared Values of Tax Policy

Let us now identify more clearly how a broad-base low-rate income tax can advance values shared by conservatives and liberals.

Fairness

Both groups insist that our tax laws be fair. As elusive as the qualities of fairness can be, conservatives and liberals have little difficulty arriving at an eminently sensible initial principle for establishing fairness: People with equal abilities to pay taxes ought to pay equal amounts. Likewise, people with equal abilities to pay before paying income taxes ought to have equal abilities to pay after paying them. Economists refer to these principles as **horizontal equity**.[16]

The flip side of horizontal equity is **vertical equity**: As our ability to pay rises, our taxes should rise by a just amount. "Fairness is generally recognized," the economist Richard Goode wrote, "as comprising equal treatment of equals and reasonable differences in the treatment of unequals."[17] Conservatives and liberals would agree.

> *Conservatives and liberals have little difficulty in arriving at an eminently sensible initial principle for establishing fairness: People with equal abilities to pay taxes ought to pay equal amounts.*

Before the New Deal, concepts of horizontal and vertical equity competed with the **benefit theory** of tax fairness. Benefit theory taught that people ought to pay taxes in accordance with the benefits they receive from government. Advocates had in mind heavily taxing the rich, whose sizeable property interests and opportunities to earn income were seen as benefiting most from federal expenditures.

Beginning with the New Deal, however, federal interventions on behalf of all Americans began growing at a pace that made it impossible (if it ever was possible) to rank each of us by the benefits we receive from most government activities. Today, for example, the Department of Labor advances the interests of workers just as the Department of Commerce advances the interests of the owners of industry; the Departments of Education, Health and Human Services, Housing and Urban Development, and Veterans' Affairs as well as a panoply of agencies from equal employment to consumer protection serve the common interest. Benefit theory remains appropriate for supporting certain forms of easily measurable government services, such as charging people for using bridges, waterways, airports, national parks, and public utilities. But even when benefits are measurable, many beneficiaries are poor or near poor and cannot afford to pay for them. Thus we turn to the ability to pay principle for implementing a fair federal tax policy.

> *Most conservatives would agree that the ability-to-pay principle is expressed far better in a broad-base low-rate income tax system than in the system we have today.*

How, then, shall we rank taxpayers' respective abilities to pay? Liberals believe that income is the best starting point. Joseph Pechman, a liberal economist writing in 1987, insisted that whereas "theoreticians may disagree about the meaning of the term 'ability to pay,' . . . the close association between a person's income and his or her taxpaying ability is commonly accepted."[18] Today, however, a growing number of conservatives believe that our level of consumption, rather than our level of income, is a preferable gauge of our ability to pay. Economists are divided on this point. We will address the debate in Chapter 13. The subject of this chapter is fixing the income tax, not replacing it. And most conservatives would agree that the ability-to-pay principle is expressed far better in a broad-base low-rate income tax system than in today's narrow-base higher-rate system.

In fact, our system is a hybrid, part income tax, part consumption tax, and part neither. For example, it operates as an income tax when it taxes salaries, interest on savings accounts, and gain from the sale of a family business. It operates like a consumption tax when it allows the tax-free exchange of stock in a corporate merger, when it exempts gain from tax on the sale of a principal residence, when it defers the tax on pension and IRA contributions and investments, and when it allows the cash value within insurance policies to accumulate free from tax. It operates as neither when it allows fringe benefits paid by an employer to be excluded from an employee's income. In view of all such inconsistencies, David Bradford, a leading conservative economist, has written: "A hybrid income tax system of the sort we now have yields results that are inferior to those produced by either a rigorous adherence to accrual-income principles [of Haig-Simons] or a consistent application of consumption-type rules."[19]

> *Even the most ardent advocates of a broad-base income tax recognize that income is an incomplete measure of one's ability to pay.*

For the vast majority of us, income is a sound indicator of our ability to pay because it closely correlates to our purchasing power—our ability to spend, save, and invest. Even the most ardent advocates of a broad-base income tax recognize, however, that income is an incomplete measure of one's ability to pay. For example, it ignores extraordinary hardships, such as unusually large medical bills and the impact of debt. We know that a college graduate with $100,000 of education loans has less ability to pay taxes on her $35,000 of income than someone earning $35,000 who is debt free. The person without a college debt may, however, never have graduated from college (only about 25 percent of the adult population has a four-year college degree) and likely will earn less over the long run than the college graduate.

Differences in ability to pay arise among households of married couples with equal incomes. If only one spouse is employed, the other can perform household chores. If both spouses are employed full-time, they may have to employ someone to help them out. Single workers living alone face the same problem. Some households may have high child-care costs; others have no children at all. One family may live in Boston, where the costs of housing are high; another may live in Oklahoma City, where housing costs are about 50 percent less.

To summarize, probably no two households with the same income have identical abilities to pay if all measurable personal factors are taken into account.[20] (It is equally true that no two households with the same consumption patterns are likely to have identical abilities to pay consumption taxes.) A broad-base low-rate system would take into account only the most important personal factors. Although inequities inevitably would arise, the lower tax rates accompanying such a system would minimize the relevance of personal factors among us. Indeed, no workable system can account for each special circumstance of each taxpayer; nor should it. Once government embarks on that course, the legislative process is likely to produce less equity rather than more, as our current system demonstrates. When the tax system also attempts to modify our economic behavior, history teaches that government typically multiplies the economic inefficiencies of the tax laws.

Like democracy, the best income tax system can claim only to be better than the other choices. The highest probability of consistent horizontal equity—fairness among equals—rests with a system that counts most income, exempts the poor and the near-poor from tax, makes other adjustments only for the most compelling special circumstances, and reduces tax rates across the board. When compared with our existing system, a broad-base system with moderate but progressive tax rates also increases the probability that people with equally high incomes will pay substantial and approximately equal taxes. Conservatives and liberals would refine these results differently if they had their own way. But a broad-base low-rate system reflects the basic principles of fairness endorsed by each.

Perception of Fairness

A broad-base low-rate system also would give taxpayers greater confidence that others bear their fair share of the tax load. More favorable perceptions about the tax system would increase taxpayer compliance with the tax laws, as discussed shortly. Such perceptions also would have important indirect benefits for the federal government. Writing in 1984, Bill Bradley, then a senator from New Jersey, put it well.

> The unfairness of the tax laws makes us doubt whether government is still capable of overseeing the way society's burdens are distributed. The less confidence we have in government, the less willing we are to pay taxes to support it. The more we try to avoid paying taxes—the more time we all devote to finding the loopholes that will reduce each of our individual tax bills—the less equitable the system appears. The less equitable the tax system and the greater the difference in taxes paid on similar incomes, the less faith there is in government and the weaker become the bonds of our American community.[21]

Conservatives and liberals would agree. A tax system widely perceived as fair is in the best interest of democracy.

Administrative Advantages

A simpler tax system with fewer and more understandable laws reduces the length of returns, the documentation and information that must accompany them, the likelihood of inadvertent mistakes by taxpayers, and the need to pay third parties to help prepare returns. Under a broad-base system, the vast majority of taxpayers would be able to file a short-form return like the short-form returns available to many taxpayers today because of information supplied to the IRS by employers and others. Many taxpayers would file no return at all.

A simpler system also would help address what Will Rogers observed—that the income tax had made more liars out of Americans than golf. Not all taxpayer errors are inadvertent. Apart from the vast amount of income from illegal activities that never gets reported, hundreds of billions of dollars currently escape taxable income each year because people intentionally underreport income that they legally earn and overstate deductions.[22] Much goes undetected by the government because the IRS audits less than 1 percent of all tax returns and less than 5 percent of returns reporting $100,000 or more of income. Some forms of tax evasion are detected without the need for an audit, such as the failure to report interest income that is covered by a form 1099 filed by a bank with the IRS. But the odds are high that most forms of tax evasion will not be caught.

> A broad-base low-rate income tax system would increase voluntary compliance.

Simplicity reduces opportunities to cheat. Fairer laws with lower tax rates also minimize incentives to cheat. For these reasons, a broad-base low-rate income tax system would increase voluntary compliance. Fred Goldberg, while commissioner of the Internal Revenue Service during President Bush's administration, had this in mind when he urged Congress to pursue simplification "with a vengeance."[23] Cutting tax rates, he advised, was the "single best thing" to reduce incentives to cheat.[24]

Finally, simpler laws would make the government's collection and oversight responsibilities far easier and less costly. Greater simplicity also would reduce the opportunities for inconsistency and error by the IRS and the consequent antagonism of so many taxpayers toward it. Conservatives and liberals would agree: When in doubt, err on the side of simplifying.

Economic Efficiency

Conservatives and liberals also share a fundamental goal that our tax system become more economically efficient. An efficient system contributes to the nation's economic growth by minimizing the adverse economic consequences of taxes to the private sector. As mentioned earlier, a tax system usually achieves **economic efficiency** by interfering as little as possible with market behavior. Tax preferences generally produce inefficiencies. Many seduce us along a path of excesses. Higher tax rates increase their seductiveness.

For example, taxpayers are seduced into acquiring more whole life insurance policies than they might need because cash values of these policies are not currently taxed and may never be taxed. High tax rates magnify the advantage of the tax deferral. If the growing cash values were taxed

> *Each exclusion and deduction, by encouraging the favored behavior, potentially is mind-altering. It can seduce us. Higher tax rates increase its seductiveness.*

currently, many taxpayers would acquire the same amount of insurance through less expensive term insurance policies and would invest the difference in ways they believe would produce higher rates of return. Other taxpayers would decide that they would be better off with less insurance. Although such economic behavior would be to the disadvantage of the insurance industry, economic theory teaches that over the long run, these market-based decisions likely would strengthen the economy as a whole.

Even tax provisions created solely to stimulate economic growth rarely do so. Mortimer Caplin's experience with the investment tax credit (ITC) is instructive about tax incentives generally. While with the Treasury Department, Caplin, a Democrat, was an architect of the ITC. Adopted in 1962 to stimulate industrial modernization, it encouraged businesses to acquire equipment and furnishings by allowing them to credit 7 percent (later 10 percent) of the purchase price against their income taxes.

Eliminated from the tax laws in 1986, the ITC remains one of the favorite options of some politicians and economists for jump-starting the economy. Caplin has become one of the ITC's most outspoken opponents. Recalling his growing

> *Tax incentives "are often less bureaucratic because they do a less effective job of directing the nation's resources toward the activity that people wish to favor." (Rudolph Penner)*

disenchantment with it while commissioner of the IRS under Presidents Kennedy and Johnson and later as a lawyer in private practice, Caplin found little proof that the ITC substantially increased investments in equipment and furnishings. What became clear, he believes, is that it offers "a strong brew for distorting normal decisionmaking and encouraging tax-motivated, noneconomic behavior. Tax avoidance and abuse are an inevitable byproduct."[25]

On the Republican side, economist Rudolph Penner, a longtime observer of Congress and former policy official at the Treasury Department, warned in 1989 about the "temptation to fix problems by offering incentives for good behavior." Too often the incentives are misleading. "Tax incentives," Penner wrote, "give the impression of being less bureaucratic than new subsidy programs on the spending side. It is easy to forget that they are often less bureaucratic because they do a less effective job of directing the nation's resources toward the activity that people wish to favor."[26]

By attempting to balance the twin goals of a fair tax and an efficient tax, liberals have been willing to concede some loss of efficiency in order to impose high tax rates on people with high taxable incomes. Liberals also are inclined to believe that the efficiency loss from high tax rates is less than what conservatives estimate it to be. Conservatives, for example, argue that the level of personal saving and investment is enhanced more significantly than liberals are willing to concede by laws that favor saving and investment. Liberals also worry that any revenue loss from savings and investment incentives that primarily benefit the rich will be recovered by raising the tax on ordinary workers.

Views about the fairness of progressive rates and the efficiency loss from them are explored at length in Chapters 8 and 9. At this juncture, we can reach at least two conclusions. First, the broad-base low-rate alternative to the existing system would give greater assurance to liberals that higher-income taxpayers would pay progressively higher rates on their income. Second, such an alternative would give greater assurance to conservatives that economic success would be encouraged and rewarded more consistently.

Stability and Flexibility

Simplification advances stability, stability promotes predictability, and predictability enhances planning. Under a stabile income tax system, taxpayers would feel far more confident about engaging in long-term planning, including investing for long-term results. All such investment and planning should enhance the nation's economic growth.

A broad-base low-rate system also produces desired flexibility in varying economic times. Because, for the most part, we would report our economic income, the system automatically would adjust well to the ebbs and flows of the economy. During a recession, tax liabilities would be reduced to reflect our lower incomes and our decreased ability to pay taxes; in turn, reduced tax burdens would give the private sector greater opportunity to regain economic strength. During times of rapid economic growth when incomes are high, the system would extract far more taxes that could be used to reduce deficits that arose during times of recession; alternatively, rates could be lowered further to maintain constant tax collections.

Again, conservatives and liberals would agree: A broad-base low-rate income tax system should respond well to the nation's economic health.

Less Politics

A system that minimizes tax programs greatly diminishes the pressure on politicians to engage in the time-consuming exercise of initiating massive numbers of tax proposals each year. Many of these proposals are mere show-pieces to satisfy lobbyists or constituents and never will be taken seriously.[27] With the proper leadership under a broad-base low-rate system, politicians could tell constituents and lobbyists who seek special tax legislation, "The game has changed; it won't fly." They could add that the new, lower rates make life without a new exclusion or deduction more tolerable than before. Both conservatives and liberals would find this stability reassuring.

The idea of minimizing Congress's role in tax policy was advanced years ago by Joseph Kraft, a leading columnist for the *Washington Post*. Having watched Congress construct the Tax Reform Act of 1969, he wrote, "It is now clear that taxes are too complicated and sensitive a matter to be decided in detail by the Congress. . . . Congress in fiscal matters is a dinosaur—huge body and tiny brain."[28] Tax professor Michael Graetz recently added, "Since then, Congress has become a more gargantuan body, but no larger of brain."[29]

An Old Idea Whose Time Has Come

The concept of a broad base low-rate system is far from new. Distinguished conservative and liberal economists advocated it many decades ago. Their numbers have multiplied greatly over time. One of the most noted conservative spokesmen, Milton Friedman, continues to reaffirm the message he gave as far back as 1956.

> A much lower set of nominal rates, plus a more comprehensive base, through more equal taxation of all sources of income could be both more progressive in average incidence, more equitable in detail, and less wasteful of resources. This judgment that the personal income tax has been arbitrary in its impact and of limited effectiveness in reducing inequality is widely shared by students of the subject, including many who strongly favor the use of graduated taxation to reduce inequality. They too urge that the top bracket rates be drastically reduced and the base broadened.[30]

Forty years later Friedman observed that a "major purpose of taxes today is to enable legislators (and presidents) to raise campaign funds by inserting or removing loopholes in our present obscenely complicated tax code."[31]

One of Friedman's most respected liberal counterparts was Joseph Pechman. Writing shortly before his death in 1989, Pechman, then president-elect of the American Economic Association, observed (wistfully, it seems): "Comprehensive income taxation seems to make so much sense, one wonders why there has been so little progress in reforming tax systems along these lines. The answer seems to be that the groups benefitting from the special provisions resist any inroads into their favored tax status. Moreover, politicians are more interested in using the tax system to promote their economic and social objectives than in improving equity and economic efficiency."[32]

Three years earlier, the 1986 Reform Act had significantly reduced the opportunities to shelter income from tax and had reduced top rates on the highest incomes to 28 percent. Unfortunately, most of the old tax programs remained, along with most of the tax losses from them. As Eugene Steuerle pointed out in *The Tax Decade,* which examined tax policies of the 1980s, "Over 80 percent of the assets of individuals . . . [still] receives some tax preference that excludes part of the income from taxation."[33] Although President Reagan and Congress deserve praise for the achievements of the 1986 Reform Act, the new code resembled a termite-riddled house that was remodeled by superimposing a new structure on it.

Legislation since 1986 has made matters much worse: Congress has considerably reduced the tax base and complicated the laws. Genuine reform still needs to be achieved. Conservatives and liberals, speaking as objective policymakers, could show the way. The public deserves to hear them.

7

Discovering the Values of Our Income Tax Laws

If you know the position a person takes on taxes, you can tell their whole philosophy. The tax code, once you get to know it, embodies all the essence of life: greed, politics, power, goodness, charity.
—Sheldon Cohen, former IRS commissioner

Five Questions * Drawing Distinctions Among Different Capital Gains * Promoting Social Behavior: Charitable Giving * Encouraging Learning: Expenses for Higher Education * Simplicity * A Closing Comment

---

The public's mounting desire for the federal government to play a declining role in our nation's domestic life has paralleled an ascending role of personal values in public discourse. That these trends have occurred simultaneously is no accident. Propelled by disillusionment with federal efforts to solve enduring social and economic problems, both trends reflect the conviction that fundamental solutions must emanate from policies rooted in beliefs of local citizens.

As a nation, we will continue to experiment regarding what we choose to retain under federal control and, indeed, what should be legislated at all rather than left to private decisionmaking. These experiments will be strongly influenced by the ebb and flow of the public's confidence in our political leaders. But the public's concern with values, public and private, likely will expand as our nation seeks to define itself for the new century. Crucial to the outcome will be a clearer understanding of values legislated by Congress.

Nowhere are these values more plentiful, inconsistent, and less understood than in federal income tax policy. So far, I have spoken about them somewhat anecdotally. This chapter will be more systematic. Initially we will consider five questions we might ask when addressing whether, and in what form, Congress should grant relief from taxation. We then will apply this methodology to a range of tax preferences by which Congress fashions economic incentives, attempts to shape social behavior, and revisits its notions of tax justice.

Five Questions

A fundamental principle of fairness in tax policy is that taxpayers ought to pay in accordance with their ability to pay. It follows that for the income tax to serve as the principal source of federal revenue, income must be a reliable measure of our ability to pay. In most cases, it is: Our level of income primarily determines what we can consume and save and determines what we can spare. Though recently challenged by consumption-tax advocates, a belief that income is the most reliable measure of our ability to pay taxes dominated congressional thinking for most of the twentieth century.

As we identify the values by which Congress has justified exceptions to the taxation of income, we need to identify the values that have led Congress to accept the problems accompanying the exceptions.

Even the most enthusiastic supporters of retaining the income tax's central fiscal role recognize, however, that taxing income without exception poses problems. But each problem does not justify an exception, because each exception poses its own problems. As we identify the values by which Congress has justified exceptions to the taxation of income, we need to identify the values that have led Congress to accept the problems accompanying the exceptions. Equally important are values embraced by Congress when it chooses not to address problems created by taxing income. Keeping the following questions in mind will help you develop your own views on the subject.

First: Which Problems Has Congress Addressed, and What Solutions Has It Chosen?

Congress legislates values by selecting which problems posed by taxing income will be ignored or addressed and by choosing solutions for problems that are addressed. Readers might ask themselves which problems they would address and what solutions they would choose that express their values.

Second: What Is the Significance of the Type of Relief That Congress Has Chosen?

The public tends to be particularly unaware of the range of choices and values Congress has when it decides to provide tax relief. With rare exception and vast consequences, Congress has delivered tax relief through income exclusions and tax deductions rather than through tax credits. Exclusions and deductions save most taxes for high-income taxpayers.

For example, whenever Congress allows all taxpayers to exclude or deduct $1,000 from income, taxpayers who would have paid a 39.6 percent tax on the $1,000 save $396; taxpayers who would have paid a 15 percent tax save only $150. A tax credit of 15 percent of $1,000 ($150) treats everyone equally who owes at least $150 of taxes, regardless of their income levels. Congress also knows that if someone does not owe taxes, an extra exclusion or deduction has no value to him. Neither does a tax credit unless it is a **refundable tax credit**. When a credit is refundable, the government sends the taxpayer a check for the excess of the credit over his taxes.

> *With rare exception and vast consequences, Congress has delivered tax relief through income exclusions and tax deductions rather than through tax credits.*

By choosing tax relief through exclusions and deductions, Congress values lowering the tax liability most for people whose income is greatest. We also know that when Congress enacts an exclusion, deduction, or nonrefundable credit, it does not intend to help lower-income households that do not owe taxes.

How are we to evaluate these government choices? Exclusions or deductions are the appropriate choice whenever they help measure income accurately. For example, if you are an independent insurance salesman, you must be entitled to deduct the rent you pay for your office and other reasonable expenses that you incur to produce your income, whether you earn millions or are barely profitable. Only then can you determine your economic gain.

When, however, Congress's goal is to provide relief from tax-

> *By choosing tax relief through exclusions and deductions, Congress values lowering the tax liability most for people whose income is greatest.*

ation to subsidize a personal hardship or expenditure, we might assume that Congress would want the relief to be no less for people who can least afford the hardship or expenditure than for people who can best afford it. Where hardship exists, Congress could deliver the relief through tax credits. In fact, Congress could focus the relief on lower-income households by reducing the credit as income rises, but that would make the tax system more complicated.

Congress's concerns for the most part have been diametrically opposed to those I have just suggested. Of the approximately 100 personal exclusions and deductions today, only a few exist to measure income accurately. Only a handful of tax credits exist. Only one credit—the earned-income tax credit—is refundable.

A telling example of Congress's values appears in one of the largest tax expenditures, the exclusion for employer-paid health insurance premiums. Like food and ordinary clothing, these premiums are widely viewed as personal expenses rather than costs of producing income. Yet a virtually unlimited exclusion is available, even for the most expensive policies, for premiums paid either as a supplement to an employee's wages or through a **salary-reduction** plan (called a **cafeteria plan**).

For the period 2000 through 2004, the Joint Committee estimates that the exclusion for employer-paid health premiums will reduce the government's income tax collections by $324 billion. These premium payments also avoid Social Security taxes at a cost to the Social Security trust fund of at least $150 billion. We are talking about a five-year, $475 billion government subsidy.

But, this upside-down subsidy, which helps people most who need the government's assistance least, never would survive congressional hearings if proposed by the Department of Health and Human Services as a direct federal grant to workers. Because of wide variations in coverage, premiums, and participants' marginal tax rates, the employee who typically receives the largest tax subsidy is a company executive. A low-paid employee—the person who can least afford health insurance and whom the government would like to keep off Medicaid—is likely to be subsidized least. Congress's articulated rationale for the income tax exclusion appears to be its desire to promote health insurance coverage for people who might not otherwise be insured or who could not afford to be adequately insured.[1]

> *The upside-down tax subsidy for employer-paid health insurance premiums never would survive if proposed by the Department of Health and Human Services.*

The reasons are clear. Only about one-third of families with income of $10,000 to $20,000 have health insurance through their employer, compared with 90 percent of families with income of $50,000 or more.[2] The low participation rate of lower-paid employees occurs because their employers frequently do not offer such a program or exclude them from coverage, or these employees elect not be covered. When these employees are covered, their premiums often are less than those for higher-paid employees because, under the tax laws, employers can favor higher-paid employees except when the premiums are paid through a cafeteria plan. When premiums are not paid through a cafeteria plan, an employer may simultaneously provide family coverage in a gold-plated plan for management that contains a small deductible, the widest variety of medical services coverage, and high levels of reimbursement; and the employer may provide single coverage in a plain vanilla plan for others that has high deductibles, only basic medical services coverage, and lower levels of reimbursement.

Even when the plan and premiums are identical for management and staff, the income exclusion produces vast differences in tax savings because of vast differences in marginal tax rates. Take Edna Executive, who earns $350,000, and Sally Secretary, who earns $25,000. Their employer pays the entire $5,000 premium for their health insurance plan. By not being taxed on the $5,000, Edna saves (and the government loses) $1,980, the tax she would have paid at her 39.6 percent tax rate on $5,000. Sally saves only $750, the tax she would have paid on $5,000 at her 15 percent tax rate.

If you believe that all employer-paid health-care expenditures should be excluded from income, you would endorse these government subsidies. Alternatively, you might believe that lower-income employees should receive the largest subsidy; that all employees should be eligible for equal subsidies, such as through a tax credit; that executives like Edna should receive no subsidy at all because they can afford to pay for their own health insurance and the government must ration its resources carefully; or that no tax subsidy should be available, at least when the employer fails to provide equal coverage for a high percentage of its workforce. In the latter case, you might believe that the government could spend its money more efficiently through a program of direct government subsidies solely to workers in need of assistance. If you believe a tax credit makes most sense, you also favor complicating taxpayers' and the IRS's jobs: Taxpayers must claim the credit on their tax return in order to benefit from it, whereas they benefit from the exclusion without any requirement to report it to the IRS. You also must recognize that the more Congress restricts an employer's ability to favor higher-compensated employees, the risk rises that an employer will eliminate all payments for health insurance.

To summarize, Congress discloses its values by identifying a problem to address, for example, the need to broaden health-care insurance coverage, and by choosing a solution, for example, a broad exclusion from income and Social Security taxes for health-care premiums paid by employers. Whether and how you would address the problem reflects your values.

Third: What Tax Burdens Should Taxpayers Tolerate?

When Congress chooses not to address certain hardships brought about by taxes, some people are hurt financially more than others. To understand the values legislated by Congress, we need to know which burdens it believes people should tolerate. The taxation of income subject to Social Security taxes is revealing.

Workers pay Social Security taxes (6.20 percent) and Medicare taxes (1.45 percent) on their wages up to a specified wage base for the year. In 2000, the wage base was $76,200; it is adjusted annually for inflation. The combined tax of 7.65 percent, referred to as FICA (Federal Insurance Contributions

Act), is matched by an equal contribution from employers. Once an employee's wages equal the year's wage base, the employer and employee pay only the Medicare tax on the balance of his wages. These rules make Social Security taxes regressive: They exact a higher percentage of wages from workers earning up to the wage base than of the wages of workers earning over it. (In contrast, Social Security benefits are progressive: Retirees with low average wages over their working years receive higher payments as a percentage of their wages than do retirees with high average wages.)

Matt Median, a single taxpayer whose $24,000 of wages in 2000 was about the median income of all taxpayers that year, paid the full 7.65 percent FICA tax on all of his wages. By comparison, FICA taxes averaged only about 5.4 percent of the $120,000 of wages earned by Tom Topps: Tom paid 7.65 percent on the first $76,200 of his wages but only the 1.45 percent Medicare tax on the balance.

For a typical worker, income used to pay FICA taxes is taxed twice more, once by the federal income tax because FICA taxes are neither deductible or entitled to a tax credit on our returns, and once again by a state income tax. This was true in Matt's case, which made him feel like a three-time loser. If Matt itemized deductions, he could have deducted the state income tax attributable to his FICA taxes; but Matt claimed a standard deduction. Tom itemized, which meant that he did not pay a federal income tax on the state income tax on wages used to pay his FICA tax. He was, so to speak, only a two-time loser.

> *For a typical worker, income used to pay FICA taxes is taxed twice more; for itemizers, it is taxed only once more.*

Congress could choose to place Matt and Tom on more equal footing. It could extend Social Security taxes to all (or more) of Tom's wages, which also would reduce future deficits in the Social Security trust fund, as discussed in Chapter 11. It could eliminate the deduction for state income taxes, which could lead Congress to lower income tax rates for Matt and Tom. It could allow Matt an earned-income tax credit on a portion of his wages, thus reducing his income tax liability and thereby indirectly offsetting a portion of his FICA costs. The government's revenue loss, however, from an enhanced earned-income tax credit could force Congress to raise income tax rates, perhaps for Matt as well as for others. As readers can see, each initiative produces new countermeasures and embraces distinct values.

Fourth: What Circumstances of Taxpayers Warrant Tax Relief?

By favoring one set of circumstances under our tax laws and not another, Congress helps some taxpayers and not others, as we have seen with Tom and

Matt. What circumstances of favored taxpayers lead Congress to grant them the advantage? Consider the tax preference for people who work abroad.

In general, Americans are subject to tax on their worldwide wages and other forms of earned income. Since 1926, however, income earned abroad by Americans who have satisfied requirements for living and working abroad has received special treatment. Today, anyone (except a federal employee) who has lived at least one year abroad may exclude up to $72,000 (and eventually $80,000) of income earned abroad, plus some or all foreign housing expenses paid by his employer. This tax preference is estimated to cost the U.S. Treasury about $14 billion from 2000 through 2004.

Originally enacted to encourage foreign trade, the exemption today is a relief measure. Although $72,000 exceeds the wages of 90 percent of all American workers, Congress assumes that all employees who work abroad suffer extra financial burdens, perhaps from maintaining a home abroad and in the United States or from large travel expenses to and from the United States. As Congress recently explained, the exclusion "is a simple way to prevent taxpayers from facing an increased tax burden when there has been no increase in economic well being by accepting an overseas assignment."[3]

The exemption, premised on the assumption that working abroad creates financial hardships, does not require any demonstration of hardship.

Simple the exclusion is, but difficult to justify. Congress grants this relief having already assured these employees that their foreign wages will not be subject to double taxation—once by the host country and again by the United States. When foreign wages are subject to taxation by the host country, workers may either deduct the taxes or claim them as a tax credit on their U.S. income tax return. In fact, the exemption does not require any demonstration that working overseas creates a financial hardship. One might receive a pay raise as inducement to work abroad, maintain a residence solely abroad, and not travel back and forth to the United States. For example, an Exxon executive earning hundreds of thousands of dollars and whose wife and children live abroad with him is fully entitled to the exemption. If his family remains in the United States, they continue to enjoy all of the protections and benefits of the U.S. government whether or not he pays any U.S. taxes.

Employees need not work in hardship posts, such as in underdeveloped countries, for charities, or for small U.S. businesses trying to gain a foothold abroad. They may even work for foreign corporations in competition with U.S. businesses, which often take the exemption into account in calculating the compensation they must pay U.S. employees living abroad. In such cases, the true beneficiaries of the exemption are foreign employers, not American employees.

Workers earning a fraction of the $72,000 exclusion within the United States must report all of their wages. They have good reason to ask why the entire wages of all Americans should not be included on their tax returns, subject to relief only in cases of demonstrable need.

Fifth: What Is the Impact of Tax-Relief Measures on Tax Rates?

When assessing which income tax problems we would address by excluding income from tax or by allowing personal deductions and credits, we must recognize the potential impact on tax rates. Each time Congress adopts a tax preference and does not reduce federal expenditures, it must impose higher tax rates to keep federal revenues constant, that is, for the reforms to be revenue neutral, unless the special provision sufficiently stimulates economic growth. Rarely do tax preferences result in such stimulation; often they have the opposite effect. By contrast, when Congress eliminates a tax preference, the resulting expansion of the tax base likely allows Congress to lower tax rates to achieve revenue neutrality.

> *Values that lead Congress to broaden the tax base under revenue-neutral reforms usually embrace lower rates and reduce the pressure on Congress to consider new tax preferences.*

If a tax preference leads to higher income tax rates, Congress has valued increasing the taxes of certain taxpayers, some of whom may include people who benefit only slightly or not at all from the tax preference. Because higher tax rates increase the cost to taxpayers of having their remaining income exposed to tax, Congress should anticipate that taxpayers and lobbyists will exert greater pressure on members for additional tax relief. In sum, values that lead Congress to protect more income from tax under revenue-neutral reforms invite consideration of even further tax preferences. Values that lead Congress to broaden the tax base under revenue-neutral reforms usually embrace lower rates and reduce the pressure on Congress to consider new tax preferences. If such a broader tax base and lower rates also strengthen the economy, Congress values a course that would allow it to lower rates further in years ahead. With these observations in mind, let us examine some significant tax preferences.

Drawing Distinctions Among Different Capital Gains

A capital gain arises when we sell or exchange an investment (a capital asset) for more than we paid for it. In most cases, our gain is taxable in the year we receive what we have bargained for, whether it is cash or other property. Two important exceptions to these rules involve real estate swaps and inherited property.

Real Estate Swaps

If you are an investor in real estate—whether in raw land, office or apartment buildings, shopping centers, or other commercial developments—you can swap your investment for another real estate investment without paying a tax on your gain. You also may repeat this process an indefinite number of times regardless of how large your gain may be. If the transaction is handled correctly, you can sell your real estate for cash and still defer the gain as long as the cash is held in escrow and is used to acquire another real estate investment within six months.

Tax-free real estate swaps are said to be justified because investors are in substantially the same economic position before and after the swap; only the identity of the real estate has changed. The proposition often tests our credulity given the variety of swaps that qualify. Who among us would believe that swapping the Empire State Building for farmland in Des Moines or Des Moines farmland for the Empire State Building would leave one's economic position unchanged? Remember, unimproved land may be swapped for improved land and vice versa, a transaction that would alter the swapper's economic position far more than if he had traded common stock in the marketplace.

> *By favoring real estate swaps, Congress has paved the way for wealthy people, who benefit most from the tax deferral, to pyramid their real estate holdings and minimize their taxes.*

Deferring the tax on real estate swaps is also said to be justified because taxing the gain could impose a hardship on swappers, who may not have the cash to pay the tax. But how much of a hardship, and for whom? Swappers who cannot afford the tax almost always have the option to sell for cash or to require enough cash in the transaction to cover their taxes. Swappers also nearly always are people of means; they can pay the tax either from other resources or by securing a loan on the property acquired.

By favoring real estate swaps, Congress has paved the way for wealthy people to pyramid their real estate holdings and minimize their taxes. The tax deferral also distorts economic behavior. It often seduces amateurs to swap for properties they otherwise never would, and never should, have acquired. Without the deferral, many people would sell their real estate for cash and use the proceeds to acquire stocks, bonds, or other investments that they believe have greater economic potential than additional investments in real estate.

Inherited Property

Congress is not averse to bestowing windfalls. One of the oldest and most generous arises from the law that forgives, at the time of death, the potential income tax on appreciated property owned by the decedent. Regardless of how large the gain might be, neither the decedent, his estate, nor his heirs ever pay an income tax on it.

What we pay for an investment becomes its **tax basis,** from which future gains or losses are measured.[4] Ted Sundland, for example, bought Intel stock years ago for $30,000. If he sold the stock today for $100,000, his taxable gain would be $70,000—the difference between his sale price and his $30,000 tax basis. If he gives the stock to his wife, Mandy, her tax basis for it also would be $30,000; and were she to sell it for $100,000, she too would realize a $70,000 gain. If, however, Ted died owning the stock, the tax laws call for *stepping up* his tax basis in the stock (as well as in his other investments) to its market value at the date of his death. If, then, Mandy inherited Ted's Intel stock when it was worth $100,000 and sold it the next day for $101,000, she would have only a $1,000 taxable gain from the sale—the difference between the sale price and her $100,000 stepped-up basis.

The **step-up-in-basis rule** extends to any heir, whether or not related and no matter how wealthy. If Ted had bequeathed his Intel stock to a friend who sold it for $101,000, he too would have had only a $1,000 gain. Thus, Ted's heirs, whoever they might be, are entitled to better income tax treatment than is Ted himself.

> *Relatively few heirs would be subject to a double federal tax on inherited property if their tax basis for determining gain or loss from such property were the same as the decedent's.*

Congress has afforded heirs this special relief in large part to protect them from double taxation of their inheritance—once from federal estate taxes, where rates on the largest estates run as high as 55 percent, and again from federal income taxes on the appreciation of a decedent's investments. This rationale is nurtured by the myth that estates commonly are subject to federal estate tax. Few estates are; and the step-up-in-basis rule applies even when they are not. In 2000, estates worth $675,000 or less were free of federal estate tax regardless of the relationship of the beneficiaries to the decedent. Only about 5 percent of estates today are worth more than $675,000. By 2006, the $675,000 exclusion will have risen to $1 million. Furthermore, the exclusion applies after unlimited deductions for property that passes either to a surviving spouse or to charity. In other words, all property passing to a surviving spouse or charity may pass estate-tax free. An additional estate-tax exclusion may exist if the estate includes a family-owned farm or business. For all these reasons, less than 2 percent of all estates can be expected to owe any federal estate tax.

To summarize, relatively few heirs would be subject to double federal tax on the appreciation of inherited property if their tax basis for determining gain or loss upon the sale of such property were the same as the decedent's. If the heir is a surviving spouse, double taxation virtually never would occur because her inheritance would be exempt from federal estate tax. The step-up-in-basis rule thereby conveys the largest income tax windfalls upon spouses who inherit property with the highest appreciation.

The step-up-in-basis rule is costly to the federal government; revenue losses from it are estimated at $136 billion for the years 2000 through 2004. In the rule's defense, supporters note its considerable administrative advantages. Often in the past, a decedent's records have been inadequate for determining his tax basis in his assets. Had heirs been required to use the decedent's tax basis for the property

> *The administrative justification for the step-up-in-basis rule is weakest in cases where windfalls from the rule are greatest.*

they inherited, their inability to prove this tax basis could force them to pay a tax, when they sell the property, on more than their actual gain.

These administrative problems are much less serious today. Costs for publicly traded stocks, bonds, and other investments are recorded by the institutions performing the transactions. Taxpayers also have become far more aware of the importance of maintaining cost records for their own income tax purposes. Finally, the wealthier you are, the more likely are your or your financial adviser's records to be complete. Thus the administrative justification for the step-up-in-basis rule is weakest in cases where windfalls from it are greatest.

To address concerns about double taxation, Congress could apply the rule solely to appreciated assets subject to federal estate tax. People who inherit property free of estate tax would use the decedent's tax basis. For administrative reasons, Congress might allow the rule in small estates such as those worth less than $100,000.[5]

If Congress restricted the rule to these situations, it would tax people more consistently on their income, raise considerable tax revenue, and create the opportunity to lower tax rates across the board. The additional income tax revenues would arise not merely because many heirs no longer would benefit from the rule. Tax collections also would be accelerated because owners of appreciated assets, anticipating that the step-up-in-basis rule would not apply to their investments, would be more inclined to realize gains on underperforming investments in order to transfer resources into more productive uses.

Promoting Social Behavior: Charitable Giving

Charitable behavior is a virtue universally recognized. Intuitively, therefore, we are likely to support a tax policy that promotes charitable giving. Far more than citizens of most nations, people in the United States depend on the work of nonprofit organizations—from churches to schools and colleges to performing and visual arts organizations to soup kitchens and homeless shelters and to charities of all sorts. For these reasons, fiddling with the deduction for charitable giving may be risky.

Issues of Fairness: The Itemized Deduction for Charitable Gifts

Why fiddle? Consider, first, an argument commonly advanced for the charitable deduction—that our ability to pay can be measured fairly only after subtracting our charitable gifts. The underlying assumption here is that because charities perform quasi-public functions, giving to them ought not to be viewed as personal consumption. For example, if your neighbor has $100,000 of income and gives $10,000 to charity and you have $90,000 of income and give none of it to charity, the deduction allows both of you to be viewed as having $90,000 of income for determining your ability to pay.

> *If a deduction for charitable gifts is necessary to measure income fairly, the deduction should not be restricted to the less than 30 percent of taxpayers who itemize.*

If, however, a deduction for gifts to charity is necessary to measure income fairly, the deduction should not be restricted to the less than 30 percent of taxpayers who itemize. Congress may assume that gifts by nonitemizers are too insignificant to worry about. Yet it is likely that nonitemizers give no smaller a percentage of their AGI than the typical itemizer. For example, itemizers in 1997 with a modest $30,000 to $40,000 of AGI gave the highest percentage (3.85 percent) of their AGI to charity compared with all but one of the higher-income groups; only itemizers with $1 million or more of AGI gave a higher percentage (see Figure 7.1). Itemizers with $200,000 to $500,000 of AGI gave only 2.67 percent of their AGI.

Nevertheless, charitable gifts by a nonitemizer typically will not be large in total dollars; and if every dollar given to charity by nonitemizers were deductible, the system would be ripe for fraud because of the IRS's inability to monitor these claims. But itemizers are entitled to claim a deduction for *every* dollar they give to charity even if they give only a dollar, which means that their returns are ripe for fraud.

One alternative would be to extend the charitable deduction to everyone whose gifts exceed a threshold that is deemed a real sacrifice. This measure also should minimize the number of minor fraudulent claims. For example, deductions might be allowed for amounts that exceed the greater of $1,000 or 3 percent of a taxpayer's AGI. (John F. Kennedy proposed in 1963 that itemized deductions be limited to amounts in excess of 5 percent of a taxpayer's AGI.[6]) Taxpayers with $100,000 of AGI could then deduct charitable gifts that exceed $3,000.

Adopting a basic threshold for the charitable deduction would be consistent with the treatment of most other itemized deductions. Personal casualty losses may be deducted only in excess of 10 percent of AGI, and no single casualty loss may be taken into account except to the extent that it exceeds

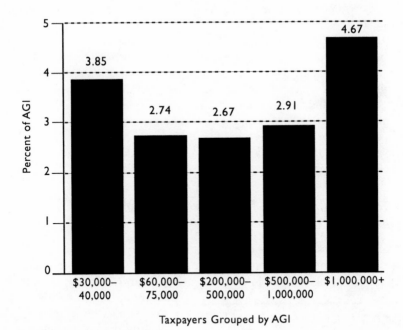

FIGURE 7.1   Charitable Contributions of Itemizers as Percentage of AGI, 1997
SOURCE: Internal Revenue Service, *Statistics of Income—1997: Individual Income Tax Returns* (Washington, D.C.: IRS, 2000), 60.

$100; out-of-pocket medical expenses are allowed only in excess of 7.5 percent of AGI; miscellaneous expenses such as for expenses of employment, tax preparation, or investment advice may be deducted only in excess of 2 percent of AGI; and the total of itemized deductions for mortgage interest, state and local taxes, charitable contributions, and miscellaneous expenses are reduced by 3 percent of the amount that a taxpayer's AGI exceeds an annual threshold ($128,950 in 2000).

I began by noting that advocates of the charitable deduction believe that our ability to pay taxes should be judged after taking into account gifts to charities. This logic should extend only to gifts that are *charitable,* that is, gifts that have no significant personal benefit. Most gifts fail this test. The most common gift is to our church, a gift that generates its own personal rewards. A great many gifts are to our children's schools, allowing the schools to hold down nondeductible tuition costs, or to museums, theaters, orchestras, dance companies, and other organizations that we attend; these gifts hold down the price of our admission.

One possibility would be to prohibit deductions to organizations from which we or our dependents directly benefit. But this rule could be unduly harsh on organizations where our personal benefit is slight, and it would be difficult for the IRS to monitor. Another possibility would be to disallow a deduction for a fixed percentage of all charitable gifts, over and above the basic threshold mentioned earlier, on the assumption that most gifts involve some personal benefit. (By analogy, Congress allows a deduction for only 50 percent of business entertainment expenses because they typically have mixed personal and business purposes.) Congress might exempt from this limit gifts to charities devoted exclusively to alleviating severe hardships, but gifts qualifying for exemption would be difficult to define and monitor. This observation reminds us that as we attempt to limit the charitable deduction, we make the laws more complicated.

The Importance of the Charitable Deduction to Charitable Giving

Economists raise an entirely different question about the value—and thus the values—of the deduction. They wonder whether it pays for itself. In other words, is the revenue lost by the government from the charitable deduction at least matched by increased charitable giving induced by the deduction? If not, the government could narrow the deduction if it felt that a more carefully focused allowance would pay for itself. If the evidence indicated that no charitable deduction was likely to pay for itself, the government might eliminate the deduction altogether or still allow some deduction because it valued the pluralistic nature of charitable giving. Alternatively, as some economists have suggested, Congress could disallow the deduction, collect the additional revenue, and distribute to charities whatever their shortfall might be that can be attributed to the absence of the charitable deduction. But shortfalls would be difficult to measure; most gifts are to churches, which generally cannot legally receive government grants; and (for better or worse) the government likely would end up allocating the subsidies differently than would the individual donors.

> *Lower tax rates, although highly desirable in general, reduce tax savings from charitable gifts and thereby reduce the tax incentive to be charitable.*

In any event, economists are right to ask how much additional charitable giving is prompted by the charitable deduction. The answer is crucial not only to whether, and how, tax subsidies should be crafted for charitable giving. It also may be crucial to the future of charitable organizations. For example, what would happen to the level of charitable giving if Congress retained some form of charitable deduction but lowered tax rates significantly in conjunction with broadening the tax base? What charitable giving would occur if Congress eliminated the charitable deduction altogether?

We know that taxes can change greatly the price of charitable giving. For example, the after-tax cost of a $10,000 gift to charity in 1980 by one who had reached the 70 percent marginal tax bracket was only $3,000 because the gift saved him $7,000 in taxes: Had he not made the gift, he would have retained only $3,000 of the $10,000 after taxes. When the top rate fell to 28 percent in 1988, a $10,000 gift by a top-bracket taxpayer cost him $7,200 because he would have retained $7,200 after taxes had he not made the gift. Thus, lower tax rates, although highly desirable in general, reduce tax savings from charitable gifts and thereby reduce the tax incentive to be charitable.

Charitable giving as a percentage of the gross domestic product has remained relatively constant over the past three decades, notwithstanding dramatic changes in the top tax rate.

We might assume, therefore, that charitable giving rises as tax rates rise and falls as tax rates fall. Yet no such pattern can be found. Charitable giving as a percentage of the gross domestic product has remained relatively constant over the past three decades. It has ranged from 2.1 percent in 1964, when the top tax rate was 90 percent, to a low of 1.7 percent from 1977 through 1980, when the top rate was 70 percent, back to 2.1 percent in 1998, when the top rate was 39.6 percent (also the current top rate).[7]

Early research suggested that the charitable deduction contributed significantly to charitable giving; the size of the effect today is highly debatable.[8] Many flat tax proponents so minimize the importance of the deduction to charitable giving that they propose to eliminate the deduction altogether.[9]

All experts agree that many factors other than tax rates bear heavily on charitable behavior. In fact, charitable patterns of the rich appear to track most closely not their level of wealth, economic outlook, or marginal tax rates but their level of income. As stated by Giving USA, which reports on philanthropic giving each year, "Giving growth rates closely parallel income growth rates."[10] The more income the rich accrue, the more generous they are. They have more income when tax rates go down, not up—that is, when the tax incentive for giving is less, not more.

Charitable patterns of the rich most closely track not their level of wealth, economic outlook, or marginal tax rates but their level of income.

Charitable giving also responds to fund-raising efforts. When tax incentives fall, charities often mount more aggressive fund-raising campaigns. Charitable giving also increases when Americans sense a greater urgency to solve the unmet needs of society; it declines when Americans feel less connected to people beyond their immediate households.

To summarize, if relief for charitable giving is appropriate to measure income accurately, it is unfair to limit the relief to itemizers. This inequity is magnified by allowing itemizers to deduct relatively small gifts. Congress could fashion a fairer and administratively workable system if it were to allow everyone tax relief, through revenue-neutral reforms, for gifts in excess of a basic dollar amount (such as $1,000) and a percentage of their AGI (such as 3 percent). If Congress wished to recognize that charitable gifts usually have mixed personal and charitable consequences, the simplest method would to be raise the deductible threshold somewhat higher, such as to amounts that exceed 4 percent of AGI. These new rules should not have much effect on the overall amount of charitable giving, the greatest inducements for which would remain a strong economy and an ethic of caring for others.

Encouraging Learning: Expenses for Higher Education

After cracking down on welfare for the poor in the mid-1990s, Congress might have allocated a significant portion of the many billions of dollars of revenue it saves each year to help lower-income households achieve the advantages of postsecondary education. After all, a college degree is the surest passport out of poverty in America. But nothing like that has occurred. Modest increases by Congress in direct grants and low-interest loans for low-income households to help with their higher-education costs pale in comparison to major new higher-education tax credits that primarily benefit middle-income households.

The substantial size of the new education tax subsidies and their minimal value for lower-income households reflect a decided shift in values of the federal government.

Historically, most higher-education subsidies have been in the form of Pell grants, which are made to students from lower-income households, and through student loans, which are available to lower- and moderate-income households; no loan is likely to be made to a household with more than $40,000 of AGI. Congress also has provided an exemption for scholarship income covering tuition and fees at a degree-granting educational institution; an exclusion by employees of up to $5,250 per year of educational expenses paid by their employers even if the expenses are not related to their job; and contributions to tax-exempt state tuition programs that will pay for a child's education at one of the state's postsecondary education institutions. None of these three provisions requires proof of need; indeed, they save the most taxes for taxpayers in the highest marginal tax brackets, but the tax subsidies never have been large.

In 1997, Congress added three more tax subsidies for the payment of higher education expenses and added a deduction for up to $1,000 of interest paid on higher-education loans. All four of the 1997 laws screen out high-income taxpayers. Three have the effect of screening out most lower-income taxpayers. Collectively, the three old laws and the four new ones create a hodgepodge of tax subsidies primarily for middle-income households. Because the new tax subsidies are sizable and have minimal value for lower-income households, they reflect a decided shift in values of the federal government. The teach a powerful lesson, one I have referred to often in these pages. Congress and presidents commonly use special provisions of the tax system to achieve objectives that probably could not be achieved through the direct budget process. We also are reminded that the poor have poor voting records. Let us consider three of the new laws.

Hope Scholarship Credits and Lifetime Learning Credits

Beginning in 1998, a Hope scholarship credit of up to $1,500 per year is available for the first two years of postsecondary education costs of a taxpayer, his spouse, and his dependents. Parents with two children beginning college can earn up to $3,000 in credits. A child who is not a dependent may claim the credit for himself.

The Lifetime Learning credit offers a tax credit of 20 percent of the first $5,000 of education expenses ($10,000 beginning in 2003) at nearly any postsecondary institution for courses to acquire or improve job skills. Only one Lifetime Learning credit may be claimed in any one year, regardless of the number of household members who incur education expenses. The expenses, however, are not limited to the first two years of college, and the credit may be claimed for an indefinite number of years. To avoid taxpayers' double-dipping, expenses that contribute to one of the credits may not contribute to the other.

Because the education tax credits benefit only people who owe taxes, many people working at lower ends of the wage scale will not benefit from them.

Congress's choice of tax credits reflects its sensitivity to the fact that each $1 credit, as distinguished from each $1 deduction, saves as much for taxpayers in the lowest marginal tax bracket as for taxpayers in a higher tax bracket. But the credits are *nonrefundable: They benefit only people who owe taxes, and only to the extent that they owe taxes.* Thus for people working at lower ends of the wage scale, the credits either have no value or, at best, can be used by them only to a limited extent. If the credits were refundable, all lower-income people would benefit because the government would issue a check to them to the extent that the credits exceeded their tax bills. A small percentage of joint filers, heads of households, and single taxpayers also will not benefit from these credits: To limit revenue losses, Congress eliminated the credits for joint filers with over $100,000 of AGI and for all other taxpayers with AGI over $50,000.

Education Individual Retirement Accounts

Up to $500 per year may be contributed to an education IRA for a child under the age of 18. Although contributions are not deductible, earnings are tax exempt; and distributions from the IRA to pay for the beneficiary's post-secondary education are tax free as long as no Hope or Lifetime Learning credit is claimed for the year that distributions are made.

Though the government's revenue losses from education IRAs may equal or exceed those from Hope or Lifetime Learning credits, joint filers with up to $150,000 of AGI and others with up to $95,000 of AGI (AGI thresholds considerably higher than those establishing eligibility for education credits) can fully fund education IRAs for an unlimited number of children, grandchildren, and others. Assuming an 8 percent return, each account can amount to $20,000 by the time a child is 18. But lower-income parents and grandparents and many with average incomes cannot afford to make an IRA contribution in the first place, which means that their children and grandchildren never will benefit from this government subsidy.

Concluding Comments

Education tax credits and IRAs will cost the government an estimated $5.4 billion in 2000, compared with the approximate $11.8 billion cost of Pell grants and student loans, which includes about $1.7 billion of recent additional funding. Eventually, education tax subsidies flowing to middle-income households may equal or exceed the direct subsidies to lower-income households, particularly as people become more familiar with the tax provisions and as education IRAs become more heavily funded. We must assume that Congress favors this outcome. Congress also deliberately has used the tax laws rather than direct grants to achieve its purposes. It would have been far more difficult to minimize the participation of lower-income households in new subsidies for higher education had the proposed subsidies been vetted through hearings of House and Senate education committees.

We can understand Congress's legitimate concerns about the costs of higher education that confront middle-class families. But we can only wonder why Congress has not found substantial additional resources, far beyond its relatively modest increases to Pell grants, to give the most needy members of society better access to higher education. A core feature of our nation's social covenant is the promise of equal opportunity to all citizens regardless of their initial station in life. By largely ignoring people most in need, who could have benefited from the new tax credits had they been made refundable, the 1997 education initiatives sharpened our sense that our national values seen through the lens of our tax laws fall short of the values that true conservatives and liberals claim to live by.

Simplicity

The goal of simplicity in the tax laws is little understood and too little pursued. In most cases, a highly simplified tax system would ignore the source of income, how it is provided, and how it is used. With few exceptions, it would tax our economic income after assuring each household that it would not pay tax on amounts deemed necessary to meet basic living costs consistent with standards appropriate for the world's most successful industrialized nation. These amounts would increase with household size but not with one's income, and they could be provided through a single tax credit rather than through separate computations of personal exemptions, standard deductions, and child credits. For example, if the tax on $18,000 of income were 10 percent, or $1,800, and Congress were to conclude that a household of two should be entitled to $18,000 of income before paying an income tax, then all households of two would be entitled to a tax credit of $1,800 whether they earned $8,000, $18,000, or $180,000.

Such an approach would be exceedingly simple and would simplify the filing of returns; in fact, most taxpayers would not have to file tax returns because the government would have the requisite tax data about them, and withholding taxes would cover their liabilities. Using a tax credit to secure each household a basic income level before the income tax applies also provides identical relief for everyone who has at least that level of income. You may prefer this approach to personal exemptions and standard deductions, which provide the greatest tax relief (and cost the government most) for households in higher tax brackets.

This highly simplified system would greatly expand what constitutes our taxable income. Fringe benefits would count as wages. All interest on state and local bonds would be taxable, as would all previously untaxed Social Security retirement benefits, which for must recipients would be about 85 percent of the benefits received. We would include as income the gain from the sale of our personal residence. We no longer could defer from income our capital gain that we realize when we swap our appreciated stock in Company A for stock in Company B in the course of Company B's takeover of Company A. Nor could we defer from income our capital gain on land or buildings that we swap for other real estate. A greatly simplified system would not allow contributions to employer-based retirement plans or to individual retirement accounts to avoid current taxation. We could not itemize deductions. We would not receive tax credits for child care or for education expenses; lower-income workers with dependents no longer would receive a refundable earned-income tax credit.

With these and many other examples of base-broadening reforms, a highly simplified tax system would accommodate much lower tax rates for all taxpayers to ensure that the reforms were revenue neutral. Much lower rates combined with a vastly broadened tax base could, if Congress agreed, maintain the same tax burden for the average taxpayer.

As must be evident, however, simplicity is not pain free, something that requires sacrifices only by others. You may not like what you must give up in order to be taxed at much lower tax rates. Russell Long's cynical comment is instructive. Recalling the high-minded testimony that always accompanied reformers' proposals before his Senate Finance Committee, he concluded "[a tax loophole] is something that benefits the other guy. If it benefits you, it is tax reform."[11]

Our cynicism aside, real tax reform ought to be guided by the public's best interest—indeed, our nation's highest values—not our narrow self-interest. And simplicity may not necessarily advance those values. When you examine tax policy, you may conclude that certain exclusions, deferrals, and deductions that cover personal expenses or investments may be warranted even though they make the laws more complex. You also may want lower-income households to continue to receive an earned-income tax credit, a form of wage supplement described in Chapter 8, to encourage work and discourage welfare. If you do, you favor a special relief provision that, by definition, must be complicated in many respects.

Many who criticize the complexity of our tax system believe that the limited number of relief provisions in a broad-based income tax should, for the most part, be available to all taxpayers, including those with high incomes. They note that although focusing tax relief on people who need it most sounds sensible, the rules for achieving these results have proliferated enormously and have added immensely to the complexity of the laws. For example, personal exemptions currently are reduced and eventually eliminated for taxpayers as their adjusted gross income rises above certain levels. In 2000, the phaseout begins for joint-return filers once their AGI exceeds $193,400 and is complete only when their AGI reaches $315,900—a range of over $120,000. A simpler approach, if Congress is to retain personal exemptions rather than move to the tax credit for household size described earlier, would be to award everyone personal exemptions regardless of income and to raise rates slightly on higher-income households to offset the revenue loss.

This observation returns us to the crucial relationship between the tax base and tax rates. If we simplify most tax-relief provisions by making them equally available to all households, we reduce the tax base and force Congress to maintain higher rates than otherwise would be necessary. If, however, Congress greatly restricts the number of relief provisions to relatively few cases that seem truly compelling, the revenue loss from them would be modest, as would the impact on tax rates. In short, if we are concerned, as we should be, about the level of tax rates, a policy that favors simplifying tax-relief provisions ought to be accompanied by a strong reluctance to enact the relief provisions in the first place.

A Closing Comment

Recognizing the values reflected in and promoted by the tax system, understanding their consequences, and weighing these values against competing values are the difficult but necessary processes by which we rationally arrive at our own ideas about what system makes most sense. Achieving a fairer, simpler, and economically sound system requires some widely shared agreement about which choices best promote the public interest.

Consider the following. Fairness sometimes requires complexity, and economic growth sometimes requires both complexity and a degree of unfairness. Each inequity, however, does not justify a solution, and each opportunity for economic growth does not warrant an incentive. History, politics, and mathematics are instructive. History teaches us to be wary of rhetoric that exaggerates hardships or assures us that a special tax measure will stimulate economic growth. Politics teaches that every special exception in the tax laws is likely to breed others. Mathematics teaches that each time Congress refuses to adopt a special tax program or eliminates an existing one, it usually has made a decision about tax rates.

Our nation cannot afford to ignore these lessons. Taking them seriously requires major new efforts to inform the electorate. Once informed, the public can engage in **cost-benefit analysis**. It can understand what can be gained, and lost, by eliminating most special provisions and simultaneously by lowering tax rates for all taxpayers. People then can appreciate, as they could not before, the competing choices among tax policies and the values embraced by each. They also will appreciate, as they could not before, why a leading tax expert would say, "If you know the position a person takes on taxes, you can tell their whole philosophy."

8

Progressive or Flat Rates:

Which Are Fairest of Them All?

> *Systems of taxation are not framed, nor is it possible to frame them, with perfect distribution of benefit and burden. Their authors must be satisfied with a rough-and-ready form of justice.*
> —Benjamin N. Cardozo, former justice of the Supreme Court

Overview * A Brief History of Progressive Rates * Shares of Tax Burdens * Who Pays Progressive Rates * Alternative Minimum Tax * Principles of Horizontal and Vertical Equity * Equity Arguments for Progressive Rates * Equity Arguments for a Flat Tax Rate * Passive Income of Children * Conclusion

---

The principle that federal income tax rates should rise as our income rises always has occupied a hallowed place in federal tax policy. Although not constitutionally mandated, progressive income tax rates were conceived as an indispensable bridge between nineteenth-century liberal and twentieth-century egalitarian beliefs that formed the uniquely American amalgam known as the American creed. Until recently, one could hardly imagine our democracy without them. Most Americans believed that allowing the rich to pay the same rate as everyone else would deny the federal government a prime instrument in our society for ameliorating excessive imbalances of income, wealth, and opportunity. Yet today, even people who benefit from progressive rates are intrigued by claims from advocates for a single flat tax rate across all returns.

Oddly enough, existing progressive rates have caused relatively few taxpayers to pay a proportion of all income taxes that is higher than their proportion of all adjusted gross income. This result suggests that the heat generated by the debate over the future of progressive rates may stem as much from their symbolic value as from their real value. Because passions and rhetoric on both sides of the debate can be at once illuminating and obfuscating, I have devoted two chapters to it. Issues of fairness, the starting point for most Americans, will be addressed here; the economics of tax rates will be addressed in the following chapter. In each, we will consider tax rates on **ordinary income**, which includes wages, salaries, commissions, profits from the operation of unincorporated businesses, rents, pensions, Social Security benefits, dividends, and interest. Chapter 12 considers the distinct issues involved in taxing capital gains. Chapter 13 examines arguments for a flat tax rate in the context of replacing the income tax with a flat tax.

Overview

Perspectives of progressive-rate and flat-rate advocates differ in political philosophies and economic analyses. Progressive-rate advocates stress such rates' valuable capacity to redistribute income from the more fortunate to those who are less fortunate. A flat rate also would be redistributive because it would claim proportionately more taxes from households with proportionately more taxable income. Progressive rates, however, can redistribute more by claiming *progressively* more taxable income as households become progressively prosperous.

Few progressive-rate advocates today propose highly progressive rates. Most realize that highly progressive rates lead high-income taxpayers to behave in ways that sharply reduce the degree of redistribution sought and can have undesirable economic consequences. Instead, advocates generally favor modest progressive rates (though they may differ about what constitutes *modest*) to achieve more limited goals. One goal is to slow the growing gap in income and wealth between the most financially successful among us and the average household. Progressive rates, by imposing higher rates on a minority of high-income taxpayers, allow the great majority of households to be subject to lower rates than would be the case with a flat rate. These lower rates, as seen by progressive-rate advocates, preserve income for such households often essential to achieving opportunities for advancement in our society. At a minimum, lower-income households should be less likely to need welfare assistance. Progressive rates also are viewed by advocates as a counterweight to the decided abilities of higher-income taxpayers to avoid taxes through legitimate tax planning. Finally, progressive rates help offset the regressive effects of Social Security taxes and federal excise taxes that claim a higher percentage of income from ordinary workers than from upper-income workers.

Flat-rate advocates respond by insisting, at the outset, on the intrinsic fairness of a tax that takes an equal proportion of each household's taxable income. If your neighbor has 20 times more taxable income than you, she will pay 20 times more taxes, which flat-rate advocates believe is redistributive enough. Advocates also note that a flat rate would discourage manipulations to allocate income or deductions to different tax years because the rate would be identical regardless of the year in which income is received or deductions are claimed. Most important, flat-rate advocates believe that a flat rate would best serve the public by stimulating economic growth. The growth, advocates claim, would create sufficient additional jobs at higher pay across the work-force to outweigh the value to ordinary workers from any income redistribu-tion that may result from progressive rates. Progressive-rate advocates dis-count such claims when applied to today's rates.

Undoubtedly, a flat rate is somewhat simpler for taxpayers to understand. Because the same tax rate applies to everyone, a flat rate also neutralizes many current tax consequences of marriage and minimizes the tax savings that can be achieved when high-income parents shift income-producing as-sets to their low-income children. Progressive-rate advocates believe that a few reforms to current laws can approximate these flat-rate advantages while retaining progressive rates' overriding redistributive rewards.

As background to the debate, I first will summarize our tax-rate history, clarify data about our tax burdens and who pays progressive rates, and elabo-rate on principles of fairness. I then will bring the debaters into the ring.

A Brief History of Progressive Rates

Ironically, progressive tax rates are in jeopardy as the gap of income and wealth between rich and poor approaches dimensions that led to the pro-gressive income tax. Unlike today, however, when there is little evidence of social unrest, the decades leading up to 1913 were marked by a bruising so-cial and economic battle. Grangers, Populists, the Pulitzer newspapers, and liberal religious leaders, fighting on behalf of ordinary households, de-manded better wages, working conditions, and housing from the owners of industry, some of whom enjoyed "fortunes swollen beyond all healthy lim-its," as President Theodore Roosevelt described them in 1906.[1] Roosevelt, a Republican, feared that the battle could mobilize a critical mass of the dis-contented to contemplate overturning the existing order.

This was the Gilded Age, an age of stark contrasts. A relative handful of American families, such as the Rockefellers, Vanderbilts, Astors, Harrimans, Carnegies, and Mellons, enjoyed unprecedented concentrations of wealth and power. At the same time, as much as 40 percent of all industrial workers lived in poverty with levels of wages and living conditions grossly inadequate to their basic economic needs.

Some people justified these disparities on the basis of insidious survival-of-the-fittest notions of social Darwinism—only the most able deserve the fruits of democracy. According to James MacGregor Burns, a leading U.S. historian, the view that "state interference to protect the weak or deprived violated the process of natural selection . . . fell with the tinkling melody of an intellectual aphrodisiac on the ears of the social and economic elites of America."[2] Even ministers suggested that wealth and virtue went hand in hand. Russell Conwell, a respected Christian minister from Philadelphia, advised his congregations in the 1890s that "ninety-eight out of one hundred of the rich men of America are honest. That is why they are rich." As good Christians, he would sermonize, "it is your duty to get rich."[3]

By 1904, life was sufficiently grim for the working class that for the first time, the Socialist Party, led by Eugene Debs, became a significant force in American politics. In the presidential election that year, handily won by Roosevelt, Debs received over 400,000 votes, up from 95,000 in 1900. This worried Roosevelt far more than did the Democratic Party.

> *By seizing the middle ground, progressive Republicans became the true conservatives of their age.*

Roosevelt had assumed leadership of the moderate wing of the Republican Party, which was determined to break big business's hold on the party. These Progressives, as they were called, sought to redefine the role of the federal government. Through regulation of big business, the protection of labor unions, and, ultimately, the taxation of the very rich, Roosevelt promised a "square deal," as he called it, for workers and employers. Along with fellow Progressives, Roosevelt was convinced that government must pursue a balanced course to secure capitalism from the growing radicalism of the working class. By seizing this middle ground, these Progressives became the true conservatives of their age.

In 1906, Roosevelt shocked the establishment by suggesting the need for progressive gift and estate taxes. As a prescriptive "Cure for the Disease of Wealth," he announced, "We shall *ultimately* have to consider a progressive tax on all fortunes, beyond a certain amount, either given in life or devised or bequeathed upon death to any individual—a tax so framed as to put it out of the power of the owner of one of these enormous fortunes to hand on more than a certain amount to any one individual" (emphasis added).[4]

"Ultimately" arrived the following year. In 1907, Roosevelt urged Congress to adopt both a progressive income tax and a progressive inheritance tax. In 1909, during the Republican administration of William Howard Taft, Congress passed the Sixteenth Amendment to eliminate constitutional impediments to the income tax found in the 1895 Pollock case. Not until 1913 did the amendment received the necessary approval of three-quarters of the states.

The House Ways and Means Committee immediately began crafting an income tax. Progressive tax rates made their way into the final legislation of 1913 largely because of efforts by John Nance Garner and Cordell Hull, Democrats in the House of Representatives who ultimately became vice president and secretary of state, respectively, under Franklin Roosevelt.

By 1916, the Supreme Court decided that Congress had the prerogative to set rates as it saw fit.[5] Thus licensed, different congresses have sent rates lurching between extreme highs (often in times of emergency) and lows. Top rates have been as low as 7 percent (1913) and as high as 94 percent (1944–1945). Bottom rates have ranged from about 1 percent (1913–1915) to as high as 23 percent (1944–1945) (see Figure 8.1).

Shares of Tax Burdens

To assess the fairness of today's progressive rates, we need to know who bears progressive tax burdens. As it turns out, a surprisingly small percentage of all taxpayers bear progressive tax burdens with respect to their adjusted gross income. In 1997, only the top 5.9 percent of taxpayers (those with $100,000 or more of AGI) owed a percentage of all taxes that was higher than their percentage of total AGI (see Table 1.2, columns C and G).

> *A surprisingly small percentage of taxpayers bear progressive tax burdens with respect to their AGI.*

Top taxpayers today, however, pay a far smaller percentage of their AGI in taxes than they did a half-century ago. In 1954, taxpayers who reported the equivalent of about $200,000 of AGI in 1997 dollars accounted for 5 percent of all AGI but paid 16 percent of all income taxes, *over three times their share of AGI*. In 1997, taxpayers with $200,000 or more of AGI accounted for about 20 percent of all AGI but paid only about 37 percent of all income taxes, *less than two times their share of AGI*. Had the 1954 ratios between AGI and taxes remained the same, these taxpayers in 1997 would have paid over *60 percent* of all income taxes.

These figures do not account for the distribution of corporate income taxes among us. All corporate income taxes ultimately are borne by individuals: shareholders, whose stock is worth less because of them; consumers, because corporations include a portion of the taxes in the prices of their goods and services; and workers, who receive lower wages because corporations have less income with which to pay them. Economists typically believe that much of the burden of the corporate income tax falls on owners of capital generally. If true, corporate income taxes fall disproportionately on the rich. Over the past half-century, however, corporate income taxes have greatly declined relative to individual income taxes and thus have far less impact on the rich than they once did. In 1954, corporate income taxes equaled nearly 75 percent of individual income taxes; in 1997, they equaled only about 25 percent.

Who Pays Progressive Rates

Each year the top rates have applied only to a tiny percentage of Americans and have reached only a fraction of their income. In fact, progressive rates apply to-

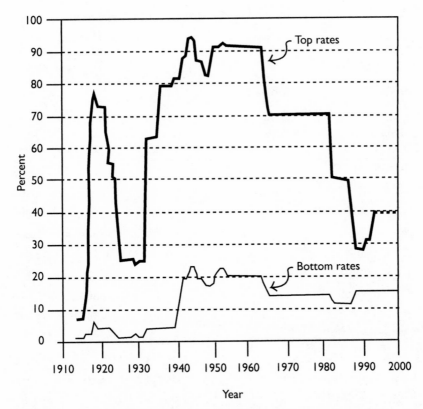

FIGURE 8.1   Chart of Top and Bottom Tax Rates on Ordinary Income from 1913 to 2000
SOURCE: Author's compilation.

day to less than one-third of all taxpayers. Over two-thirds of all taxpayers pay no higher than the bottom rate of 15 percent. Also remarkable, average tax rates paid by most upper-income taxpayers nearly always have been closer to the bottom than to the top tax rate. For example, as Table 1.2 (column E) demonstrates, although rates ranged from 15 to 28 to 31 to 36 to 39.6 percent, the total income taxes of only the top 1.5 percent of all taxpayers (those with $200,000 or more of

> *Each year the top rates have applied only to a tiny percentage of Americans and have reached only a small fraction of their income.*

AGI) in 1997 exceeded 20 percent of their AGI. All other taxpayers—including nearly all with under $200,000 of AGI—paid less than 20 percent.

The critical importance of the lowest rate to most taxpayers and its relevance even to top taxpayers suggests that the debate about tax rates must consider equally where rates *begin* and where they *end*. If Congress consider-

TABLE 8.1 Tax Burden Using Actual Tax Rates and a Revenue-Neutral Flat Rate
of 21.3 Percent , 1997

(A)	(B)	(C)	(D)	(E)	(F)
	Tax as % of Taxable Income		Average Tax Paid		Average Tax Increase/ Decrease with Flat Rate
Taxpayers Grouped by Income[a] ($)	Progressive Rate	Flat Rate	Progressive Rate ($)	Flat Rate ($)	($)
(1) 0–9,999	14.8	21.3	92	130	38
(2) 10,000–19,999	13.2	21.3	641	933	292
(3) 20,000–29,999	14.1	21.3	1,870	2,769	899
(4) 30,000–39,999	15.4	21.3	3,344	4,594	1,250
(5) 40,000–49,999	16.2	21.3	4,797	6,282	1,485
(6) 50,000–74,999	17.1	21.3	7,281	9,081	1,800
(7) 75,000–99,999	19.8	21.3	12,438	13,366	928
(8) 100,000–199,999	23.0	21.3	23,495	21,746	(1,749)
(9) 200,000–999,999	30.0	21.3	89,431	64,535	(24,896)
(10) 1,000,000–	32.0	21.3	844,813	562,201	(282,612)

[a]*Income* as used here refers to adjusted gross income, or AGI, which is the income
before deductions reported on all tax returns.
SOURCE: Internal Revenue Service, *Statistics of Income–1997: Individual Income
Tax Returns* (Washington, D.C.: IRS, 2000).

ably broadened the tax base, today's bottom 15 percent rate could be much
lower without altering total tax revenues. If Congress were to adopt a flat tax
rate on today's tax base, the rate would have to be considerably higher than
15 percent in order to be revenue neutral. In 1997, had all other provisions
of the tax laws remained the same, that rate would have been *21.3 percent*
(see Table 8.1). In such case, taxpayers with under $100,000 of adjusted
gross income—94.1 percent of all taxpayers—would on average have paid
more taxes (compare columns D and F of Table 8.1). For example, taxpayers
with between $75,000 and $99,999 of AGI would have seen their taxes rise
an average of *$928.* By contrast, taxpayers with $1 million or more of AGI
would have enjoyed an average decrease in taxes of *$282,612.*

Alternative Minimum Tax

To increase the taxes paid by people who seemed to benefit excessively from
tax exclusions and deductions, Congress in 1976 adopted an **alternative**

minimum tax (AMT). Taxpayers must pay the AMT to the extent that it exceeds their regular tax. Under a complex set of rules, the AMT applies a small range of rates—from 26 to 28 percent—against a tax base that is somewhat broader than under our laws.

The AMT's inroads on tax preferences, however, are modest. Because its tax rates also are modest, the AMT primarily camouflages Congress's unwillingness to address directly the flawed rationale of so many tax preferences. As Sheldon Pollock, professor of business law, has written, "In the end, the alternative minimum tax reflects the worst tendency of incremental policymaking, tinkering with change at the margins and thereby further complicating the tax laws, rather than abandoning an unwarranted tax preference altogether."[6] In 1997, only 618,000 out of 122 million tax returns owed an AMT. Worse, the AMT produced only $4 billion of revenue, compared to $731 billion of income taxes due overall. Quite possibly, the amount of taxes collected from the AMT was less than the combined costs incurred by over 4.4 million taxpayers who were required to comply with AMT filing requirements and by the IRS to administer the program.

Current estimates indicate that up to 6 million taxpayers might pay the AMT 10 years from now. But as the AMT threatens to become more effective, we can expect more effective pressures on Congress to contain its grasp. Proposals to eliminate the AMT already abound.

Principles of Horizontal and Vertical Equity

Horizontal Equity

As readers may recall, a guiding, though not inviolate, principle of tax justice is that people with equal abilities to pay income taxes ought to pay equal amounts. Known as horizontal equity, this principle applies equally to both flat and progressive tax rates.

Horizontal equity, however, precedes tax rates; it is not determined by them. Hori-

Horizontal equity: People with equal abilities to pay should pay equal amounts.

zontal equity requires defining taxable income so as to group people together who have equal abilities to pay. Then, either a single rate or progressive rates will treat everyone in the same group similarly. For example, all single people with $100,000 of taxable income will pay the same tax whether they pay a flat rate of 25 percent or progressive rates that yield a tax of $25,000.

Vertical Equity

The flip side of identifying equals is identifying unequals. For unequals, whether rates are progressive or flat matters greatly. Which is fairer depends on

our view of vertical equity—the principle that tax burdens should increase appropriately with our increasing ability to pay.

Vertical equity: People with greater abilities to pay should pay appropriately more.

Achieving vertical equity, therefore, requires answers to two questions. First, what criteria are used to determine ability to pay? Second, what increases in tax burdens are appropriate for people who have greater abilities to pay?

Achieving Vertical Equity Through Progressive, Flat (Proportional), or Regressive Rates

In theory, vertical equity might be achieved with progressive rates, a flat rate, or regressive rates. In each case, your neighbor will pay more taxes than you will pay if she has more taxable income. But what is *appropriately* more?

Taxpayers will pay disproportionately more taxes on their taxable income if tax rates progress from a lower rate to one or more higher rates. A progressive-rate system can exist, however, with as few as two rates, such as 10 percent on

A progressive-rate system can exist with as few as two rates.

the first $40,000 of taxable income and 20 percent on the balance. Remember: With progressive rates, higher rates apply solely to higher levels of taxable income. The lowest

rate, for example, continues to apply to the lowest level of taxable income. For this reason, no taxpayer today, even with millions of dollars of taxable income, pays an average tax of 39.6 percent because portions of her taxable income have been taxed at 15, 28, and 36 percent.

A flat-rate system imposes one rate on all taxable income. A flat rate is said to be proportional because it claims the same proportion of each dollar of taxable income. Regressive rates are the obverse of progressive rates, declining as income increases. The rate might be 20 percent on the first $40,000 of taxable income and 10 percent on the balance.

Although today's tax rates on ordinary income are progressive, the special tax rates on long-term capital gains—gains from the sale of investments held for more than 12 months—can produce regressive results. The maximum long-term capital gains rate for higher-income taxpayers is now 20 percent. This means, for example, that in 1999 a single person with $200,000 of taxable income, all of which is capital gains subject to the 20 percent rate, paid less tax ($40,000) than did a single person with $150,000 of taxable income, all of which was from wages ($42,267). Capital gains aside, no notable case has been made for regressive income tax rates. I will ignore any argument for them here.

As mentioned earlier, few progressive-rate advocates favor steeply progressive rates, but reminders of such rates often skew the fundamental debate between the merits of progressive rates and the merits of a single rate. Let us be clear. The threshold issue is whether *some* progressivity in rates is fairer than a single flat rate for raising the same amount of tax revenue. If so, we can debate how progressive the rates should be.

Equity Arguments for Progressive Rates

Progressive Rates on the Rich

The first hurdle for progressive-rate advocates is to establish it is fair to tax the rich at a higher tax rate than applies to others. If so, we must decide whether some people who are not rich also should be subject to progressive rates.[7]

Who are the so-called rich? Our perspectives vary greatly in good part because they are so subjective. They are complicated further because public records do not and cannot adequately track all of the income and wealth of the wealthiest among us. For discussion purposes, let us refer to the rich as the top 1 percent of all income as identified in public documents, which today means households with somewhat more than $200,000 of income.

What is life like for the top 1 percent? While they enjoy a vastly disproportionate share of all income—in 1997, taxpayers with over $200,000 of income represented 1.5 percent of all taxpayers but had 20.2 percent of all AGI—most enjoyed a far greater concentration of our nation's wealth. According to economist Edward N. Wolff, wealth data of the Federal Reserve Board for 1992 indicated that the richest 1 percent of all households owned 35.9 percent of all household net worth and 45.6 percent of all financial wealth (defined for these purposed as net worth minus houses and automobiles).[8]

Many of the rich become increasingly rich by saving and investing significant portions of their annual incomes. People also can be very rich and have little taxable income. They might live on tax-exempt income or borrowed money, or they might raise cash by selling stocks for which they have no taxable gain or by realizing in the same year an equal amount of capital losses and capital gains. Whatever their source of cash, their combined income and wealth provide them with enormous lifestyle advantages. They and their families are assured of excellent nutrition and medical treatment, of living in safe neighborhoods, and of the best education and training. As a result, they are likely to be healthier and better educated than others. Their immeasurable opportunities to network through personal, college, graduate school, and other connections advance their careers and, thereby, their finances. They often have special access to politicians and can use their wealth to influence political outcomes. To summarize, the rich enjoy vastly disproportionate mastery over their destinies compared with most people.

Consider the bottom half of all households as measured by their income. In 1992, median household income was $29,000. (Household income will average more than taxpayer income because the former aggregates the income of all related people residing in a single house, including parents and adult children who file separate tax returns.) In other words, half of all households had less than $29,000 of income. Median household wealth also was modest— $51,000—or about 2 percent of the wealth of the richest 1 percent of all households. Most median household wealth was tied up in the family home; only $10,000 constituted financial wealth.[9] In short, few households in the bottom half have any spendable wealth to speak of. Most

> *Median household wealth in 1992 equaled about 2 percent of household wealth held by the richest 1 percent.*

are in debt. Many, though not most, children raised in these households live on substandard diets, receive substandard medical care, live in substandard housing, and receive substandard education and training. To summarize, members of these families often must overcome, rather than capitalize on, the predominant conditions of their lives in order to succeed in America.

Politicians have generated multiple justifications for progressive tax rates in order to lessen the chasm between the lifestyles and opportunities of the rich and those experienced by the rest of society. The simplest borrows on Willie Sutton's explanation for robbing banks: "That's where the money is!" Teddy Roosevelt viewed progressive rates as part of the arsenal to restrain the excessive power and influence of the rich and to ensure for ordinary workers a promising future within the capitalistic system. Franklin Roosevelt felt that steeply progressive rates on the rich also were a fair exchange for the benefits they received from government. In FDR's view, "vast personal incomes come not only through the effort or ability or luck of those who receive them, but also because of the opportunities for advantage which Government itself contributes. Therefore, the duty rests upon the Government to restrict such incomes by very high taxes."[10]

Today, advocates of progressive rates tend to offer a threefold justification for them. First, progressive rates generate additional revenue that the rich can relinquish without sacrificing their basic lifestyles and that the government may use to improve the welfare of lower- and moderate-income households. Second, by paying higher taxes, the rich make it possible for lower- and middle-income households to pay less. Progressive-rate advocates believe that the combination of additional government assistance and lower tax burdens for these households are essential to fulfill this na-

> *"Progressive taxation can trade off the benefits of ensuring a broader distribution of opportunity against the modest costs of higher tax rates and higher tax burdens on some to finance it." (Robert Shapiro)*

tion's sacred promise that everyone should have the opportunity to succeed. That opportunity is elusive for many members of the bottom half often because they lack financial resources to extricate themselves and their children

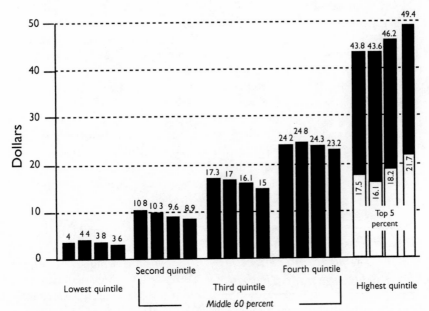

FIGURE 8.2   Share of Aggregate Household Income by Quintile, 1967, 1977, 1987, and 1997 (in percent)
SOURCE: U.S. Bureau of the Census, *Money Income in the United States: 1997*, Current Population Report, P60-200, September 1998, xii.

from their predicaments. As Robert Shapiro of the Progressive Foundation has written, "Progressive taxation can trade off the benefits of ensuring a broader distribution of opportunity against the modest costs of higher tax rates and higher tax burdens on some to finance it."[11] Third, progressive-rate advocates believe that the sacrifice by the rich of a higher percentage of their taxable income does not result in a disproportionate sacrifice of their personal welfare; I will explain this argument in the **utility of income** terminology used by economists when I analyze the application of progressive rates to people who are not rich.

Progressive-rate advocates point to income trends over the past 30 to 40 years. Since 1967, according to the Bureau of the Census, the share of household income belonging only to the top quintile of households has increased; the share of all other quintiles has declined. Interestingly, only the share of the bottom quintile of households increased from 1967 to 1977 (from 4.0 percent to 4.4 percent), but its share fell to 3.6 percent by 1997, the largest relative decline of all households. The share of income of the highest quintile, which fell slightly from 43.8 percent in 1967 to 43.6 percent in 1977, has risen since then to 49.4 percent. The share of the middle quintile of households has fallen from 17.3 percent in 1967 to 15.0 percent in 1997 (see Figure 8.2).

In fact, between 1977 and 1994, according to the Center on Budget and Policy Priorities in Washington, D.C., the average after-tax income of the wealthiest 1 percent of Americans rose 72 percent (adjusted for inflation); that of the poorest fifth of families shrank 16 percent. "In 1977," the center reported, "the bottom 35 percent of the population had nearly twice as much after-tax income as the top one percent. . . . By 1994, these two groups had essentially the same amount of income."[12] As the economist Gary Burtless recently observed, "Permanent inequality is going up."[13]

The foregoing statistics ignore income mobility. Over their lifetimes, people move about economically, both into higher income quintiles and into lower ones. But even income mobility in the lower quintiles may be declining. A study of income trends among younger workers from 1979 through 1990 documented this decline: Someone in the bottom income quintile in 1980 was nearly twice as likely to move into a higher income quintile by 1982 than someone in the bottom income quintile in 1990 was likely to move into a higher quintile by 1992. When upward movements from the lower quintiles occurred, they were likely to be smaller in 1990 than in 1980.[14]

Between 1980 and 1990, movement out of the bottom income quintile apparently became more difficult.

Little evidence suggests that the income gap between the rich and ordinary working households will not continue to expand. Much suggests otherwise: the global economy that offers businesses increasingly easier access to inexpensive labor; the disgraceful underpreparation of students by our public elementary and secondary schools for an information age that increasingly requires a skilled workforce; and low memberships of unions, which weaken the bargaining power of rank-and-file workers.

Nonetheless, most champions of progressive rates also champion capitalism. They seek only to temper its extremes. Even Adam Smith, while advocating proportionate taxation as a general principle, hastened to add in his *Wealth of Nations* that "it is not very unreasonable that the rich should contribute to the public expense, not only in proportion to their revenue, but something more than in proportion."[15] Capitalism rewards people who are best able to make money, even when the impact on society may be unfavorable. Progressive rates redirect some of this success to people who have modest earnings but who may work as hard or harder than many of the rich, may be as or more creative and talented, and may contribute as much or more to the betterment of society. Highly trained and skilled artists and musicians, for example, might struggle to make ends meet, whereas a young stockbroker only a few years out of college might make hundreds of thousands of dollars by executing commonplace trades for customers. A laboratory scientist may discover a drug that will earn her a raise but will make the stockholders of her company small fortunes. Schoolteachers play at least as vital a role in the future of our country as professional basketball players and work as hard, but they earn annually less than a basketball star earns for one game. Progressive rates help correct for these consequences.

Progressive rates also help correct for the disproportionate ability of the rich to exclude their income from AGI, to maximize itemized deductions, and to take advantage of low capital gains rates. Last, advocates believe that without progressive income tax rates, federal tax burdens overall might not be progressive because the other major federal tax, Social Security, is regressive. A study by Treasury's Office of Tax Analysis illustrates this point: Using a comprehensive definition of income, it found that the top 1 percent of families in 1996 received 14.3 percent of all income and paid 17.4 percent of all federal taxes.[16] A flat tax rate might have lowered their percentage of all federal taxes close to or even below 14.3 percent.

Progressive Tax Rates Across the Income Spectrum

Let us assume momentarily that sound equitable grounds exist to apply progressive rates to the rich. Do we have grounds to apply progressive-rate differentials among taxpayers who are not rich? The issue was academic during early decades of the income tax because only top-income earners owed taxes. Since World War II, however, when most households became taxable, rates have progressed on modest levels of taxable income. In fact, since 1986 the most significant jump in rates was from 15 percent to 28 percent, which occurred in 2000 when taxable income exceeded $26,250 for single taxpayers and $43,850 for joint taxpayers. What theory supports making these, or any, rate distinctions among a range of economically unexceptional taxpayers?

One of the most radical theories, articulated by the philosopher John Rawls, argues that the welfare of a society is to be judged by the well-being of its least well off members. According to Rawls, "Social and economic inequalities, for example inequalities of wealth and authority, are just only if they result in compensating benefits for everyone and in particular for the least advantaged members of society."[17] Concluding that few inequalities are just, Rawls argues that income must be massively redistributed from all other segments of society to raise the welfare of the least well off.

Rawls's justification for such massive redistribution has roots in the teachings of John Stuart Mill, the nineteenth-century English utilitarian philosopher and economist. Mill proposed that fair taxation required equal sacrifice from each taxpayer. Taken literally, equal sacrifice could require extreme sacrifices by the rich because such sacrifices would cause them less pain than would small sacrifices for people with modest incomes and wealth.

Viewed less radically to justify progressive rates, and viewed with more interest by this country, has been the principle of **equal proportional sacrifice**. Equal proportional sacrifice is determined by estimating what economists refer to as the **marginal utility of income** among us, that is, the degree that additional income increases our personal welfare—our well-being. When economists refer to the **declining marginal utility of income**, they mean that the additional value (or marginal utility) to us of each dollar of income decreases disproportionately once income has climbed above a basic threshold. Our welfare is enhanced most by income that covers our basic needs, such as for food, shelter, clothing, health care, and education. As our income increasingly serves discretionary needs—as we move, in effect, from acquiring our first pair of shoes to acquiring our tenth or twentieth—its utility declines at an accelerating rate. Consequently, if we look at two people with disparate incomes and consider their very next dollar of income, the person with more income must pay a higher percentage in taxes in order for each person's sacrifice to be proportionally equal.

Take the case of Ms. Manager, who has an income of $50,000 and receives a year-end bonus of $1,000, compared to the case of Ms. Secretary, who has an income of $15,000 and also receives a bonus of $1,000. According to the declining marginal utility of income, $1,000 is likely to increase Ms. Secretary's welfare disproportionately more than it increases Ms. Manager's. For each to sacrifice equally, Ms. Manager must pay a higher tax rate on the $1,000 than would Ms. Secretary.

But how much? Here lies the problem. No two people experience exactly the same rate of declining marginal utility. You may be miserable without certain products and services, whereas your neighbor is not. Income may buy power and fame, which attract some and repel others. Ms. Entrepreneur may work 80 hours a week to develop her business, which she values above all else. Ms. Leisure, who never would want the responsibility of running her own business, refuses to work overtime at her 35-hour-per-week job because she places greater value on spending time with family and friends.

We know, too, that as our incomes increase, our needs change, complicating our experience of marginal utility even more. What seemed a luxury when one's income was less may now be viewed as a necessity. Furthermore,

> *Distinctions in tax rates based on the theory of diminishing marginal utility are as legitimate as distinctions in the standard deduction for different-sized households.*

some people (including some who pay progressive rates) use their money more constructively than others; inevitably, some who benefit from progressive rates may squander their benefits.

All these observations compel us to conclude that although declining marginal utility makes intuitive sense, wide variations in our needs for income and our uses of it preclude any scientific basis on which to configure a utility curve for progressive tax rates. Unfortunately, this difficulty has led many analysts to reject entirely the relevance of declining marginal utility to tax rate policy. Were scientific standards applied throughout the tax laws, all the laws would flunk.

Consider a provision as basic as the standard deduction and distinctions drawn between a single taxpayer and a married couple. The deduction helps establish a threshold of income below which taxpayers who do not itemize deserve to be spared from taxation in order to meet basic living costs. Congress provides a higher standard deduction for a married couple than for a single individual because the typical couple requires more income to pay for basic living costs than does the typical single individual. Yet there is no exact calculus for determining the differential. We also know that there always will be exceptions to the rule: The needs of some single individuals will exceed those of some married couples with the same income. Nonetheless, most people, including flat tax advocates, accept the principle that a larger standard deduction for married couples than for single people can achieve rough but admittedly imperfect justice and should be included in our tax laws.

We should expect nothing more from the theory of diminishing marginal utility of income. It posits that for typical individuals, the value of income begins to decline above a basic income threshold; and at some point, the decline occurs more rapidly than the percentage increase in their income. (If the decline occurred proportional to the increase in their income, a proportional, or flat, tax rate would suffice.) If you agree, fairness requires taxpayers who have reached that threshold to pay a progressive tax rate on their next dollar of taxable income. Only then can their sacrifice of a portion of that dollar be equal to the sacrifice of lower-income taxpayers with respect to a portion of their next dollar. As in the case of the standard deduction, Congress must draw the lines, which always will be subject to debate.

Progressive tax rates also maximize the number of people who pay an income tax by permitting tax burdens to be affordable by everyone who can

> *Progressive rates maximize the number of people who pay an income tax by permitting tax burdens to be affordable by everyone who can pay something.*

pay something. This strategy perpetuates a core principle promoted by Dwight Eisenhower when, as president, he rejected a 1954 proposal that would have exempted one out of every three taxpayers from the federal income tax: "I am for everybody paying his fair share."[18]

To summarize, progressive-rate advocates seem less ambitious about what progressive rates can achieve today compared with their ambitions many years ago. Most expect only that progressive rates will temper great inequalities of income or at least the growth of these inequalities. Shortly before his death in 1989, Joseph Pechman, an advocate of progressive rates, seems to have expressed these views best: "The basic justification for the progressive income tax is now probably the socio-economic objective of reducing great

disparities of welfare, opportunity and economic power arising from the unequal distribution of income" (emphasis added).[19] This paradigm seems to
limit progressive rates to people with high incomes, though not necessarily
only the rich as defined here.

Equity Arguments for a Flat Tax Rate

General Principles

A **flat (or proportional) tax rate** applied to all taxable income intrigues advocates mostly because of its economic and administrative advantages. But
advocates also view it as fairer than progressive rates. Their argument proceeds from two initial propositions: People are entitled to what they have
justly earned, and most income is justly earned. It follows that taxation in
proportion to income ought to be a limiting principle of tax policy. To tax
successful people's income disproportionately is seen as unwarranted taking
of their private property, a violation of their personal liberty.

As these assumptions suggest, flat-rate advocates, compared with progressive-rate advocates, tend to credit far less any contributions from "silent
partners," the ordinary workers of whom Carnegie spoke; or protections
given to them and to their property by the government, of which Franklin
Roosevelt spoke; or circumstances of birth and environment. Instead, flat-
rate advocates believe that individual financial success results primarily from
one's willingness to take risks, from one's ingenuity,
and, most important, from one's hard work. Underlying these beliefs is the assumption that most
people have the ability and opportunities to become
successful.

> *Flat-rate advocates*
> *believe more in*
> *celebrating great*
> *inequalities than in*
> *constraining them.*

Understandably, then, flat-rate advocates are
more inclined to celebrate inequalities than to constrain them. Listen to Irving Kristol, a leading con-
servative spokesman and flat-rate advocate: "A just and legitimate society, according to Aristotle, is one in which inequalities—of property, station, or
power—are generally perceived by the citizenry as necessary for the common good. I do not see that this definition has ever been improved on."[20]
By this reasoning, inequalities in the tax system favor people who are the
most worthy.

Flat-rate advocates also maintain that a flat rate would end political bicker-
ing about what is the fairest schedule of progressive rates. In the view of
nineteenth-century commentator James McCullough, progressive rates put
the tax system "at sea without a rudder or compass." By contrast, "proportional taxes," the economist Lawrence Lindsey explains, "at least unite the
interest of the nation behind a specific standard."[21]

Flat-rate advocates remind us that with a flat rate, people with high taxable incomes pay much more than do people with much lower taxable incomes. In concrete terms, if you have $40,000 of taxable income and your neighbor has $400,000, or 10 times as much, a flat rate of 20 percent takes $8,000 from you and $80,000, or 10 times as much, from her.

That such a result is fair, Lindsey believes, can be seen by examining the case of identical twins, equally endowed and with equal career opportunities. One chooses to be a college professor. He (Lindsey posits) has a much lighter workload plus far more vacation time than does the other, who starts his own business, "works fourteen hours per day, six or seven days per week, and is amazingly successful, making lots of money." Lindsey argues that the "equal proportionate sacrifice" test ought to be satisfied if the wealthier brother pays proportionately more tax. To ask him to pay progressively more ignores the importance of their career choices and their judgments about the utility of income. The "college professor," writes Lindsey, "is paid not only in money but also in free time. In effect, the extra money the businessman earns compensates him for the extra hours he works."[22] If one accepts this analysis, progressive rates unjustifiably redistribute income to people who have chosen to earn less because of personal tastes.

Even if we accept Lindsey's example, the question becomes how well these twins represent the general workforce. Flat-rate advocates and progressive-rate advocates sharply disagree. Flat-rate advocates such as Gregory Fossedal, chairman of the Alexis de Tocqueville Institution of Washington, D.C., cite statistics supporting their view that most of us can and do move up the income scale if we put our minds to it.[23] Progressive-rate advocates counter that even if that were true, most people lack the combination of skills and opportunity to "make lots of money," unlike the businessman's twin.

Lindsey's example is provocative as well as controversial. It echoes Kristol's description of "class struggle" between professors and the business community.[24] Anyone who has spent time on a college campus notices it. Minimizing the skills and energy of successful businesspeople and critical of the extremes of capitalism and the spiritual emptiness of an ethic of materialism, many members of the academic community sharply discount the right of a successful businessperson to the fruits of her enterprise. Such unbalanced, and often unwarranted, animus toward the business community complicates any discussion about tax rates.

No less complicating is the resistance of flat-rate advocates to justifying scientifically their claim that a flat rate is fair while simultaneously criticizing the scientific shortcomings of theories about the utility of income. Flat-rate advocates seem to assume that a flat rate is more neutral or natural than progressive rates, and they cast the burden on progressive-rate advocates to justify their "unnatural" scheme.[25] Robert Hall and Alvin Rabushka summarily conclude that a flat rate "avoids penalizing success,"[26] but they fail to provide a theory that would help us identify a tax penalty. Would they argue, for example, that the top progressive rate of 7 percent in 1913 penalized the rich but not a flat 10 percent rate? What about the ordinary worker who receives a substantial raise that would be taxed at the 15 percent rate today but may well be taxed at a higher rate under a flat tax? Would not a flat rate penalize her success?

Flat-rate advocates correctly note that a flat rate can result in progressive tax burdens.

Whereas progressive-rate advocates may legitimately question presumptions that proportionate rates are presumptively fair, flat-rate advocates correctly note that a flat rate can result in **progressive tax burdens:** When combined with a basic income exclusion, a flat rate can claim a larger percentage from the income of higher-income taxpayers than from the income of lower-income taxpayers. Consider Judy Recht and Jill Neury, who live in Marin County, California. Judy's adjusted gross income is $50,000, Jill's $100,000. If each were entitled to a basic exemption of $20,000 and no other deductions, Judy's taxable income would be $30,000 and Jill's $80,000. With a flat tax rate of 20 percent, Judy would pay a tax of $6,000, or 12 percent of her AGI, and Jill would pay a tax of $16,000, or 16 percent of her AGI. Jill's progressive tax burden follows because the personal exemption eliminates a smaller percentage of her AGI than of Judy's.

The likelihood that a basic exemption combined with a flat rate would consistently result in progressive tax burdens depends, however, on the tax base.

Whether a flat rate combined with a basic exemption for all taxpayers would produce progressive results depends on how Congress defines the tax base.

If Judy has no other income, but Jill has an additional $100,000 of tax-exempt gain from the sale of her principal residence, Jill's actual income is $200,000. In that case, her $16,000 of taxes represents only 8 percent of her income, compared to Judy's 12 percent, a distinctly regressive result.

In sum, whether a flat rate combined with a basic exclusion consistently produces progressive results depends on what income exclusions and other deductions enter into the computation of taxable income. That computation varies enormously among taxpayers today. It can vary enormously under a flat tax that calls for a flat tax rate but exempts returns on savings and investment, an exemption that would apply to a great deal of high-income taxpayers' income and little of the income of ordinary taxpayers (see Chapter 13).

Finally, what cannot be disputed are two additional points made by flat-rate advocates. A flat rate would minimize the income tax consequences of marriage. It also would minimize the tax savings from shifting income-producing assets to lower-income members of a family.

Marriage Bonuses and Penalties
from Progressive Tax Rates

Samuel Butler, the English satirist, cautioned in "Higgledy-Piggledy" that "in matrimony, to hesitate is sometimes to be saved." Hesitating also may save taxes. Marriage, it turns out, can result in a tax penalty—it may increase the combined income tax liabilities of partners. Marriage also may produce a tax bonus—it may decrease their combined tax liabilities. Progressive rates play a role. To understand Congress's dilemma, we must understand a bit of history, including distinctions between common law and community property states.

According to the common law that applies in most states, earnings of a spouse are treated as the property of that sole spouse. In community-property states, these earnings usually belong equally to each spouse and are taxed accordingly. These differences often meant, prior to 1948, that one-earner couples in a community-property state such as California paid less in taxes than one-earner couples in a common-law state such as Massachusetts, though the couples had identical income and deductions. This injustice occurred because husbands and wives filed separate returns, each reporting their own income; and by splitting their income on two returns, the California couple took advantage of the lowest rates twice. Conversely, the Massachusetts earner spouse was required to report all of the income on a single return, which caused the income to progress more quickly to the higher rates.

Congress solved the problem in 1948 by adopting a joint return for married couples on which the tax rates progressed half as fast as did the rates on a single return. This gave common-law couples the equivalent of income splitting under community-property laws and achieved marriage neutrality: consistent tax treatment of couples regardless of the sources of their income or where they live.

Single taxpayers soon complained that it was unfair that their tax rates climbed twice as fast for the same amount of taxable income as the tax rates available to married couples. In 1969, Congress agreed; but like all congresses since, it believed that tax rates for married couples on the same income ought to progress somewhat more slowly than for singles. As with the standard deduction, Congress reasoned that married couples needed more income to live on than did a single person. (As precedent, Congress in 1951 had created a special tax schedule for a head of household—an unmarried individual with one or more dependent children—that roughly split the difference between the rate schedule for single and joint returns.)

Congress's compromise in 1969, and since, was to establish tax rates for singles that progressed slightly faster than those for heads of households and even faster, but less than twice as fast, than those for joint returns. Married couples in all states have filed either a joint return, which combines all of their income and deductions on one return, or a married-filing-separately return, in which case each reports his or her income on a separate return. (Separate filing is distinguished from filing as single individuals, which is prohibited for married couples.)

To encourage joint filing in order that couples with the same taxable income pay the same tax, Congress has set the tax rates on married-filing-separately returns to progress twice as fast as under a joint return. Thus separate returns rarely save taxes. For example, in 2000, the 15 percent tax rate extends to $43,850 of taxable income if a couple files jointly, but it extends only to $21,925 if they file separately. Consequently, the tax decision for the typical prospective bride and groom is whether they would be better off by marrying and filing jointly or by remaining unmarried and filing single or head of household returns. The answer depends on their respective incomes.

> *Depending on their incomes, a prospective bride and groom may collectively owe more taxes by marrying and filing jointly or by remaining unmarried.*

Progressive rates typically produce a marriage penalty when both partners have comparable incomes. Take Reuben, a filmmaker, and Lois, a real estate broker, who, unmarried, share a house in St. Paul, Minnesota. Each has $120,000 of taxable income. As single taxpayers, their top rate in 1999 (see Table 8.2) did not exceed 31 percent. If they had married and reported $240,000 of taxable income on a joint return, the amount above $158,550 would have been taxed at 36 percent. Overall, they would have incurred a **marriage penalty** of nearly $5,800.

A marriage penalty also could apply were their income modest. For example, if each had $25,000 of taxable income, all of it would have been subject solely to the 15 percent rate if unmarried. Married, their taxable income above $43,050 would have been subject to the 28 percent tax, costing them over $900.

Progressive rates typically produce a marriage bonus when only one partner has substantial income. For example, if in 1999 Lois had $120,000 of taxable income and Reuben had none, Lois, as a single taxpayer, would have been subject to the 31 percent rate on all of her taxable income above $62,450. If they were married and filed a joint return, only their taxable income above $104,050 would have been taxed at the 31 percent rate, which would have yielded a **marriage bonus** of nearly $3,500.

For 1999, the Office of Tax Analysis (OTA) of the Treasury Department estimated (taking into account all income tax laws) that 48 percent of all joint returns would have a marriage penalty; 41 percent would have a marriage bonus. Average marriage penalties ($1,141) would be slightly less than average marriage bonuses ($1,274). Marriage penalties and, to a lesser extent, marriage bonuses would be highly concentrated among higher-income couples. Couples with over $100,000 of adjusted gross income, though rep-

TABLE 8.2 Individual Income Tax Rates and Liabilities for Single and Joint Returns, 1999

Tax Rate (%)	Taxable Income ($)	
	Single Return	Joint Return
15.0	0–25,750	0–43,050
28.0	25,751–62,450	43,051–104,050
31.0	62,451–130,250	104,051–158,550
36.0	130,251–283,150	158,551–283,150
39.6	283,151–	283,151–

SOURCE: Internal Revenue code.

resenting only 15 percent of all couples, would suffer 42 percent of aggregate marriage penalties while enjoying 30 percent of aggregate marriage bonuses. By comparison, couples with under $30,000 of AGI were far more likely to enjoy marriage bonuses (42 percent) than to suffer marriage penalties (27 percent).[27] OTA's data also made clear that virtually all couples that suffered marriage penalties were two-earner couples.

Congress could eliminate the marriage penalty caused by progressive rates by returning the tax rate brackets for joint returns to twice that for single returns. In such case, the 15 percent tax bracket for a joint return in 1999 would have extended to $51,550 (rather than to $43,050), twice the limit of the 15 percent bracket for a single return. By **eliminating the penalty,** Congress would magnify marriage bonuses even for couples who already enjoy them, which would deplete government tax revenues by billions of dollars. To recover the revenue, Congress might impose higher tax rates on singles, but singles likely would view this measure as unjust for the same reasons that led to the 1969 reforms.

If Congress eliminated the joint return and required married couples to file as two single taxpayers, we would return to the situation that existed prior to 1948. Then, tax policy in common-law states would favor many two-earner couples over one-earner couples who have the same incomes. The same tax policy also would favor one-earner couples living in community-property states over one-earner couples living in common-law states.

Finally, a single-taxpayer system would encourage spousal tax manipulations. By making sure, each year, the spouse with the least income owned all of their income-producing investments, the couple could report investment income exclusively on the return of the spouse in the lowest tax bracket. By titling their residence in the name of the higher-income spouse, they would save more from deductions for mortgage interest and real estate taxes.

On balance, a single-taxpayer system would create at least as many problems as it solves. In my view, the joint return is a sensible if imperfect means to make legitimate distinctions between the income needs of single and married couples, to recognize that marriage involves a great deal of sharing, and to tax all married couples equally who have equal taxable income.

> *A flat rate would advance the tax principle of couples neutrality.*

A flat rate, however, clearly advances the tax principle of **couples neutrality**. By subjecting all couples to the same rate, couples with equal taxable income would pay the same percentage of their taxable income in taxes regardless of the state in which they live, the distribution of income between them, or whether they are married. In contrast, progressive rates always have the potential to create a marriage bonus or penalty when applied to a joint return. Congress could reduce this likelihood, however, as well as the size of the bonus or penalty by greatly broadening the tax base. Then, rates could be flat or nearly flat for the majority of taxpayers and progressive only for a minority of higher-income taxpayers.

To ease any remaining two-earner tax penalty attributable to progressive tax rates, Congress might reestablish a tax deduction for the spouse who earns less. Such a deduction existed during the early Reagan years; this "two-earner deduction" allowed a couple to deduct a maximum of $3,000—10 percent of up to $30,000 of earned income. Only a minuscule portion of the tax savings, however, would be for couples with under $30,000 of income; nearly one-third of the tax savings would be for couples with over $100,000 of income.

If tax relief for two-earner couples focused on couples that needed it most, as I believe would be appropriate, Congress could increase the standard deduction, thereby confining the relief to couples who do not itemize. A larger standard deduction for all married couples, however, would save additional taxes for couples who do not suffer a marriage penalty. Furthermore, the tax savings from the deduction would be greater for couples who face higher marginal tax rates. For these reasons, a tax credit would be more fair and more efficient. If applied to a portion of the earnings of the second spouse would confine relief to two-earner couples; and each dollar of earned income entitled to the credit would produce the same tax savings regardless of a couple's marginal tax bracket. For example, a tax credit of 15 percent on the first $10,000 of earned income of the second spouse would save $1,500 for all couples in these circumstances rather than saving more taxes for couples whose marginal tax rates rise above 15 percent.

We also must note that progressive tax rates by no means solely determine marriage penalties and bonuses. The standard deduction for a married couple is less than twice the standard deduction of two single people. Marriage may reduce or eliminate one's right to take advantage of education tax credits, to contribute to education IRAs, to deduct contributions to regular

IRAs, or to make contributions to Roth IRAs. The greatest marriage penalty, however, measured as a percentage of a taxpayer's income, is suffered by two heads of households who marry and, prior to marriage, are each entitled to the maximum **earned-income tax credit (EITC)**.

The EITC supplements the earnings of low-income working parents who have one or more qualifying children (typically a dependent who lives with the parent). In 1999 the maximum EITC for a parent with earnings up to $12,460 was $2,312 if she had one qualifying child and $3,816 if she had two or more qualifying children. The credit declines (eventually to zero)

> *The greatest marriage penalty, measured as a percentage of a taxpayer's income, is suffered by two heads of households who marry and, prior to marriage, are each entitled to the maximum earned-income tax credit.*

as a parent's income rises; no EITC was available in 1999 once a parent's income reached $26,928, if she had one qualifying child, or $30,580 if she had two or more.

Consider the marriage penalty in the case of two single parents who lived together, each with two qualifying children and an income of $12,000. Their combined EITCs totaled $7,632. If they married, they would have been entitled to an EITC for only two children; and because their combined incomes would become $24,000, the EITC would have shrunk to $1,386, for a cash loss in excess of $6,200.[28]

In addressing marriage penalties, Congress should at least extend the full EITC to working parents with somewhat more income than $12,460. A working parent with one or more dependent children needs considerably more than $12,460 plus the EITC to cover basic living costs if we expect her to be able to pay for child care. For example, typical day-care costs for a preschool child will exceed $20 per day, or $9,000 per year. If we also want a working parent to afford health insurance, the EITC must be expanded even further. Finally, the living expenses of a married couple with one or two children typically are larger than those for a single parent with one or two children; it follows that the EITC should be larger for a married couple than for a single parent with the same number of qualifying children. All of these reforms have particular urgency as our nation moves to policies that discourage welfare and encourage work.

Passive Income of Children

Progressive tax rates reward transfers of income-producing assets from high-tax-bracket parents to low-tax-bracket children. Every $1,000 of investment income that can be taxed at a child's 15 percent rate rather than at the parents'

39.6 percent rate saves the family about $250. In the case of large investment accounts for a child, the annual savings per child can exceed $6,000.

A family can achieve only small savings from such transfers before a child is 14; until then, nearly all investment income in a child's name is taxed at her parents' highest marginal tax bracket. Once she becomes 14, her investment income, such as from an account under the uniform-gifts-to-minors laws, is taxed at her rate, with one exception: If the income is used to discharge her parents' support obligations, the income is taxed at her parents' highest bracket. Support obligations typically exclude expenses such as for summer camps, music lessons, trips to see relatives, private schooling, and college, all of which can be paid from the child's account.

A flat rate would also eliminate the opportunities for families to play this tax rate game. Congress could minimize these opportunities under a progressive-rate system if it applied the rules for children under 14 to all dependent children. Then, nearly all investment income of the household would be taxed at the same rate whether it belonged to parents or to their dependent children. Reforms of this sort advance the sound principle that households with equal abilities to pay should be taxed equally.

Conclusion

Just as the case for progressive rates is "uneasy," as some commentators have written,[29] so, too, is the case for a flat rate. Progressive rates have the distinct advantage of allowing Congress to tax people more lightly who can afford to pay something, but not very much, while taxing people progressively who have substantial discretionary income. A single, flat rate that is revenue neutral must eliminate from taxation many people who could afford to pay something, or it must force them to pay more than they can afford. If the initial tax threshold under a flat-rate system eliminates from taxation a large percentage of taxpayers, many middle-income taxpayers are forced to shoulder a much larger tax burden than before. Under any of these flat-rate scenarios, tax burdens would be gentler for people who can afford to pay the most. Yet in recent decades, the inflation-adjusted income of this segment of the population has risen dramatically, whereas the inflation-adjusted income of most taxpayers has remained constant or declined. On balance, such outcomes support the view that at least some progressivity in tax rates remains fairer than a single, flat rate.

Progressive rates alone, however, are unlikely to close our country's chasm in income and wealth between the rich and everyone else. As mentioned,

> *Progressive rates allow Congress to tax people more lightly who can afford to pay something, but not very much, while taxing people progressively more who have substantial discretionary income.*

they may do no more than slow the increase in that gap, although this achievement in itself would be important. Real progress in the growth of income and wealth across the workforce will depend on our nation's economic growth and the level of real wages for most workers.

This observation returns us to a basic theme. Congress should lower all tax rates in conjunction with extensive reforms that broaden the tax base. A much broader base would enable Congress to raise the same revenue as under our current system with two integrated strategies. First, Congress could impose a low flat rate on the taxable income of a majority of taxpayers—small variations in their rates would not warrant the complications, and a flat rate for them would achieve couples neutrality and eliminate any significant tax savings from intrafamily transfers. Second, Congress could impose moderately progressive rates on the income of the top 20 percent or so of all taxpayers. By keeping the rates moderate, Congress would advance the cause of a just society while respecting the diversity of judgments on the subject.

> *Moderately progressive income tax rates advance the cause of a just society while respecting the diversity of judgments on the subject.*

Through these reforms, tax burdens would be more consistently progressive, the economy more likely would grow faster, and financial success would be more consistently rewarded than under our existing system. In this balanced manner, the federal income tax system also would promote far better the twin goals of equality and liberty for all.

9

Are We Creatures of Taxation?

Demystifying the Effect of Taxes on Economic Behavior

The income tax laws do not profess to embody perfect economic theory.
—Oliver Wendell Holmes Jr., former justice of the Supreme Court

---

Overview: Conflicting Theories About the Economic
Effects of Lowering Top Tax Rates * Meaning of Efficiency
in Taxation * Tax Rates and Economic Efficiency * Three
Possible Responses to Rate Changes: Timing, Avoidance,
and Real Responses * Actual Real Responses to Changes in
Tax Rates in the 1980s and 1990s * Reducing the Top
39.6 Percent Rate * Conclusions

We turn now to a central concern of federal tax policy: To what extent are we and the economy creatures of taxation? In other words, how does the prospect of paying taxes influence our economic behavior—our decisions about how much and where to work; how much and in what ways to save, invest, and consume; and how much to arrange our affairs so as to minimize our tax bills? In turn, how do our responses influence the economy?

Answers to these questions have great urgency today in light of challenges to the income tax and, in particular, to progressive tax rates. Some proposals to lower tax rates are part of a strategy to reduce tax revenues and thereby the size of the federal government; these strategies are beyond the focus of this chapter. What concerns us here is proposals that purport to be revenue neutral—that is, to be able to raise as much revenue as today's rates—or purport to be capable even of increasing tax revenue, all *without* broadening the tax base. The proposals either would lower top rates within our progressive-rate structure or would eliminate progressive rates in favor of a single (flat) rate. The appeal of either strategy depends on its ability to strengthen the economy sufficiently to raise the after-tax income of the great majority of Americans, not simply higher-income taxpayers.

> *This chapter is an attempt to demystify the ways economists think about the relationship between tax rates and the economy and to demythologize the historical record.*

How is the public to judge these economic issues? My goal is ambitious here, but I believe you are ready now for what I have in mind—to invite you on a journey both foreign and, at first blush, intimidating. It is a journey into the world of economic theory, economic data, and debates among economists about the impact of tax rates. I hope to demystify this world for you. If I prove to be an effective guide, you will be equipped, by the end, to think critically when you hear conflicting claims about the economic and revenue consequences from lowering or raising rates.

As in the previous chapter, we will focus on tax rates for ordinary income. You will learn what it means, and why it is desirable, to have an economically *efficient* tax system. You also will learn how lowering tax rates can promote economic efficiency yet lose tax revenue. In this connection, we will consider the seductive but largely discredited claim of supply-siders that the solitary act of lowering today's top ordinary income tax rates can actually increase tax revenue over the long run. The evidence also is inadequate to demonstrate that a single, flat tax rate unaccompanied by reforms that would broaden the tax base would achieve sufficient economic growth to improve the welfare of most Americans. Most Americans, however, should benefit at least to some extent from the economic growth that likely would follow if Congress trimmed or eliminated most tax preferences and lowered all tax rates on a revenue-neutral basis. Therefore, liberals should not ignore the advantages of lower rates in the context of responsible tax reform, and conservatives should couch the advantages of lower rates in that context.

Overview: Conflicting Theories About the Economic Effects of Lowering Top Tax Rates

Economists generally agree that if lower top progressive rates are revenue neutral or actually increase tax revenues, the economy will benefit over the long run even if these lower rates produce deficits over the short run. Most economists expect that significantly lowering today's top rates without also broadening the tax base would reduce the taxes paid by high-income taxpayers for the foreseeable future. Still, lowering top progressive rates could be revenue neutral over the long run if the lower rates stimulate sufficient positive economic behavior by high-income taxpayers.

Economists who believe such outcomes are likely make the following argument: High-income taxpayers would save and invest more, a greater proportion of their savings and investments would be in capital and technology that would fuel stronger economic growth, and they would be more entrepreneurial, all of which would raise business productivity; higher business productivity would raise the wages of the workforce; these higher wages would increase the taxes workers pay, particularly the taxes of middle-income workers; and largely because of these higher taxes, the original rate decrease on high-income taxpayers ultimately would be revenue neutral. If this scenario materialized, high-income taxpayers would be better off because their tax rates would be lower and the value of their investments would grow faster; but the majority of workers also would be better off because their net after-tax wages would be higher. If wages rose sufficiently, Congress eventually could lower tax rates on workers without creating deficits.

Opponents of proposals to lower top tax rates without broadening the tax base doubt that high-income taxpayers would alter their economic behavior nearly to the extent anticipated by advocates of the lower rates. Relevant to these opponents' doubts, and crucial to their analyses of the economic and revenue impacts of the lower rates, are the following expectations: The government's revenue losses would be significant if Congress significantly lowered top rates; these losses would force the government to borrow more; this additional borrowing would drive up interest rates that the private sector must pay in order to gain access to capital; because the government competes for capital with the private sector, additional borrowing by the government would reduce the amount of capital available to the private sector; and all of these developments would sufficiently constrain productivity gains to render them inadequate to overcome the government's revenue losses. Thus government deficits would continue to grow, forcing Congress to raise tax rates, quite possibly on all taxpayers, or to reduce government programs, some of which benefit ordinary workers. In the end, rather than everyone winning, most workers would be worse off; only high-income taxpayers might be better off.

If Congress replaced progressive rates with a revenue-neutral flat rate but did not significantly broaden the tax base, high-income taxpayers initially would pay far less taxes. Until productivity gains were evident, ordinary and middle-income workers would pay more taxes because their average tax rate would have risen; thus, they would be worse off because their earnings would not have improved. In Chapter 8, I noted that had a revenue-neutral flat rate been imposed for 1997, income taxes paid by the *bottom 94 percent* of taxpayers would have increased, whereas income taxes paid by the *top 6 percent* would have declined. Whether households that paid more taxes would view their additional burdens as fair would depend on their expectations about how quickly and how much productivity increased and how much any increased productivity would translate into better wages.

Meaning of Efficiency in Taxation

A perfectly efficient tax reduces private incomes by $1 for each $1 of tax collected. When a $1 tax reduces private incomes by more than $1, it produces what economists call an excess burden, a **deadweight loss**, or (as used here) an **efficiency cost**.[1] A less elegant phrase might be economic waste.

The textbook example of an efficient tax is the old-fashioned head tax—such as a $10 tax imposed on every citizen regardless of income, wealth, or other factors. It was efficient because no one could legally maneuver to avoid it short of abandoning citizenship. For the income tax to be perfectly efficient, your taxes would not discourage your work or saving or induce you to reduce the tax in some other way. The money simply would move from you to the government. But the income tax never can be perfectly efficient because we always can elect to reduce our income. Some efficiency cost may be justified to make the tax laws fairer or to achieve an overriding social objective. Thus when we speak of strengthening the economy by making the income tax more efficient, we mean extracting income through tax policies that minimize but not necessarily eliminate economic harm.[2]

Tax Rates and Economic Efficiency

Reducing unjustified efficiency costs of the income tax is desirable whether we favor shrinking, maintaining, or enlarging the federal government. Because this book is about fixing the income tax, not changing the size of the federal government, we will assume that reforms to enhance the efficiency of the income tax would be revenue neutral.

Most liberal and conservative economists believe that to make the tax laws more efficient, Congress must remove the laws (and thus itself) from the business of attempting to micromanage our behavior. As economists Joel Slemrod and John Bakija have written, economists believe

Most economists believe that to make the tax laws more efficient, Congress must remove the laws (and thus itself) from the business of micromanaging our behavior.

> that firms and individuals, aided by the signals given by market prices, are generally the best judges of what goods and services should be produced, and how

resources should be allocated. . . . For their part, individuals will spend, or save, their income the best they can to maximize their well-being, according to their own preferences. . . . Taxes interfere with that *natural efficiency*, causing economic choices to be distorted away from taxed activities to relatively untaxed ones, keeping us from making the best use of our resources. (italics added)[3]

Sometimes market choices are inefficient, such as when we lack adequate information to make rational decisions about the best uses of our resources or when we are confronted by monopolies. Typically, however, economic efficiency is advanced by a tax system that is neutral toward our market decisions. Were Congress to adopt reforms that, as popularly phrased, created a more level playing field for our economic choices, our tax burdens would be far less dependent on the source of our income, the method that it is paid, or how we use it. Achieving a more level playing field requires eliminating most special provisions (tax preferences) that protect income from tax. For the most part, we would be taxed on our economic income, however earned, received, or used. Such a system would encourage us to act according to the intrinsic merits of choices before us rather than on the basis of conflicting and highly arbitrary rewards and penalties under the tax laws. The advantages of neutrality are sufficiently promising that, according to economist Dale Jorgenson, "achieving neutrality in the taxation of income from all assets in the U.S. economy is the most important goal for future tax reform."[4]

> *Increasing the economic efficiency of the tax system requires making the system more neutral with respect to our economic behavior.*

Making the taxation of income more neutral through revenue-neutral reforms would greatly increase the amount of income subject to tax. This process involves a twofold benefit from what economists call **feedback effects.** First, fewer tax preferences automatically expose more income to tax. Second, with more income to tax, Congress would lower tax rates, presumably across the board, in order for the reforms to be revenue neutral. Lower rates might induce us to work and save more, to become more entrepreneurial, and to allocate our resources more on the basis of pretax rather than after-tax returns. Whether and how much we might behave in these ways is highly controversial; but to the extent we did, we would increase our pretax income.

Congress might, however, simply lower tax rates without reducing tax preferences. Then, the tax base would be broadened only to the extent that we voluntarily decided to generate more taxable income through work and saving. The danger is that the tax on any additional income would be inadequate to offset the **static revenue loss** from the lower rates, meaning that tax revenue would be less overall. As previously discussed, substantial and persistent reductions in tax collections could seriously undermine the opportunity to achieve productivity gains counted on by advocates of lower tax rates. Understanding the concept of a static revenue loss, therefore, is crucial to understanding controversies over tax rates.

Static revenue loss refers to the loss of revenue from taxing the same level of income at a lower rate. Assume, for example, that taxpayers average $40,000 of taxable income. A flat 25 percent rate would raise, on average, $10,000 per taxpayer. If Congress lowered the rate to 20 percent, it would raise only $8,000 per taxpayer on $40,000 of taxable income, for a static revenue loss of $2,000 per taxpayer. If the feedback effects from the lower rate increased average taxable income to $46,000, the 20 percent tax on the extra $6,000 would recover only $1,200 of the $2,000 static revenue loss, leaving the government with a net revenue loss of $800 per taxpayer. Thus if you believe that lowering rates will increase taxable income, you still must ask, "By how much?" Only then can you calculate whether the lower rate would be at least revenue neutral.

> *Lowered tax rates can increase tax revenue only if they produce sufficient additional taxable income to offset the static revenue loss.*

To summarize, achieving a more efficient tax system has important implications for tax rates, which in turn have important implications for achieving economic efficiency and higher productivity. A broader tax base makes the tax system more neutral with respect to our economic choices and increases the amount of income subject to taxation. Congress then can lower tax rates without sacrificing tax revenue, which would make the tax system even more efficient. We arrive, therefore, at the following propositions for revenue-neutral reforms: Increasing the economic efficiency of the income tax by broadening the tax base promotes lower rates; increasing inefficiency by narrowing the tax base promotes higher rates. Solely lowering today's top tax rates without substantially broadening the tax base means that efficiency gains sufficient to achieve revenue neutrality depend largely on how much high-income taxpayers would increase their productive economic behavior.

The dilemma for policymakers and the public is that experts have been unable to measure with satisfactory precision the inefficiency of higher rates. Because these difficulties have led to sharp disagreements within the economics profession, the public understandably does not know what to believe. Yet the subject is one the public cannot avoid; Americans take a stand on it each time they vote for one political candidate over another. Thus, we turn here to the great debate about how, and how much, tax rates influence our economic behavior.

Three Possible Responses to Rate Changes: Timing, Avoidance, and Real Responses

For certain Americans, no action by Congress short of a declaration of war so causes their hearts to palpitate or mobilizes their imaginations as when

Congress announces new tax rates. Joel Slemrod has classified the potential economic reactions as short-term *timing* responses, longer-term *avoidance* responses, and long-term *real* responses.[5] Of the three, timing responses are the most dramatic and likely but the least problematic; avoidance responses are less evident than timing responses but more evident than real responses; and real responses, though least evident of the three, currently receive the most political attention.

Timing Responses

Short-term timing responses involve playing games with the tax system. When tax rates are in transition, we might allocate more income to years when it will be taxed least and more deductions to years when they are most valuable.

The relevant tax rate that influences our responses is the marginal tax rate, not the average tax rate on our taxable income. Our **average tax rate**, determined by dividing our total taxes by our taxable income, takes into account all rates that apply against our taxable income. When we are about to make a decision that has tax implications, however, the tax rate that matters is the rate that applies to our *next dollar* of income or deduction—our **marginal tax rate**. If our uppermost income (our income at the margin) is subject to the 31 percent rate (our marginal rate), each additional $1 deduction will save us 31 cents of tax even though our average tax rate on all our taxable income is less. Thus we might borrow against our home equity line of credit to buy a new car because our interest payments will offset income that would be taxed at 31 percent. In effect, the government pays 31 percent of the interest; we pay 69 percent. We might postpone the purchase if our marginal tax rate were only 15 percent, because our share of the after-tax cost of all interest payments—85 percent—may exceed our budget. Common sense teaches that as our marginal tax rate rises, our motivation rises to avoid it.

In theory, everyone may participate in these tax games. Most taxpayers, however, are bit players. In the real world, the great majority of workers receive nearly all of their income from wages they cannot manipulate from one year to the next; most retirees receive Social Security, interest, dividends, or pensions they either cannot or cannot afford to manipulate; and over 70 percent of taxpayers do not itemize their deductions. If tax rates will be higher next year, which means that each $1 deducted will save more taxes, bit players who itemize might postpone until January of next year paying this December's mortgage-interest and real estate taxes. If tax rates will be lower next year, bit players will make those payments this December and might accelerate into December the payment of state income taxes as well as charitable contributions that otherwise would be made next year.

Wealthier taxpayers engage in such actions as a matter of course. Take the reaction of Dr. John Belkor of Houston to the Tax Reform Act of 1986. A highly successful sports medicine physician, Belkor aggressively played the movement from the maximum 50 percent tax rate in 1986 to the maximum 38.5 percent rate in 1987 to the maximum 28 percent rate in 1988. One strategy was to have his corporation defer paying him $200,000 of compensation in 1986 and in 1987. The corporation then paid him the deferred $400,000 as compensation in 1988, when it was taxed at only 28 percent, for an overall tax savings of $65,000.[6] Variations on these games were pursued with gusto by taxpayers with $1 million or more of income; as a group, they reported only $12 billion of wages and salaries in 1986 versus an impressive $45 billion in 1988.

The opposite game was played in 1992. Wall Street anticipated that president-elect Clinton would persuade Congress to raise the top tax rates in 1993. Reversing past practices, brokerage houses apparently paid in December 1992 two-thirds, rather than the usual one-third, of year-end bonuses owed to stockbrokers and dealers. The 1992 bonuses were taxed at no more than the top 31 percent rate rather than at the top 1993 rates of 36 percent or 39.6 percent.

As these examples indicate, short-term timing decisions in response to changes in tax rates can significantly reduce the short-term tax liabilities of successful taxpayers. Of the three responses, however, they bear least on the economy over the long term.

Avoidance Responses

Avoidance responses, as explained by Slemrod, include illegal evasion of taxes as well as spending time and money, such as by hiring lawyers and accountants, to find legal ways to minimize taxes. For example, we might be able to convert ordinary income into capital gains, which allows us to take advantage of favorable tax rates on capital gains. We might shift income to lower-income members of a family or to business entities that may be taxed less or not at all. We might arrange for more of our wages to be paid through tax-free fringe benefits and tax-favored stock options, or we might transfer wages to a retirement plan or to an individual retirement account in order to postpone the tax on our earnings. In these and other ways, raising tax rates encourages us to try to beat the system; lowering tax rates lessens the incentives because it lessens the rewards.

In case we are unaware of the plentiful opportunities for legitimate tax avoidance, the vast complex of financial institutions and planners across the country will intervene on our behalf. Their cleverly packaged promotions of tax-avoidance opportunities, marketed like vitamins essential to good health, can make us feel foolish, if not unpatriotic, for not partaking. A 1998 Merrill Lynch pamphlet, for example, invited us to exploit "Ninety-eight Tax Savings Ideas for Investors;" in 1999, Merrill Lynch offered "ninety-nine."

Real Responses: Substitution and Income Effects, in Theory

By far the most intriguing aspect of the economics of tax rates is the extent to which tax rates produce what Slemrod calls *real responses*. These cover long-term alterations in the *quantity* of our work, in the *quality* and *quantity* of our *saving and investing,* and in our willingness to be entrepreneurial.

> *Changing rates may alter the equilibrium we had established between work and leisure and between saving and consumption.*

Taxes represent a cost of producing income. Raising tax rates increases the cost and thereby lessens the reward from work and saving. Lowering rates increases the reward from work and saving. It follows that changing tax rates may alter our equilibrium between *work* (the term economists use to describe compensated time) and *leisure* (the term economists use to describe uncompensated time) and between *saving* and *consumption.* Whether and how much the equilibrium changes has crucial implications for the progressive tax-rate debate. As economist Robert Triest has commented about the trade-off between work and leisure, "In general, the more responsive labor supply is to economic incentives, the greater will be the efficiency cost of increased progressivity."[7] The less the work–leisure and saving–consumption equilibriums in our lives depend on taxes, the more dominant will be issues of fairness in the debate about tax rates. Progressive-rate advocates consider the fairness issues to their advantage, but arguments that progressive rates promote a fairer society become less persuasive if such rates significantly impair economic growth— that is, if higher taxes would induce people to work and save much less efficiently.

> *The less the work–leisure and saving–consumption equilibriums depend on taxes, the more the case for progressive rates turns on issues of fairness.*

The argument that lowering tax rates would induce us to work more emphasizes what economists call the **substitution effect**. That is, with lower tax rates, taxpayers would perceive work as being relatively more valuable than before in relation to its counterpart, leisure. Consequently, they would substitute work for some of their leisure time. But matters are not so simple. When tax rates are lowered, economists also recognize an **income effect**. Because we have more after-tax income than before from the same amount of work, we could work less yet end up with the same income after taxes. Indeed, rather than continue to work overtime Friday nights, you could be home with your family or could party with your friends and still have, after taxes, the same amount of income left to cover your expenses. If the substitution effect controlled, you would continue to work Friday nights and also another night or weekend day to earn additional income. If the substitution and income effects cancel each other out, you would not change your work habits at all; in that case, the government would collect less in taxes from you because you would pay a lower rate on the same amount of labor income.

The saving–consumption equilibrium encounters similar conflicts when tax rates are changed. According to the substitution effect, lowering tax rates, by increasing the after-tax return on savings, will induce us to save more now and forgo some current consumption. But lowering tax rates also means that we could reduce our present level of savings yet end up with the same amount of savings after taxes.

The substitution effect leads us to seek more of the thing that has become relatively less expensive. The income effect leads us the other way. The question is, Which effect is stronger?

For example, assume that you save $10,000 of your $100,000 of pretax income and that your marginal tax rate is 36 percent. After taxes, you would have $6,400 of that $10,000 left. If your marginal tax rate was reduced to 25 percent, you would have $7,500 left of the $10,000, confronting you with these questions: Would you continue to set aside $10,000? Would you set aside more (the substitution effect) because of the higher after-tax return on saving? Or might you reduce your pretax saving (the income effect) to $8,333 because you would be left with the same $6,400 after taxes ($8,333 x 25 percent = $6,400), and you could then consume the remaining $1,667? In this last case, the lower marginal tax rate would have reduced your saving rate from 10.000 percent to 8.333 percent of your pretax income.

Raising tax rates produces opposite pressures. Because the after-tax return to working and saving becomes relatively less, we might work less and consume more (the substitution effect). By diminishing our after-tax income, however, higher tax rates reduce resources to meet current or future needs unless we are willing to work more and consume less (the income effect).

At a minimum, higher tax rates, by reducing the after-tax return from savings, increase the short-term advantage of consumption over saving. Consider receiving a $100 gift. You could consume it—you could buy a sweater that you have eyed for months—or you could deposit the $100 in a savings account that pays 6 percent interest.

Higher tax rates increase the short-term advantage of consumption over saving.

If you buy the sweater, you enjoy owning it without diminution by income taxes. If you deposit the $100 in your savings account, its future value is reduced by the taxes you pay on the interest. When tax rates increase, the return on your savings shrinks even further, testing your resolve to resist the sweater.

Emotions matter greatly here. Saving, after all, requires a combination of discretionary income and the willpower to defer gratification, not exactly an

American strength. Because the rewards are postponed, tenuous, and abstract, saving requires rationality, a rational investment in our future. By saving now, we guard against unexpected setbacks such as the loss of a job or a sudden illness; we also plan for expected future needs, such as acquiring a home, educating our children, and having adequate income at retirement. In sum, current saving ensures future consumption, both unplanned and planned. By contrast, current consumption in no sense ensures future saving, notwithstanding promises we make to ourselves.

> *Current saving ensures future consumption. Current consumption in no sense ensures future saving.*

Saving personally also means acting responsibly toward our economy. As Slemrod and Bakija have explained, "The savings of individuals—often funneled through a financial intermediary such as a bank, a savings and loan, or an insurance company—eventually are used by businesses to finance real investment in plants, equipment, inventories, and know-how. Through this process, individual savings add to the productive capacity of the country and increase the productivity of the workforce."[8]

Actual Real Responses to Changes in Tax Rates in the 1980s and 1990s

Theory aside, what impact of taxes on work and saving should policymakers *expect* from observations about the past and predictions about the future? Their enterprise is maddeningly complicated: The relationship between tax rates and economic growth exists in the murkiest cosmos because of powerful variables other than tax rates that inevitably are at play whenever rates rise or fall. These include the entire composition of federal, state, and local tax laws, much of which may be undergoing change. They also include economic, social, and political conditions and trends as well as the cultural norms of the day. Our country may be at war; budget deficits may be growing; a recession may be brewing; the stock market may be booming; unemployment may be shrinking; wage levels may be stagnant; trade deficits may be large; foreign capital may be pouring into U.S. markets; consumer confidence may be high; married women may prefer or need employment more than before; an educated workforce may be in greater demand; or the Federal Reserve may be pursuing a restrictive monetary policy.

> *The equation between tax rates and economic growth exists in the murkiest cosmos because of powerful variables other than rates that inevitably are at play any time rates rise or fall.*

The economist Patric Hendershott had such variables in mind when, asked to evaluate efforts by other economists to measure the impact of the Tax Reform Act of 1986 on personal saving, he wrote, "Though I admire the courage of the authors, I question their sanity in agreeing to undertake this task."[9] Measuring the impact of tax reforms is no easier today. Profound uncertainties about the past impact of tax rates and about the future cosmos in which they will operate teach at least one, clear lesson: We should have modest expectations about what economic benefits will accrue simply from lowering today's

> *Accusations about the evil perpetuated on the economy because of today's tax rates appear overblown.*

rates. Indeed, accusations about the evil perpetrated on the economy by today's tax rates appear greatly overblown. This conclusion is most compelling for the bottom 99 percent of all taxpayers. So much has been written about the behavior of the top 1 percent that we will consider this sector separately.

Supply-Side Economics and Revenue Predictions: The Economic Recovery Tax Act of 1981

The 1980s produced about as good an experiment as we have had for examining the relationship between tax rates, economic growth and productivity, and tax revenues. Not since the 1920s had supply-side convictions about the advantages of low tax rates so dominated government policy.

Fueling supply-side theory was the **Laffer curve**, developed in the 1970s by economist Arthur Laffer, who became a principal mentor to Ronald Reagan in 1980. The Laffer curve taught that at any particular time, a revenue-maximizing tax rate existed above which tax revenue would be less, not more. Laffer and fellow believers in **supply-side economics** insisted that lowering 1980 tax rates would increase tax revenue because people would work, save, and invest more and more creatively, thereby increasing the resources *supplied* to the economy. As the economist Lawrence Lindsey explained in *The Growth Experiment*, these "extra efforts and investments [would] yield more economic activity, more income, and more tax revenue."[10]

> *The Laffer curve taught that lowering rates across the board at the beginning of the 1980s would increase tax revenue.*

The experiment to which Lindsey referred began with the Economic Recovery Tax Act of 1981 (ERTA), which dramatically reduced all tax rates. By 1982, the top rate on ordinary income had fallen from 70 percent to 50 percent, and the top capital gains rate from 28 percent to 20 percent. Between 1981 and 1984 all other ordinary income rates were reduced by 23 percent; and beginning in 1985, personal exemptions, standard deductions, and tax brackets were increased for inflation. If ever supply-side theory had an opportunity to validate itself, this was the time.

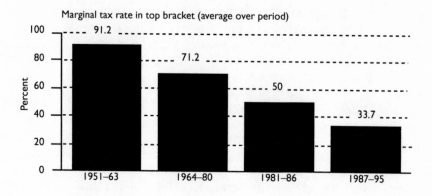

Marginal tax rate in top bracket (average over period)

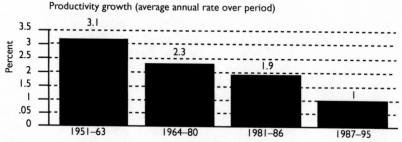

Productivity growth (average annual rate over period)

FIGURE 9.1   Comparison of Top Marginal Income Tax Rates and Productivity Growth in the United States for the Period 1951–1995
SOURCE: Joel Slemrod and Jon Bakija, *Taxing Ourselves,* 2nd ed. (Cambridge: MIT, 2000), 100, figure 4.1.

But that validation never came, either in economic growth, worker productivity, or tax revenues. From 1981 to 1985, our economy—measured by the gross domestic product (GDP)—grew at a healthy average annual rate of *2.6 percent.* But the growth rate had been *3.2 percent* from 1976 through 1980, when tax rates were higher.[11] In fact, from the mid-1900s through 1986, declines in top marginal tax rates were accompanied by declines in productivity, just the opposite of the seesaw relationship between rates and productivity—when rates go down, productivity goes up—that supply-siders would have predicted (see Figure 9.1). Productivity growth, measured by how much workers produce for each hour worked in the nonfarm private sector, was *1.9 percent* from 1981 to 1986, when the top individual income tax rate was 50 percent. This growth rate compares unfavorably with the *2.3 percent* rate from 1964 to 1980, when the top individual rate averaged 71.2 percent, and with the *3.1 percent* rate from 1951 to 1963, when the top individual rate averaged 91.2 percent.

Such data should not be interpreted to mean that productivity gains are larger when tax rates are higher. Rather, productivity gains depend on a great many factors other than tax rates. Recent technological developments, for example, have contributed enormously to productivity gains, which averaged nearly 3 percent annually from 1996 through 1999.

If their estimates of economic growth were only disappointing, supply-siders failed abysmally as revenue forecasters. Even Lindsey conceded that "income tax collections were lower under ERTA than they would have been had tax rates never been cut."[12] Much lower! As a percentage of GDP, income taxes fell from 9.7 percent in 1981 to 8.3 percent by 1986, which represents a decline of 14 percent. According to President Bush's 1990 budget report, had ERTA remained in effect from 1981 through 1990, its rate reductions (compared to pre-ERTA rates) would have cut tax collections for 1990 alone by a staggering $164 billion.[13] In sum, ERTA demonstrated the revenue risks of lowering all tax rates without adequately broadening the tax base or reducing direct budget outlays.

Actual Effect of Tax Rates on Labor Supply for All but the Top Taxpayers

The effects of lower rates on labor supply over the course of the 1980s are ambiguous. Marginal federal tax rates, including Social Security, were reduced during the 1980s for the great bulk of taxpayers.[14] Consistent with predictions of supply-siders and certain other less ideological labor economists,[15] the average number of hours worked by men and women in the 1980s rose above the pre-ERTA trend. There is good reason to doubt, however, that the rise was attributable to the substitution effect. If it were, workers in the higher-income quintiles should have increased their work hours most because their marginal tax rates (counting all federal taxes) declined the most. But the greatest increase in work hours (particularly for men) occurred among workers in the *lowest income quintile* (see Table 9.1); their marginal rates, rather than declining the most, either stayed the same or even increased, at least through 1987.[16]

These data demonstrated either the prominence of the income effect or, as is most likely, that factors other than taxes dominated male workforce behavior in the 1980s.[17] As documented by Robert Triest's survey of recent research, most economists now widely agree that "overall, the bulk of the evidence on male labor supply suggests that there are only minor incentive effects" from lowering tax rates.[18]

> "The bulk of the evidence on male labor supply suggests that there are only minor incentive effects" from lowering tax rates. (Robert Triest)

Earlier studies suggested that female labor supply was more responsive than male labor supply to changes in tax rates. More recent studies question these results with one important exception:[19] Marginal tax rates appear to have noticeably affected decisions by

TABLE 9.1 Effects of Changes in Marginal Tax Rates on Labor Income and Hours Worked During the 1980s

Income Quintile	Marginal Tax Rate on Labor Income[a]		Estimated Percentage Change in Hours Worked, 1981–1989[b]	
	1980	1989	Men, Aged 25–64	Women, Aged 25–64
All quintiles	35.0	34.6	6.0	5.4
Bottom	14.7	19.3	31.0	16.7
Second	26.2	28.0	3.6	-6.9
Middle	28.7	27.3	4.1	6.4
Fourth	32.1	31.1	2.5	10.5
Highest	41.2	33.8	3.2	11.8

[a]Includes personal income tax and Social Security payroll tax.
[b]Percent change in hours worked between 1981 and 1989 relative to what would have been predicted by the trend since 1967, holding unemployment constant.
SOURCE: Joel Slemrod and Jon Bakija, *Taxing Ourselves,* 2nd ed. (Cambridge: MIT, 2000), 108, table 4.2.

married women about whether to work at all if their first dollar of earnings would be taxed at a high rate.[20] The principal culprit is the joint tax return.

Joint returns tax the first dollar earned by a newly employed spouse at the highest-rate bracket applicable to the couple's combined income. (Rarely can spouses save taxes by filing separate returns.) When Berry Stein contemplated a job offer in 1983 from a computer software consulting firm in Tucson, she considered that all of her earnings would fall within the top 50 percent bracket. Her earnings would also be subject to Social Security taxes and state income taxes, and she would incur child-care costs and other work-related expenses. Berry and her husband, Ian, lived well on his $300,000 salary from his designer-clothes business; and though she liked the idea of working part-time outside her home, she felt too little of her earnings would be left after taxes and expenses to warrant taking the job.

Women like Berry, who do not need a paid job to maintain a comfortable standard of living and whose first dollar of earnings would be taxed at a high marginal bracket, constitute a small percentage of the potential female workforce. The great majority of married women today feel that they must be employed to help pay household expenses. Women's attitudes toward work also have evolved considerably in recent decades. Married women increasingly choose paid work, even if part time, instead of unpaid household chores and full-time care for young children. For all of these reasons, the workforce participation rate of married women with minor children has risen dramatically in recent decades, from 48 percent in 1977 to 71 percent in 1997.[21]

To summarize, employment decisions continue to be influenced by tax rates in the case of married women who can afford not to be in the workforce more than in the case of comparably situated married men.[22] Otherwise, changes in tax rates have little bearing on most people's decisions about whether and how much to work.

These conclusions have enormous relevance to our consideration of tax-rate reductions because labor income constitutes about three-quarters of national income. For the vast majority of workers, reduced tax rates without a comparable broadening of their tax base likely would reduce the amount of taxes they pay. Increased tax rates, as would apply to most workers if Congress adopted a flat rate, likely would increase the amount of taxes workers would pay unless Congress comparably shrank their tax base.

Martin Feldstein suggests we might discover greater responsiveness of labor supply to tax rates if we understood the effect of rates on "education, occupational choice, effort, location, and all of the other aspects of behavior that affect the short-run and long-run productivity and income of the individual." We have much to learn. For now, revenue projections from these possible effects would be purely speculative. As Feldstein admits, "We still know very little about how taxes affect labor supply defined in this way."[23]

Actual Effect of Tax Rates on Level of Savings for All but the Top Taxpayers

Some economists continue to believe that saving levels respond more to tax rates than do workforce levels and that personal savings would increase materially if savings were taxed less.[24] These economists share concerns about the distressing decline in our rate of personal saving over the past decade. The great majority of economic studies, however, find that quantifying the effect of tax policies on the amount of personal saving has been more diffi-cult than quantifying the effect of tax policies on work and that any effect is likely to have been relatively small.[25] As Eric Engen and William Gale have concluded in a comprehensive summary of the economic literature, "Virtually no empirical study suggests a large saving response by households to changes in the after-tax return."[26] Even Robert Hall, a great exponent of the flat tax, wrote in 1988 that a "detailed study of data for the twentieth-century United States shows no strong evidence" of a positive saving response to an increased real rate of return on savings. Instead, according to Hall, when the proper estimation methods are used, the substitution effect on the rate of savings is small and "may well be zero."[27]

> "Virtually no empirical study suggests a large saving response by households to changes in the after-tax return [to savings]."
> (Eric Engen and William Gale)

It remains possible that favorable tax policies toward saving, consistently applied over a long time, could cumulatively increase the rate of personal saving rather significantly. But tax policies have been too unstable for us to know. Such policies also could have the opposite effect. Figure 9.2 charts the relationship since 1960 between rates of return and rates of private saving (which includes both personal, or household, saving and business saving). On balance, the chart suggests that private saving rates are more likely to decline rather than increase when the return to savings (such as through higher interest rates or lower taxes) increases. We know, however, that a great many factors other than the return to savings determine private saving rates, such as budget deficits, changes in real wages and wealth, and unemployment rates.

As in the case of labor supply, ERTA provided probably the best opportunity so far to test the proposition that lower tax rates raise personal saving rates. ERTA lowered rates on ordinary income and capital gains and also encouraged saving by expanding the opportunity of workers to make tax-deductible contributions to individual retirement accounts. Previously, the deduction was available only to workers who did not participate in an employer-sponsored retirement plan, and the deduction was limited annually to $1,750 per worker plus $250 for a nonworking spouse. ERTA made tax-deductible IRA contributions available to all workers and increased the $1,750 limit to $2,000.

Personal saving rates declined after ERTA.

Nonetheless, personal savings fell from 8.8 percent of disposable personal income in 1981 to 6.8 percent by 1983 and eventually to 6.0 percent by 1986.[28] If ERTA had not been so quickly modified by subsequent legislation, personal saving rates might have risen. They also might have declined even further. Economists cannot even agree on whether the increased opportunities under ERTA to deduct IRA contributions, which were intended to increase personal savings, had much impact on new savings. IRA contributions increased enormously after ERTA, which some economists believe represented a substantial increase in new savings. Other economists believe it equally plausible that most of the increased contributions to IRAs represented a shuffling of taxable forms of savings to IRAs or were offset by lower contributions to employer-based retirement plans.[29]

The impact of the Tax Reform Act of 1986 on the quantity of personal savings also has been difficult to detect, in part because the act mixed saving incentives with disincentives. Overall, tax burdens on savings probably were lessened slightly. If true, and if the substitution effect dominates, the slight reduction in the taxation of savings should have slightly increased the rate of personal saving. But personal saving rates declined as a percentage of disposable income, from 6.5 percent in 1986 to as low as 5.1 percent by 1989. In fact, after legislation in 1990 raised the top ordinary tax rate for high-income taxpayers, personal saving rates increased, reaching 6.2 percent in

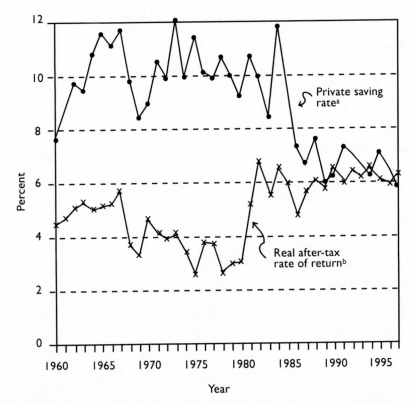

FIGURE 9.2   Savings Rates and the Reward for Saving in the U.S., 1960–1997
[a]Net private saving as a percent of disposable income (GNP less depreciation and taxes).
[b]Interest rate on Baa corporate bonds, adjusted for expected inflation and the average marginal tax rate on personal interest income, plus a fixed equity premium.
SOURCE: Joel Slemrod and Jon Bakija, *Taxing Ourselves*, 2nd ed. (Cambridge: MIT, 2000) 113, figure 4.4.

1992, again contrary to supply-side theory. After the 1993 increase in the top tax rates, however, personal saving rates began to plummet, falling to 5 percent, consistent with supply-side theory.[30]

The very existence of such inconsistent data teaches us, as economist Douglas Bernheim has written, that "it is difficult to find any reliable evidence that points to a substantial *elasticity*" (that is, responsiveness) of saving patterns to tax rates.[31] Rather, a great many nontax factors contributed to the decline in personal savings rates after the 1970s. Simply paying bills became an increasing challenge for many households. For people with discretionary income, the boom in real estate and in the stock market in the 1980s meant that the growth rate of their wealth typically exceeded the growth rate of their income. As traditional economic theory predicted, their saving rate declined because they borrowed heavily against their newfound wealth to engage in high levels of consumption.[32]

Personal saving may be declining because the elderly are receiving a growing percentage of our nation's resources.

Economist Laurence Kotlikoff offers a very different explanation for the decline in personal saving. In his profoundly unsettling view, the principal culprits are Social Security and Medicare. These programs have allocated a growing percentage of the nation's resources to older generations, who have high propensities to consume.[33] Because our population is aging, Kotlikoff's explanation delivers a particularly grim prognosis for the future of personal saving.

Effect of Tax Rates on Top Taxpayers

When the federal government needs additional revenue, raising the tax rate on people with the highest incomes (I will call them the rich) seems, at first blush, an easy call. They have so much more discretionary income than anyone else. In 1997, for example, a year that reflected a trend of the 1990s, the top 1 percent of taxpayers had slightly more AGI than did the bottom 50 percent. If their *economic incomes* were compared, the top 1 percent would have had considerably more because much of the income of the top 1 percent was not captured in AGI. Yet from the mid-1960s until 1990, the trend of Congress was to lower tax rates on the rich. High rates were considered counterproductive (as well as unfair), yielding too little revenue compared to the assumed costs from their distortionary effects on the economic behavior of the rich.

The top 1 percent of all taxpayers has somewhat more AGI than does the bottom 50 percent.

No one doubts that the rich have the resources and skill to avoid taxes more effectively than do the rest of us. What sharply divides economists, politicians, and other analysts is judging how athletic at dodging taxes the rich have been or are inclined to be and how dependent the economy is on their efforts. Take, for example, George Gilder, who, according to Kevin Phillips, "wrote . . . the comprehensive theology of the Reagan era."[34] Gilder argued in 1981 that "to help the poor and middle classes, one must cut the taxes of the rich." Why? Because "a successful economy depends upon the proliferation of the rich."[35] But according to Peter Drucker, the international management guru, "If all the super-rich disappeared, the world economy would not even notice. The super-rich are irrelevant to the economy."[36]

Behavior of the Rich in the 1980s.   Neither Gilder nor Drucker happens to be an economist. But consider the dispute between these economic experts—Lawrence Lindsey, one of the most respected advocates of lowering tax rates on the rich, and the Congressional Budget Office, about the impact of ERTA (the 1981 tax legislation) on the top 1 percent of taxpayers. Lindsay admits that ERTA's lower tax rates on ordinary income and capital gains lost tax revenue overall, but he insists that the lower rates on the top 1 percent increased the taxes they paid. As evidence, he notes that their percentage of all income taxes, compared with the percentage paid by all other taxpayers, increased for 1982 and 1983 as a result of increases in their taxable income.[37] CBO agreed that the top 1 percent paid relatively more taxes for these years. It concluded, however, that the top 1 percent would have paid even more under the income tax laws that existed before ERTA.[38]

From 1962 through 1988, the fraction of compensation of the affluent in the form of wages and salaries did not increase as their marginal tax rate declined.

The premise of supply-siders that the rich respond significantly to significant changes in tax rates is not substantiated by data uncovered by Joel Slemrod in his study of the behavior of the rich from 1962 through 1988. Slemrod found, surprisingly, that "with respect to two aspects that differentiate the rich from the nonrich—the importance of capital income and the flexibility of the form of compensation—I have uncovered no evidence of a significant behavioral response to the marginal tax rate." For example, marginal tax rates for the top 1 percent were higher in the 1960s than in the 1980s, yet Slemrod saw "no noticeable shift out of tax-exempt securities into taxable securities." He also found "no indication that the fraction of compensation of the affluent that is received in the form of wages and salaries has increased as their marginal tax rate has declined." On the other hand, he could not find data that would preclude such a trend.[39]

The evidence is elusive. For example, the gross income of top taxpayers increased sharply after the Tax Reform Act of 1986. Yet economists Daniel Feenberg and James Poterba concluded that it was "impossible" to determine whether top taxpayers worked harder, were compensated more for their services (such as from the emergence of "superstar" salaries and bonuses), or received higher returns on their capital.[40] According to the economist Nada Eissa, the evidence was clearer in the case of the top 1 percent of married women: The drop in their marginal tax rate from 50 to 28 percent, Eissa found, materially increased their labor supply.[41]

Behavior of the Rich in the 1990s.   The 1990s have reversed the tax-rate experiment on the top taxpayers. Whereas the 1980s tested whether they would react favorably to rate decreases, the 1990s tested whether they would react unfavorably to rate increases. In 1990, Congress increased the top tax rate on ordinary income from 28 percent to 31 percent. It also raised the wage ceiling against which the 2.90 percent Medicare tax (half of which is paid by the employee) applied from $51,300 of wages to $125,000. In 1993, Congress increased the top tax rate on ordinary income to 39.6 percent and made the 2.90 percent Medicare tax applicable to wages at all levels. In 1993, therefore, top taxpayers paid a top federal tax rate on their wages of 41.05 percent (39.60 percent for income taxes plus 1.45 percent for Medicare taxes), compared with a top rate of 31 percent in 1992 and 28 percent in 1990. Furthermore, the top income tax rate has been effectively higher than 39.6 percent rate (which made the top federal tax rate on their wages higher than 41.05 percent) because certain itemized deductions and credits have been phased down or eliminated for top taxpayers.

The 1993 laws relevant to the top 1 percent remain substantially unchanged except for 1997 legislation that reduced their capital gains tax. Thus the 1993 increases offer a rare opportunity to observe behavioral patterns of the top 1 percent when their tax rates are increased. Yet forecasting and analyzing their behavior predictably has been complicated, leading to verbal wars among some of the nation's leading economists. Consider the forecasts of Martin Feldstein and Daniel Feenberg, on the one hand, and those by Jane Gravelle, on the other.

Feldstein and Feenberg insisted that the rate increases would backfire. Writing in 1993, they predicted that the higher rates would produce "very little, if any, . . . additional revenue" because top taxpayers would work less, be less entrepreneurial, and avoid taxes more. Feldstein and Feenberg also maintained that the higher rates would impose "a significant burden on the economy" not only because of their negative impact on the top taxpayers' work patterns but also because saving and investment decisions by top taxpayers would be driven more by their tax consequences than by their pretax (economic) return.[42]

Not so, Gravelle fired back. Responses of the top taxpayers to these rate changes would be limited. Not only would changes in their work patterns likely be small; they might even work more in order to maintain their after-tax income. Gravelle also believed that top taxpayers probably already had maximized their tax-free or tax-deferred benefits at work, and their portfolios still likely would be taxed to some extent.[43]

Who was right? Feldstein and Feenberg pointed to a decline in the incomes of the top 1 percent on their 1993 returns. But CBO and Treasury Department experts noted, as Feldstein had not, that top taxpayers apparently anticipated the 1993 rate increases. To take advantage of the lower 1992 rates, they materially accelerated into 1992 income that otherwise would have been taxed in 1993. This caused their tax liability for 1992 to be higher and their tax liability for 1993 to be lower than otherwise would have been the case. After accounting for such income shifting through 1994, a Treasury Department study estimated that the income of the top taxpayers declined only slightly in 1993 and 1994, far less than Feldstein and Feenberg expected or found.[44] And their incomes have grown greatly since. In 1995, the top 1 percent of all taxpayers received about 15.3 percent of all AGI; by 1997, they received about 20 percent, or nearly one-third more.[45]

These figures strongly suggest that Gravelle was right: Any decline in the income of top taxpayers, after accounting for interyear manipulations, appears to have been modest and shortlived, in which case top taxpayers paid substantially more taxes because of the higher tax rates installed in 1993. What is not controversial is that the percentage of all income taxes paid by the top 1 percent rose considerably in the 1990s. In 1990, the last year that the top rate was still 28 percent, the top 1 percent paid about 24 percent of all income taxes. In 1997, when the top rate was 39.6 percent, they paid close to 30 percent of all income taxes. Although factors such as the strong stock market help explain this phenomenon, so too, it seems, do the higher rates.

Reducing the Top 39.6 Percent Rate

As expected, economists debate with equal vigor the possible effects of lowering today's top rate. Advocates believe that the government would sacrifice little tax revenue, if any. The Treasury Department's own study strongly suggests otherwise. Treasury calculated that the feedback effects from reducing the top rate from roughly 40 percent to 32 percent would recover only about one-third of the static revenue loss—the loss from taxing income at 32 percent that would have been taxable under the former system at 40 percent. In other words, Treasury estimates that about two-thirds of the large static revenue loss would become a real revenue loss.[46] Such a loss might result in Congress imposing higher taxes on other, less able taxpayers.

Conclusions

Except for periods of transition from one set of tax rates to another, the impact of tax rates on our economic behavior is difficult to detect. Even for periods when rates have been very high, economists have difficulty establishing a clear connection between the rates and distortions of our real economic behavior. Yet the difficulty of proving such connection does not mean that excessive rates do not discourage work, saving, and entrepreneurship. And nearly all policy analysts agree that excessive rates corrupt income tax policy by justifying more and larger tax preferences that whittle away at the tax base and at taxpayer trust.

Some view today's top tax rates as unnecessarily high, particularly in times of peace; others note that these rates are not high compared to top rates historically, including during times of peace. This debate aside, reducing today's top rates without substantially broadening the tax base or reducing federal expenditures runs the serious risk of increasing federal deficits; and our memories need not be long to fear the resumption of federal deficits, which from 1981 through 1997 alone added nearly $3 trillion to the government's public debt. Determined that rate reduction occur responsibly, Barber Conable, a leading Republican member of the House Ways and Means Committee in the 1970s and early 1980s, remarked in the mid-1980s that the reformer's goal should be "to strike a balance in which [there are] fewer preferences, more moderate progressivity, and a tax base as broad as possible."[47] Congress could achieve revenue neutrality by adopting a flat rate without broadening the tax base. But the remaining economic distortions would remain large from today's panoply of tax preferences. Their existence would make the economic consequences more uncertain and thus more risky. This is particularly true for the vast number of taxpayers whose tax burdens would increase (at least temporarily) under a flat tax rate.

Let us be clear. Although revenue-neutral reforms involving lower rates and a broader tax base would create a healthier climate for long-term economic growth, the tax consequences would vary greatly. Some people—typically those with the largest tax savings from tax preferences—would pay more, many people would pay about the same, and some would pay less. But linking judicious broadening of the tax base with lower rates across the board should (absent intervening considerations) gradually produce favorable feedback effects because taxpayers would have fewer opportunities and less reason to avoid taxation when they make choices about work, saving, and investment. These effects would strengthen the economy and give Congress the opportunity to lower tax rates even further, potentially making winners of us all.

If, however, Congress wants to cut rates substantially across the board without broadening the tax base, responsible budgeting necessitates that it anticipate substantial revenue losses. Then, it must delineate the public programs that would have to be cut or eliminated, some of which are likely to be for low- and moderate-income households. A shadow thereby would be cast, as Henry Aaron argues, over attempts to discredit the public welfare arguments behind progressive rates. While recognizing the arguments for a flat rate, Aaron accuses his own economics profession of being "part of a large and powerful intellectual movement that has undermined the respectability of egalitarian impulses," making the case for progressive taxation "seem to be a product of hormonal excess rather than clear thinking."[48]

In fairness, both sides of the progressive tax-rate debate need to address their own excesses. Whereas liberals too often have been indifferent to efficiency arguments against highly progressive rates, conservatives often have exaggerated the likely efficiency gains from lowering tax rates from today's levels. Much can be said for a middle ground.

10

Myths and Realities:
Tax Subsidies for the Family Home

The most fortunate of men,
Be he a king or commoner, is he
Whose welfare is assured in his own home.

—Goethe

Owners, Renters, and Government Subsidies: An Overview
* The Home-Mortgage Interest Deduction * The Real Estate Tax Deduction * The Exclusion of Gain upon Sale of a Principal Residence * The Economics of Homeownership Tax Subsidies * Recommendations * Tax Values

---

Few Americans would disagree with Goethe's observation: Our well-being depends to a large extent on our home. If our home is secure, if it is adequate to our household needs, and if it is affordable, our lives benefit greatly. If our home is unsafe, if it cannot accommodate the number of people who live there, or if it consumes an excessive portion of our income, our risks abound. They may be risks to our family's health, to our children's ability to be good students, to our relationships within the household, to our ability to function well at work. These risks spill over to the community—to its health, the quality of its public schools, the safety of neighbors and other residents, the strength of its economy.

Yet on the subject of the tax benefits we derive from our homes, federal income tax policy is, and always has been, troubling. The massive tax subsidies for homeownership could help heal deep social and economic divisions within this country. Regrettably, Congress never has shaped tax policy toward that end. Tax policy for homeownership remains largely indifferent to the plight of people whose housing welfare is least assured. Instead, the laws principally expand the comforts of people who are capable, and often extremely capable, of owning a home without government assistance.

Though representing over one-third of all households, renters receive no tax relief for the rent they pay. Tax subsidies for homeownership are only modest for most homeowners because they own modest homes and have modest mortgages. They also have modest incomes taxed at the 15 percent or at most the 28 percent marginal rate, which means that deductions and exclusions for homeownership have much less value for them than for people taxed at the highest marginal rate. By comparison, tax subsidies for owners of large homes who have large mortgages and incomes can vastly exceed the *income* of most households. Owning one or two expensive houses can be the best of all possible tax worlds.

Contrary to popular belief, current tax policies promoting homeownership have undesirable economic consequences. By attracting so much capital to homeownership, they indirectly reduce the number of rental units and thereby probably raise the price of rents; both effects magnify the growing housing crisis for many people who cannot afford to buy a house. The tax subsidies indirectly lead to higher mortgage-interest rates and higher property taxes, and, most likely, higher prices for houses. The extensive tax advantages of owner-occupied housing, and expensive housing in particular, also have drawn money away from investments that would be more economically productive. With less money available to them, businesses must pay more to borrow money or to attract investors. These added costs slow business growth and thus the opportunity for better jobs at better pay. Economists widely agree that our economy would be strengthened by tax laws more neutral in their treatment of owner-occupied housing vis-à-vis other investments.

Contrary to popular belief, current tax policies that promote homeownership have undesirable economic consequences.

Such outcomes invite the fundamental questions posed by this chapter. Should the income tax laws provide any relief for our use, ownership, or sale of the place where we live? If so, who should benefit from this relief and to what extent?

Owners, Renters, and Government Subsidies: An Overview

Tax relief for homeowners has become among the most expensive of all tax-relief measures. In 2000 alone, taxpayers will have saved approximately $87 billion from the three principal subsidies: (1) the itemized deduction for

TABLE 10.1 Three Major Federal Tax Expenditures for Home Ownership (in $billions)

	2000	2000–2004	2000–2004 (% of Total)
Mortgage interest deduction	55.2	301.4	64.4
Real estate tax deduction	18.9	101.3	21.7
Exclusion of gain	12.9	65.1	13.9
Total	87.0	467.8	100.0

SOURCE: Joint Committee on Taxation, *Estimates of Federal Tax Expenditures for Fiscal Years 2000–2004*, JCS–13–99 (Washington, DC: GPO, 1999), 17–18.

home-mortgage interest payments for a principal and secondary residence, (2) the itemized deduction for real estate tax payments for all personal residences, and (3) the exclusion of gain upon the sale of a principal residence. Over five years, according to the Joint Committee on Taxation, homeowners' tax savings from these subsidies will total an estimated $468 billion, growing on average about 4 percent annually (see Table 10.1).

By comparison, the Department of Housing and Urban Development, the federal agency responsible for providing direct housing subsidies, will spend about $32 billion for the years 2000 and 2001 on housing subsidies, for an average of $16 billion per year.[1] The figure is not projected to change much over the following years, which means that HUD's housing budget for the years 2000 through 2004 will be less than 20 percent of tax expenditures for homeownership. Clearly, Congress has chosen tax relief, rather than funding through HUD, as the predominant method for helping people to meet their housing costs.

Whether tax relief should play this dominant role will be addressed later in the chapter. While it plays this role, Congress ought to use the tax laws to promote the public interest most. Congress largely justifies the mortgage-interest deduction and, to a lesser extent, the real estate tax deduction, as promoting homeownership,[2] but the deductions never have helped low- and even moderate-income households more than minimally to become and remain homeowners. Consider the tax expenditures attributable to these deductions in 1999. Together, these deductions produced 92 percent of the tax savings from homeownership tax preferences. As in the past, less than *2 percent* of the tax savings were for the *bottom half* of all taxpayers. By comparison, about 73 percent of the tax savings was for the top 14 percent of taxpayers. Over 20 percent of the tax savings was for the top 1 percent of taxpayers (see Table 10.2).

As one commentator observed about federal housing policy, Congress offers "the middle and upper classes exactly what it tells the poor it can no

TABLE 10.2   Distribution of Federal Tax Expenditures by Income Group for
Mortgage Interest Deduction and Real Estate Tax Deduction, 1999

Taxpayers by Income Percentile[a]	% of Mortgage Interest Tax Expenditure	% of Real Estate Tax Expenditure
Bottom 50%	1.3	1.5
Top 50%	98.7	98.5
Top 14%	72.7	73.7
Top 7%	51.8	54.7
Top 1%	20.6	24.5

[a]As used by the Joint Committee, "income" means the total of AGI plus tax-
exempt interest, employer contributions for health plans and life insurance, the
employer's share of FICA tax, nontaxable Social Security benefits, and several
other items.
SOURCE: Joint Committee on Taxation, *Estimates of Federal Expenditures for
Fiscal Years 2000–2004,* JCS-13-99 (Washington, D.C.: GPO, 1999), JCS 13–19,
25–26, 30.

longer afford: generous Government subsidies."[3] We are reminded of the
maxim "Banks will lend money only if you don't need it."

Data in Table 10.2 show only part of the total picture because they give
only a snapshot of taxpayers in a single year. Many taxpayers who received
few benefits in 1999 will receive larger benefits in subsequent years as their
income levels rise and their opportunities for tax savings grow. In other
words, as people move up the income scale, many will become homeowners,
own more expensive houses, have larger mortgages, and move into higher
marginal tax brackets. As they do, homeowners' tax subsidies will have increasing value to them.

Such a trend raises questions about Congress's values: Why does Congress
believe that tax relief for housing costs should increase in proportion to our
well-being? No clear answer appears. We might assume the influence of politics. We should not assume that sound economic policy underlies subsidizing
ownership of sizable principal residences and second houses for middle- and
upper-income households. As explored elsewhere in this chapter, no such
justification can be found in the economic literature.

Despite our flawed tax policy in relation to homeownership, it remains a
national hallmark. Though the record falls short of Thomas Jefferson's goal
that "fifty acres of land be granted to every person of full age," a remarkable
66 percent of all households own their own houses. The figure climbs to 79
percent for households headed by someone 65 or older and to 86 percent of
households in the top-income quintile.[4] Owner-occupied houses also are in
remarkably good repair; according to a recent American Housing Survey,
only about 5 percent are considered structurally inadequate.[5]

Whether modest or grand, the American home is expected to convey security and status. As James Otis declared in 1761 in a Boston courtroom, "A man's house is his castle."[6] The family residence represents an important boundary between public and private domains. In our house, we are masters of our destiny. There, we may conduct our lives as we like. Others may enter only if invited in. Homeownership long has been a sign of coming of age, evidence that we are living the American dream. One tangible reason is that we consider homeownership a good investment. While sheltering us, our house may appreciate in value. It also can help protect us from the vagaries of inflation and eviction, to which renters are so vulnerable; and by gaining these protections, we achieve greater household stability.

> "For most . . . housing is a dream fulfilled; but for too many others, housing is unavailable, unaffordable and unfit." (National Housing Task Force)

To justify a government tax subsidy for homeownership, homeownership must have value beyond our individual self-interests. It needs to generate what economists call "positive externalities": It must promote the public good. Most Americans would say that homeownership does so by promoting good citizenship. Invested in our home, we are more likely to feel a stake in our community and to make sacrifices for its long-term health.[7] Communities, and their economies, prosper as a result.

Housing also is an American paradox. "For most," concluded the congressionally appointed National Housing Task Force in 1988, "housing is a dream fulfilled; but for too many others, housing is unavailable, unaffordable and unfit."[8] Since 1988, the plight of renters, whose average income is less than 50 percent of homeowners' income, has grown steadily worse. The Joint Center for Housing Studies of Harvard University reports that from 1985 to 1995, the number of very low income renter households (defined as having incomes less than 50 percent of the area median) jumped by 13.5 percent to a total of 14.4 million households. Most live in central cities. By 1995, they represented one out of every four central-city households.[9]

Eighty percent of households with incomes *30 percent* or more below area medians pay more than half of their income in rent or live in structurally inadequate housing. Experts generally regard rent as excessive when it exceeds 30 percent of a household's income: Too little income remains to cover other essential living costs. Yet only about one-third of the 15 million households that qualify for federal housing assistance because of their low incomes actually get it.[10] According to the Center on Budget and Policy Priorities of Washington, D.C., "The shortage of low-rent housing . . . reached a record high in 1995 when the number of low-income renter households exceeded the number of low-cost rental units by 4.4 million."[11] By comparison, in 1970 the number of housing units available for the poor *exceeded* the number of poor households.[12]

The situation of median-income renter households has been in decline as well. From 1970 to 1994, their income fell by 16 percent while their gross rents increased by more than 14 percent.[13] Conditions have not improved since.

Only about one-third of the 15 million households that qualify for federal housing assistance because of their low incomes actually get it.

Direct assistance to renters from the federal government rarely has included a component that would foster their transition to homeownership, such as funds to help make the initial down payment for the purchase of a starter home.[14] Instead, the government offers vouchers that help pay rent or offers the opportunity to live in subsidized apartment buildings owned by others. These forms of government assistance have been extremely valuable. Still, with their destinies dictated by distant landlords and their lives humbled by the circumstances of their typically disadvantaged community, inner-city residents long to move out rather than settle in.

The most significant indirect tax relief that helps renters become homeowners is a little-known Mortgage Revenue Bond program. State housing authorities are authorized by the federal government to issue tax-exempt bonds, the proceeds of which are lent at below-market interest rates to low-income people to help them finance acquisition of their first home. By working through state agencies that screen and counsel applicants, the program in many ways serves as a model to effectively move low-income renters into homeownership. For reasons that are unclear, Congress always has kept the program small. In 1999, the government lost $2.3 billion from exempting the bond interest from taxation, less than 4 percent of its loss from itemized mortgage-interest and real estate tax deductions.

Congress also provides tax incentives for higher-income taxpayers to invest in the construction of low-cost rental housing. These incentives, though still having widespread congressional support because they appealed to investors and the building industry, were sharply curtailed by the Tax Reform Act of 1986. Partly as a consequence, fewer low-cost rental housing units are being constructed. Growing numbers of low- and moderate-income households must pay higher rents as they compete for serendipitously available rental housing.[15] Congress has come to view vouchers, which help low-income households pay rent, as a more efficient use of the government's money. Low-income renters simply have lacked the political clout to persuade Congress to do more.

Congress could advance the health and stability of households, their communities, and the economy far better if it focused tax subsidies for homeownership on maximizing the number of first-time homeowners of starter homes.

These observations suggest the need to question our government's values and, ultimately, our own values as they relate to two major areas of housing policy. First, we ought to reassess our government's refusal to devote more resources to ameliorate the rental plight of low- and moderate-income households. Second, we ought to re-assess our government's insistence on providing massive tax subsidies for middle- and upper-income housing. As discussed later in the chapter, Con-gress could advance the health and stability of households, their communi-ties, and the economy far better if tax subsidies for homeownership focused on maximizing the number of first-time owners of starter homes. Much also can be said for vastly reducing homeownership tax subsidies overall and, cor-respondingly, reducing tax rates to achieve revenue-neutral reforms.

With these issues in mind, we now turn to a close look at the three princi-pal homeownership tax subsidies.

The Home-Mortgage Interest Deduction

Home-mortgage interest and real estate taxes were deductible by every tax-payer until the standard deduction appeared during World War II. Since then, only itemizers can claim the two deductions. High-income taxpayers nearly always itemize. Relatively few middle-income taxpayers would if they could not deduct their home-mortgage interest—the Big Bertha of all de-ductions—and real estate tax payments on their houses. Collectively, these two deductions (see Table 10.3) represent about 60 percent of all itemized deductions claimed by taxpayers each year.

Rules for Deduction; Limits and Opportunities for Higher-Income Taxpayers

Homeowners may deduct interest they pay on up to $1.1 million of loans, called **acquisition indebtedness**, to acquire, construct, or substantially im-prove up to two personal residences—a principal residence plus one sec-ondary residence. Each loan must be se-cured by a mortgage on the applicable residence. Up to $100,000 of the $1.1 million may be a **home equity loan** that does not qualify as acquisition indebted-ness yet is secured by a mortgage on one of the residences. A home equity loan can pay for anything, from golf clubs to yachts, from schooling to vacations abroad.

The $1.1 million ceiling reflects our government's choice to subsidize lifestyles of the wealthy.

Less than 1 percent of all households test the $1.1 million ceiling. For ex-ample, itemizers with $100,000 to $200,000 of AGI in 1997 claimed on av-erage only about a $11,000 mortgage-interest deduction. Nevertheless, the mortgage-interest deduction for households with $200,000 or more of AGI currently saves them over $7 billion of federal income taxes, and some por-tion (no official statistics exist) of the savings is attributable to loans at the $1.1 million ceiling. The Congressional Budget Office has estimated that re-

TABLE 10.3 Itemized Deductions, 1997

Category of Deduction	Amount of Deduction (in $billions)	Percentage of All Deductions
Mortgage interest	236.0	38.0
State and local income taxes	137.0	22.1
Charitable gifts	99.2	16.0
Real estate taxes	75.0	12.1
Other	73.6	11.8
Total	620.8	100.0

SOURCE: Internal Revenue Service, *Statistics of Income—1997: Individual Income Tax Returns* (Washington, D.C.: IRS, 1999).

ducing the maximum mortgage loan eligible for the deduction to $300,000 would have increased tax collections for 1999 by as much as $2.3 billion.[16] The $1.1 million ceiling, therefore, reflects our government's choice to subsidize, at considerable government expense, the purchase of expensive houses by the wealthiest taxpayers rather than to eliminate their subsidy and use the tax revenue to fund other social causes, reduce the deficit, or lower tax rates across the board. Perhaps Congress believes that granting the wealthiest taxpayers enormous mortgage-interest deductions is necessary to measure fairly their ability to pay.

Peter and Sarah Pawley, like many of their extremely successful New York peers, are grateful for these values. With several million dollars of mortgages on their New York City condominium and country house in western Massachusetts, they deducted $88,000 in 1999, the 8 percent interest they paid on $1.1 million of the loans. The deduction saved them over $30,000 in income taxes, more than the median income in 1999 of all taxpayers.

Still, the 1986–1987 limitations on the home-mortgage interest deduction represent progress of sorts. Before the Tax Reform Act of 1986, homeowners could borrow unlimited amounts and deduct the interest whether the money was spent on a family home or for any other purpose. The loan simply had to be secured by a family home. They also could refinance the loan at any time and continue to deduct the interest. Since 1987, the interest on any refinanced loan may not be deducted to the extent that the loan proceeds exceed the prior loan balance plus the $100,000 home equity loan limit and are not used to make substantial home improvements.

A small percentage of homeowners must contend with one other limitation. In 1990, Congress selectively pruned some itemized deductions (let's call them "tainted deductions"), including deductions for home-mortgage interest and real estate taxes, for taxpayers with more than $100,000 of AGI.

(The $100,000 figure is adjusted annually for cost-of-living increases.) Such taxpayers must reduce the total of their tainted deductions by 3 percent of the amount that their AGI exceeds the year's AGI threshold. For example, in 1999 when the AGI threshold had equaled $126,000, a taxpayer with $326,000 of AGI (or $200,000 more than the threshold) had to reduce her tainted deductions by only $6,000 (3 percent of $200,000). Not surprisingly, this pruning is more complicated than painful for all but a relative handful of taxpayers.

The Mortgage-Interest Deduction for Ordinary Taxpayers

Homeowners who have paid off their mortgage or who do not itemize obtain no tax savings from the mortgage-interest deduction. Tax savings from the deduction typically are only modest for itemizers in the 15 percent marginal tax bracket. For example, in 1997 itemizers with $45,000 to $50,000 of AGI, most of whom reached only the 15 percent marginal tax bracket, claimed on average a $6,250 mortgage-interest deduction. The average deduction in those cases saved only $938, or $78 per month. Itemizers with $60,000 to $75,000 of AGI averaged $6,800 in mortgage-interest deductions. Today, the typical mortgage for a first-time house buyer is about $80,000. At an 8 percent annual interest rate, the initial year's interest deduction is $6,400, saving the typical taxpayer about $53 per month.

Even such modest subsidies, though, may help many Americans purchase a starter house. The first-time homeowner typically has little cash for a down payment and must borrow heavily to pay the purchase price. The mortgage-interest deduction reduces her net out-of-pocket interest expense. In theory, then, without the mortgage-interest deduction, homeownership among younger Americans would be confined increasingly to people who have independent wealth or gifts from their families.

A 1997 Census Bureau study concluded, however, that modestly reducing mortgage-interest costs barely increases the number of homeowners. What low- and moderate-income taxpayers need to convert them into homeowners is the money to make the initial down payment.[17]

The mortgage-interest deduction also produces unintended consequences. Just as the new college tuition tax credits, by making tuitions more affordable,

> *Whether the benefits of the mortgage-interest deduction for the ordinary taxpayer exceed the related costs is a matter of considerable debate.*

likely will induce colleges to raise tuitions, the mortgage-interest deduction, by making interest payments less burdensome, has made it possible for sellers of houses to escalate the sales price. It also has enabled lenders to charge higher interest rates. Markets work these ways. In short, the mortgage-interest deduction is not a free lunch. Whether the tax savings for the ordinary taxpayer are more valuable than these indirect costs is difficult to measure and is a matter of considerable debate among economists.

Economic Theories for and Against the Deduction

We begin with the principle that just as interest received is income under Haig-Simons because it increases our wealth, interest paid is deductible, at least to the extent that its payment relates to income-generating activities. Allowing interest deductions even when the payments are unrelated to income-generating activities also generally is seen by economists as fair and efficient, and probably consistent with Haig-Simons, because the deductions advance the principle of **tax neutrality:** The deductions neutralize the economic outcomes of alternative methods for financing an activity.[18]

Consider a couple who wants to purchase a $300,000 house and owns a $300,000 corporate bond that pays 8 percent interest. One option is for them to sell the bond and use the cash to purchase the house. In that case, they have neither interest income nor interest expense. Alternatively, they might retain the bond and pay the purchase price through an 8 percent, $300,000 mortgage loan. The economic outcome is identical to their first option: The $24,000 of interest income is offset by $24,000 of interest expense, leaving them with zero net interest income. But interest on corporate bonds is taxable. For the second option to produce the same after-tax outcome—the same economic outcome—as the first, the couple must deduct its mortgage-interest payments against its interest income.

For the tax laws to follow economic theory, however, interest income and deductions, including the mortgage-interest deduction, would be reduced by the annual increase in the cost of living; in that way, the income and deductions reflect *real* gains and losses (see Chapter 2). Our tax laws do not require cost-of-living adjustments in either case. Thus homeowners claim much larger mortgage-interest deductions, particularly in times of high inflation, than is economically justified.

The allowance of any mortgage-interest deduction, however, is questionable once we understand another basic economic theory. Homeowners enjoy what economists refer to as **imputed rental income** from the personal use of their residences. While the concept (introduced in Chapter 2) is familiar to few noneconomists, imputed rental income is as real to economists as is rent paid to a homeowner by a third-party tenant. The concept recognizes that our personal occupancy of our residence has real economic value. In effect, economists see a homeowner who lives in her house as wearing two hats, one as occupant, the other as landlord. As landlord, she receives the net economic value of her occupancy each year as if she rented the house to a third party. This net economic value equals the gross rental value of the house minus the costs of owning and maintaining it, including interest on her house-acquisition loan.

For sound political and administrative reasons, Congress never has taxed imputed rental income. Americans would be outraged at the thought. Massive underreporting could be expected, and enforcing such a law would test the IRS's oversight resources. Yet homeowners gain an enormous advantage in avoiding tax on their imputed rental income while deducting home-mortgage interest payments. The advantage increases with the value of one's house and the size of one's mortgage: Houses with greatest value have the largest imputed rental income, and their owners generally claim the largest mortgage-interest deductions. Moreover, the net imputed income and mortgage-interest deduction often would be comparable, which under Haig-Simons would eliminate any net tax savings from the mortgage-interest deduction.[19] In sum, as long as imputed rental income is untaxed, it would not be inequitable to deny them the mortgage-interest deduction, that is, if tax laws are to be guided by economic principles.

Home Equity Loans

A principal casualty of tax reforms in 1986 and 1987 was the deduction for personal interest. Unless they are homeowners, taxpayers no longer can deduct interest on loans to acquire automobiles, clothes, and other goods and services for personal use.

Before, homeowners typically deducted all of their mortgage-interest payments regardless of how they used the loan proceeds; Congress was persuaded that limiting the home-mortgage deduction solely to house-related expenses would be harsh. Therefore, it allowed homeowners, including future homeowners, to deduct interest on up to $100,000 of loans used for any personal purpose, as long as the loans are secured by a principal or secondary residence. These *home equity loans* are responsible for perhaps 20 percent of the home-mortgage interest tax expenditure and are concentrated among the most favored homeowners. As reported in a 1998 Federal Reserve Bulletin, "Households who have a home equity line of credit typically own relatively expensive homes, have higher incomes, and have substantially more equity in their homes than most other homeowners."[20]

Households without home equity loans, including by definition all renters, may not deduct interest on loans to pay their rent, health insurance premiums, car loans, or other consumption expenses except for a small amount of interest for certain education loans. These households are further disadvantaged because loans unsecured by a house usually carry a higher interest rate. Finally, these households also may pay higher tax rates because the government must raise rates to compensate for revenue lost from the deduction. For all these reasons, the deduction for interest payments on home equity loans unfairly favors homeowners and defies a core principle that people ought to pay taxes in accordance with their ability to pay.

The Real Estate Tax Deduction

Itemizers may deduct real estate taxes paid on *all* of their personal residences. At an estimated cost to the government of $101 billion from 2000 through 2004 (see Table 10.1). This revenue loss is difficult to justify. In 1985, President Reagan proposed eliminating the deduction, along with all deductions for state and local taxes, in his comprehensive *Tax Proposals to the Congress for Fairness, Growth, and Simplicity* (the *Proposals*). According to his *Proposals*, the "current deduction for State and local taxes disproportionately benefits high-income taxpayers residing in high-tax States, . . . the cost of the deduction is borne by all taxpayers in the form of significantly higher marginal tax rates, [and] provision of the subsidy through a deduction . . . is neither cost effective nor fair."[21]

To tax archeologists, however, deductions for real estate taxes and for state and local income taxes are valued artifacts: They are the only significant deductions for taxes that remain since the 1913 laws, when all state, local, and federal taxes were deductible. The last to be eliminated was for state sales taxes, a casualty of the 1986 Reform Act. Deductions for real estate taxes and for state and local income taxes survived the act because of claims by many states and localities that they depended heavily on the revenues and that the taxes were not regressive, unlike sales taxes.

Although these arguments carried the day, many people questioned whether state and local revenues would suffer much without the deductions. Critics of the real estate tax deduction also noted its considerable disadvantages, as had Reagan's *Proposals*. First, it effectively converts the real estate tax from a proportionate to a regressive tax: The after-tax cost of each dollar deducted is least for homeowners in the highest tax bracket.

Further inequities arise among states and localities. Those with the highest per capita income have the highest percentage of itemizers, including taxpayers who save the most from itemizing. These states and localities thus can bump up their real estate taxes the most because the federal government absorbs a disproportionate share of the cost. As Reagan's *Proposals* noted, "In effect, the deduction requires taxpayers in certain communities to subsidize taxpayers in other communities."[22]

For example, the deduction favors states such as New York and New Jersey that combine high real estate taxes with a higher-than-average percentage of citizens who deduct them. It penalizes states such as West Virginia and Alabama that have low real estate taxes and have relatively few people who itemize. West Virginians and Alabamians also receive lower levels of public services because of their states' lower real estate taxes. Consider the funding of public education through property taxes. Families that live in communities with high property values can more easily afford high property taxes to support their schools because many of the families itemize their deductions and gain relief from the highest marginal tax rates. For such communities, the federal

> *The real estate tax deduction favors states that combine high real estate taxes with a higher-than-average percentage of citizens who deduct them. It penalizes states that have low real estate taxes have relatively few people who itemize.*

government's per student tax subsidy is substantial. By contrast, families in poor communities with low property values struggle to pay modest property taxes, and relatively few of such families itemize. In such communities, the federal government's per student tax subsidy is far less. Families in poor communities also probably pay higher federal income tax rates than would be necessary were the deduction eliminated.

The deduction also appears to be an inefficient way for the federal government to subsidize local services. Leading studies suggest that the ability of states and localities to increase property taxes because of the deduction is considerably less than the loss of tax revenue to the federal government because of the deduction. In other words, states and localities pick up far less than an extra $1 of revenue for each $1 of revenue loss to the government attributable to the deduction. If Congress eliminated the deduction, states and localities would lose some revenue because people who benefited from the deduction would insist on paying less; but the federal government could collect sufficient additional income taxes from eliminating the deduction to reimburse localities for their loss of tax revenue and still have substantial revenue left over.[23]

Critics of this analysis note correctly that reimbursing states and localities for revenue that they may lose from elimination of the deduction would be difficult to calculate, politicized, and uncertain. But no precise quid pro quo should be necessary to justify eliminating the deduction. Federal subsidies to states and localities ought to be based on need, and the deduction yields the greatest subsidies typically for places least in need.

Richard Musgrave and others believe, however, that partial deductions for real estate taxes can be justified because to some extent they pay for services that do not involve personal gain. For example, we know that real estate taxes pay for police and fire departments, courts of law, roads, and schools that benefit people who do not pay the taxes, such as renters and people who work in the community but live elsewhere.[24] But the taxes are distinctly local, which means that homeowners benefit directly from many of these services and indirectly from all. The taxes help businesses thrive and in some fashion are likely to enhance a homeowner's quality of life. In sum, they deserve to be characterized as nondeductible consumption expenses because they are inseparable from homeowners' personal welfare.

The Exclusion of Gain upon Sale of a Principal Residence

In 1997, Congress greatly simplified provisions relieving homeowners from tax on their gain from selling their principal residence. In doing so, Congress replaced one set of poorly focused and excessive subsidies for another. The new rules pander to owners of expensive houses, excessively favor joint filers over others, encourage people to overinvest in their houses, cause tax rates to be higher than otherwise would be necessary, and constrain economic growth. Congress's justification of the new laws turns not on their intrinsic merit but on comparison to prior law.

Pre-1997 Legislation: The Tax-Free Rollover Rule and the $125,000 Exclusion

From 1951 until 1997, homeowners were entitled to defer paying tax on their gain from the sale of their principal residence regardless of how large the gain might be if they satisfied the "rollover" rule. The final version of the rule required that within two years of the date when they sold their principal residence, homeowners buy or build another principal residence at a cost that at least equaled the sale price of their prior residence. For example, if you bought residence A for $200,000 and sold it for $1 million, you could defer ("roll over") the tax on your $800,000 gain as long as you bought or built residence B for at least $1 million within two years of selling residence A. You also could engage in future sales and deferrals an indefinite number of times.

> Not surprisingly, the typical family received little of the tax savings from the tax-free rollover rule.

Though Congress's rationale for adopting the rollover rule in 1951 was to address the plight of ordinary homeowners who had to move because of a change in jobs or family size, Congress never confined the tax-free rollover to the typical family. Not surprisingly, the typical family received little of the tax savings because its gains are small and would have been lightly taxed without the relief; most of the tax savings belonged to high-income households.[25]

As we also know, one tax preference typically begets another. The rollover rule was no exception. The elderly, often preferring simpler and smaller accommodations, might "buy down." Alternatively, they might rent, possibly in the growing number of retirement communities, or might move in with their children. The rollover rule gave them only partial protection if they bought a less-expensive house and none at all if they failed to buy. Yet they were no less deserving of tax relief than homeowners engaged in tax-free rollovers.

Congress responded in 1964 by allowing people who were 65 or older a modest, one-time permanent exemption of up to $20,000 of their gain that was not protected by the rollover rules. By 1981, the relief extended to people 55 and older and covered up to $125,000 of gain, which remained the rule until the 1997 legislation. These expanded rules dramatically expanded the government's revenue loss and shifted much of the relief to middle- and upper-income taxpayers.[26]

Together, the rollover and the exemption nearly eliminated tax on gains from the sale of a principal residence.[27] In this context, Congress and Clinton found appealing the notion of adopting simpler rules that would allow nearly everyone to avoid tax on the sale of their principal residence.

The New $250,000–$500,000 Exemption

The Taxpayer Relief Act of 1997 discarded the tax-free rollover rule and the $125,000 exemption. Instead, all taxpayers of any age who have owned and used a house as their principal residence for at least two of the five years before selling it now may exclude up to $500,000 of gain if they are joint filers; they may exclude up to $250,000 if they are not. None of the proceeds need be reinvested in another principal residence. The exemptions may be used unlimited times—even every two years. Taxpayers who fail to satisfy the two-out-of-five-year requirement because of a change of place of employment, health, or unforeseen circumstances may exclude a fraction of the exempt amount.[28]

Congress enacted the new law because it viewed the old laws as excessively burdensome for taxpayers. Though few gains from the sale of a principal residence had been taxed, many sellers had to compute their gain. This required them to maintain records to establish the house's original cost, the cost of all improvements, and any depreciation for business usage. If they had rolled over their gain to a new house, similar records would have to be maintained for their second house. Congress considered these computations "among the most complex tasks faced by a typical taxpayer." Exemptions under the new law are sufficiently high so as to spare the typical taxpayer, as a practical matter, from worrying about such record keeping.

> The taxation of gain from the sale of a principal residence should be guided by the basic principle of tax justice that people ought to pay taxes in proportion to their abilities to pay.

Congress also assumes that the new law offers less encouragement to homeowners than did the rollover rule "to purchase larger and more expensive houses than [they] otherwise would in order to avoid a tax liability. . . . This [encouragement] promotes an inefficient use of taxpayer's financial resources." Last, Congress was concerned that the $125,000 exemption discouraged sales by some elderly, who might have a gain in excess of $125,000 or who might already have used their exemption and would like to move to a smaller house or rent. "By raising the $125,000 limit and allowing multiple exclusions," Congress explained, "this constraint to the mobility of the elderly would be removed."[29]

Congress was quite right that the old rules were not sound. The modest revenues from taxing relatively few sales of principal residences did not warrant the social-welfare costs to homeowners or warrant the IRS's oversight responsibilities. But the policy question ought to be whether our house merits being treated as a castle effectively sheltered from the capital gains tax rolls. By providing such blanket and substantial exemptions for gains on the sale of a principal residence, Congress has again overridden the basic principle that people ought to pay taxes in proportion to their abilities to pay.

Consider the proposition, now endorsed by the new legislation, that single, 33-year-old Holly Newark, who sold her principal residence this year for $400,000 that she bought two years ago for $150,000 at a foreclosure sale in Reno, Nevada, should automatically be exempt from tax on her $250,000 gain. Why is it irrelevant to Congress that Holly, who expects to earn $135,000 this year from her law practice, could easily afford the $50,000 tax (20 percent of $250,000), which would leave her with $200,000 of net profit from the sale after taxes? At the same time, Congress requires Gloria Royal, a full-time, single housekeeper, to pay income taxes on a portion of her $10,000 in wages. Does anyone doubt who between them is better able to pay?

The blanket $250,000–$500,000 exemption also invites builders and others to game the system, thus breeding contempt for the system. For example, Dunn Samuels, who builds expensive houses in Sarasota, Florida, might realize a $500,000 profit from constructing and, two years later, selling the house he owns jointly with his wife and retain all $500,000 of the profit after federal taxes. If he realizes $500,000 of profits from constructing *your* house, typically he will be left with less than $300,000 of cash after income and Social Security taxes. Congress has authored such tax games within a set of rules that are

> The blanket $250,000–$500,000 exemption invites builders and others to game the system, thus breeding contempt for the system.

distinctly regressive. People with the largest gains, who almost always live in the most expensive houses and have the highest incomes, will receive many times the relief of ordinary homeowners.

Congress's assumption that the $125,000 exemption commonly was inadequate was equally flawed. In 1993, the median gain of those claiming the exemption was only $28,000. The average gain of elderly taxpayers with AGI of $200,000 or more was about $110,000.[30]

Congress also seems mistaken in believing that the new legislation will not induce taxpayers to "buy up" to the extent of the prior laws. The tax-free rollover allowed the deferral of an unlimited amount of gain, but the new $250,000–$500,000 ceilings will be inadequate for only a relative handful of taxpayers. To realize a $500,000 gain from the sale of a principal residence requires acquiring a very expensive house; and the massive potential savings from this exemption, acting like a magnet, will attract people to acquire far more house than they need. Such a strategy seems particularly attractive now because, compared with the

> *The strongest argument for providing tax relief upon the sale of a principal residence is that much of the gain usually is attributable to inflation.*

rollover, the $250,000– $500,000 ceilings provide permanent tax exemptions. Also, compared with the former $125,000 *one-time exemption* for people 55 or over, the new, much higher exemptions may be claimed unlimited times by people of any age. Tax relief of this kind inevitably distorts economic behavior away from other, less-favored forms of investments, as will be discussed shortly.

The strongest argument for providing tax relief upon the sale of a principal residence is that much of the gain usually is attributable to inflation. Protecting homeowners from paying tax on inflationary gains would be consistent with Haig-Simons. Haig-Simons, however, calls for real gains to be taxed annually even when there is no sale; alternatively, the deferred gain should accrue interest until the tax is paid. Thus if our tax laws followed basic economic theory, inflationary gains on personal residences would be untaxed; but each year's real, deferred gains would accrue interest if not taxed. In turn, a homeowner would be entitled to receive interest from the government on her deferred losses if her house declined in value. (For how the tax laws might sensibly respond to all of these considerations, see recommendations below.)

The Economics of Homeownership Tax Subsidies

Home building occupies a central place in our economy. It directly involves an extraordinary number of trades and materials, and it has a ripple effect on collateral economic activities that serve homeowners, from manufacturing to road building to the development of commercial ventures. For these reasons, people widely believe that our economy would weaken if we devoted fewer resources to homeownership. Yet all major economic studies conclude otherwise. Although home building stimulates economic growth, our economy would grow even faster, producing more profits for business, more jobs, and higher wages, if we allocated less of our savings to private homeownership and more to a range of business and other investments.[31]

Some economic studies indicate that allocating less of our savings to homeownership would only modestly affect the growth of businesses, jobs, and wages.[32] Other studies, particularly during the 1990s, find that the economic effect would be significant, "suggesting," as the nonprofit Committee for Economic Development of Washington, D.C., said in 1992, "a gross misallocation of capital" to homeownership.[33] Writing in 1996, the economist Jonathan Skinner suggested "that the welfare cost of preferential treatment of housing is nearly five times that measured by earlier studies." Skinner posited that the welfare cost could amount to as much as 2.2 percent of the gross national product.[34] In 1999, that would have meant a loss to the economy of over $150 billion.

> *Our economy would grow even faster, producing more profits for business, more jobs, and higher wages, if less of our private savings were allocated to private homeownership and more were allocated to a range of business and other investments.*

Tax subsidies for homeownership distort economic behavior. By greatly increasing the after-tax return from homeownership and ownership of expensive houses in particular, the tax subsidies encourage everyone who can, but particularly middle- and upper-income households, to devote a higher percentage of their savings to homeownership than they would if the tax laws were neutral among competing investments. As Skinner explains, "By stimulating the price of tax-preferred owner-occupied housing, the capital income tax causes the now more valuable housing stock to soak up a larger fraction of total saving, leaving less for investment in (non-housing) physical capital."[35] The lower supply of savings available to businesses forces businesses to compete more actively for it. This competition increases the cost of their capital: Businesses must pay lenders higher interest rates and must pay potential investors higher rates of return on their investments for using their money. In turn, these higher costs reduce business resources available for upgrading existing plant and equipment, for research and development, for engaging in new projects, for hiring more employees, and for paying higher wages.

> *The reduction of homeowner tax subsidies tops the list compiled by economist Dale Jorgenson of tax reforms needed to stimulate economic growth.*

The reduction of homeownership tax subsidies tops the list compiled by economist Dale Jorgenson of tax reforms needed to stimulate economic growth. "Very significant opportunities for U.S. economic growth can be created," he wrote in 1993, if "Congress . . . would 'level the playing field' between business assets and owner-occupied housing by sharply curtailing the tax benefits to housing provided through deductions for mortgage interest and state and local property taxes."[36]

If Congress created a level playing field for the after-tax returns from housing and other investments, people who receive little or none of the savings from the existing homeownership tax subsidies would be among the many beneficiaries. For one thing, the price of houses likely would fall, helping people become homeowners, because fewer subsidies for homeownership would make houses less affordable at their old prices. A minority of commentators believe, however, that existing house prices might not fall at all or would fall only slightly, because they expect that eliminating the deductions would cause a significant drop in mortgage-interest rates and property taxes.

If the elimination of homeownership tax subsidies were accompanied by lower tax rates that made the reforms revenue neutral, renters would have more income after taxes with which to purchase a home. The same may be true for homeowners who want to purchase a different home and who benefit little today from the subsidies. Homeowners who benefit a great deal from today's homeownership tax subsidies likely would experience increased after-tax costs of homeownership, even with across-the-board reductions in tax rates. Among this group of homeowners, the wealthiest would continue to afford whatever home they chose; others might elect to own somewhat less expensive homes in order to devote more of their personal savings to investments that promise higher returns.

Fewer tax subsidies for homeownership should increase investment in rental housing.

Finally, fewer tax subsidies for homeownership should increase private investment in rental housing. As the Congressional Budget Office has written, existing subsidies "reduce the demand for rental housing by decreasing the relative cost of homeownership as a consumption good and increasing its attractiveness as an investment. This lower demand, in turn, leads to the construction of less rental housing."[37]

Let me, then, summarize what appear to be the most respected economic views about homeownership. The subsidies hurt renters because they reduce indirectly the amount of rental housing and cause rents and income tax rates to be higher than they otherwise would be. The subsidies hurt a significant minority of homeowners who do not itemize by increasing their mortgage-interest rates, their property taxes, and their income tax rates. For many homeowners who itemize but whose tax rate does not exceed 15 percent, the tax savings for homeownership may approximate the higher housing costs attributable to the tax subsidies. The tax outcomes of homeowners who itemize and are subject to higher marginal tax brackets vary considerably. Homeowners in the highest tax brackets who have expensive houses and large mortgages are likely to benefit significantly from the subsidies. Even so, the story may differ considerably after accounting for adverse effects of subsidies on the economy and thus on each homeowner's level of income.

Recommendations

To be fair to existing homeowners and to minimize disruption to the economy, any blueprint for reforming homeownership tax subsidies must provide an orderly transition to a new system. But what should the ultimate goal be? We began the chapter with a question: If federal subsidies for homeownership make sense, should they be provided primarily through the tax laws, as they are today, or through direct government grants? In either case, the goals should be clear and the subsidies highly focused. Most middle-income households, and all upper-income households, could afford to own a house without a subsidy, though the house may be more modest than the one in which they live. Rather than enable people to buy larger homes, homeownership tax subsidies ought to maximize the number of homeowners. The social and economic payoffs likely would be large. Conservatives and liberals widely agree that homeownership encourages family stability and, by increasing a family's long-term stake in its community, promotes behavior that advances the health and vitality of the community.

Consider our inner cities, where the rate of homeownership falls far below that in the suburbs. With larger subsidies for first-time home buyers, owners of apartment buildings would have incentives to convert the buildings into condominiums that residents and others could afford to acquire. The larger market for modest dwellings also likely would lead to more construction of modest houses and condominiums appropriate for first-time home buyers. Because many more inner-city residents would become homeowners, the favorable effects would ripple up as well as down, benefiting the new owners, their communities, and neighboring communities as well.

According to an extensive U.S. Census Bureau study, the principal obstacle to renters' becoming homeowners is their inability to make the down payment. The number of renters in 1993 who could have afforded a modest home (one valued in the bottom 25 percent of all owner-occupied homes in the renter's area) would have more than tripled—from 12 percent to 36 percent—had renters been given (rather than lent) a subsidy of $10,000 for the down payment and received conventional, 30-year fixed-rate financing for the balance of the purchase price. The number would have more than doubled—to 28 percent—had the subsidy been $5,000. Surprisingly, lending renters the down payment without also substantially lowering their mortgage-interest rate on the loan would have increased the number of renters qualified to buy a modest home by only 3 percent.[38]

Subsidies for down payments or for below-market-interest-rate loans to cover down payments could be made available through HUD, which could work with state and local housing offices to administer the program. These subsidies also could be made through tax relief to the prospective homeowner, such as through tax credits toward the down payment and for mortgage-interest payments. Finally, tax subsidies could be offered to investors who would be willing to acquire interests in publicly traded, below-market mortgages that would be made available to a prospective homeowner toward her down payment. None of these alternatives has been studied extensively by the government or by economists. All deserve to be. We need to understand far better what approaches likely would produce the largest payoffs through subsidies that the government could afford. In short, we know too little at this time to resolve whether direct government funding or tax subsidies would be preferable.

We do know, however, that important timing problems would result from tax subsidies made directly to prospective homeowners in order to help them with their down payment. For example, a refundable tax credit, the greatest help to lower-income taxpayers, for the purchase of a house in 1999 would not have been issued until after purchasers filed their tax returns in 2000, long after they needed the money. Lenders would have to advance the down payment with an agreement that it would be repaid by the borrower once she received the credit. Understandably, lenders would be reluctant to enter into such agreements without government guarantees, which in turn would be complicated. Refundable credits to subsidize mortgage-interest payments also would be available only after the year in which the interest payments were made; the delay would limit the number of renters who could afford the payments.

An alternative and highly promising strategy has been outlined by the Joint Center for Housing Studies of Harvard University,[39] which calls for the creation of low-income second-mortgage tax credits. The credits would be allocated to states according to a formula based on their population and the government's overall budget for the program. A state agency then would allocate its credits to regulated financial institutions and others who would be the top bidders for the credits in public-auction markets. The tax credits would compensate successful bidders for making second-mortgage loans— loans that would stand behind, and thus be riskier than, primary or first-mortgage loans—to qualified low-income renters. Each loan to purchasers would cover between 18 and 22 percent of a home's purchase price and would bear interest rates of only 3 percent. Conventional loans (the first-mortgage loans) would be made by other lenders for the balance of the purchase price except that all prospective purchasers would be required to make some down payment with their own resources. Even a small down payment made by a buyer from her own funds vastly reduces loan-default rates.

The center estimates that $300 million of tax credits allocated annually to investors over 10 years (for a total cost of $3 billion) could help approximately 200,000 households become first-home buyers. If the center is correct, and if Congress were to reallocate *annually* only $3 billion of the $87 billion of homeownership tax expenditures to this cause, Congress could convert millions of renters into homeowners. By doing so, Congress would transform the social and economic fabric of cities and towns throughout the country. With this background, let us now turn to the three principal home-ownership tax subsidies.

Home-Mortgage Interest Deduction

Congress ought to focus homeownership subsidies on multiplying the number of first-time buyers of starter homes. We have seen that the most effective method would be to help renters pay the initial down payment and set-tlement costs, possibly through the low-income second-mortgage credit just described. This focus would justify eliminating the mortgage-interest deduc-tion, though a transition period should be provided for homeowners with current mortgages in order for the new laws not to be punitive or too dis-ruptive to the housing market.

The enormous popularity of home-mortgage interest deductions sug-gests, however, that voters would insist on retaining at least some tax subsidy for home-mortgage interest. In that case, the subsidy should be through a refundable tax credit that applies to a basic amount of home-acquisition in-debtedness. The credit would assure each eligible taxpayer that she would receive $1 of tax relief for each $1 of tax liability, whereas each $1 deduction ensures the highest tax relief for taxpayers whose income falls in the highest marginal tax bracket. By making the credit refundable, Congress would help subsidize the interest costs of low-income households that do not owe taxes.

Congress might, for example, allow a refundable credit on the interest paid on a basic amount of home-acquisition indebtedness, such as a mortgage up to $100,000, which is about $20,000 above the median mortgage for first-time home buyers today. The size of the credit would depend on how much Congress wanted to allocate to the program. For example, if the credit was 15 percent of eligible interest payments, and interest was 8 percent, or $8,000, on a $100,000 mortgage, a homeowner would receive a maximum credit that year of $1,200 (15 percent x $8,000). Limiting the credit to taxpayers whose income falls below certain levels would focus the credit on households most in need and would limit the cost of the program to the government; but phase-outs of special tax provisions create enormous complexity for taxpayers and the IRS, and I would oppose such a phaseout here for that reason.

Real Estate Taxes

Deductions for real estate taxes on private residences are regressive among taxpayers and operate arbitrarily in their indirect consequences among local-ities. Property taxes, however, represent a significant percentage of most lo-cal governments' tax bases. Many local governments have few other produc-tive sources of tax revenue, partly because many states prohibit local governments from adopting income taxes that would compete with the state income tax. For these reasons, many jurisdictions with high property taxes, such as in the northeast and north-central parts of the country, are particu-larly opposed to any immediate elimination of the deduction. Nonetheless, the deduction cannot be justified for the nation as a whole, as discussed ear-lier. Congress should eliminate the deduction, but the effective date should be sufficiently prospective to allow state and local governments time to plan for the possibility that they may have to lower property taxes.

If voters insist on retaining some subsidy for real estate tax payments, the subsidy should be in the form of a refundable tax credit, such as 15 percent, of real estate taxes up to a basic level. The basic level might be 120 percent of the median real estate tax paid by homeowners nationwide.

Exemption of Gain upon Sale of Principal Residence

Congress adopted both the tax-free rollover and the $125,000 exclusion primarily to address hardships that occur if ordinary homeowners are taxed fully when they sell their principal residences. For these households, all or most of their gain likely reflects inflation, such homeowners' houses represent a major portion of their net worth, which itself is modest. By comparison, wealthy homeowners' more expensive houses partly reflect a discretionary investment. The owner might have bought a basic house, one equivalent to that of the ordinary homeowner, and invested the rest in stocks or bonds. Viewing more expensive houses in this fashion justifies a bifurcated approach to the taxation of gain upon the sale of a principal residence.

Congress should replace the $250,000–$500,000 exclusion with a provision that divides the value of a house into a *basic value* and a *discretionary value*. Every homeowner should be protected from tax on inflationary ("nominal") gains up to a basic value (as set by Congress) of her principal residence. Gains on the discretionary value—the portion that should be equated to investments in stocks and bonds—should not be protected from inflation as long as inflationary gains on stocks and bonds continue to be taxed.

For the sake of illustration, let us assume that Congress sets the value of a basic house at $200,000, which is about 25 percent above the median value of houses nationally. (Because basic house costs vary greatly, Congress might establish different values for a basic house depending on the location of the house, just as it establishes different business travel allowances depending on the place of travel; such variations, however, would make the rules more complex.) Let us also assume a current and past inflation rate of 3 percent. Thus the basic house is rising in value, because of inflation, at the rate of about $6,000 (3 percent of $200,000) per year. For transition to the new law, Congress might allow everyone who sells her principal residence this year to add to her actual house cost $6,000 for every year that she has owned the house. In future years, the $6,000 annual adjustment would be adjusted for inflation according to tables that accompany tax-return materials. For example, if you bought your house this year and sell it in 10 years, the table would tell you exactly how much to add to the cost basis of your house. Thus the ordinary house value would be exempt from tax on inflationary gains; the excess value would not.[41]

These measures would make the laws more complicated than they are today, but I believe that the current laws are unfair and do not make economic sense.

This is an example, therefore, where the goal of achieving a fair and economically sound tax system conflicts with the goal of simplifying the tax laws.

Tax Values

By enacting these reforms, Congress would advance a number of values that would serve the public's best interests. It would tailor the tax subsidies more closely to standards of need. It would promote the idea that increasing the number of homeowners is advantageous for individuals, their communities, and communities beyond. It also would reduce incentives to overinvest in one's personal residence, which should increase the availability and lower the cost of capital for alternative, more economically useful purposes, including investments in rental housing. As noted, however, achieving these goals may in some cases complicate the tax system.

Finally, assuming that Congress reduced total tax subsidies for homeownership, Congress could use the opportunity to reduce tax rates across the board. In all these ways, Congress would legislate more broadly from the principle that people ought to be taxed in accordance with their ability to pay.

11

The Troubling Shortfalls and Excesses of Tax-Subsidized Pension Plans

Cessation of work is not accompanied by cessation of expenses.
—Cato the Elder (2nd century B.C.)

Our Inadequate Personal Savings * Tax Relief for Pension Plans * Government's Revenue Losses from Subsidizing Pension Plans * Employers Who Adopt Pension Plans * Employees Who Participate in Pension Plans * Demographics of Tax Expenditures for Pension Plans * An Overview: Why Pension Plans Have Fallen So Short * The Skewed Results: Rules for Participation and Benefits * Excessive Complexity of Pension Plans * Pensions and Net National Savings * The Case for Deferring the Tax on Pension-Plan Deferrals Under a Normal Tax * Recommendations

A massive financial crisis is building in this country: Too few of us have saved enough for retirement. Worse still, we refuse to take the matter seriously.

For the past 25 years, Congress has hoped that employer-sponsored retirement plans (called *pension plans*, for simplicity) would overcome much of the savings gap for the typical worker. But pension plans largely have failed this expectation. They are likely to fail in the future. Too few typical workers ever participate in a plan. When they do, too often their accounts are modest. As economist Eugene Steuerle has observed, "It appears that at least

one-half of the workforce will be without significant private retirement benefits as we move well into the next century."[1]

In contrast, most middle- and upper-income workers can expect to receive
considerable benefits from pension plans, at considerable government expense
and with mixed economic benefit. Congress massively subsidizes pension
plans by allowing contributions to the plans and plan earnings to escape taxation until participants receive them. These tax concessions are intended to
stimulate workers' savings. Yet the evidence is uncertain as to whether pension
plans increase personal savings of plan participants because once they participate in a plan, participants may decrease other forms of savings. If we assume,
however, that pension plans increase participants' overall personal savings,
pension plans might not contribute meaningfully to **national savings** (the
sum of public and private savings): Any increase in participants' personal savings may come close to approximating the government's associated revenue
losses from the income tax relief for pension plans and from exempting most
plan contributions and all plan distributions from Social Security taxes.

Like the mortgage-interest deduction, tax subsidies for pension plans have
enormous political support. To its credit, Congress frequently has attempted,
by a range of reforms, to extend the reach of pension plans to a much larger
percentage of ordinary workers. Yet the laws and outcomes remain distinctly
flawed. Very little of the tax subsidies for pension plans benefits workers who
need the assistance most. Furthermore, the government's enormous revenue
losses from the subsidies limit its ability to provide new forms of retirement assistance that could be more fairly distributed among the workforce.

In light of these problems, Congress should adopt reforms to try to
broaden participation by and benefits of ordinary workers. It also should
stop subsidizing contributions and benefits for highly compensated workers
beyond a basic retirement amount that it believes is reasonable for the average worker. Subsidizing much higher retirement benefits for these workers is
unlikely to increase national savings and cannot be justified as a matter of social policy any more than Congress can justify subsidizing expensive health
insurance policies and expensive personal residences. If these suggested reforms are unacceptable, or if they fail to produce adequate results for most ordinary workers, Congress should consider making pension plans pay their way,
as discussed at the end of this chapter.

Our Inadequate Personal Savings

A 1995 survey by the Employees Benefit Research Institute of Washington,
D.C., found that 84 percent of workers "believe most Americans do not save
enough money to live comfortably throughout retirement," yet only 35 percent of workers who had saved something for retirement "said they have tried
to determine how much they will need to save by the time they retire."[2] Most
will need to save a great deal more than they are saving currently.

A 1997 study for Merrill Lynch by economist B. Douglas Bernheim concluded that baby boomers—the 76 million Americans born between 1946 and 1964—ought to *nearly triple* their rate of saving, on average, if they wish to retire at age 65 and maintain their standard of living. Bernheim added that his study "probably underestimates the problem of retirement savings" because he assumed, for purposes of his study, that Social Security benefits will not diminish. Critics of his study note that it ignored the financial value of baby boomers' homes, many of which have substantial value. If these homes were heavily refinanced, rented, or sold when the owners retired, the savings rates of baby boomers might be about 80 percent of what they need.[3] But most people, if they have dreamed the American dream of retiring in comfort and dignity, do not have in mind being forced to take out large mortgages on their homes or rent out rooms to make ends meet or sell their homes and become renters.

> *Baby boomers—the 76 million Americans born between 1946 and 1964—may need to save far more than they are if they wish to retire at age 65 and maintain their standard of living.*

The Risk of Lower Social Security Benefits

When considering their retirement needs, young and middle-aged workers no longer prudently may assume that their Social Security retirement benefits will be the same as provided under current law. Beginning in about 35 years, the Social Security trust fund is expected to be exhausted, and Social Security taxes collected thereafter will be inadequate to fund benefits fully. To mitigate the shortfall, policymakers are considering a range of strategies: raising Social Security taxes on workers; allowing a portion of the trust funds, currently invested solely in U.S. government securities, to be invested in the stock market in order to increase the rate of return; privatizing Social Security; and adopting some form of national sales tax to supplement or replace the Social Security tax. None of these offers a quick fix. Each alternative invites its own set of problems. For example, although the opportunity to invest funds in the stock market seems promising in light of the bull market of recent years, seasoned analysts remind us, as we witnessed in 2000, that the stock market guarantees nothing. Periods of stock market feasting often have been followed by periods of famine.

To summarize, solutions to the future Social Security shortfall may be pain free, but workers ought to anticipate otherwise. Their Social Security retirement benefits may be curtailed, taxed more, or both. Congress already has extended the age by which workers are entitled to their full retirement benefits; by the year 2022, a worker will become eligible to receive full benefits only if he has reached the age of 67.

Current Household Savings Data

Even if we assume no reduction of Social Security benefits, at least *half* of this country's civilian workers of 120 million still need to make major changes in their savings patterns if they wish to maintain their standard of living when they retire. Evidence of the dangerously low level of savings by baby boomers was evident in wealth data accumulated by the U.S. Census Bureau for 1993, the most recent year that it published such data. Half of all married-couple households led by people age 35 to 54 owned net assets (assets minus liabilities) worth less than $18,000, excluding their house, corporate retirement plan accounts, and the cash value of insurance policies. Included in the $18,000 were motor vehicles; business properties; and financial assets owned personally such as cash, stocks and bonds, individual retirement accounts, and self-employment, or **Keogh**, retirement accounts. Households headed by a single male averaged less than $7,000 of such net assets; the figure was less than $3,000 if the household was headed by a single female.

> *At least half of this country's civilian workers need to make major changes in their savings patterns if they wish to maintain their standard of living when they retire.*

Net asset figures for households headed by someone 55 to 64 years old were little better. Married couples averaged about $44,000 in such net assets, male-headed households averaged about $11,000, and female-headed households averaged about $7,000.[4] None of these sums can produce much retirement income, and some of the assets such as motor vehicles will produce none. As we will examine shortly, including corporate retirement plan accounts in the net asset figures would have made little or no difference for the majority of these households. Let it suffice here to say that in 1995, according to the *Survey of Current Finances*, prepared by staff of the Federal Reserve Board, the median net worth of households headed by someone 55 to 64 years old was only $111,000, *including* the value of their houses, the cash value of their insurance policies, and most retirement plan accounts.[5]

The picture may be somewhat rosier in recent years because of the booming stock market. But flat or declining real wages for many members of the workforce have been accompanied by the megatrend of corporate America toward downsizing, often after a merger and acquisition has made many jobs expendable. Though the national unemployment rate has been steadily declining and today nears historic lows, millions of workers have lost jobs with corporations that historically provided good pay, job security,

> *In 1995, the median net worth of households headed by someone 55 to 64 years old was only $111,000, including the value of their houses, the cash value of their insurance policies, and most retirement plan accounts.*

and retirement plans. Many baby boomers who have been laid off have been forced to spend their savings while they seek new employment. When they have gotten a new job, often their new employers do not offer a retirement plan or they are hired as independent contractors rather than as employees and are ineligible for their employer's retirement plan even if one exists. If independent contractors, they may adopt their own pension plan. Alternatively, anyone not covered by a pension plan may contribute to an individual retirement account. Workers strapped for cash rarely do.

Our Savings Needs for Retirement

The stark reality is that most workers need to save a portion of every paycheck. For each year that they delay, the portion grows geometrically. Consider Joseph Renard, 35, who earns $30,000 working for a political consulting firm in Minneapolis that does not have a pension plan. Joseph has no personal savings. His goal is to retire at age 65 without reducing his standard of living, which he has been advised typically requires income equal to at least 70 percent of his annual earnings before retirement. Joseph assumes, perhaps conservatively, that Social Security will cover about 20 percent of his needs. Without a pension plan, he must make up the remaining amount through his own savings. According to a T. Rowe Price Associates study, Joseph must save 10 percent of each paycheck before taxes. If he does not begin saving until he is 40, he then must save 15 percent; if he waits until he is 45, he must save 22 percent.[6]

We are left with the inescapable conclusion that if a middle-class baby boomer's savings and retirement plan accumulations are meager by age 40 to 45, they likely will be inadequate by the time of retirement. Furthermore, the 70 percent formula assumes that, once retired, we will consume less. Maybe so: We probably have paid off the mortgage on our house; we will be covered by Medicare; we no longer will have work-related expenses; and our retirement income will not be subject to Social Security and Medicare taxes. However, with more leisure time, we may travel and otherwise consume more. Most important, because of advances in health care, we will outlive every generation that has gone before us; and we will need personal care for more years than did earlier generations. Whether in nursing homes or at home, such care can be staggeringly expensive. The 70 percent formula takes little of these costs into account.

In 1996, 40 percent of people 65 or older received less than $11,200 of cash income.

If baby boomers need a wake-up call about their future, they need look only at today's retirees. In 1996, according to the Social Security Administration's data on income quintiles of people 65 and over, 40 percent of the elderly received less than $11,200 of cash income. The bottom 20 percent received less than $7,200. These figures count cash income from all sources—wages, welfare, Social Security, pensions, and investment returns. On average, the bottom 40 percent of the elderly received about 80 percent of their income from Social Security. Less than 4 percent came from private pensions,[7] though in some cases retirees have already cashed in their pension savings. What will happen to future generations in the bottom 40 percent if Social Security benefits are cut or further delayed?

Our Culture of Consumption

The dramatic shortfall of retirement income for so many Americans can be explained in part by circumstances they cannot control. But Americans also must take responsibility for what they can control—their seemingly insatiable appetite to consume and their growing willingness to borrow in order to feed their appetite. Consumption has become our national pastime, the enclosed shopping mall America's neighborhood playground.

The flip side of a workforce willing to buy anything is a society that refuses to acknowledge the consequences of not saving—both personally and nationally. Increasing our savings will help the economy, which for most of us is a form of self-help in the long run. As summarized by the nonpartisan Competitiveness Policy Council, "Saving a greater proportion of current income will make more capital available for investment. By increasing the share of investment . . . *and* by shifting more investment into activities with high productivity growth, . . . Americans can earn higher incomes in the future. In turn, higher incomes will enable individuals to consume more, in absolute terms, than they do today."[8]

Our federal government shares responsibility for our consumption behavior. Only during World War II has it mounted a consistent campaign urging Americans to save. Buying war bonds became our patriotic duty. We rallied at the opportunity for good citizenship; and in lending the government money, we saved. Ever since, the government has allowed the consumption craze to take hold without effectively extolling the virtues of adopting a balanced program of saving.

Understanding the Importance of Compound Interest

Reforming the tax laws can help; but to turn our habit of conspicuous consumption around, we need nothing short of a cultural revolution. "Just save it!" must become as compelling as Nike's "Just do it!" Jointly, our government and schools must show the way. The government might begin by explaining to the public, as all schools should teach, the simple principle of **compound interest**. Compounding interest means that interest is earned on interest, that new earnings are earned on prior earnings. If you earn 5 percent on your $100 savings account this year, and you reinvest the entire

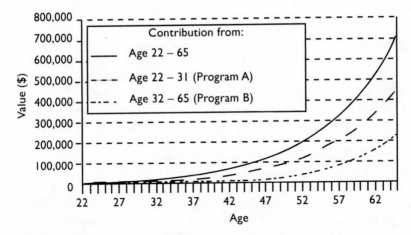

FIGURE 11.1   Value of IRA Accounts: Contribution of $1,000 per Year, Earning
10 Percent Compound Interest Each Year
SOURCE: Author's computations.

$105, you will earn interest on the original $100 plus interest on $5 (interest on interest) next year. The growth is small and unexciting at first. Over the long run, it is magical.

Margaret Field of Chicago, 22 and fresh out of college, has just begun employment as a litigation aide in the law firm of Elwood and Curtis. She will receive a salary of $18,000 plus health insurance benefits. If she makes contributions of $1,000 each year for 44 years to an individual retirement account that compounds at 8 percent per annum, her *$44,000* of contributions would be worth *$357,000* by the time she is 65. As seen in Figure 11.1, if her IRA compounds at 10 percent per year (about the historic yield of publicly traded common stocks), her IRA would amount to *$718,000.*

The key is to begin an aggressive savings program when young. For example, Margaret might choose Program A—investing $1,000 per year in an IRA for 10 years, stopping at age 31, and allowing the fund simply to grow until she is 65. Alternatively, she might begin her $1,000 per year savings program at age 32 and continue it until she is 65 (Program B). She should know that by age 65, her IRA will be 45 percent larger under Program A ($448,000) than under Program B ($245,000), assuming both accounts earn the same rate of return (see Figure 11.1).

Of course, the ordinary worker cannot afford to set aside $1,000 at age 22, but the mathematics of compound interest emphasize the critical importance of beginning and adhering to a savings program—whatever the amount—at an early age. As you will see, the value of compound interest is an important part of the story of employer-sponsored retirement plans.

Tax Relief for Pension Plans

For its part, the government encourages the adoption of pension plans through four interrelated tax laws. *First,* to protect employers from being taxed on the income they contribute, Congress allows employers to deduct their contributions. *Second,* pension trusts, which are separate legal entities and receive, invest, and distribute pension funds, are tax exempt and thus are not taxed on the contributions or their earnings. *Third,* with the exception of **401(k) plans** and SIMPLE IRAs, neither employers nor employees are subject to Social Security taxes on contributions to the trusts; and all trust distributions are exempt from Social Security taxes. In the case of 401(k) plans and SIMPLE IRAs, Social Security taxes apply to payroll deductions—that is, amounts contributed out of a participant's salary—but not to additional amounts contributed by employers. *Fourth,* the tax on contributions and their earnings is deferred until participants receive their pensions.

Readers might ask: If the income tax ultimately is paid, why is the government worse off than if it collected the tax currently? The answer lies in the *time value of money.* Taxes in hand are worth more to the government than taxes paid in the future because the government does not collect interest on the deferred taxes. In effect, participants receive an interest-free loan from the government on the taxes they ultimately must pay.

Consider Chris Lyle, who is hypothetically entitled to an additional $10,000 this year that would be subject to the 36 percent marginal tax bracket if paid directly to him; in such case, he would owe $3,600 in taxes, leaving $6,400 to invest. Alternatively, he could elect to have the $10,000 added to his pension plan and then distributed to him after one year. With $10,000 in the pension plan, he will have his $6,400 plus the government's $3,600 to invest for the year. Let us assume he will earn 10 percent interest on his money. In both cases, by the end of the year, he will have earned $640 on the $6,400, and he will pay the tax on it. In the pension example, however, he also will have earned $360 on the government's $3,600. He then will pay the $3,600 to the government; but instead of paying the government the full $360 earned on its $3,600, he will pay only the 36 percent tax on the $360, or $130. Chris will keep the remaining $230. Thus by deferring the tax for only one year, Chris comes out $230 ahead, the government $230 behind. Chris's benefit and the government's loss from the tax deferral grows geometrically as the deferral is prolonged.

Government's Revenue Losses from Subsidizing Pension Plans

The government would not lose revenue in a particular year on the taxes it defers on pension accumulations if the total taxes deferred did not exceed the total tax collections on all current pension distributions. But pension accumulations exceed pension distributions. This imbalance, which is vast and has been growing for decades, is projected to continue to grow well into the twenty-first century. The government's resulting tax losses—the tax expenditures for pension plans—are estimated at *$81 billion* in *2000* and *$442 billion* from *2000 through 2004*.[9] During this period, the exemption for Social Security taxes ought to add over $250 billion to that cost.[10] In short, the relief from income taxes and Social Security taxes afforded pension plans is likely to cost the government close to *$700 billion* over these five years.

> *Over the next five years, the government stands to lose in excess of $600* billion *by deferring all pension-plan contributions and earnings from income tax and exempting most contributions and all distributions from Social Security tax.*

At a minimum, we can expect this enormous loss to keep income and Social Security tax rates higher than they otherwise would be. Because these higher rates are paid by all workers, including those who do not participate in pension plans, we would like to believe that pension plans play a major role in resolving the financial dilemma of retirement for most members of the workforce, particularly because pension plans owned nearly *8 trillion* of assets at the end of 1998.[11] But for many reasons, pension plans have never played that role, and they are unlikely to do so in the future.

Employers Who Adopt Pension Plans

Pension plans fail to meet most retirees' needs primarily because private-sector employers are not required to offer plans, and most opt out. Though large employers usually offer a plan, most small employers—and most employers are small—do not. They cannot afford pension plans; the plans seem too complicated to administer; management lacks knowledge of plans that might make sense for the firm; or employees prefer to receive any extra money as wages. Many employers, however, fail to see such plans as part of a fundamental compact workers are entitled to expect: Workers have pension plans, along with decent working conditions and pay, in exchange for which the employer is entitled to expect good work.

No data exist about the number of employers who adopt plans today or in recent years. But in 1985, only about 23 percent of private employers had adopted a plan; the percentage probably is not much different today.[12] Some indication of the discrepancy of coverage between large employers and small ones can be seen in the case of 401(k) plans. In 1993, 56 percent of workers in companies with 1,000 or more employees were offered 401(k) plans; the figure was only 5 percent for companies with fewer than 10 workers.[13]

As we think about pension-plan tax subsidies, we should keep in mind that employees of large companies, on average, receive higher pay and are offered a substantial package of other benefits—health insurance, child care, employee training and education, leave for sickness or other reasons, on-site fitness centers—that are far more extensive than what the typical small company even contemplates. In other words, employees of large firms are disproportionately advantaged by their employment circumstances *before* taking into account their disproportionately high share of pension-plan tax subsidies. As a Labor Department study pointed out, people more likely to be employed by smaller employers "include young workers, old workers, minorities (particularly Hispanics), less-educated workers (especially with less than 12 years of schooling), . . . single workers, . . . [workers who] are less likely to be covered by a union contract and are more likely to be part-time, lower-wage workers and . . . [workers who] more frequently change jobs."[14]

These more vulnerable workers have the greatest difficulty saving for retirement and could use income supplements when they retire, such as an amount equal to the lifetime pension-plan tax subsidy for the typical plan participant. But because of the narrow view that Congress appears to have about welfare, it sends money (and sparingly, at that) only to the elderly who are officially poor. That payment is labeled welfare; by contrast, Congress does not characterize as welfare its generous tax subsidies for pension plans that supplement workers' incomes when they are elderly, though few of these workers are expected to be officially poor at retirement. Viewing these subsidies differently would require Congress to examine more carefully its own, substantial pension program (discussed later).

Spencer Rich of the *Washington Post* wrote about one vulnerable worker several years ago. Teena West began working in Chicago at the age of 14. Over the next 50 years, she worked as a secretary, a clerk, a bookkeeper, and a credit manager for about 20 employers. "Yet in all these jobs," Rich reported, "with only one year off for childbearing, West earned just one small pension." In 1996, the pension "pays her $381 a month, which, combined with the $800 she gets from Social Security, is all the 70-year-old woman has to show for her lifetime of work."[15]

Employees Who Participate in Pension Plans

An assortment of government data establishes that pension plans bypass or marginalize a great many workers. The most recent government data arise from complementary studies by the Department of Labor on the workforce for 1993 and 1994. Forty-nine percent of all workers (public and private, part time and full time) participated in a plan. These figures were skewed upward by a participation rate of 77 percent for workers in the public sector, where virtually every employer offers a pension plan. The participation rate for the private sector, which employs about 83 percent of all workers, was only 43 percent.[16]

Plan participation rates also differ widely between full-time and part-time employees. Part-time employees, who often must split their time between work and caring for children at home or between two jobs, are classified in government pension statistics as working less than 35 hours per week. In 1993, a mere 12 percent of part-time employees in the private sector participated in a plan, compared with 50 percent of full-time employees. The much lower rate for part-time employees is largely explainable by plan eligibility barriers that Congress allows employers to impose. Yet Congress knows that few part-time workers, who represent about 18 percent of the private-sector workforce, have resources of their own to save for retirement. Equally troubling are recent studies suggesting that participation rates of younger and less-educated workers, full time as well as part time, have declined compared with participation rates 10 or 15 years ago.[17]

> *In 1993, 12 percent of part-time employees—those working under 35 hours per week—in the private sector participated in a plan, compared to 50 percent of full-time employees.*

More encouraging data are suggested by a study that sampled households with one or more members in the workforce between the ages of 21 and 55 (the government figures above were for individual workers ages 16 to 65). Nearly 62 percent of these households in 1993 had one or more members covered by a pension plan.[18] But such data must be read in conjunction with other data. In 1994, for example, only 40 percent of workers and retirees ages 65 and over formerly employed in a private-sector job were receiving, had received, or expected to receive a pension.[19] This discrepancy underscores the importance of distinguishing data on *coverage,* which counts employees included in a pension plan, from data on *nonforfeitable* pension benefits of covered participants, as explained shortly. Twenty-three percent of employees in 1994 who participated in a former employer's pension plan reported they did not expect to receive any benefits.[20]

Even the lucky ones—the elderly who receive pensions—typically receive extremely modest amounts. Consider these statistics for 1996 compiled by the Social Security Administration (SSA) about the population 65 and older, whom the SSA divides into quintiles based on income levels. Only 2.8 percent of those in the bottom quintile—the bottom 20 percent—received a pension or annuity; their median payment for the year was $1,473. Only 11.5 percent in the next quintile received a private pension or annuity; their median annual pension was only $1,897. The figures improved for the middle-income quintile: Twenty-four percent received a pension or annuity with a median annual payment of

> *In 1995, of the population 65 and older, only 2.8 percent of those in the bottom income quintile and only 11.5 percent of those in the next income quintile received a private pension or annuity.*

$3,690. A slightly higher percentage of the top quintile—28.7 percent—received private pension or annuity payments, and, most important, their median annual payment amounted to $11,776.[21]

Policymakers also must be concerned that contributions by private employers to pension plans have declined as a percentage of workers' compensation. In 1986, the percentage was 3.8. In 1990, it had fallen to 3.0, the same as in 1998.[22] Part of the decline can be explained by the rising rates of return achieved by pension plans, which reduced the amount employers had to contribute to certain plans. The trend also reflects a decline in pension coverage largely resulting from the rising popularity of 401(k) plans. Because contributions are voluntary and reduce a worker's salary, 401(k) plans have been popular with workers who can afford to contribute some of their salary. Few low- and moderate-income workers can afford to participate. Previously, at least some of them benefited from a traditional pension plan to which their employer contributed.

Demographics of Tax Expenditures for Pension Plans

Great disparities among income groups in the *distribution of pensions* are accompanied by far greater disparities among income groups in the *distribution of tax expenditures* for pension plans. For this analysis, we must turn to private research. Although pension-plan tax expenditures always have been the largest or one of the largest of all tax expenditures tracked by Congress, the Joint Committee on Taxation never has allocated pension-plan tax expenditures among income classes. Congress never has requested it to, quite possibly because of what the data tell.

The most recent data, produced by the Employee Benefit Research Institute for the year 1992, involve pension-plan tax expenditures amounting to $56.5 billion. Only 1.4 percent of the tax savings was for people in the bottom 41 percent—people with under $20,000 of income. Nearly 63 percent of the tax savings was for the top 21 percent—people with $50,000 or more of income. Over 20 percent of the tax savings was for the top 4 percent—people with $100,000 or more of income (see Table 11.1).

The commanding size of pension assets, their revenue drain, and their failure to distribute the rewards sufficiently among a high percentage of the ordinary workforce invite voters to question the rules that produce these results, and to consider alternatives.

An Overview: Why Pension Plans Have Fallen So Short

With only modest success, Congress has tried numerous times and ways to broaden workers' pension-plan participation and benefits. The primary obstacle is that pension plans always have been, and probably always will be, optional in the private sector because of fierce objections by smaller employ-

TABLE 11.1 Distribution of $56.5 Billion of Tax Expenditures for Employer-Based Pension Plans, by Income Class, 1992

Income Class[a] ($)	Percentage of All Tax Returns	Percentage of Tax Expenditures	Amount of All Tax Expenditures ($billions)
Less than 10,000	19.7	0.0	.335
10,000–19,999	21.3	1.4	.775
20,000–29,999	16.7	7.1	4.000
30,000–49,999	21.2	28.1	15.870
50,000–99,999	17.2	42.8	24.210
100,000–199,999	3.0	13.4	7.550
200,000–	1.0	6.7	3.760
Total	100.0	100.0	56.500

[a]As used by EBRI, "income" means AGI plus tax-exempt interest, employer contributions for health plans and life insurance, inside buildup on life insurance, workers' compensation, nontaxable Social Security benefits, deductible contributions to individual retirement accounts, and several other items.
SOURCE: Employee Benefit Research Institute, *Pension Tax Expenditures: Are They Worth the Cost?* February 1993, no. 134, 14, table 7.

ers to any government mandate.[23] Unless many more employers adopt pension plans, employee participation rates will remain disturbingly low.

Terms of the plans themselves, however, must share a considerable portion of the blame. To achieve favorable tax advantages, pension plans must must satisfy rules of the income tax code and regulations. Many of these rules protect the ordinary worker. Nonetheless, employers may exclude from their plans many employees and may adopt provisions that cause participants to forfeit benefits, including employees who are terminated without cause, who often can least afford to lose their pensions. Employers also may adopt formulas that ensure extremely high benefits for a firm's most valued employees.

From an employer's perspective, giving pensions only to full-time, longer-term employees and giving very large pensions to key employees may make good business sense. The strategy of granting tax relief for pension plans at great government expense must be based, however, on the best interest of employers and employees generally, not selectively on the best interest of a minority of employers who tend to be large, successful enterprises.

Congress has a legitimate dilemma. As it has broadened the rights of rank-and-file workers to benefit from pension plans and has expanded reporting requirements for plans to ensure their compliance, many businesses have terminated their pension plans, unwilling to assume the additional costs or the expanded administrative responsibilities. Businesses also have turned to plans that require smaller employer contributions: The major growth in pension plans over the past decades has been in 401(k) plans, which allow employees to contribute a portion of their wages. Although employers also may contribute their own funds, they generally view 401(k) plans as opportunities to reduce the overall level of their pension contributions. In short, if Congress experiments with more stringent pension rules that promote participation by ordinary workers, accelerate vesting schedules, and restrict benefit levels for key employees, many firms may stop offering pension plans or reduce their own contributions. But Congress should experiment. Current rules and outcomes insufficiently benefit ordinary workers to justify the special tax concessions for pension plans.

> *The strategy of granting tax relief for pension plans at great government expense must be based on the best interest of employers and employees generally, not selectively on the best interest of a minority of employers who tend to be large, successful enterprises.*

The Skewed Results: Rules for Participation and Benefits

Confronted by the low rate of rank-and-file participation in pension plans, Congress in the 1940s began its trek to establish rules about plan eligibility and benefits.[24] Focused on prohibiting excessive discrimination in favor of highly compensated employees rather than on ensuring broad participation and benefits for rank-and-file members, the rules have only tempered the Darwinian quality of plans. The fittest—those with the highest pay and longevity—continue to reap disproportionately great rewards.

Rules Limiting Participation

Employers may exclude all employees who are seasonal, who are younger than 21, who work less than 1,000 hours per year (which is about 20 hours per week), or who have not yet been employed at least one year. Most plans adopt all of these exclusions.[25] (Employers may require two years of employment to become eligible; they rarely do because none of the employee's pension can then be forfeited.) In addition, employers often may exclude large numbers of the remaining employees under classifications too complicated to explore here. Each of the rules limiting participation represents a concession by Congress to induce employers to provide pension plans for their employees.

For long-term employees who work less than 20 hours per week, such as Gloria Royal during her child-rearing years, participation rates are likely below 1 percent. As a single parent, Gloria worked 15 hours a week, or about 700 hours per year, for a national food chain over a period of 10 years while she raised her son, Topher. Never sick, willing to pitch in if others were ill, and always at work on time, she received high marks in annual reviews. But Gloria never participated in the company's pension plan because she could not satisfy the requirement that she work at least 1,000 hours during the year. If the government is to continue to subsidize substantial pensions for other workers, it must insist that pension plans cover workers such as Gloria who have little chance of living comfortably in retirement without a pension.

For long-term employees who work less than 20 hours per week, plan participation rates are likely to fall below 1 percent.

Rules Governing Forfeitures

Employers always can make pension accounts nonforfeitable. (Amounts that cannot be forfeited are deemed *vested*.) Few employers ever do so. Most maximize pension forfeitures. Among Congress's past failures in overseeing pension-plan policies, none is as glaring as its failure to protect participants adequately from this risk of forfeiture.

After pension plans first were recognized by the tax laws in 1921, over half a century passed before Congress limited the number of years during which employees could forfeit their pensions. Forfeitures occurred in many plans even for people who had been employed 30 or 40 years. The Employment Retirement Security Act of 1974 (ERISA) drastically changed the rules. A participant's account might vest gradually over a 15-year period, after which his pension became forever fully vested. The alternative was a do-or-die schedule, appropriately referred to as *cliff vesting*. A participant's entire pension was forfeited if his employment terminated before he performed 10 years of service; the pension figuratively fell over the cliff. After 10 years, his pension was fully vested.

Though an improvement from the lawless past, ERISA vesting rules still produced too many draconian results. Over time, Congress reined them in. Today, for the great majority of private plans, the graduated vesting period for employer contributions may extend up to six or seven (rather than 15) years, and the cliff vesting period may extend up to five (rather than 10) years. Contributions made by employees to 401(k) plans, based on reductions in their salaries, never can be forfeited.

Forfeitures still hurt workers badly, often inflicting the greatest pain on the most vulnerable employees. Young workers and unskilled workers are unlikely to stay in their first jobs for five years. Yet we know, from the teachings of compound interest, that savings accumulated while workers are young can be crucial to their retirement security. Furthermore, millions of workers at all levels of the employment ladder change jobs from time to time throughout their working careers. They may have to forfeit all or part of their pensions whether their employment terminates voluntarily or involuntarily, *even if they are fired without cause.*

Plan participants can forfeit all or part of their pensions whether their employment terminates voluntarily or involuntarily, even if fired without cause.

Take Marco Landly. Marco was hired in 1994 as a janitor by Bali Laboratory, Inc. of Fairfax, Virginia. He would be entitled to join Bali's pension plan in 1995. Bali was obligated to contribute 4 percent of Marco's salary each year. A colorful graph on the plan's brochure charted the growth of a dollar per year until a worker reached the normal retirement age of 65. When, however, in the fall of 1998, Bali decided to contract out all of its janitorial services and fired the entire maintenance staff, Marco's pension fell off the cliff.

One argument to justify pension forfeitures is that employees are less productive in their early years; and one way for an employer to compensate them initially at a higher level than they may be worth is through contributions to pension plans that they will become entitled to if they stay but will lose if they leave. Pension-plan forfeiture rules thereby assist employers to invest in human capital—their employees.[26] However true—many would dispute that most entry-level jobs in the market today are overcompensated—the public policy issues are threefold: Should the government subsidize employers' costs in such cases? If so, should the subsidy be through the tax laws? If so, should the subsidy be through pension-plan forfeitures? In such case, the only employers who are subsidized are the minority who adopt pension plans, and the largest subsidies are for the largest companies.

These observations suggest that subsidizing employers' investment in entry-level employees by allowing five-year cliff vesting or vesting over six or seven years is a highly inefficient choice by the government to accomplish its objective, assuming the government should be involved in the first place. And the harm to these workers is considerable. Most workers must begin to accumulate savings early in their employment years in order to save adequately for retirement. They cannot afford *any* forfeitures, let alone major ones that can occur under today's typical vesting schedules. Unless Congress adopts pension reforms that result in the coverage of a significant majority of ordinary workers whose pension accumulations vest far more quickly, most workers would be better off if Congress eliminated all tax subsidies for pension plans and lowered tax rates across the board.

Rules Setting Maximum Contributions or Benefits

Pension contributions may be tiny or enormous. Outside limits depend on whether contributions are to a defined *contribution* plan or to a defined *benefit* plan. In all cases, Congress prohibits contribution or benefit formulas that "discriminate in favor of highly compensated employees." Plans are not deemed to engage in discriminatory policies, however, if contributions or benefits are *in proportion to compensation.* In 2000, compensation up to $170,000 could be taken into account for determining contributions and applying nondiscrimination rules. Because the compensation ceiling is so high, most of the government's tax subsidies for pension plans redound to the benefit of middle- and upper-income participants, the very class of workers who least need government assistance in order to prepare for retirement.

As the words suggest, a defined contribution plan defines what the employer *must* or *may* contribute to the plan each year. Participants' accounts rise and fall with the value of plan investments. No pension is guaranteed. At normal retirement, a participant is entitled to the value of his account, whatever it might be. Almost always the contribution is a percentage of participants' compensation. The percentage will be identical for every participant except for plans that take Social Security taxes into account (as subsequently explained) or contribute more for older participants because of the shorter time remaining to fund for their retirement. In other words, with these exceptions, a plan cannot, for example, contribute 10 percent of an executive's compensation and only 5 percent of a secretary's. Because plans may take into account compensation as high as $170,000, however, a contribution formula of 10 percent of participants' compensation means the contribution will be $1,700 for an employee who earns $17,000 and $17,000 for an employee who earns $170,000.

By comparison, a defined benefit pension plan guarantees the annual benefit a participant will receive when he reaches normal retirement age, typically 65. The benefit is a fixed amount regardless of the plan's investment performance. A participant's benefit is defined as a percentage of his highest average wages, usually measured over any three consecutive years. For example, if the benefit equals 10 percent of the average of a participant's highest three years of wages and if such average is $35,000, the participant is entitled to $3,500 per year when he reaches age 65.

> *A defined benefit pension plan as of 2000 may provide an annual retirement benefit of $135,000 per year for as long as the employee lives if the average of his highest three years of wages is $135,000 or more.*

Unless a defined benefit pension plan takes into account Social Security taxes, its benefit formula must be identical for all participants.

To limit the government's revenue losses, Congress has established ceilings on annual contributions to defined contribution plans and on benefits from defined benefit plans. The ceilings, however, allow for enormous pension accumulations for well-compensated employees. The maximum annual contribution by an employer to a defined contribution pension plan in 2000 was the lesser of 25 percent of a participant's compensation or $30,000.[27] (The $30,000 is to be periodically adjusted for cost-of-living increases.) This means that if an employee's compensation is $120,000 or more, the employer may contribute $30,000 (25 percent x $120,000) to his account each year even if his account already is worth millions. The maximum annual benefit under a defined benefit pension plan can be as high as 100 percent of a participant's high average wages, subject to a dollar ceiling of $135,000 in 2000, which also is adjusted for cost-of-living increases. Thus, in 2000 a plan could provide an annual retirement benefit of $135,000 per year for as long as the employee lives if his highest three years of wages averaged $135,000 or more.

Policy Issues Arising from Contribution and Benefit Formulas and Limits

Everyone can agree to the reasonableness of prohibiting plans from adopting contribution or benefit percentages that unfairly discriminate in favor of higher-compensated workers. What remains at issue is the maximum contribution or benefit that should be allowed for them.

Consider Abby, Barbara, and Carol. They earn, respectively, $10,000, $40,000, and $120,000 as the sole employees of ABC Enterprises. Each participates in ABC's pension plan, which calls for contributions equal to 25 percent of each participant's wages. This year, ABC will contribute $2,500 for Abby, $10,000 for Barbara, and $30,000 for Carol. As seen in Table 11.2, the deferral of tax on Abby's $2,500 costs the government only $375 because Abby would have paid a tax of 15 percent on the $2,500 had it been deemed income to her. The deferral of tax on Barbara's $10,000 costs the government $2,800 because her marginal tax bracket is 28 percent. The government's revenue loss in Carol's case, however, is $11,880, because on the joint return she files with her husband, the $30,000 contribution for her avoids their marginal tax bracket of 39.6 percent. In short, although Carol's contribution is 12 times larger than Abby's because her salary is 12 times greater, the government's revenue loss is over 31 times greater for Carol's contribution than for Abby's.

People like Carol—executives of all kinds, doctors, lawyers, accountants, and others—can afford to set aside $30,000 tax free year after year, but can the government afford to give them such tax relief? The government's revenue loss for each Carol could reach over $1 million by the time she retires.

Consider a 30-year program that Carol begins when she is age 35. In Example A, she receives $30,000 each year as compensation, pays taxes on it at

TABLE 11.2 Federal Income Tax Savings from Proportional Contributions to a Pension Plan for Abby, Barbara, and Carol

Participant	Contribution ($)	Tax Bracket (%)	Tax Saving ($)	Percentage of Tax Savings
Abby	2,500	15.0	375	2.5
Barbara	10,000	28.0	2,800	18.5
Carol	30,000	39.6	11,880	79.0
Total	42,500	–	$15,055	100.0

SOURCE: Author's calculations.

her 39.6 percent marginal tax bracket, and invests the balance at a 10 percent pretax rate of return, on which she also pays taxes. At age 65, her investment account will be worth *$1.5 million,* all fully taxed.[28] In Example B, her employer contributes $30,000 to her pension account, which earns 10 percent per year. When she is 65, her account will be worth $5.4 million. If the entire $5.4 million is then distributed to her (though she could defer the distribution if she wished) and taxed at 39.6 percent, she would have *$3.3 million* left after taxes. The *difference of $1.8 million* over Example A theoretically would have be-

> *The government's revenue loss for each Carol could reach over $1 million by the time she retires.*

longed to the government had her pension account been taxed each year. In other words, the government's tax relief for Carol's pension made her $1.8 million richer and the government $1.8 million poorer.

The spectacle of the tax system subsidizing an executive's annual retirement benefit of as much as $135,000 through a defined benefit pension plan also is problematic. Why does Congress feel that it is an appropriate use of government resources to assure high-income, high-tax-bracket workers of a retirement at that level? Politics obviously plays a role: These people help finance campaigns. Self-interest also plays a role. If Congress lowered the ceiling on tax-qualified private pensions, it likely would have to reduce pensions for its own members. In 1998, according to the National Taxpayers Union Foundation, pensions of members of Congress who would retire that year included initial annual benefits as high as $98,694.[29]

Congress believes, however, that unless it subsidizes large pensions for key employees, many firms would elect to disband or sharply curtail their pension plans, which could hurt rank-and-file workers. Congress reasons that its rules mandating plan coverage of a certain percentage of rank-and-file workers redistributes them some meaningful portion of the employer's profits and Congress likes the idea that this redistribution is in the form of retirement savings.

History teaches that the overall redistribution has been modest at best. Economists generally believe that any pension contribution for rank-and file workers is reflected, at least over time, in lower wages or other benefits for these workers unless the minimum wage or market factors prevent the employer from playing such zero-sum games. Furthermore, most rank-and-file workers either do not participate in plans or receive very small benefits.

Skewing the Results Even Further: Integrating Pension Plans with Social Security

Incredibly, Congress does not believe that it has done enough for higher-income workers by subsidizing their pensions up to the levels so far discussed. To the contrary, Congress bestows special additional pension plan advantages on higher-income workers because, in its view, they are disadvantaged under Social Security. Why? Because they do not accrue Social Security benefits on their wages above the annually adjusted Social Security taxable wage base, which in 2000 was $76,200. But highly compensated workers are delighted to forgo the benefits because they are spared paying Social Security taxes on their wages above the taxable wage base. Indeed, they lobby vigorously to retain the cutoff because they believe, with good reason, that the Social Security taxes they save, plus the investment return on them, will far exceed any Social Security benefits they might accrue were they to pay Social Security taxes on all their wages.

Yet because of the Social Security cutoff, Congress allows pension plans to make contributions for wages above the Social Security wage base. Plans that adopt such a provision are called *integrated with Social Security*. For example, a defined contribution plan in 2000 that contributed 10 percent of each participant's wages up to $170,000 could contribute an additional 5.7 percent of wages between $76,200 and $170,000. Each participant who earned $170,000 or more received an additional contribution of *$5,347*. Participants who earned less than $76,200 received nothing extra.

> Congress could prohibit plan integration, subject all wages to Social Security taxes, and pay modest additional retirement benefits on these higher levels of wages. These reforms would have the net effect of increasing Social Security trust funds and raising tax revenue.

To summarize, plan integration with Social Security further magnifies the substantial tilt of the pension system in favor of higher-income workers and is costly to the government. It should be eliminated. If Congress felt that higher-income workers then would be short-changed, it could subject all wages to Social Security taxes up to a much higher ceiling than the current wage base and pay additional retirement benefits, which would be modest, on these higher levels of wages consistent with current benefit formulas. These reforms would have the net effect of increasing Social Security trust funds and raising tax revenue. To be sure, highly compensated workers would much prefer just eliminating plan integration.

Excessive Complexity of Pension Plans

To enjoy tax-qualified status, pension plans must comply with several thousand pages of fine print spread through the Internal Revenue code, Treasury Department regulations, and Department of Labor laws and regulations. One is reminded of *King of Hearts,* in which, as World War I ends, unsuspecting British soldiers enter an abandoned French town that has been taken over by inmates of the local insane asylum who pose as respectable citizens. Meticulously crafted pension-plan rules have the trappings of respectability. On inspection, they reveal a system out of control. The interlocking and cross-referencing code sections and regulations are mind-boggling for all but a relative handful of experts. Employers also periodically must update their plans at considerable expense because of technical changes in the laws or regulations. These considerations discourage many employers from adopting pension plans even though banks, brokerage houses, and insurance companies offer preapproved plans without charge.

A great deal of the complexity exists because Congress has accommodated employers' desires to tailor plans to their individual circumstances. Each accommodation has bred multiple others. But like so much else in life, most employers would accommodate themselves to something far simpler if they had no other choice. That is why Congress should offer a limited number of prototype plans with limited options, all published by the Internal Revenue Service. Some employers would opt out altogether because none of the prototypes satisfied them, but few large employers would: Pension plans are too ingrained in their corporate culture. Also, many smaller employers, attracted by the simplicity and minimal costs, might opt in. An emphasis on prototype plans also would greatly reduce the IRS's responsibilities and costs for overseeing the pension-plan system.

In a modest way, Congress already has moved in this direction. For example, employers may adopt a simplified employee pension (SEP) as an alternative to a regular pension plan.[30] To have a SEP, an employer need only file a simple form that adopts the model SEP drafted by the IRS. Thereafter, SEPs require minimal administrative time and sophistication from employers. Still, SEPs have been adopted by a statistically insignificant number of employers. Many employers are unfamiliar with SEPs, and many resist them because nearly all employees must be covered and no contributions may be forfeited. Employers much prefer to adopt regular pension plans that exclude a great many employees and impose harsh forfeiture provi-

sions. If regular pension plans had to broaden their coverage and limit forfeitures, SEPs might become far more popular.

Pensions and Net National Savings

Given the historic failure of pension plans to provide adequately for rank-
and-file workers, the only justification for maintaining the existing program
of tax subsidies would be if pension plans significantly strengthened the
economy. Remarkably few economists have demonstrated interest in the
broad economic consequence of pension
plans beyond their impact on savings. For
example, their work has hardly explored
whether pension plans affect a worker's
productivity.[31] Economists have extensively examined, however, whether pension plans increase or decrease net national savings—the total of private and
government savings. A material increase
in net national savings could be expected
to strengthen the economy by providing

> *Given the historic failure of
> pension plans to provide
> adequately for rank-and-file
> workers, the only justification
> for maintaining the existing
> program of tax subsidies would
> be if pension plans significantly
> strengthened the economy.*

more capital for investment in new businesses, new equipment, research and
development, the creation of more jobs and, perhaps, better pay.

Pension-plan subsidies increase net national savings if any increase in personal savings they generate exceeds the government's revenue loss from subsidizing pension plans. If the increase in personal savings equals the government's revenue loss, no real change in net national savings occurs.
Participants (mainly middle- and upper-income workers) become richer, and
the government becomes correspondingly poorer.

The initial question is whether pension plans increase personal savings at
least to some extent. The answer depends on the relative pull of the *substitution* and *income effects*. Tax relief for pension plans increases the return from
savings. If the substitution effect holds, participants would view contributions to their pension accounts as an oppor-
tunity to save more, in which event they
would not decrease their nonpension savings by an equivalent amount. The tax deferral of pension-plan savings, however, allows a participant to save less annually to
meet his retirement savings goal (if he has
one) than he would have to save in a taxed,
nonpension account. If the income effect

> *Still inconclusive is whether
> participants set aside more
> for savings once they
> participate in pension plans,
> counting both their pension
> and personal savings.*

holds, he would reduce what he sets aside in his nonpension savings by the
amount of annual additions to his pension account.

For example, suppose your employer has just adopted a 401(k) plan that allows you to contribute up to $9,000 each year. Suppose further that you had anticipated having to save $12,000 each year in order to reach your retirement savings goal. You now realize that by contributing $9,000 to your 401(k) plan, you will end up with the same savings (taking into account the taxes you eventually will pay on distributions from the plan) than you would have had if you saved $12,000 per year personally. Assuming that you contribute $9,000 to the plan each year, will you continue to set aside $3,000 personally, which means that you will maintain your former rate of savings? Will you set aside more than $3,000, which means that you will have increased your rate of savings? Or will you set aside less than $3,000, knowing that you can reduce your nonpension savings by as much as $3,000 and still achieve your original savings goal?

Three leading economists, Alicia Munnell, Jane Gravelle, and William Gale, have reached some interesting conclusions. Munnell, writing in 1991 while senior vice president and director of research for the Federal Reserve Bank of Boston, suggested that one-third of pension saving represented new savings;[32] Gravelle, writing in 1994, concluded that pensions probably did not increase personal savings and may actually lower personal savings overall because of the income effect;[33] and Gale, writing in 1998, suggested that between 20 percent and 60 percent of pensions represent net additions to personal saving, but he warned that his figures may be high.[34]

If Gravelle is right, pensions clearly reduce national savings because of the revenue loss to the federal government from tax subsidies for pension plans. Munnell concluded that pensions probably had no impact on national savings because the increase in net personal savings from pensions probably approximated the government's revenue loss. Gale's figures allowed for a modest increase in national savings, perhaps 10 percent. To summarize, at this juncture, the case is unconvincing that pension plans materially increase national savings and thereby deserve to be subsidized at today's levels.

The Case for Deferring the Tax on Pension-Plan Deferrals Under a Normal Tax

Some tax experts object to the very premise that tax deferrals for pension accruals are tax preferences. These experts argue that, for several reasons, the deferrals fit within the government's own definition of a normal tax. They note that income under Haig-Simons exists only when it is measurable, and that measuring the present value of all defined benefit accounts on a consistent basis is difficult and likely would lead to very inconsistent results because of different approaches by actuaries. These experts also note that forfeitable pensions should not be counted as income.

Both points have merit but are solvable. If pension accounts become currently taxable, participants should be taxed only on annual increases in nonforfeitable amounts. (Participants also could deduct annual decreases of such amounts.) Defined benefit plan accumulations already must be valued annually; but to make the valuations consistent among different plans, Congress would have to require all actuaries to adopt uniform procedures and assumptions, and some of the more complicated features of defined benefit plans might have to be eliminated. In short, the problems, though complicated, can be solved even if not to everyone's satisfaction.[35]

Recommendations

Tax subsidies for pension plans deserve the same rigorous evaluation as direct subsidies for welfare programs. Whether or not you view the subsidies as welfare, they spare participants from being taxed currently on their vested pension accumulations, and they are massive. What does the tax relief buy?

Pension plans primarily buy better retirements for middle- and upper-income workers. At the same time, the huge revenue losses from exempting pension contributions and distributions from Social Security taxes and from deferring income tax collections impede the ability of Congress to reduce Social Security and income tax rates for all workers, and they severely limit other government programs that might help ordinary workers. Without clear evidence that the subsidies as currently distributed significantly increase national savings, they appear difficult to justify. Law school professor Louis Kaplow expressed the intellectual dilemma of pension-plan advocates some years ago. Writing in 1988 after reviewing each assumption that underlies endorsement of the system of retirement savings incentives, Kaplow concluded that "whatever the precise rationale or one's confidence in any particular step in the argument, it clearly takes quite a leap of faith to accept simultaneously the requisite combination of necessary conditions."[36]

Because the system is so vast and the consequences of abolishing the subsidies so serious, Congress should revise the rules one last time to see if employer-based pension plans deserve to be subsidized. The goals of the new rules should be to expand coverage, to reduce forfeitures, and to set much lower ceilings on contributions and benefits for workers who receive above-average compensation. Inevitably, many businesses would find these new rules unacceptable and would opt out. If too many businesses opt out and too few opt in, the experiment will fail and the subsidies should end.

At least six basic reforms seem essential to achieve these goals.

Eligibility.   To accelerate the coverage of workers and allow more part-time workers to participate, all plans should include workers after they have been employed for one year or longer and have performed at least 500 hours of service (about 10 hours per week) during that year. Companies still could exclude short-term workers and casual labor.

Vesting. To minimize forfeitures that most workers can ill afford, all contributions and benefits should be at least 50 percent vested after the first year of participation and 100 percent vested after the second.

Portability. All vested benefits must be portable. Upon termination of their employment, participants would be entitled to have their vested benefits transferred tax free to their new employer's pension plan or to their own IRA.

Benefits. Pension funding for higher-income workers should be capped at levels that provide a basic retirement income for the typical worker at retirement age, which we will assume is 65 for discussion purposes. Such limits might be guided by principles that Congress, since 1978, has applied to allow a highly compensated employee to receive tax-free reimbursements by his employer of his out-of-pocket medical expenses. The reimbursement is tax free only if the employer adopts a plan that "does not discriminate in favor of highly compensated individuals as to eligibility to participate; and . . . benefits provided under the plan do not discriminate in favor of participants who are highly compensated individuals." Eligibility rules are somewhat comparable to those for pension plans. But in order for benefits not to discriminate, all eligible employees must be entitled to the *same* maximum reimbursement amount. In other words, if the CEO is entitled to be reimbursed for up to $5,000 of out-of-pocket medical expenses, so too must every other eligible employee regardless of his relative wage levels.[38]

Congress might temper this rule in the case of pension-plan contributions and benefits. For example, maximum contributions to defined contribution plans might be 15 percent of a basic wage level, such as $30,000, for a maximum contribution of $6,000, adjusted for cost-of-living increases ($6,000 per year, earning 8 percent per year, would amount to $730,000 after 30 years, ignoring inflation). Defined benefit plans might fund no higher than a basic retirement amount, such as $30,000 per year, also adjusted for cost-of-living increases. Plans should be prohibited from integrating with Social Security.

If employers contributed less than the allowable amount, employees could be permitted to make up the difference through their own tax-deductible contributions. Highly compensated employees, however, would not be allowed to contribute more than the average contribution of other workers, in compliance with rules now in place for 401(k) plans. Without this limitation, employers could regularly make very small contributions, knowing that highly compensated employees would always make up the difference themselves, whereas other employees would not.

Prototype Plans.   The government should establish a short list of highly simplified, prototype pension plans for employers to choose from, including
SEPs. The simplicity might encourage far more businesses, particularly small
businesses, to adopt plans, for they would be easier to understand and to administer. Because further changes in the laws automatically would be incor-
porated into the plans, businesses also would avoid the sizable expense of
employing lawyers to make the plans conform to the new laws.

Government Oversight.   Only one government agency—the IRS—should
oversee pension plans. The Department of Labor, which currently shares
oversight responsibilities with the IRS, would continue to provide data and
analysis about plans that are crucial to evaluating whether the tax subsidies
are sound.

*   *   *

If these suggested reforms are unacceptable, or if they fail to produce adequate results for most ordinary workers, Congress should consider making
pension plans pay their way by imposing an annual income tax on the plans
themselves based on their annual net growth. Alternately, Congress could
tax individual participants annually on the net increase in their vested accounts; the tax payments could be made from plan assets in order to assure
participants of funds necessary to pay the tax. (While either of these approaches poses certain administrative problems, the problems are manageable.) Congress then could afford to reduce income tax rates for all workers,
including those who benefit little or none at all from pension plans. These
results seem clearly preferable to the status quo, although a pension-plan system that truly and fairly served a much larger universe of workers in this
country would be best.

12

The Great Capital
Gains Tax Debate

*There's been so much misinformation, and even more misleading informa-
tion, about capital gains that even the best-intentioned demagogue might
get confused.*

—Leonard E. Burman, deputy assistant secretary,
U.S. Treasury Department

The Policy Dilemma * The Special Tax Treatment for Net
Capital Gains * Review of Special Tax Rates on Capital
Gains * Who Claims a Special Tax Rate on Capital Gains? *
Should Capital Gains Be Taxed at All? * How a Lower
Capital Gains Tax Would Affect Federal Revenue * The
Unlocking Effect from Lowering the Capital Gains Tax *
The Economic Effects of Lowering the Capital Gains Tax *
The Capital Gains Tax, Entrepreneurs, and Venture Capi-
talists * Fairness of Lowering the Capital Gains Tax * Con-
clusions and Recommendations

No income tax issue has so deeply and consistently divided politicians and
tax experts as the taxation of capital gains. At one end of the spectrum are
those who favor exempting capital gains from tax. Those at the opposite end
favor taxing capital gains and ordinary income at the same rates. People in
the vast middle believe in taxing capital gains but at rates lower than for ordinary income. Within this middle group, controversies rage over how low
the rates should be as well as the appropriateness of special deferrals and exemptions for particular capital gains. All factions would be drawn closer together if economists could agree on which tax rates on capital gains would

maximize tax revenue *and* our nation's economic growth. Yet sharp disagreements among economists on this subject make the answer seem as elusive as the Holy Grail.

The Policy Dilemma

That these controversies continue to command so much attention is itself intriguing because each year only a distinct minority among us owes taxes on capital gains, and the taxes always have been a minor source of total income tax revenues. Yet getting capital gains taxation right remains such a compelling undertaking because the richest among us have such enormous capital gains. What's more, they, not the government, always have decided if and when they would pay tax on their gains. As long as they do not *realize* their gain, that is, engage in a taxable sale or exchange, they can continue to postpone the tax indefinitely. And if they hold an appreciated asset until death, they and their heirs will have

> *The power of the rich to time their tax liability for capital gains always has provided them with a formidable defense against efforts to redistribute substantial portions of their wealth to the rest of society.*

permanently avoided the tax because of the step-up-in-basis rule. These powers always have provided the rich with a formidable defense against efforts to redistribute substantial portions of their wealth to the rest of society.

To be sure, all owners of capital assets potentially benefit from the same tax laws. But for most investors, the day of reckoning ordinarily arrives. At some point, they must sell to pay bills, perhaps for their children's schooling or medical expenses. In contrast, the rich—the top few percent of all wealth-holders—have so many sources of income that they can be selective about what investments to sell if they need cash. They might sell stocks that have no gain; they might sell a mix of stocks on which their losses offset their gains; or they might pledge their investments as collateral to borrow funds they need. Most important, they have the prerogative to retain their most highly appreciated investments indefinitely, forestalling the tax indefinitely.

Thus Congress has a policy dilemma. Congress knows that capital gains taxes discourage selling. It wants the rich to invest, but it also wants them to sell and pay taxes. This chapter explores Congress's dilemma. The context will be proposals to lower today's top rates, a measure advocates believe would strengthen the economy and produce at least as much, if not more, tax revenue than do current rates.

Readers will become familiar with some definitions and with the trade-off between the advantage of deferring taxes on capital gains without paying interest on the taxes deferred and the disadvantage of paying taxes on inflationary gains. They will understand why experts disagree about whether **real** (noninflationary) **capital gains** are income. Assuming that at least real capital gains are income and thus properly subject to tax, I will address two major economic questions.

First, should we expect that if tax rates on capital gains were lowered, tax revenues would grow or at least not decline because the lower rate would induce people to sell more of their investments? This question recognizes that lowering rates would induce *some* additional sales, but these sales might not be enough to bring revenues up to the level they would have been at the higher tax rate. The answer is important because revenue shortfalls attributable to the lower tax rate, if not offset by higher taxes on other income or lower government spending, could minimize or nullify favorable economic effects from a lower tax rate; worse, the shortfalls could negatively affect the economy.

The second question assumes, for the sake of discussion, that a lower rate does *not* increase the *number* of sales sufficiently to achieve revenue neutrality. A lower rate, however, might stimulate economic growth. If it does, should we assume that a lower rate would increase the *size* of capital gains as well the amount of other income to such an extent that the combination of *more capital gains* with *higher values,* plus *more ordinary income,* would yield revenue-neutral results or even produce revenue surpluses? An important aspect of this question is how much a lower capital gains tax would affect entrepreneurship and venture capitalists' investments.

Last, we will turn to another seminal question: Would lowering the capital gains tax rate be fair? The answer may turn not only on the economic and revenue consequences but also on which taxpayers and capital gains we have in mind.

One considerable disadvantage of any special tax rate on capital gains and today's special laws that allow for the deferral or permanent exemption of many gains is the immense complexity and economic distortions they generate. One solution, advocated by proponents of a flat tax, is to eliminate all taxes on capital gains from personal investments. Policy experts who do not want to eliminate the taxation of capital gains but want to reform the rules explore many options. As discussed in "Conclusions and Recommendations" at the end of this chapter, I favor comprehensive reforms that, on one hand, protect the ordinary taxpayer from tax on inflationary gains and on the other eliminate most special deferrals and exemptions for capital gains: these reforms could occur in connection with others that significantly broaden the overall income tax base. To make these reforms revenue neutral, they would be accompanied by substantially lower tax rates on ordinary income. Capital gains thereafter would be taxed at new, lower rates for ordinary income rather than at special rates. The double taxation of corporate income (covered later in this chapter) would be minimized but only in connection with revenue-neutral reforms that make up for the lost revenue by taxing people most who can be expected to benefit most from minimizing the double tax. Finally, I would continue modest experimentation with tax incentives to invest in certain new enterprises.

A point of clarification. Because this book, for the most part, addresses taxation of individuals, not corporations, I will not discuss taxation of a corporation's capital gains from the sale of its investments such as the stock of a subsidiary corporation, though the topic becomes relevant in Chapter 13 on the flat tax. I note here only that a corporation's capital gains typically are taxed at the same tax rate as applies to its operating income.

The Special Tax Treatment for Net Capital Gains

Debates about maximum capital gains rates concern *net* capital gains: Only net capital gains benefit from the special rates. Net capital gains for the year represent the excess of net long-term gains over net short-term losses. Long-term currently refers to investments held for more than one year.

Computing this excess sounds complicated, but the mathematics are simple. First, add long-term gains and subtract long-term losses; any balance of long-term gains equals net long-term gains. Second, add short-term losses and subtract short-term gains; any balance of short-term losses equals net short-term losses. Therefore, if you have $10,000 of net long-term gains and $2,000 of net short-term losses, you have $8,000 of net capital gains. If you had no net short-term losses, your net capital gains would be $10,000.

> *We have no evidence that the economy grows faster or that people invest more wisely because of laws that distinguish between short- and long-term capital gains.*

Net short-term gains (the excess of short-term gains over short-term losses) are taxed at ordinary income rates. Congress thereby rewards longer-term investing, believing it good for the stock market and the economy, and discourages short-term trading and speculation. The one-year demarcation is purely arbitrary. Holding periods for long-term capital gains have in the past been as little as six months or as long as two years. More important, we have no evidence that the economy grows faster or that people invest more wisely because of laws that distinguish between short- and long-term capital gains.[1]

Review of Special Tax Rates on Capital Gains

For higher-income taxpayers, net capital gains nearly always have been subject to favorable tax rates or have been partially exempt from tax. Only from 1913 through 1921 and from 1987 through 1990 did the same tax rates apply to ordinary income and to all net capital gains. The top, special capital gains rate has ranged from a low of 12.5 percent, from 1922 through 1933, to a high of 39.9 percent, from 1972 through 1977. The top rate today is

10 percent for taxpayers whose ordinary income is taxed at no more than 15 percent, and 20 percent for everyone else. These rates are scheduled to decline to 8 percent and 18 percent, respectively, in certain circumstances.

In some cases, the top rate is effectively higher than the explicit rate. Such a case occurs, for example, when we pay a 20 percent tax (the explicit rate) on inflationary gains, because the tax deprives us of a portion of our underlying investment as well as a portion of our real gains. Conversely, the top rate may be effectively lower than the nominal rate because of interest-free tax deferrals of gains; the top rate always is effectively lower than the nominal rate for gains that are exempt from tax.

Last, and contrary to what we often hear, our maximum capital gains rates are not higher than those of most developed countries. Capital gains are untaxed in Belgium, Germany, and the Netherlands; they are taxed at only 12.5 percent in Italy. The maximum rate rises, however, to 20 percent in Japan (where provincial and territorial taxes increase the top marginal rate to as high as 53 percent), 23.5 percent in Canada, 26 percent in France, 30 percent in Sweden, 40 percent in the United Kingdom, and 48.5 percent in Australia, though gains are indexed for inflation in the United Kingdom and in Australia.[2]

Who Claims a Special Tax Rate on Capital Gains?

You might believe that a special capital gains tax primarily serves the middle class if you were told that "there are many more taxpayers with *moderate* incomes who realize capital gains than there are in higher brackets [italics added]," as Congressman Ed Jenkins, a Democrat from Georgia, stated in 1989 to support a proposed reduction of the capital gains tax.[3] Jenkins may have had in mind that 61 percent of all returns that reported net capital gains in 1988 had less than $50,000 of adjusted gross income (AGI). Though $50,000 was nearly three times the median income of taxpayers that year, let us assume for our purposes here that all 61 percent had *moderate* incomes, which would make Jenkins technically correct. But Jenkins failed to convey two important points. First, *only 9 percent* of all taxpayers reported capital gains. Second, within the 9 percent, people with moderate incomes enjoyed little of the tax savings from special capital gains rates.

From 1989 until 1997, no more than 10 percent of all taxpayers reported net capital gains. In 1997, the figure jumped to 16 percent, in part

People with moderate incomes enjoy little of the tax savings from special capital gains rates.

because of the new, lower capital gains tax rates and in part because of the rapid rise of the stock market and the growing popularity of mutual funds, most of which regularly realize capital gains each year. The *greatest portion* of net capital gains was heavily concentrated among the highest-income taxpayers. The top *5.9 percent* of all returns—those with $100,000 or more of AGI—reported *80 percent* of all net capital gains. The *top 0.1 percent* of all returns—those with $1 million or more of AGI—reported *45 percent* of all net capital gains. Tax returns with under $50,000 AGI, representing *76 percent* of all returns, reported only *10 percent* of all net capital gains.[4] Some middle-income taxpayers fell into the higher-income range because of a one-time sale, yet their inclusion did not alter the general picture. Over a 10-year period, no more than one-third of all taxpayers can be expected to have even one capital gain.[5] In short, tax savings from favorable capital gains tax rates overwhelmingly redound to high-income taxpayers.

> *Returns with $1 million or more of AGI in 1997 reported 45 percent of all net capital gains.*

Should Capital Gains Be Taxed at All?

Opposition to taxing capital gains takes several paths. Some opponents advance the cause of a consumption tax, defined as a tax on all forms of income except that from savings and investment. Consumption refers to what we spend on things we use up, such as rent, food, clothing, tuition, and health insurance premiums. Our savings and investments are resources that we can turn to for future consumption. The case for and against adopting a consumption tax, such as a flat tax, is the topic of Chapter 13 and will not be considered further here. Other critics of the capital gains tax want it limited to *real* gains—capital gains adjusted for inflation—which I will discuss when considering the fairness of taxing capital gains.

Finally, some opponents of the capital gains tax believe that even real capital gains from personal investments are not income; if true, real capital gains should not be taxed under any income tax system. These opponents advance a range of arguments.[6] The most intellectually rigorous one views taxing capital gains as often taxing twice the same economic enhancement. Although this argument usually has some truth in the case of corporate stock, as explained in the discussion of fairness, would it be so for gains from other investments? An office building, for example, may appreciate in value because of increased rents. Since rents received are taxable income, would taxing the realized appreciation of the building, when the building is sold, amount to double taxation? Law professor Walter Blum explained years ago why this would not be so. "Though there would be two impositions of tax," he noted, "there also would be two separate increments of economic enhancement, each subject to tax only once. The economic position of the taxpayer first improves when his capital rises in value [above the value when the asset was acquired]. It further improves when he receives increased revenues from his appreciated property."[7] In sum, the owner enjoys the rent *plus* the appreciation.

Blum's logic is consistent with the teachings of Haig-Simons. Indeed, under Haig-Simons, each year's real appreciation of the building would be taxed even though not realized, along with the net rent.

How a Lower Capital Gains Tax Would Affect Federal Revenue

Three distinct schools of thought exist about whether the current maximum 20 percent tax rate on capital gains for middle- and upper-income taxpayers is the optimum maximum rate to raise revenue *and* promote economic growth.

First School

The first school confidently maintains that substantially reducing today's top rate of 20 percent would help everyone. This school is represented by many politicians—mostly Republicans, who historically have favored low capital gains rates, along with some Democrats—and by some economists.[8] The case the first school makes can be summarized as follows:

- The lower rate, by raising the after-tax rate of return from capital gains, would increase tax revenue because investors would invest more, sell more, and have larger gains.
- As capital gains revenue rises, the government would need to borrow less. People then would invest less in government bonds and notes; instead, they would loan or invest more in businesses or put more of their money into savings accounts with banks, savings and loans, and other institutions that lend money to businesses. The greater supply of lendable funds would give businesses the power to borrow money at lower interest rates and to offer lower dividend rates to stockholders. Also, with a lower **cost of capital**—what businesses must pay to lenders to borrow from them and to investors to attract their investment—businesses would be able to retain more profits for their own growth and development.
- Lower capital gains rates would attract more of us to become entrepreneurial—to start or join new businesses. This activity would help supercharge the economy and also increase capital gains.
- All of the foregoing would multiply the number of businesses and jobs, accelerate the growth of existing businesses, and increase wages for ordinary workers. In short, everyone would win!

Second School

Before betting the farm on these views, you will want to hear from the other schools. Many politicians—almost always Democrats—and many economists believe that lowering the maximum capital gains tax rate below 20 percent is likely to hurt everyone except possibly the rich. According to this school,

- The lower tax rate likely would reduce, rather than increase, government revenue from capital gains over the long run. Tax revenues from any additional capital gains realizations brought about by the new rate would not compensate for revenue losses incurred as a result of the lower rate. This loss of revenue would lead to larger federal deficits, requiring the government to borrow a higher percentage of our personal savings, thereby leaving a lower percentage of our savings available for loans to and investments in businesses.
- The lower capital gains tax rate also would not induce much additional personal savings, investment, or entrepreneurship because individual decisions to save, or to start or invest in new businesses, are not very responsive to changes in capital gains tax rates. Also, the lower rate would be inapplicable to many investors, such as employment-based retirement plans, that do not pay federal income taxes.
- Lowering the capital gains rate exacerbates its disparity with top ordinary income tax rates that apply to investment income such as interest and dividends. This greater disparity is likely to distort economic decisions, encourage tax-avoidance schemes, and increase compliance costs that will slow economic growth.

To summarize, growing government revenue losses from the lower capital gains rate, along with economic distortions from disparities between the maximum capital gains rate and maximum ordinary income rates, would outweigh the value of any growth in personal savings and would result in higher rather than lower interest and dividend rates. Under all of these circumstances, businesses would grow more slowly; there would be fewer of them, including fewer entrepreneurial undertakings; and there would be fewer jobs and lower wages.

Members of the second school also warn that if the gamble of a lower capital gains tax rate boomerangs, ordinary workers, the poor, and the typical small business would be among those sure to be hurt. The rich would benefit from the tax savings, but slower economic growth might mean that their wealth would be affected adversely overall.

Third School

A third and highly respected school of thought, with its own mix of economists and politicians, adopts the much-ado-about-nothing view. According to this school, any positive or negative impact on government tax revenue or on personal savings and investment patterns arising from some further reduction in the capital gains tax would appear like a fly on the back of an elephant. The elephant is our $8 trillion economy. The fly—the capital gains tax—generates less than 1 percent of that amount in revenue. The only noticeable effect of the lower tax rate would be on the rich, who would receive most of the relief and probably would be made richer.

Why Are Economic Predictions So Disparate?

How can it be that the nation's most established economists disagree so profoundly on a subject they have shared such profound interest in for so many years? The answer, as all but the most self-assured admit, is "They don't know enough!" They never have tracked adequately the patterns of investors over time that might reveal predictable patterns when tax rates on capital gains change. In truth, tax revenue rises and falls, and the economy moves about in response to so many factors that it is impossible to isolate the role played by capital gains rates.

Economists lack the data to predict, with the precision they would like, the long-term impact on tax revenue or the economy from lowering or raising the maximum capital gains rate.

To be more definitive, economists must be able to predict multiple reactions to a change in the maximum capital gains tax rate: reactions by people who have different amounts and types of appreciated assets, different incomes, and other varied personal circumstances. No prediction can be reliable unless economists can control for the likely impact of other factors that may affect behavior, an extraordinarily difficult task. We might choose to sell our stock or not depending on our view of the future of the stock market. We may need money to pay unexpected expenses. We may defer selling because we have become more secure economically as the result of a new job or a pay increase, or we may elect to sell because we have lost our job or have received a pay cut. Wealthier taxpayers also have become far more sophisticated in finding ways to enjoy the fruits of their appreciated investments without, for tax purposes, realizing their gains.

With these observations in mind, let us examine the argument that lowering tax rates would increase revenue from net capital gains because people would elect to realize more of their gains. Economists call such a response the *unlocking effect* from lowering the tax rate.

The Unlocking Effect from Lowering the Capital Gains Tax

When we decide not to sell an investment because of the capital gains tax, the tax is said to *lock in* our gain. The higher the tax, the greater the **lock-in effect**. Lowering the tax would induce us to sell more of our appreciated investments. It does not necessarily follow, however, that more capital gains taxed at a lower rate would yield as much tax revenue as would fewer realizations taxed at a higher rate.

Over the short term, capital gains realizations tend to become atypical when investors anticipate a change in capital gains rates. In 1986, once taxpayers knew that, in 1987, the top rate would rise from 20 to 28 percent, they unloaded an extraordinary amount of their capital gains to take advantage of the lower rate. Guessing that Congress might lower the maximum rate in 1997, some taxpayers who could postpone their sales in 1996 did so and were rewarded by the lower rate that was enacted the next year.

To make a convincing case, however, that Congress should lower the maximum tax rate on capital gains in order to unlock additional capital gains, proponents must persuade us not merely that capital gains realizations will be substantially higher in the year or two following the tax reduction or that *some* unlocking of capital gains will occur thereafter. We must believe that the unlocking will be sufficient over many years to bring about a sustained increase in the sum of government and household savings. Proponents have then made their case in spades. But after the transition years, the lower tax rate may decrease government revenues, and household savings may not increase sufficiently to offset the mounting government deficit.

> *To make a convincing case that Congress should lower the maximum tax rate on capital gains in order to unlock additional capital gains, proponents must persuade us that the unlocking will be sufficient over many years in order to bring about a sustained increase in the sum of government and household savings.*

Which of these scenarios would occur depends on the **elasticity** of our reaction to the lower rate. If we react a lot, which means that our response is very elastic, a lower tax is more likely to pay for itself. We can understand the mathematics of the unlocking effect with an example. Suppose that $200,000 billion in capital gains is taxed at a new rate of 15 percent, rather than at the old rate of 20 percent. A 20 percent tax on $200 billion would have yielded $40 billion; a 15 percent tax would yield only $30 billion. For the unlocking effect to be at least revenue neutral, it must offset this $10 billion static loss. [9]

For increased realizations to raise $10 billion, they would have to reach $67 billion (15 percent x $67 billion = $10 billion). Thus total realizations would be $267 billion compared with $200 billion, an increase of *33 percent*. In short, for the unlocking effect to work, realizations must go *way up*, not simply up. And they must go way up *year after year*.

Experts divide sharply on these revenue effects. People who have believed that rate reductions, even from 28 percent, would produce too little unlocking over the long run to overcome the static revenue loss include Jane Gravelle, chief economist at the Congressional Research Service; Henry Aaron, an economist at the Brookings Institution in Washington, D.C.; and Alan Auerbach, an economist at the University of California at Berkeley. They have been concerned that the overall revenue loss could be substantial.[10] Writing in 1989, Auerbach concluded that a careful review of the literature reveals "essentially no measurable permanent response of capital gains realizations to changes in capital

> *For the unlocking effect to work, realizations must go way up, not simply up. And they must go way up year after year.*

gains rates."[11] Leonard Burman, deputy assistant secretary of the Treasury for Tax Analysis, recently updated the literature in *The Labyrinth of Capital Gains Tax Policy* and concurred: "Careful economic studies find that capital gains are relatively unresponsive to statutory changes in tax rates, even though the timing of gains is highly sensitive to year-to-year variations in rates." Burman thus concludes that "a capital gains preference almost surely reduces tax revenues."[12]

Past advocates of the opposite viewpoint have included economists Martin Feldstein, former chairman of the Council of Economic Advisors under President Reagan; Lawrence Lindsey, former member of the Federal Reserve Board; and Michael Boskin, former chairman of the Council of Economic Advisors under President Bush.[13] Lindsey, for example, has suggested that the revenue-maximizing rate may be about 16 percent.[14]

Although the warring mathematical models used to estimate unlocking effects are too technical for our purposes here,[15] we can understand pessimism about the revenue-generating ability of the unlocking effect. As Burman notes, "A large difference between the rates on capital gains and other income gives taxpayers a strong incentive to convert other income into capital gains. The reduction in other income, which would otherwise be taxed at higher rates, produces a revenue loss to the government not measured in the empirical studies of capital gains." This revenue loss alone, Burman believes, may equal the additional revenue from the unlocking effect.[16]

Second, as unlocking occurs, the pool of previously locked-in gains diminishes. With each passing year, it becomes increasingly difficult to wrench loose sufficient additional realizations to overcome the ongoing static loss. The pool, however, is large. Only about 14 percent of stocks held by individuals is sold each year.[17]

Third, a significant portion of the unlocking (how much is unclear) merely involves investors realizing gains sooner than they would otherwise. The earlier tax collections on these accelerated gains allow the government to collect interest on the money for a longer period of time, but the government profits only if that interest exceeds the loss from the lower rates, which would occur only if the lower tax rate accelerated realizations by many years. Consider 1993, when the top rate was 28 percent. Let us assume, for sake of illustration, that reducing the tax rate to 15 percent would have shortened the average holding period by seven years. If a taxpayer's gain had been $1,000, a 15 percent tax would have produced $150 in taxes. If the government earned 8 percent interest for seven years on the $150, it would have gained approximately $107, for a total *of $257 after seven years.* At the end of that time, however, under the old 28 percent rate, the government would have collected *$280* on the $1,000 gain. Thus the government's net revenue loss as a result of the lower rate is *$23* ($280 – $257).[18]

Finally, the unlocking effect is severely hampered because so many realized gains under existing laws are deferred or exempt from tax. Nearly all gains from the sale of a principal residence—the largest investment for most taxpayers—are tax exempt. Gains such as from real estate swaps and the exchange of stock in corporate mergers and acquisitions are tax deferred. Most important, about one-half of all gains escape tax because of the step-up-in-basis rule—what writer Michael Kinsley nicknamed the "angel of death loophole"[19]—or because appreciated assets are contributed, tax free, to charity at death.[20]

Let's take as an example Warren Buffett, who owns about $30 billion of Berkshire Hathaway stock that he bought decades ago for a tiny fraction of its current value. If he sold the stock, he would owe capital gains taxes of about $6 billion at the current 20 percent tax rate and $4.5 billion if the rate were 15 percent. It appears highly unlikely that Buffett would sell the stock at any tax rate. He knows that if he owns the stock at death, the step-up-in-basis rule would exempt him and his heirs from ever paying an *income* tax on his massive gain. If he bequeaths the stock to his wife, the stock also will be exempt from federal *estate* taxes because of the unlimited estate-tax deduction for bequests to a surviving spouse. In other words, Mrs. Buffett could inherit all $30 billion of the stock and sell it the next day without owing any federal income or estate taxes. If she retained it and it continued to increase in value, she also could avoid the capital gains tax on such appreciation by giving the stock to charity when she died. In short, for the rich, and particularly the elderly rich, the possibility of achieving a zero tax rate on their capital gains makes even a 15 percent rate look expensive.

> *Mrs. Buffett could inherit all $30 billion of the stock and sell it the next day without owing any federal income or estate taxes.*

To summarize, estimating the revenue consequences of the unlocking effect is a perilous business. Even Martin Feldstein, after years of predicting that huge and permanent unlocking would occur if the top rate on capital gains was substantially reduced, seems to have reevaluated his position.[21] In 1990, he dismissed an estimate by the Joint Committee on Taxation that President

Bush's proposal to exclude up to 30 percent of net capital gains from taxation would lose revenues over the long run: "The difficulty of estimating the [unlocking] effects of the capital gains exclusion is far too great to put any confidence in the . . . [JCT's] estimate."[22] The same presumably would be true of optimistic estimates. As Treasury economists have conceded, "Without understanding the effects of capital gains tax policies on GNP, interest rates, dividend payouts, and asset values, predictions about revenue consequences [from lowering capital gains rates] must be viewed as tenuous."[23]

We must conclude that although the unlocking effect may lead to higher tax collections over the long run, a prudent Congress should assume otherwise. The risk is substantial that lowering the top rate on capital gains will lose revenue if only the unlocking effect is considered. The argument that a rate reduction will increase tax revenues should turn, therefore, on the likely economic effects.

The Economic Effects of Lowering the Capital Gains Tax

Proponents of lowering the tax rate on capital gains believe that this measure would stimulate economic growth, referred to as the **feedback effect,** or **economic effect**: They expect the lower tax to *feed* the economy. This returns us to a discussion of old competitors, the *substitution effect* and the *income effect,* which determine how we behave when confronted by a change in tax rates. As a separate part of that discussion, we will consider the capacity of the lower rate to stimulate entrepreneurship and the investment of venture capital in entrepreneurial undertakings. Let us begin with an overview of possible outcomes.

Possible Outcomes of a Lowered Capital Gains Tax

A lower tax rate on capital gains should set off a series of favorable economic consequences if it causes national savings (the sum of private and government savings) to rise. National savings will rise if any increase in household savings exceeds any loss in tax revenue attributable to the lower rate. Then, more capital will be available to businesses for two reasons: More savings by households will be available for businesses to borrow, and individuals will increase their investments in businesses. This larger supply of available capital should lower the cost of capital, what businesses must pay in interest to lenders and in dividends to investors. With a lower cost and greater availability of capital, businesses can be expected to engage in more research and development, to expand, and to create more jobs at higher pay, all of which will stimulate economic growth. Stronger economic growth will increase capital gains and capital gains realizations.

If household savings increase insufficiently to offset a loss in tax revenue because of the lower tax rate, the government, which competes with the private sector to borrow funds, will be expected to borrow the additional household savings to cover its increased deficits. The additional government borrowing will drain funds away from the private marketplace, just the opposite of what is required in order for the lower rate to stimulate economic growth.

Increased Savings Through the Substitution Effect

As economist Joseph Stiglitz explains, "Whenever a government program lowers the price of some commodity, we [economists] say there is a substitution effect. The individual substitutes the cheaper good for other goods."[24] In this case, the competition is between consuming today or saving and investing today and consuming at a future date. By increasing the after-tax rate of return on investments subject to capital gains taxes, a lower capital gains tax would make capital gains *cheaper* for investors than before and thereby enhance the value of current saving and investing relative to current consumption. According to the substitution effect, we would save and invest more and consume less, as advocates of lowering the tax rate maintain.

But the lower tax also makes us better off: We will have more after-tax income, and thus more wealth, from the same level of saving and investing as before (assuming the lower tax does not change the price of investments). This increased wealth produces an income effect: Because we feel richer, we might reduce our saving and investing to a level where the amount that we save and invest, plus the after-tax return, equals what we would have had after taxes at the higher capital gains rate. Lowering the tax rate on capital gains thus would have both a substitution and income effect, each pulling us in the opposite direction. Which would be stronger, and by how much?

Most economists expect that the substitution effect would prevail, but not by much.

Economists who have trumpeted the substitution effect include Michael Boskin, who examined President Bush's proposal to reduce the maximum tax rate from 28 percent to 15 percent,[25] and most recently David Wyss of DRI Resources, who examined a 1998 proposal to reduce the current top rate from 20 percent to 15 percent. They believe that the substitution effect would be far stronger than the income effect, driving down the cost of capital and driving up the gross domestic product, producing increased tax revenues over the long run. In his estimates, Wyss relies heavily on the expectation that the lower tax rate would stimulate substantial new entrepreneurial undertakings and financing, discussed shortly.[26]

Most economists, including Henry Aaron,[27] Eugene Steuerle, and economists at the Congressional Budget Office (CBO), expect that the substitution effect would prevail, but not by much. Steuerle, a principal economist in the Treasury Department under President Reagan, believed that Bush's proposal to reduce the top capital gains rate from 28 percent to 15 percent would involve such modest tax savings (perhaps $10 billion) in an economy of about $20 trillion that "to argue that these small tax cuts would have a dramatic impact on the economy is absurd."[28] The tax savings would be modest, as CBO has explained, in good part because the individual capital gains tax affects only about one-quarter of all income attributable to business capital. The remaining three-quarters consists of dividends and interest taxed at ordinary income rates, income of corporations taxed at corporate rates, and income that is tax sheltered because it belongs to tax-exempt pension plans, 401(k) plans, individual retirement accounts, charities, and other such entities.[29] CBO also expects that the Federal Reserve Bank would interrupt any significant increase in consumption and investment, if triggered by a lower tax on capital gains, so as to thwart most of the economic gains expected by advocates of a lower rate;[30] David Wyss ignores this possibility.

Some economists warn that because of how the elderly might respond, household savings actually might *fall* after a cut in the capital gains tax rate. The elderly not only own most investment assets held by households; they also tend to be consumers rather than savers. According to economists Barry Bosworth and Lawrence Kotlikoff, the elderly likely would consume more if they could achieve the same after-tax return from a smaller investment, which would be true in the case of a cut in the capital gains rate.[31] Kotlikoff also cautions that if a reduction of the capital gains tax rate lost revenue, the government might make up the deficit by taxing wages more, which would likely depress the savings rates of workers. Because workers are net savers, their lower savings rate could cause a decline in the savings rate of households overall.

> *The elderly would likely consume more if they could achieve the same after-tax return from a smaller investment, which would be true in the case of a cut in the capital gains rate.*

We also must recognize that if U.S. corporations pay lower dividends in response to increased investments by U.S. households, foreigners, who are exempt from capital gains taxes on their U.S. stocks,[32] might move their capital to countries where their rate of return is greater. In that case, the private U.S.-based market might have access to fewer funds.

To summarize, as with the unlocking effect, neither economic theory nor existing data allow us confidently to predict whether, and by how much, a lower capital gains tax would stimulate household investment. Policymakers would be mistaken to assume that any government deficits resulting from inadequate unlocking of capital gains would be more than offset by feedback effects on household saving.

One other point rarely is mentioned. All leading proposals to lower the capital gains tax rate make the lower rate available to investments abroad, including investments in foreign-based and foreign-controlled companies. As long as proposals to lower the capital gains rate are not limited to investments in the United States, estimates of economic benefits from the lower tax must account for the possibility that only a portion would accrue directly to our economy.

With so much uncertainty about the ability of a lower capital gains tax to stimulate additional household saving through a conventional substitution effect, we turn to what has become the most animated argument from proponents of the lower tax rate. The lower rate, they maintain, would overcome revenue shortfalls over the long run because of its favorable impact on entrepreneurship and venture-capital investments in new enterprises.

The Capital Gains Tax, Entrepreneurs, and Venture Capitalists

The successful innovations of entrepreneurs can have enormous value—what economists call a positive **externality** (or a positive spillover effect)—for many of us without our having devoted time or risked our capital to advance their work. We also know that many, and probably most, attempts at innovation have failed, often at great cost in the innovators' time and their investors' capital. Providing special tax treatment for successful entrepreneurial undertakings, therefore, has appeal as a way of encouraging their efforts.

Proponents of a lower capital gains tax believe that it would inspire many creative people to leave their jobs to start or join new enterprises and would prompt far greater investment in new enterprises by third parties. At issue is not whether future entrepreneurs or venture capitalists would *prefer* to be taxed at a lower rate when they achieve capital gains. All would. The dispute centers on whether individuals' decisions to become entrepreneurs or invest (or invest more) in new enterprises depend on the adoption of a lower capital gains rate.

One preliminary observation: Advocates of government policies that encourage people to take risks with their money assume that such policies pay off for society as a whole. This assumption is not well supported in the economic literature. We know that about two-thirds of new start-ups fail; about one-quarter fail within the first two years. These failures cause extensive and painful losses of jobs and investments.[33] Assuming for discussion purposes, however, that such policies may pay off, let us begin our inquiry with entrepreneurs.

Any capital gains tax discourages entrepreneurial undertakings by reducing the after-tax return from the eventual sale of an entrepreneur's new enterprise. The higher the tax, the greater the discouragement.[34] But to what extent? Consider the ordinary entrepreneur—the individual who wants to start, alone or with others, a hardware store, dry-cleaning establishment, insurance agency, or dental practice. She and her cofounders usually work full-time in the business. They expect to make their living from it, to use profits that remain after all costs and capital investments to pay their salaries and fringe benefits. When the business matures and has sufficient profits, they also would like to set aside funds in a retirement plan. None of these objectives is affected by the capital gains tax, which would apply only if they sold the business some time in the distant future. Rarely, therefore, would a lower capital gains tax rate play a pivotal role in determining whether they stake out a course on their own or remain at their existing employment.

Advocates of a lower capital gains rate have a different entrepreneur in mind—the dynamic, Silicon valley model of the 1980s and 1990s, the next Bill Gates (Microsoft), Steve Jobs (Apple Computers), or Steve Case (America Online). We could hardly imagine, however, the real Bill Gates, Steve Jobs, or Steve Case saying that the level of the capital gains tax was material, let alone pivotal, to their decisions to become entrepreneurs. (If the data were available, perhaps we would learn that numbers of other potential entrepreneurs backed off because of the capital gains tax.) But what can we expect as we look ahead? Many future leading entrepreneurs will be driven by factors other than money: desires to run their own businesses, to invent something, to deliver a new service, or to compete successfully in an area already developed. Those driven by money—who have in mind forming a company that will be sold in the next three to seven years—typically expect a payoff that will dwarf whatever tax savings they might achieve through a lower capital gains rate. For example, Desh Deshpande, the chairman of Sycamore Networks, a small Massachusetts company engaged in improving optical communications networks, suddenly owned stock worth about $3 billion following his company's public offering in October 1999. If he were to sell all of his stock and pay a 15 percent capital gains tax, he would be left with $2.55 billion. At today's 20 percent rate, he would have *only* $2.40 billion. Are such entrepreneurs of tomorrow depending on the $2.55 billion, or, as I suspect, would the prospect of $2.4 billion suffice for most?

Most new entrepreneurs, according to a study of the NFIB Foundation, an affiliate of the National Federation of Independent Business, "rely heavily on their own resources to finance their ventures." But what about financing of start-up companies from institutional lenders, family and friends, and outside investors. Much of the capital is in the form of loans from banks and other lending institutions to whom individual capital gains taxes do not apply. Still, "families and friends," according to NFIB, "helped capitalize about one-quarter" of all new firms. How important was the capital gains rate to their decision to invest, and to the decisions of other family and friends not to invest? We can expect that personal relationship was a factor (and in some cases the controlling factor) in the decision to invest, but we also can assume that most relatives and friends wish to make money. Because we lack data about their decisions, we can only speculate about the importance of the capital gains rate.

According to NFIB, "only about one new firm in 10" included investors other than entrepreneurs, family and friends. Some are "angels," wealthy people who are attracted to the enterprise; again, we know too little about their investment decisions. Most interesting, "the number of new business owners who used either institutionalized venture capital or government programs was negligible."[35] Venture-capital firms are professionally run partnerships or other entities that raise money from individuals and others to invest in enterprises. Within venture-capital firms, nearly 90 percent of the capital is provided by existing corporations or nontaxable organizations such as pension plans, foundations, endowments, and foreign investors, none of whom are subject to the individual capital gains tax.[36]

Notwithstanding this less-than-convincing evidence, many economists and politicians believe the capital gains tax has a noticeable, negative impact on the financing of new businesses.[37] In fact, June O'Neill, while director of CBO under President Clinton, conceded in 1998 that reducing the capital gains tax should spur innovation, even that the effect could be "significant." In its 1998 study of the potential impact of a capital gains rate reduction, however, CBO would not factor in any effect because "other than anecdotal evidence nobody could put a number on it."[38] Mark Bloomfield of the American Council for Capital Formation (ACCF), one of the most vocal advocates for reducing taxes on capital gains, refused to accept her explanation: "Just because you can't quantify it doesn't mean it's not an important element." Bloomfeld and Margo Thorning, an ACCF staff member, complained that CBO had not given sufficient weight to studies by Martin Feldstein, Lawrence Lindsey, Patric Hendershott, and Allen Sinai, among others, about the impact of capital gains tax reductions on innovation.[39]

Most recently, even ACCF conceded that a lower capital gains tax actually could *reduce* equity investments in new, traditional small firms such as restaurants, construction businesses, and retail shops. But ACCF insists that typical new technology-based firms, which depend heavily on equity financing, would have more of it if capital gains rates were lower.[40]

Even assuming that lowering the top capital gains tax rate for investments in new enterprises would materially advance the rate of economic growth, Congress should not use that outcome as a basis for lowering the capital gains rate on other investments. As noted by Jane Gravelle, "Only a small fraction of capital gains and a small fraction of investment are associated with investment in new innovative firms. Most capital gains taxes stem from real estate, mature corporate firms, or new businesses that are unlikely to be associated with innovation."[41] For example, when you sell Merck stock to me through your broker, and I sell Bristol Myers stock to you through my broker, neither Merck nor Bristol Myers receives a penny from these transactions. For all these reasons, economist James Poterba concluded, on the basis of his 1990 study of the relationship between capital gains tax rates and entrepreneurship, "An across-the-board capital gains tax cut is . . . a relatively blunt device for encouraging venture investment." Such a tax cut (at a time when the top rate was 28 percent) "would have a small effect on the total tax burden on venture capital financiers, while conveying large benefits on many assets other than venture capital investments."[42]

> *Even if lowering the top capital gains tax rate for investments in new enterprises would significantly increase the allocation of capital to them and would materially advance the rate of economic growth, this outcome should not be used as a basis for lowering the capital gains rate on other investments.*

Given our heated debates about capital gains rates, readers likely will be surprised to learn that a (virtually overlooked) 1993 law cuts the capital gains rate in half for many investments in new enterprises. The stock must be acquired from a *qualified small business* (new technology companies would qualify) when it first issued stock; the business cannot have more than $50 million of assets when the stock is acquired; and the stock must be held for more than five years. If so, half of all capital gains, up to the greater of $10 million or 10 times what an investor paid for the stock, will be tax exempt.[43] The law is too new, and apparently still too obscure, for us to understand its impact on the influx of capital to new ventures.

Fairness of Lowering the Capital Gains Tax

The debate about which capital gains policies produce the most revenues and make the most economic sense is matched in intensity by the debate about which capital gains policies are fairest. I will defer to Chapter 13 the proposal from consumption-tax advocates to eliminate the taxation of personal capital gains. I also will assume for purposes of the discussion here that the economic and revenue consequences of lowering the capital gains rate are uncertain. Were we to assume that a rate cut would be at least revenue neutral and would increase the number of jobs, wage levels, and savings, the rate cut would be fair to most people. Were we to assume that the rate cut would lose revenue and would not increase the number of jobs, wage levels, and savings, the rate cut would be unfair to most people. Leaving these issues unsettled, as they are in the economic literature, allows us to focus on four questions involving the fairness of a cut in the capital gains tax rate.

1. Would the Tax Savings from Lowering the Capital Gains Tax Rate Be Distributed Fairly Among Taxpayers? Proponents of lowering the capital gains tax rate emphasize that most taxpayers with capital gains do not have high incomes. Although this assertion is true, the key demographic data concern the distribution among taxpayers of the actual tax savings from a lower capital gains tax. If most taxpayers who do not have high incomes receive, collectively, only a small percentage of the savings, the lower capital gains rate has little value to them. By analogy, a direct grant program that doles out tiny amounts to a great many average households but devotes most of its resources to the rich ought not to be viewed as primarily serving average households.

> *A program that doles out tiny subsidies to a great many average households but devotes most of its resources to the rich ought not to be viewed as primarily serving the average household.*

As mentioned earlier, savings from the special capital gains tax rate typically have been spread among 10 percent or fewer of all tax returns. Predictably, within this group, net capital gains constitute a significant percentage of the AGI of high-income taxpayers and an insignificant percentage of the AGI of ordinary taxpayers. In 1997, net capital gains represented 38.5 percent of the AGI of taxpayers with $1 million or more of AGI and represented only 1.7 percent of the AGI of taxpayers with $40,000 to $50,000 of AGI.[44]

Proponents of a lower capital gains tax argue that these statistics are misleading because over any 10-year period, about one-third of all taxpayers have some capital gains. These occasional gains tilt the statistics to an extent, but most people who have only occasional capital gains tend to have small gains.[45] By contrast, most net capital gains are realized by high-income taxpayers who have net capital gains every year.[46] In a study for the period 1979 to 1988, CBO found that among families with capital gains, those whose income averaged from $40,000 to $50,000 per year had average capital gains of $1,671, whereas those whose income averaged at least $200,000 per year had average capital gains of $179,041.[47] When we group households by their asset holdings, we can see why. The top 10 percent own about 80 percent of the value of all publicly traded stock and about 90 percent of the value of all bonds and businesses.[48]

In short, the great preponderance of tax savings from a lower tax on capital gains would belong to the taxpayers whose income is consistently high.[49] Whether you believe this is fair depends on whether you believe that high-income taxpayers currently are overtaxed. The remaining discussion may help you form your views on the subject.

2. If the Lower Capital Gains Tax Rate Induced the Rich to Realize More Capital Gains and Pay More Taxes, Why Should Anyone Oppose It? Assume that cutting the capital gains tax rate would result in the rich paying more capital gains taxes because they would realize a great deal more of their capital gains, but that most other taxpayers would not pay more capital gains taxes because they have so few capital gains. Given this scenario, the rich would pay a higher percentage of all income taxes than they did before. In such case, Congress should adopt the rate cut. Some people might complain that the rich then would pay a smaller percentage of their income in taxes because more of their income would be represented by capital gains that benefit from low capital gains taxes. Although the observation is true, it is irrelevant to whether the rate cut improves the welfare of the nonrich. Simply put, if the rich pay a higher percentage of all taxes, everyone else is better off.

3. Is It Unfair to Tax Inflationary Gains in the Context of Existing Income Tax Laws?   Inflation is the rise in the price of goods and services. If inflation is 3 percent this year, we must have $1.03 at the beginning of next year to buy the same goods and services that we bought for $1 at the beginning of this year. The extra 3 cents is not income in economic terms; it keeps us even rather than putting us ahead. Likewise, if you sell Exxon stock for $100 that you bought years ago for $60 but your $60 adjusted for inflation would be worth $90 today, your economic gain is only $10; the remaining $30 maintains the real value of your original purchase. Our tax laws treat the entire nominal gain of $40 as a capital gain.

The direct solution would be to index capital gains for inflation, leaving only real gains subject to tax. Short of that, establishing a special, low rate for taxing capital gains is seen as a rough form of justice.[50] Before we conclude, however, that being taxed on inflationary gains is unfair, we must also consider other violations of economic principles, many of which benefit us. If our tax laws, to be fair, must be consistent with economic principles, laws that help us by ignoring these principles also must be reformed. Faced with that choice, many people, including the rich, may prefer that the tax laws continue to apply to inflationary capital gains.

> *Before we conclude that being taxed on inflationary gains is unfair, we must consider other violations of economic principles under the tax laws, many of which benefit us.*

For example, economists define income for a year as any increase in our net wealth, such as the real appreciation of our investments. This means that we should pay taxes each year on the real appreciation of our *unsold* as well as our sold investments. Conversely, any decrease in the value of our unsold investments would be treated as a loss for the year. Economists are not merely being devilish here, though you may think so. Our appreciated assets can be meaningful to us long before we realize the gain for tax purposes. Our appreciated home allows us to borrow additional funds under a new mortgage in order to make home improvements or to finance something else; we might pledge our appreciated stock to acquire more stock; and we might lease our appreciated office building at higher rents. Economists also teach that if our tax laws allow the deferral of capital gains until realized, any tax deferred on our real gains should bear interest.[51] Under our laws, we never owe interest on our deferred capital gains taxes.

Economic principles would not exempt the real gain from the sale of our principal residence or allow us to defer our gains when we swap our stock in mergers and acquisitions or when we exchange one parcel of real estate for another. Nor would we be allowed to defer from income the annual growth of our individual retirement accounts or of the vested portion of our pension accounts and 401(k) plans. Interest payments on our business loans would be deductible only to the extent that they exceeded the rate of inflation. Our heirs would not be entitled to an automatic step-up in basis of our assets when we die.

> *President Kennedy linked his advocacy of a lower capital gains tax with the taxation of all accrued capital gains at death or by gift, with limited exceptions.*

President Kennedy's views are relevant here. Often, advocates of a lower capital gains tax align themselves with Kennedy's 1963 proposal to lower the maximum capital gains rate from 25 to 19.6 percent; yet they fail to mention that he linked the lower rate to the taxation of "all net gains [with certain exceptions] accrued on capital assets at the time of transfer at death or by gift." Without this "essential element," he said, "there would be no justification for any reduction of present capital gain rate schedules."[52]

When all capital gains taxation is taken into account, "many capital gains are taxed at excessive rates," as Eugene Steuerle has written, "but, at the same time, many of those with substantial capital gains pay very little in the way of income taxation. An honest debate would recognize both sides of this issue. It is a debate that almost never occurs."[53]

Those opposed to any taxation of capital gains can point to past evidence that if all capital gains were aggregated in a single pot, no real capital gains would go untaxed. A study in the early 1990s by Steuerle and professor of taxation Daniel Halperin indicated that "total capital gains accruing in the economy were approximately equal to the inflationary increases in the value of all property, plus increases in the value of corporate stock due to the retention of earnings. . . . [This] meant that if a tax system were successful in taxing all real income once, then there would be no reason, at least in aggregate, to tax capital gains." Steuerle and Halperin then added, "The future, of course, could turn out differently,"[54] as indeed it did: The rapid growth of the stock market since then has far exceeded the rate of inflation plus corporate retained earnings.

Steuerle and Halperin also warned of "the fallacy of aggregation. Many individuals and firms benefit from . . . [real] types of gains every year." Advocates of a blanket relief for all capital gains taxes often overlook this crucial distinction. People with large *real* gains "are likely to be in higher income classes than those with real losses."[55] Furthermore, higher-income people can afford to hold their investments longer; and by deferring the tax for a long time, they gain the interest-free use of the ultimate tax payment. In fact, Jane Gravelle and Lawrence Lindsey, who strongly disagree about most aspects of capital gains policies, wrote jointly in 1988 that the advantage of deferring the tax for a long time exceeded the disadvantage of paying tax on inflationary gains.[56]

> *To summarize, high-income taxpayers tend to have substantial real capital gains, whereas ordinary taxpayers tend to have either real losses or at most very modest real gains.*

To summarize, high-income taxpayers tend to have substantial real capital gains, whereas ordinary taxpayers tend to have either real losses or modest real gains. High-income taxpayers also take great advantage of opportunities in the tax laws to avoid current taxation of their economic income, including the opportunity to defer or exempt from tax substantial amounts of their capital gains. It seems on balance, therefore, that taxing inflationary gains is likely to be unfair for the typical ordinary taxpayer but not for the typical high-income taxpayer.

Indexing any gains for inflation would be complicated. Some experts, such as Alan Auerbach, believe that the problems can be managed.[57] But none other than the Tax Committee of the New York State Bar Association, whose members are highly versed in the art of legitimate tax avoidance, has warned against indexing, expressing "grave concern" that "an indexation regime would create intolerable administrative burdens for taxpayers and tax administrators as well as offer numerous tax arbitrage and avoidance opportunities for aggressive tax planners."[58]

Finally, if capital gains are indexed for inflation, interest and dividends should also be. Some economists have concluded that "the interaction of taxes and inflation penalizes other kinds of income from capital, such as interest and dividends, more than it penalizes capital gains."[59] Indexing capital gains but not interest and dividends also would distort economic decisions, shifting investments away from assets that yield interest and dividends and toward those that produce capital gains.

4. Is It Unfair to Tax Individual Stockholders of a Corporation on their Entire Capital Gains When a Portion of Their Gains Is Attributable to the Corporation's Previously Taxed Profits? This question involves what is commonly referred to as the double taxation of corporate profits, which raises issues of fairness and tax efficiency. Both are addressed here.

Except for certain small corporations, every for-profit corporation must pay an income tax on its net profits. The profits that remain after the corporate income tax (the *net after-tax profits*) may then be taxed again in either of two ways, not to the corporation but to stockholders (the double tax). When the net after-tax profits are distributed as dividends to individual stockholders, the stockholders must report the dividends as ordinary income. The double tax occurs because corporations cannot deduct the dividend payment. The other form of double taxation occurs indirectly when a corporation retains net after-tax profits and an individual later sells her stock for a gain. The stockholder must count the entire gain as income even though part or all resulted from an increase in the value of the corporation attributable to the previously taxed profits.

Both forms of double taxation occur frequently. Martin Feldstein calculated that if someone bought publicly held stock of a corporation in 1973 and sold it in 1993, the after-tax earnings for the typical corporation actually exceeded the increase in the stock's price, if both were adjusted for inflation.[60] Steuerle's earlier warning, however, about the danger of aggregating statistics is relevant here. Many stockholders have substantial real gains on their stocks that far exceed the value of the corporation's retained earnings after adjustments for inflation. Netscape, for example, earned only a few million dollars of profits the year that it went public, but the stock's price made its principal stockholder a billionaire. Amazon.com never has had profits, but its principal stockholders have become billionaires. Many other companies have substantial earnings that have not been taxed because of special provisions of the tax laws.[61]

We also know that a stockholder's capital gain may exceed her share of a corporation's pretax accumulated profits. In that case, she pays a tax on that excess only once. For example, if you own 1 percent of ABC corporation, which has $1 million of accumulated pretax profits, your 1 percent share of that amount is $10,000. If you sell your stock for a $100,000 gain, the 20 percent tax on your gain means that you have effectively paid a double tax only on $10,000, not on the remaining $90,000. Critics of this analysis note that you have paid an *implicit tax* on your $90,000 gain as well as the actual tax. By this they mean that the market discounted the price of your stock because prospective purchasers took into account the risk of double taxation in valuing your stock; and this market reduction can be considered a tax. For example, you might have received 20 percent more for your stock if the risk of double taxation did not exist. But when you purchased the stock, you probably received a comparable percentage price discount—what we might call an *implicit tax refund*—because of the risk of double taxation. To summarize, the implicit tax on your gain roughly corresponded to the implicit tax refund you received at the time of purchase, which should mean that you received a fair return on your investment.

Indeed, this analysis suggests that you have not been unfairly taxed even when the corporation has paid tax on accumulated profits equal to your entire capital gain, because the discounted price you paid for your stock—your bargained-for exchange—anticipated the double tax. You got what you paid for. The result would be unfair only if, after you purchased your stock, Congress increased the corporate tax or the individual capital gains tax; you would receive a windfall if Congress reduced (or eliminated) either tax after your purchase.

> *You have not been unfairly taxed even when the corporation has paid tax on accumulated profits equal to your entire capital gain, because the discounted price you paid for your stock—your bargained-for exchange—anticipated the double tax.*

Moreover, although corporations pay the entire corporate tax, the ultimate **tax incidence**, or burden, of the tax falls only in part on stockholders. Corporations typically pass on a portion of the tax to consumers by raising prices for goods and services, and to workers by reducing wages. Economists are uncertain about what portion of the tax incidence is transferred in these ways, but to the extent that it is, stock values are not adversely affected by the corporate tax. In other words, to the extent consumers and workers ultimately bear the corporate tax, the corporate tax does not result in a double tax on stockholders.

Though counterintuitive, the incidence of the corporate tax to some extent also is borne by owners of partnerships, limited liability companies, and other businesses whose income is taxed only once. Readers may understand this outcome best by imagining a time when the corporate income tax did not exist. Then, when the tax was imposed, it initially drove investments away from corporations to businesses whose income was taxed only once, because, on the same amount of income, such businesses produced higher after-tax returns for their owners. Over time, however, the additional supply of resources to these other businesses drives down the return they offer, just as a higher supply of labor drives down what employers must pay workers. As Joel Slemrod and Jon Bakija have noted, "Once the reallocation of investment is completed, the after-tax, risk-adjusted return on investment will be the

> *The corporate double tax drags down the value of all businesses, not just the value of corporations.*

same for corporate investments as it is for noncorporate investments."[62] Thus the corporate double tax drags down the value of all businesses, not just the value of corporations.

The double tax also encourages corporations to become undercapitalized: they depend too much on loans and too little on the issuance of stock to meet their financial needs. Loans are attractive because corporations may deduct their interest payments, whereas corporations may not deduct dividends they pay with respect to stock. A corporation's overdependence on loans, however, can endanger its future. In financially stressful times, interest always must be paid; dividends, being discretionary, can be reduced or eliminated.

Lowering the individual capital gains tax would reduce the double-tax problem. But the lower tax would trigger other economic distortions. Because it would widen the gap with tax rates on ordinary income, it would encourage corporations to retain earnings rather than pay dividends that would be taxed at ordinary income rates, even when a dividend distribution made economic sense. People would be encouraged to allocate more of their savings to investments that pay off by their potential capital gains rather than by producing ordinary income, though the latter may generate more pretax income. Such incentives can slow economic growth.

Conclusions and Recommendations

The issues, as we have seen, are exceedingly complex. Economic outcomes from lowering the capital gains rate revolve around our personal behavior. Yet economists lack sufficient evidence of our personal behavior to allow at least the great majority of them to agree about how much more we might save and invest, realize our gains, become entrepreneurial, or invest in new companies as the capital gains rate falls. What evidence we have does not allow us to conclude that lowering the rate would significantly raise government tax revenue and strengthen the economy. Both government revenue and the economy are at least equally at risk of declining as a result of a rate cut.

This risk must be taken seriously. If the experiment failed, a number of ordinary workers could lose wages or jobs. The rich, however, could afford the setback, particularly because they would receive most of the tax relief. However, any decline in government revenue and the economy likely would not be severe because of the limited role played by capital gains rates.

My recommendations follow several conclusions. First, to adjust all capital gains for inflation would provide a windfall for many high-income taxpayers because they tend to neutralize taxes on inflationary gains by maximizing opportunities to defer the tax, interest free, on their appreciated investments. Ordinary taxpayers, on average, defer the tax for much shorter periods of time, which means that they are more likely to suffer a real economic loss when they pay tax on their inflationary gains. For these reasons, Congress should consider a lifetime exemption from tax on realized capital gains in an amount that would be significant to the average taxpayer but insignificant to high-income taxpayers. (This exemption would be in addition to a limited exemption for gain from the sale of a principal residence, described in Chapter 11.) I say "consider" because such an exemption would be difficult to administer today. We may not be far from a time, however, when our capital gains are entered in IRS data banks that would automatically track any prior use of such an exemption.

Second, tax deferrals such as for stock swaps in corporate mergers or for real estate swaps cannot be justified on equity or economic grounds and should be eliminated. Third, the step-up-in-basis rule for assets at death provides an unnecessary windfall to heirs and also should be eliminated. Instead, heirs should assume the same tax basis for computing gain as the decedent had in each asset they inherit.[63] To avoid double taxation, any estate tax attributable to the asset should be subtracted from the capital gains tax that heirs might owe when they eventually sell the asset. For administrative purposes, Congress should grant a limited step-up that would protect a modest amount of inherited gain from capital gains tax.

Congress also could continue to experiment with the opportunity that exists under current laws to exclude up to half of capital gains from tax for certain investments in new enterprises; indeed, Congress might expand the relief somewhat, but the relief should be limited to enterprises operating in the United States.[64] This exclusion is unlikely to be very costly and would test the proposition of a number of economists that the tax relief could provide a substantial stimulus to economic growth.

To achieve greater economic efficiency, relief also should be provided from the double tax of corporate profits resulting from corporate dividends. Corporations should continue to pay taxes on their profits, but stockholders who owe tax on dividend distributions should receive a tax credit for the share of the corporate tax allocable to such dividends. Before instituting the credit, however, Congress must decide what taxes to raise to cover the substantial revenues that it may lose each year from these tax credits. Because higher-income stockholders primarily would benefit from the relief, they ought to shoulder the major part of any compensating tax increase by paying somewhat higher tax rates on their other income.

Along with these reforms, Congress should consider the far more ambitious program advocated throughout this book—broadening the entire income tax base by eliminating most tax preferences and lowering all tax rates across the board to achieve revenue-neutral reforms. With these comprehensive changes, capital gains would become subject to the same tax rates as ordinary income. Then, top rates on all income would be considerably lower than today's top rates on ordinary income but somewhat higher than today's top capital gains rates. These reforms would serve the economy. They also would make it more likely that equals would be taxed equally and that people with greater abilities to pay would pay appropriately more.[65] Congress also might consider reintroducing income averaging, which would allow a taxpayer with an unusually large capital gain in one year to compute her tax by treating the gain as if received in that year and several previous years. Although income averaging adds to the complexity of the tax laws, the fairness of recognizing that large gains usually accrue over many years might have overriding value.

13

Flat Tax Versus Income Tax

The flat tax. . . would be honest. . . . It would be fair. Millions of people would be off the federal income tax rolls.

—Steve Forbes

Under the Forbes flat tax, should Bill Gates. . . decide to retire early, he would never again pay a dime in income taxes for the defense of his country. But the men and women who continued to work at Microsoft would have to pay. . . . A tax idea that produces such inequity would be laughed out of Congress.

—Patrick J. Buchanan

Overview * Characteristics of a Pure Armey-Shelby * Why a Pure Flat Tax Is a Form of Consumption Tax * The Effect of the Flat Tax on Compliance Costs * How a Flat Tax Could Alter Individual Tax Burdens * The Flat Tax and Economic Growth * How the Flat Tax Might Be Compromised, and the Consequences * A Better Alternative: Reforming the Income Tax

Both statements by these controversial men were at least partly correct. Forbes's flat tax would eliminate millions from the federal income tax rolls primarily because households would receive much larger personal deductions than are available through current standard deductions and personal exemptions.[1] What troubled Buchanan, who was responding to Forbes during their 1996 Republican presidential campaigns, was that a retired Bill Gates could be part of the newly exempt group.

Like most flat tax proponents, Forbes would exempt individuals from tax on all investment income, such as interest, dividends, and capital gains. This

254

exemption means that if Gates sold all of his Microsoft stock and lived in retirement on the proceeds, he would not owe any capital gains taxes on the sale;[2] also tax exempt would be his future gains, dividends, and interest from reinvesting the funds. Under these circumstances, as Buchanan suggested, he might "never again pay a dime in income taxes for the defense of his country."[3]

Buchanan was wrong, however, in believing that the flat tax would be "laughed out of Congress," though it was dismissed summarily by the Clinton administration, whose Treasury secretary, Lawrence Summers, referred to it as "a bad idea whose time should never come."[4] Prior to Forbes's bid for the 1996 presidential nomination, the flat tax thrived only within the economic literature, where it has received extensive attention since Robert Hall and Alvin Rabushka's *Low Tax, Simple Tax, Flat Tax* appeared in 1983.[5] Forbes pushed the flat tax to the forefront of national politics, where it remains today. It also remains widely misunderstood.

This chapter addresses those misunderstandings and attempts to put in clearer perspective the choice between a flat tax and an income tax. The choice is complicated not merely because political rhetoric tends to obfuscate rather than inform. Flat tax proposals vary; many issues are technical; economists reach different conclusions about the economic consequences of a flat tax and about which tax rate would produce as much tax revenue as today's rates; were Congress to enact a flat tax, it likely would look a lot different from ones we currently are asked to consider; and distinctions from today's income tax can be overdrawn because our income tax already has many characteristics of a flat tax.

We begin, however, with the purest and most widely discussed flat tax. I will call it the Armey-Shelby flat tax, or just *Armey-Shelby*, after its authors, Representative Richard Armey and Senator Richard Shelby. Proposed in 1995 and updated in 1999,[6] Armey-Shelby follows principles articulated by Hall and Rabushka. It is *pure* in the sense that it does not offer relief for special hardships or for particular social or economic behavior other than for saving and investing.

We first will survey supporters' and critics' claims. Then we will examine in detail how taxable income would be defined and taxed under the Armey-Shelby flat tax, a major source of public misunderstanding. Readers

> *Though advocates usually compare a flat tax with today's extraordinarily complicated income tax, readers may be surprised by frequent similarities between a pure flat tax and a pure income tax.*

will learn why Armey-Shelby is a consumption tax. Though advocates usually compare a flat tax with today's extraordinarily complicated income tax, readers may be surprised by frequent similarities between a *pure* flat tax and a *pure* income tax, which will be covered next. Then we will analyze how Armey-

Shelby could reduce compliance costs, alter our relative tax burdens, and stimulate economic growth. Because Congress would be under enormous political pressure to modify Armey-Shelby in order to soften some of its harsher consequences and to stimulate certain taxpayer behavior, we will consider the dilemma these issues pose for flat tax supporters. We will conclude by considering tax-policy reforms that draw upon many principles of Armey-Shelby for achieving a fairer, more efficient, and simplified income tax.

As mentioned, a range of other flat tax proposals exist, including one by the National Commission on Economic Growth and Tax Reform, which was headed by Jack Kemp, and a cash flow consumption tax proposed by David Bradford. All are worth studying. I have not explored them here because of constraints on the length of this book and because you can understand their fundamental principles if you understand Armey-Shelby, which contains many provisions common to all flat tax proposals.

Overview

A flat tax sounds like, could be, and often is described as any tax system that imposes a single, flat tax rate. "The flat tax—having a single income tax rate for all American taxpayers instead of the current graduated set of rates—" began a front-page story in the *New York Times* in November 1999.[7] Nothing in the name suggests that it would replace the income tax with a *consumption tax;* that it would change drastically the definition of *taxable income* and the availability of *personal deductions;* that the single tax rate applied to *individuals* also would apply to *corporations;* and that it would *shift tax burdens,* sometimes substantially, among taxpayers. The Armey-Shelby flat tax would involve all the above.

Armey-Shelby would stimulate the economy, supporters believe, by two means: by increasing the economic efficiency of the tax laws and by not taxing saving and investing.

Its principal virtues, according to supporters, begin with its simplicity—tax returns would be short enough to fit on a postcard. Such simplicity would be accompanied by far lower compliance costs for taxpayers and the Internal Revenue Service. Equally important, Armey-Shelby would stimulate the economy, supporters believe, by increasing the economic efficiency of the tax laws. It would promote economic efficiency primarily by eliminating the tax on saving and investing and by including few other tax preferences; gone would be all personal itemized deductions and all employer deductions for fringe benefits. All of these simplifications and efficiencies would supposedly make most households more prosperous across income levels.

Supporters also insist that Armey-Shelby would be fairer than existing laws. Its high personal allowances would exempt many low- and moderate-income households from tax. Also, supporters believe that a single (flat) rate applied to all taxpayers would be fairer than progressive tax rates. Moreover, for several reasons, supporters claim that households would be taxed more fairly if taxed on their level of consumption rather than on their level of income. First, according to supporters, personal expenditures—stemming as they do from current income, savings, and borrowing—more accurately reflect normal or permanent income than does current income alone, which may be more subject to peaks and valleys. Second, as even opponents agree, a flat-rate consumption tax achieves horizontal equity between people who have identical patterns of labor income and no distinctions in wealth but who consume their incomes at different times. As David Bradford argues, the tax system should not "bear more heavily on the individual who chooses to apply his endowment of labor abilities to purchase of consumption late in life (by saving early in life) than it does on the one who consumes early in life."[8] By comparison, an income tax taxes more heavily the person who saves early and consumes later.

Exempting income from savings and investments is fair, supporters of the flat tax argue, because such income arises from business profits (of corporations and other entities) or from wages and salaries that already have been taxed.

Consider a 20 percent consumption tax (ignoring personal deductions). If you earn and spend $10,000 this year, you will pay a $2,000 tax. If you save the $10,000 for a year, earn 5 percent interest on it (or $500), and then consume, you would have the full $10,500 to consume, on which you would pay a tax of $2,100, leaving you with a net of *$8,400* to spend. Now compare a 20 percent income tax (also ignoring personal deductions): Your $10,000 will be reduced this year to $8,000 after taxes even if you save it. At 5 percent interest, you will earn $400 on the saved $8,000, but the $400 will be reduced by the 20 percent income tax, leaving you with $320, or a total of *$8,320* to spend, compared to $8,400 under the consumption tax. As stated by Slemrod and Bakija, "Income taxes have a negative impact on the incentive to save, whereas consumption taxes do not."[9]

Finally, supporters of a flat tax believe that it is fair to exempt from tax the income from savings and investments because, they argue, such income arises from business profits or from wages and salaries, all of which previously has been taxed. Viewed this way, the tax exemption for savings and investments shields people from double taxation.

Although sharing the goal of replacing the income tax, flat tax advocates are at odds over the future of estate and gift taxes. Some believe that these taxes must remain to help constrain concentrations of wealth, which could be magnified by a consumption tax. Others view gifts and bequests as a form of consumption and thus taxable under a flat tax. But Armey-Shelby would eliminate estate and gift taxes. The authors consider wealth already taxed once under its system, and they view taxing its transfer as another inappropriate case of double taxation.

Concerns about Armey-Shelby vary, beginning with beliefs that it would be unfair. One common observation is that Armey-Shelby would reduce tax burdens of the rich and increase tax burdens of most other households. Critics particularly worry about low- and moderate-income households with dependent children, who would lose the earned-income tax credit. Many critics also believe that because consumption as a percentage of income declines as income rises, Armey-Shelby would strike taxpayers hardest when they are most vulnerable, that is, when they are young and must consume all of their income or when they are old and must live on (consume) their savings. Critics note also that an income tax responds far better than does a flat tax to our ability to pay in a particular year. If our income falls, so too does our tax liability, whereas our tax liability may not change under a consumption tax—in fact, our liability could even rise—because we may be forced to borrow to meet basic or emergency consumption needs.

> *Because consumption as a percentage of income declines as income rises, many critics believe that Armey-Shelby would strike households hardest when they are most vulnerable, that is, when they are young and earn too little to save or when they are old and must live on their savings.*

Critics concede that Armey-Shelby would be far simpler than today's system. Indeed, its elimination of most tax preferences, such as for fringe benefits and itemized deductions, would be favored by many of us who advocate retaining the income tax but greatly broadening its tax base. But critics do not expect Armey-Shelby to emerge pure. Congress would hear powerful protests that the elimination of the mortgage-interest deduction, the charitable deduction, and other itemized deductions and the nondeductibility of certain fringe benefits would be unfair, cause excessive hardship, damage the economy, or all of the above. Independent of these considerations would be those of businesses that, prior to the new law, invested heavily in plant and equipment or borrowed heavily; such businesses could suffer badly under Armey-Shelby's proposal to prohibit them from deducting any of their old investment costs or their interest payments. How many of these and other complaints, backed by well-financed lobbyists and special-interest groups, might compromise Armey-Shelby, making it more complex and less capable of achieving the economic growth it promises?

> *Critics also believe flat tax supporters mislead by claiming that all income is taxed once under the flat tax.*

Critics also believe that flat tax supporters mislead by claiming that all income is taxed once under the flat tax. Critics view the flat tax as actually or effectively exempting a great deal of income from *any* tax, such as the normal return businesses realize from investments they make in plant and equipment. Such outcomes add to misgivings about the fairness of Armey-Shelby. These misgivings are further magnified by Armey-Shelby's elimination of estate and gift taxes, which would allow unlimited wealth—much of which never has been effectively taxed, critics maintain—to pass from one generation to the next.

Supporters of Armey-Shelby view the particular concerns of critics as exaggerated or as acceptable one-time costs for realizing Armey-Shelby's considerable advantages. Other supporters recommend provisions that would temper some of the more dire consequences. Each relief measure, however, would shrink the tax base. Each shrinkage distresses purists because Congress then would have to raise the tax rate higher

> *As the purity of Armey-Shelby erodes, so too does its opportunity to stimulate economic growth.*

and higher to maintain revenue neutrality. As the rate rises, it would become less attractive to many households compared with the top rate of 15 percent paid today by over two-thirds of all taxpayers. Each impurity and higher rate also erodes Armey-Shelby's opportunity to stimulate economic growth.

Characteristics of a Pure Armey-Shelby

Individuals: Taxable Income

Armey-Shelby appeals to us immediately because our entire tax return could fit onto a postcard (Figure 13.1). Gross income would consist solely of cash income from *wages, salary,* and *pensions.* Wages and salary would include all unemployment compensation but would exclude self-employment earnings, which would appear on the tax return for businesses.

Apparently for administrative reasons, Armey-Shelby chooses to treat fringe benefits not as employee income (a form of wages) but as nondeductible business expenses. Although this approach literally means that businesses pay a tax on fringe benefits, economists assume that employers will shift the real tax burden to employees by decreasing their wages by the size of the tax. Pensions, including individual retirement accounts and all forms of tax-favored employment-based retirement plans, would be taxable only when received, as they are today. Similarly, pension trusts would continue to accumulate contributions and earnings tax free. All Social Security benefits would be tax exempt because (as I will note shortly) payment of Social Security taxes even by employers would not be deductible.

Armey-Shelby would eliminate standard deductions, itemized deductions, personal exemptions, and all tax credits, including the refundable earned-income tax credit. Instead, taxpayers would be entitled to deductions—called

Form I **ARMEY-SHELBY FLAT TAX FORM** 2001

Your first name and initial	Last name	Your social security number

Present home address	Spouse's social security number

City, Town or Post Office Box, State and ZIP Code	Your occupation
	Spouse's occupation

1. Wages, Salary, and Pensions.	1	
2. Personal Allowance		
a. $24,400 for married filing jointly.	2(a)	
b. $12,200 for single	2(b)	
c. $15,650 for single head of household.	2(c)	
3. Number of dependents, not including spouse	3	
4. Personal allowances for dependents (line 3 multiplied by $5,500)	4	
5. Total personal allowances (line 2 plus line 4)	5	
6. Taxable wages (line 1 less line 5, if positive, otherwise zero).	6	
7. Tax (17 percent of line 6)	7	
8. Tax already paid.	8	
9. Tax due (line 7 less line 8, if positive)	9	
10. Refund due (line 8 less line 7, if positive)	10	

FIGURE 13.1   The Armey-Shelby Individual Flat Tax Form for 2001
SOURCE: Obtained from the Internet: http://flattax.gov/proposal/form.asp.

personal allowances—for themselves and each dependent. For 2001, personal allowances would be $24,400 if married, $12,200 if single, and $15,650 for a head of household; the allowance for each dependent would be $5,500.

> *Armey-Shelby would eliminate standard deductions, itemized deductions, personal exemptions, and all tax credits. In their place would be personal allowances for the taxpayer and dependents.*

Under Armey-Shelby in 2001, then, George and Sherry Crist of Charleston, West Virginia, who have two young children, would not be taxed on their first *$35,400* of income (the sum of personal allowances of $24,400 for the parents plus $11,000 for two dependents). By comparison, if the Crists claimed a standard deduction and personal exemptions under current law (adjusted for estimated inflation to 2001), plus child credits and the maximum dependent-care credits for their children, they would not be taxed on approximately their first *$32,000* of income. The Crists, however, itemize their deductions, which protects them from tax on over $40,000 of their income. Under Armey-Shelby, they no longer would be entitled to deduct a portion of their health insurance premiums and out-of-pocket medical expenses that they pay personally, interest payments on the large mortgage they took out when they recently acquired their house, real estate taxes on the house, West Virginia income taxes, and charitable contributions.

Individuals: Tax Rates

Because of deductions for personal allowances and dependents, Armey-Shelby effectively would have two rates: a zero rate that applies to all labor income protected by personal allowances ($35,400 in the Crist example) and a second rate that applies to the excess. That second rate initially would be 19 percent, falling to 17 percent after two years. Higher-income households no longer would worry about an alternative minimum tax, which Armey-Shelby eliminates. Supporters expect that because of Armey-Shelby's ability to generate economic growth, tax collections from individuals and business taxes under these low rates would be revenue neutral by Armey-Shelby's third year.[10]

Critics, and even some supporters, believe that a revenue-neutral rate for Armey-Shelby must be closer to 21 percent. Hall and Rabushka have calculated that the rate would need to be 22 percent.[11] We cannot resolve the dispute here. To minimize the risk of incurring large deficits, Congress would be wise to begin at a higher rate, knowing that it could always move to a lower rate if sufficient revenue materialized.

Businesses: Taxable Income

I have discussed business income taxes in this book only when necessary to explain aspects of individual taxation. Some discussion is unavoidable here because it completes the flat tax picture.

Under existing laws, a business formed in the United States must include on its tax return its worldwide income from all sources—from sales of goods, services, and investments and from returns on investments, such as interest, dividends, and capital gains.[12] Deductions are permitted for all ordinary and necessary expenses incurred to produce income, such as the cost of goods sold, salaries, rent, advertising, insurance, contributions to pension plans, interest on loans, and half of all Social Security and Medicare taxes. Corporations also may deduct employee fringe benefits; these deductions are more restricted in the case of unincorporated businesses.

Property that is likely to be consumed in one year is deducted in full for the year of purchase. All other property, such as a building, tractor, or copying machine, generally must be depreciated, that is, deducted a bit each year over its useful life as specified by the Internal Revenue code. In this way, businesses deduct their entire investment cost over the period in which the property is *expected* to wear out; no proof is required that the property actually wears out. For example, an office building may be depreciated over 39 years even if it appreciates in value each year. Land cannot be depreciated because, in theory, it does not wear out.

Depreciation deductions often underestimate the real economic loss from a depreciating asset because only its original cost may be depreciated. When it eventually is to be replaced, the price usually has risen because of inflation. Congress could correct the problem by allowing an annual inflation adjustment for the undepreciated cost of an asset, but Congress has resisted largely because the adjustments would be complicated to administer. Instead, as a sort of rough justice, businesses may claim extra depreciation deductions in the early years after purchase (**accelerated depreciation**), such as two thirty-ninths of a building's cost rather than one thirty-ninth, which accelerates the tax savings.

> *Business income under Armey-Shelby would exclude inactive (commonly called passive) income, typically interest, dividends, royalties, and capital gains from financial assets.*

Armey-Shelby would radically change most rules. A business's tax return, like the individual return, would fit onto a postcard. Gross income, referred to as *gross active income,* would consist of *gross revenue from sales* of property or services (Figure 13.2).[13] This definition excludes *inactive* (or *passive*) income: Interest, dividends, royalties, and capital gains from financial assets would be tax free, except perhaps in the case of banks and other financial institutions engaged in the business of lending. Armey-Shelby also would exclude income from importing property or services into the United States. (Armey-Shelby's tax treatment of financial institutions and income from imports is complicated and beyond the scope of this chapter.)

A business would be entitled to deduct *wages, salaries, and pensions,* including pension-plan contributions; *purchases of goods, services, and materials;* and *purchases of capital equipment, structures, and land.* So that Armey-Shelby not tax a tax, a business also could deduct any excise tax, sales tax, customs duty, or other levy imposed by a federal, state, or local government on the business's purchase of property or services. As mentioned earlier, businesses no longer could deduct fringe benefits, such as health insurance premiums, for their employees. Businesses also could not deduct interest on their loans or their half of Social Security and Medicare taxes, which parallels the proposed tax-free treatment of interest income and of Social Security and Medicare benefits.

Depreciation deductions would be replaced by a far more valuable deduction—the right to deduct, in the year of purchase, the entire cost of assets to

Form 2 ARMEY-SHELBY FLAT TAX FORM 1999

Business name	Employer ID Number
Street address	County
City, State and ZIP Code	Principal Product

1. Gross revenue from sales	1	
2. Allowable costs		
a. Purchases of goods, services, and materials	2(a)	
b. Wages, salaries, and pensions	2(b)	
c. Purchases of capital equipment, structures, and land	2(c)	
3. Total of allowable costs (sum of lines 2(a), 2(b), 2(c)	3	
4. Taxable income (line 1 less line 3).	4	
5. Tax (17% of line 4).	5	
6. Carry forward from 1998	6	
7. Interest on carry-forward (6% of line 6).	7	
8. Carry-forward into 1999 (line 6 plus line 7).	8	
9. Tax due (line 5 less line 8, if positive)	9	
10. Carry-forward to 2000 (line 8 less line 5, if positive).	10	

FIGURE 13.2   The Armey-Shelby Business Flat Tax Form for 1999
SOURCE: Obtained from the Internet: http://flattax.gov/proposal/form2.asp.

be used in the business—goods, materials, capital equipment, structures, and land. Yes, even land costs would be deducted in the year when land is acquired. No longer would businesses, or the IRS, concern themselves with complicated depreciation rules or records. The advantages to businesses, however, are far more than administrative. As explained shortly, the value of immediately deducting the full cost of all assets used in the business equals—and thereby neutralizes—the ultimate burden of paying tax on the normal return from such assets.

Businesses no longer could deduct interest on loans, fringe benefits, and their one-half of Social Security and Medicare taxes.

Nevertheless, some businesses will find transition to the new rules highly problematic. Consider a business that makes major property acquisitions and incurs substantial debt prior to Armey-Shelby. Implementation of Armey-Shelby would render interest payments on the debt no longer deductible. The business also would lose the right to deduct the undepreciated cost (the original cost minus depreciation deductions) of the property. This follows because Armey-Shelby eliminates depreciation deductions, and only property acquired *after* Armey-Shelby is enacted may be deducted in the year of purchase. To make matters worse, if the business was forced to sell the plant and equipment, the entire proceeds would be income even if they had to be paid to the lender in order to retire debt. Remember, *gross active income* consists of gross revenue from sales of property or services.

> *After Armey-Shelby, businesses would not be able to deduct the undepreciated cost of property acquired before Armey-Shelby or interest on any loans that arise prior to (or after) Armey-Shelby.*

Finally, businesses, like individuals, could not deduct the cost of financial investments, such as stocks and bonds, but only because proceeds from their sale would not be considered income. In sum, neither the investment in stocks, bonds, or other financial investments nor the return from them would be reported on tax returns for businesses or individuals.

Businesses: Tax Rates

Medium and large corporations today pay a flat tax rate of 34 or 35 percent on their taxable profits. Certain small corporations pay graduated rates, running from 15 to 25 to 34 percent. The profits of unincorporated businesses are taxed to their owners at their individual income tax rates.

Armey-Shelby stipulates that all businesses, including corporations large and small, would pay the same flat rate on their profits. The same rate would apply to individuals.

Why a Pure Flat Tax Is a Form of Consumption Tax

Consumption equals income minus saving and investment. It follows that a consumption tax is assessed on income consumed rather than saved and invested. To understand why Armey-Shelby is a consumption tax, let us look briefly at two classic consumption taxes, a sales tax and a value-added tax (VAT).

If Congress replaced the income tax with a national sales tax, all our income except what we consumed would be tax free. Only when we bought something would we pay the tax. If we earned $100,000, bought $40,000 of goods and services, and paid a 20 percent tax rate, our tax would be $8,000 (20 percent x $40,000), or 8 percent of our income. If we earned $40,000 and consumed it all, we also would pay $8,000 in taxes; in this case the tax would be a full 20 percent of our income. These examples suggest why a flat-rate consumption tax would be regressive unless accompanied by special relief provisions: Lower-income households, compared with higher-income households, would pay the flat sales tax rate on a higher percentage of their income because they spend a greater percentage of their income on consumption. Furthermore, the national sales tax would be much harsher on a great many households than would progressive rates.

Defenders of the flat-rate consumption tax note that people with equal incomes over their lifetimes and no other differences in wealth or inheritance would pay equally, assuming they spend all of their income during their lifetimes, and that this achievement—known as horizontal equity—is a prime goal of any tax system. But no one knows in advance what people's income, wealth, or inheritances will be over their lifetimes, which leaves to enormous speculation whether horizontal equity between particular taxpayers will be achieved. Furthermore, achieving vertical equity is equally important, and critics believe that a flat-rate consumption tax without adequate relief for low- and moderate-income households fails that test.

A value-added tax, or VAT, functions like a sales tax. Only the payer is different. The government collects a national sales tax from the ultimate consumer when he acquires the finished product or service. With a VAT, the government collects a portion of the tax from each business in the chain of production, which pays tax on *the value it adds* to the product or service. If Jerry Fleiss, who fabricates doors, sold 10 doors to Building Supply Company for $1,000 and Jerry paid $250 for materials and $50 to have them delivered, he would pay a VAT on $700, the value he added to the doors above his $300 of purchases. If Building Supply Company sold the doors to Thayer Builders for $1,500, Building Supply would pay a tax on $500, the value it added to the doors above the $1,000 it paid for them.

Armey-Shelby would function like a typical VAT *if* businesses alone were taxed. Then, a business, not its employees, would pay tax on wages, salary, and pensions because these items no longer would be deductible; they would be part of the value added to the business, which is what a VAT taxes. Remember, with a VAT, a business may deduct the costs of acquiring assets and services from third parties but not what it pays to its own workers (see Figure 13.2).

As proposed, Armey-Shelby would function as a two-part VAT. Businesses would pay tax on their profits after deducting not only their purchases of assets and services from third parties but also after deducting wages, salaries, and pensions, which would be taxed to individuals. Why, you might ask, does Armey-Shelby tax these three items to individuals, since the tax rate on individuals and businesses would be identical? By doing so, Armey-Shelby can include personal allowances that relieve households from tax on income deemed necessary to pay for basic living costs.[14]

Indeed, Armey-Shelby would be a progressive VAT for lower- and moderate-income households, which would be shielded from tax on all or most of their wages, salary, and pensions because of Armey-Shelby's large personal allowances. When the tax burdens of the highest-income households are compared with those of households some notches below them, however, Armey-Shelby is regressive. Although personal allowances would protect from tax a smaller percentage of the income of highest-income households than of these other households, this relative disadvantage for highest-income households would be dwarfed by their enormous advantage of receiving all income from savings and investments tax free.

Armey-Shelby would be a progressive tax for lower- and moderate-income households. When tax burdens of the highest-income households are compared with those of households some notches below, however, Armey-Shelby is regressive.

Note that Armey-Shelby protects savings and investments from tax in either of two ways, both of which yield comparable tax savings. Neither individuals nor businesses may deduct their purchases of stocks, bonds, and other financial investments, but all returns from financial investments are tax free. Businesses alone may immediately deduct all acquisitions of property used in the business, such as plant and equipment; in turn, they must recognize as income the entire proceeds from the sale of such property.[15]

Economists agree that the value of the savings for businesses from immediately deducting these acquisition costs generally equates with the cost of paying taxes on the income normally generated by such assets; in most cases, therefore, the income from such assets effectively would be received tax free. This observation leads to the important conclusion, as Richard Musgrave has written, that Armey-Shelby, like similar flat tax proposals, "exempts the normal return to capital [the profits from plant and equipment] from taxation," an outcome that Musgrave believes is widely misunderstood.[16] In fact, businesses would be subject to a *net* tax burden only on extraordinary returns from their property. Hall and Rabushka have made the identical point in an example in which the flat tax rate is 19 percent: "The tax benefit of the write-off in the first year [of capital purchases] counterbalances the taxes that will be paid from its productivity in the future—the 19 percent deduction for investment write-off equals the 19 percent tax on future higher earnings."[17]

The only taxes that would impose a net tax burden on businesses under Armey-Shelby would be those on extraordinary returns from their property.

One final observation. We should not forget that our income tax often functions like a consumption tax by treating favorably a great many forms of savings and investments. For example, amounts contributed to and invested in pension plans are not currently taxed; in nearly all cases, the proceeds from the sale of our principal residence are tax exempt; and all gain on investments owned by a decedent at death are tax exempt. In sum, the charge that our income tax punishes savings and investments often is untrue.

Differences Between a Pure Flat Tax and a Pure Income Tax

Without trivializing the importance of their differences, we can observe, to the surprise of most people, that a pure flat tax and a pure income tax have much in common. Differences occur solely in defining the tax base, not the tax rate: A pure income tax always can include a flat rate. A pure income tax would be based on principles of Haig-Simons, limited by practical considerations (see Chapter 2).[18] Like a pure flat tax, the tax base of a pure income tax would include fringe benefits as well as salaries and wages. To avoid taxing households that are poor and avoid taxing households into poverty, both tax systems would exempt from tax a basic amount of income that would vary with household size. Neither tax system would allow itemized deductions; nor would either allow vested pension accounts to accumulate tax free (contrary to Armey-Shelby).

> *A pure flat tax and a pure income tax have much in common.*

Both tax systems would allow businesses to deduct costs of producing income. Unlike a pure flat tax, however, which allows all acquisition costs of plant and equipment to be deducted fully in the year of purchase, a pure income tax would allow businesses to deduct the costs only over an asset's expected useful life, with the undepreciated cost adjusted annually for inflation. In this important respect, a pure flat tax, by eliminating depreciation schedules and inflation adjustments, is far simpler than a pure income tax. Both tax systems would apply to the sale of the property. Under a pure flat tax, the entire proceeds would be taxed as gain. Under a pure income tax, taxable gain would be limited to the excess of the proceeds over the undepreciated cost of the property after appropriate adjustments for inflation; again, the flat tax approach would be much simpler.

> *A pure income tax would look like a pure flat tax except for the taxation of capital income—the income from plant and equipment and financial investments.*

These distinctions aside, the principal differences between a pure flat tax and a pure income tax, and the only difference for individual taxation, lie in their treatment of savings and investments. A pure flat tax exempts the returns from financial investments on the premise that all savings and investments have previously been taxed to businesses or to individuals. Principles of Haig-

Simons reject the concept that taxing these returns taxes the same income twice. Instead, Haig-Simons recognizes the return from financial investments as new economic income after adjustment for inflation.

To summarize, a pure income tax would look like a pure flat tax except for the taxation of financial investments and the income from plant and equipment. If you like the simplicity of the flat tax for its elimination of most tax preferences but do not like its exclusion of income from financial investments, you would like a pure income tax. You would have to accept, however, the considerable complexity of calculating and taxing capital gains. You also would sacrifice the simplicity of the flat tax's immediate deduction for the purchase of plant and equipment; instead, you would encounter complicated depreciation deduction rules. In the case of a pure income tax, you also might consider the alternative of moderately progressive tax rates to the flat tax's single rate. We will return to this subject at the end of the chapter.

The Effect of a Flat Tax on Compliance Costs

People disagree about the magnitude of the compliance costs of taxpayers and the IRS under our income tax laws, but everyone agrees they are enormous and excessive. People also disagree about the magnitude of compliance-cost savings that could be achieved by a pure flat tax, but everyone agrees they would be large. According to William Gale of the Brookings Institution and Kevin Hassett of the American Enterprise Institute, "Responsible estimates suggest that the compliance costs of the current income tax are about 10 percent of revenue raised, or 1 percent of GDP," and that a "flat tax would cut compliance costs in half."[19] These estimates suggest the cost of taxpayers to comply with the income tax and for the IRS to enforce it for 1999 would have been about $80 billion. If so, a flat tax would have saved about $40 billion, enough to remove from poverty over half of all people deemed poor by the federal government in 1999.

People disagree about the magnitude of compliance-cost savings that could be achieved by a pure flat tax, but everyone agrees they would be large.

Such savings, however, would not be realized in the early years, when transition costs to the new system would be enormous. The IRS would have to develop all new tax forms and instructions, train its employees about the new laws, develop regulations to implement them, and adapt computers to the new system. Businesses would have to learn the new laws, adapt their accounting and reporting systems, and develop new strategies in light of the new laws, not least of which would be deciding the future of their fringe benefit programs. Businesses would need extra meetings with tax advisers, who in turn would need to educate themselves about the new laws and the strategies they believed were in their clients' best interest. The only reasonably simple adaptation would be to the individual return; individuals would record figures only for wages, salaries, pensions, and personal allowances before making the tax computation.

Of course, if the flat tax became less pure through the inclusion of special relief measures, the long-term potential savings in compliance costs could erode quickly. And if the existing income tax became far purer, it could achieve much of the compliance-cost savings noted for a pure flat tax.

How a Flat Tax Could Alter Individual Tax Burdens

Most economists expect that a *pure* flat tax could raise economic growth impressively, though they differ widely in their estimates. We will explore their views shortly. If the economy grew in response to the flat tax at a rate that substantially increased the income of households at all income levels, most households' living standards would rise. But the rise could take time. We also cannot know in advance how the benefits of a stronger economy overall would be distributed among households— indeed, how much of the benefits would trickle down to middle- and lower-income households.

What we will address here is the impact of Armey-Shelby on our individual tax burdens were Armey-Shelby to have little impact on the nation's economic growth or on our individual incomes. For such circumstances, economists appear to agree on three generalizations, subject always to caveats about the uncertainty of the world in which any tax changes occur. First, most low-income households that include dependents and that qualify for the earned-income tax credit would be worse off, and many much worse off. Second, some low-income households and most moderate-income households that do not have dependents would be better off. Third, most highest-income households would be better off, and many much better off. Most controversial is the impact of Armey-Shelby on middle- and higher-income (as distinguished from *highest-income*) taxpayers.

Low-Income Households with Dependents

Low-income households with dependents do not owe taxes today and would not owe taxes under Armey-Shelby, given its personal allowances. But today, millions of these households receive sizable checks from the IRS through the refundable earned-income tax credit (EITC). They would receive no such checks under Armey-Shelby, which would eliminate the EITC. Lawrence Summers has estimated that the 1995 Armey-Shelby proposal would cause about 15 million workers and their families who had income below the 1995 tax thresholds "to lose an average of $1,360 per taxpayer in benefits."[20] Summers's estimate would not be materially altered by the most recent Armey-Shelby proposal.

Take Nancy Lanier, who lives in Nyack, New York. Recently widowed at the age of 24, she is the single parent of children ages two and three. Nancy works full-time as an aide at a local hospice for the elderly and earned $11,000 in 1999, including overtime. All $11,000 was protected from income tax by basic deductions and credits. Moreover, she was entitled to the maximum EITC, a sum of *$3,816* for working parents with two or more dependent children who earned between $9,540 and $12,460. Nancy uses her entire EITC to pay for child care; without the EITC, her job would be jeopardized because she could afford only a few hours of child care each workday.

Low- and Moderate-Income Households
Without Dependents

In 1999, households without dependents that did not itemize became taxable once their adjusted gross income exceeded $8,100 if single and $12,700 if married. Millions of such households that have somewhat higher adjusted gross income would have saved taxes under Armey-Shelby because of its much higher personal allowances.

Highest-Income Households

Armey-Shelby would bring substantial tax relief to the typical households with the highest incomes. Although these households would lose their right to itemize deductions, they would gain far more by excluding income from their financial investments. For example, in 1997, tax returns with $1 million or more of adjusted gross income reported total AGI of $424 billion, of which $184 billion (43 percent) derived from interest, dividends, capital gains, and royalties. Their itemized deductions totaled only $42 billion, less than one-quarter of their capital income. These households paid 32 percent of their taxable income in taxes; on their much smaller taxable income under Armey-Shelby, they would pay a much lower flat rate.

According to the Treasury Department, families with income in 1996 that exceeded $200,000—the top few percent of all families—would have seen their taxes lowered, on average, by 28.1 percent in 1996 had a revenue-neutral version of the 1995 Armey-Shelby proposal been adopted, which Treasury believed required a flat rate of 20.8 percent. Taxes would have fallen by 36 percent for the top 1 percent of families.[21] These tax savings would have been far larger had the tax rate been 17 percent, as proposed by Armey-Shelby.

Highest-income families would have had even lower tax burdens except that when Armey-Shelby hypothetically was adopted, they suffered a one-time loss of wealth. Readers will recall that no deduction for business property acquired before Armey-Shelby is available after Armey-Shelby, whereas property acquired after Armey-Shelby is deducted fully in the year of purchase. These rules place *old capital*—capital acquired prior to Armey-Shelby—and the businesses that own it at a competitive disadvantage with businesses that acquire *new capital*—capital acquired after Armey-Shelby.

Assume, for example, that Armey-Shelby is to be adopted next week, that its tax rate will be 20 percent, and that Company A and Company B are for sale. Both are in the same business, expect to have $10 million of income after all expenses (other than for capital purchases), and have the same value with one exception: Company A acquired $10 million of equipment this week, whereas Company B will acquire $10 million of equipment the day after Armey-Shelby is enacted. On that day, Company B will be worth *$2 million more* than Company A. Company B will retain all *$10 million of income after taxes* because all of its income will be sheltered from tax by the $10 million deduction for new capital. *Company A*, unable to deduct any of the $10 million it has spent on old capital, will have to pay $2 million of taxes on its income, leaving it with *$8 million of income after taxes.*

Company A's owners understandably would feel aggrieved; indeed, we could expect them to lobby for transition rules that would reduce or eliminate the punitive nature of the foregoing result. This result also explains why Armey-Shelby has been characterized as an ongoing tax on wages and pensions and a one-time tax on old capital. That one-time tax, however, is progressive: It mainly strikes higher-income taxpayers, those who own the great majority of business capital in this country. The tax on old capital also strikes the elderly hardest because they own most of the wealth in this country.

Families in Between

According to the Treasury Department study just referred to, the 1995 Armey-Shelby proposal, at the 20.8 percent flat rate that Treasury deemed necessary to achieve revenue neutrality, on average would have lowered taxes for households with over $200,000 of income and would have increased federal taxes—by between 5 and 70.7 percent—for all other families. Treasury's figures are only averages. Many families with income under $200,000 would pay less in taxes under Armey-Shelby. But there is considerable disagreement on the subject. A study by William G. Gale, Scott Houser, and John Karl Scholz, for example, concluded that, on average, "families in the 50th percentile to the 99th percentile of the income distribution will see small tax changes under the flat tax because the effect of eliminating the charitable contributions and home-mortgage interest deductions is offset by lower rates and larger exemptions."[22]

The Treasury Department disagrees. It believes that the impact of Armey-Shelby on most workers would be more significant because it expects businesses to reduce workers' wages or fringe benefits by the extra taxes businesses would pay on fringe benefits and one-half of FICA taxes, which would no longer be deductible. Indirectly, then, workers would pay these extra taxes. Treasury concluded that had Armey-Shelby been implemented in 1999, a typical married couple with two children, $50,000 of wages, and employer-provided health insurance would have paid *$1,604* more in federal taxes—including the couple's indirect share of federal taxes paid by businesses—than under our current tax system. Only by excluding their indirect share of business taxes would their federal tax burdens have been less under Armey-Shelby. Had each spouse earned $50,000, giving them total earnings of $100,000, Treasury calculated that they would have paid $2,683 more in federal taxes under Armey-Shelby.[23]

> *The Treasury Department expects that businesses would reduce workers' wages or fringe benefits by the extra taxes businesses would pay under Armey-Shelby on fringe benefits and FICA taxes.*

Armey-Shelby supporters could be expected to challenge Treasury's methodology in various respects, including the proposition that businesses would pass on to employees *all* of the additional taxes associated with their loss of deductions for FICA taxes and fringe benefits. Supporters also expect that a stronger economy under Armey-Shelby, resulting from economic efficiencies and incentives to save and invest, would more than compensate most families for any additional taxes they might pay.

> *Supporters expect that a stronger economy under Armey-Shelby, resulting from economic efficiencies and incentives to save and invest, would more than compensate most families for any additional taxes it might cause them to pay.*

Business Tax Burdens

We have noted previously that individuals, not businesses, ultimately pay the taxes imposed on businesses. Knowing which businesses would be helped or hurt by Armey-Shelby would help us identify which individuals would be helped or hurt.

We know that Armey-Shelby likely would impose exceptional tax burdens on businesses that, at the time of enactment, had significant, undepreciated investments in old capital and had borrowed heavily. Armey-Shelby supporters note that market pressures might bring interest rates down because borrowers no longer could afford the same interest payments once they become nondeductible. Even so, the new interest rates would not be immediately available to many recent borrowers because lenders typically prohibit prepayment for a number of years or impose high prepayment penalties. Businesses with lots of old capital and heavily in debt might also come under pressure to sell some or all of their old capital to reduce their debt. The results could be devastating both because used property typically is heavily discounted when sold and because all proceeds from any sale would be fully taxable as *gross active income.*

Armey-Shelby likely would impose exceptional tax burdens on businesses that, at the time of enactment, had significant undepreciated investments in old capital and had borrowed heavily.

Apart from transition problems, we know little about how Armey-Shelby, or other versions of a flat tax, would impact the ultimate tax burden of different kinds of businesses. Perhaps that is why we have heard surprisingly little from the business community about the potential consequences to them of replacing the income tax with a consumption tax.

The Flat Tax and Economic Growth

As readers have heard often in these pages, economists widely agree that our economy would benefit from a vastly simplified tax system, whether based on income or consumption, accompanied by lower progressive tax rates or a single flat rate. Efforts by Congress to advance seemingly endless social and economic objectives in our income tax system through deductions, exclusions, deferrals, and credits have greatly diminished the tax base, forced tax rates much higher than they otherwise need be, driven up compliance costs, and created a nation cynical about the tax system. On balance, these efforts have slowed the rate of economic growth and too often have failed to advance social justice. As Henry Aaron and William Gale have noted, "To encourage every sort of behavior is to encourage none."[24]

"Unless the [flat] tax improves the performance of the economy, it will let a minority of high-income families off the hook for the very high taxes they are now paying and finance the move by slightly raising everybody else's taxes." (Hall and Rabushka)

The principal promise of a flat tax, and the trump card of the flat tax movement, is that it will increase our nation's rate of economic growth. Otherwise, the movement itself likely would fall flat, though the cause of a flat tax *rate* would linger. As Hall and Rabushka admitted when they advanced the flat tax cause in 1983, "The simple tax is not immediately a good deal for most Americans. Unless the tax improves the performance of the economy, it will let a minority of high-income families off the hook for the very high taxes they are now paying and finance the move by slightly raising everybody else's taxes."[25] Adds William Gale, who has written extensively about flat-tax proposals: "Without a significant gain in living standards, uprooting the entire tax system is probably not worth the risks, redistributions, and adjustment costs [that moving to a flat tax] would impose."[26]

Let us turn our attention to the three reasons that a pure flat tax might spur economic growth. The initial stimulus, according to supporters, would come from an increase in work performed by people whose tax was lowered—a substitution effect. Second, by eliminating the tax on saving and investment, a pure flat tax would reduce economic distortions: No longer would the tax laws treat different kinds of assets differently. People then would choose investments on the basis of their underlying value. Last, the simpler tax system would reduce compliance costs by decreasing opportunities for and rewards from avoiding or evading taxes.

Most recently, Armey and Shelby have referred to two studies that estimate remarkable gains under a flat tax. (The studies do not clearly refer to *their* flat tax, an important distinction we will consider shortly.) One study, by "a former chief economist for Congress's Joint Committee on Taxation," expects that "under the flat tax the economy would be 5.7 percent larger after five years than under the current system." According to Armey and Shelby, "This translates into $522 billion in higher output, or $3,000 in higher income for the typical family of four." We also learn that "Michael Boskin, a former chairman of the Council of Economic Advisors, estimates that the flat tax would increase the size of the economy by 10 percent."[27]

Among other economists who share exuberant economic expectations for a flat tax is Dale Jorgensen, a longtime advocate of a consumption tax. Jorgensen has predicted that the "economic impact of a consumption tax would be truly staggering." Testifying before the House Ways and Means Committee in 1996, Jorgensen predicted that in the first two years of a consumption tax, the gross domestic product would grow at an annual rate of about 13 percent, "leveling off" thereafter at a growth rate of about 9 percent per year over the following 25 years.[28]

Boskin and Jorgensen forecast results way at the high end of leading economists' range of expectations.[29] No developed country ever has grown at a rate anywhere near Jorgensen's estimates. The skepticism of many economists begins with claims that economic growth would be triggered in good part by a sharp change in labor supply. Viewing any sharp change unlikely, they believe, instead, as Henry Aaron and William Gale have written, "the primary way to raise economic growth is to boost national saving, and advocates have claimed that fundamental tax reform would dramatically boost saving by reducing the effective tax rate on capital income." But according to Aaron and Gale, the most respected studies suggest that a flat tax would have a small impact on saving primarily because a very large percentage of savings, such as through pension plans, IRAs, life insurance vehicles, and the family residence, already receives the same favorable treatment that would be available under a flat tax.[30] Aaron and Gale also note that if tax reform lowered interest rates, "the return on such investments would decline, which may reduce saving." Finally, they warn that any transition relief—and they believe some is likely—would further diminish the impact of a flat tax on saving.[31]

Jorgensen agrees that transition relief would dampen expectations for a strong economic response to a flat tax. He also would agree that any economic forecasts must be specific to flat tax proposals because different flat taxes can prompt very different outcomes.

Alan Auerbach underscores this point in his comprehensive study of the possible effect of tax reform on capital allocation, efficiency, and economic growth. Writing in 1998, Auerbach compared economic outcomes from a national sales tax/VAT, the Hall-Rabushka flat tax, and the Armey-Shelby flat tax.[32] Armey-Shelby differs from Hall-Rabushka by offering much larger personal deductions for household size. The resulting smaller tax base of Armey-Shelby requires a higher tax rate to raise the same revenue as Hall-Rabushka, which places Armey-Shelby at a comparative economic disadvantage: The higher tax rate distorts economic behavior and thereby produces a slower rate of economic growth. Auerbach also estimated the economic results if Hall-Rabushka and Armey-Shelby allowed businesses transition relief by allowing them to continue to depreciate assets acquired prior to the flat tax.

Auerbach measured two economic outcomes—what he calls "efficiency gains"—for each proposal (Table 13.1). In layman's terms, we have an efficiency gain if, overall, we are better off from the new tax. Auerbach made this determination by taking into account, on the plus side, how much more in earnings and thus more ability to consume we likely would have as a result of the new tax system. On the minus side, Auerbach considered how much more we must work and save to achieve these results; thus we would have to sacrifice some leisure and some benefits of current consumption. In all comparisons, Armey-Shelby produced the least economic stimulus. Efficiency gains from a national sales tax/VAT would be the largest and substantial, according to Auerbach, ranging between 6.4 percent and 5.7 percent across households; gains under Armey-Shelby would be modest or nonexistent.

Auerbach's national sales tax/VAT performs so well economically because it maintains the lowest tax rate. The low rate is possible because the tax is a pure, regressive consumption tax, containing no relief provisions that might take into account a household's ability to pay or special adversities brought about by the new law. Large personal deductions for household size reduced the Armey-Shelby efficiency gain to between 1.4 and 1.0 percent; transition relief for old capital drops its efficiency gain to 0.4 percent or to zero. In sum, Auerbach estimates that the combination of large personal deductions under Armey-Shelby and transition relief for old capital "very nearly eliminates the efficiency gains from tax reform."[33]

Auerbach has not resolved the debate. Too many variables are at play that could alter the results, as Auerbach knows well. Glenn Hubbard, who was

TABLE 13.1 Efficiency Gains from VAT, Hall-Rabushka Flat Tax, and Armey-Shelby Flat Tax

Type of Tax	Percent Efficiency Gain Without Adjustment Costs [a]	Percent Efficiency Gain With Adjustment Costs
VAT	6.4	5.7
Hall-Rabushka		
No transition provision for old capital [b]	2.8	2.2
Transition provision for old capital	2.2	1.6
Armey-Shelby		
No transition provision for old capital	1.4	1.0
Transition provision for old capital	0.4	0.0

[a] Adjustment costs means costs to the economy, arising from problems of moving from the existing system to the new one, that would reduce efficiency gains.
[b] No transition for old capital means that the particular flat tax did not provide special relief for undepreciated property acquired before the flat tax became law.
SOURCE: Alan J. Auerbach, "Tax Reform, Capital Allocation, Efficiency, and Growth," in *Economic Effects of Fundamental Tax Reform,* ed. Henry J. Aaron and William G. Gale (Washington, D.C.: Brookings Institution, 1996), 58–62, tables 2-3 and 2-4.

asked to review Auerbach's work, takes issue with some of Auerbach's assumptions, though he believes Auerbach's economic model provides "a useful basis for starting to analyze the economic consequences of tax reform." Hubbard concludes what I believe all thoughtful planners ought to conclude: "More thorough analysis of efficiency and distributional analysis of tax reform is still needed to guide the policy debate."[34] Put differently, Auerbach may or may not be right; but the evidence surely is inadequate for Congress to assume that Armey-Shelby holds the economic trump card that its supporters claim to wield.

How the Flat Tax Might Be Compromised, and the Consequences

Auerbach considered only one modification of Armey-Shelby—permitting businesses to continue to depreciate old (pre–Armey-Shelby) capital. Including that provision alone virtually eliminated Armey-Shelby's economic advantages, according to Auerbach's calculations. To test the viability of Armey-Shelby, let us assume that Auerbach is wrong; instead, let us assume that even with the modification for old capital, Armey-Shelby would promote greater economic growth than would our current income tax. But the treatment of old capital would be but one of dozens of highly charged issues that Congress would be under pressure to address were it contemplating a flat tax. As the somewhat liberal economist William Gale and the somewhat conservative economist Kevin Hassett observed in *A Framework for Evaluating the Flat Tax,*

> *The treatment of old capital would be but one of dozens of highly charged issues that Congress would be under pressure to address were it contemplating a flat tax.*

"Any tax system that exists in the real world has survived efforts to patch loopholes, efforts to impose fairness and social policy, and changes made for political reasons."[35]

Consider seven possible changes. Homeowners, fearing life without the mortgage-interest deduction, would produce studies by the National Association of Realtors and others predicting a 12 to 15 percent decline in housing prices if the deduction were eliminated;[36] At a minimum, homeowners would argue, old mortgages should be grandfathered. Congress would hear from employers, employees, and the entire health insurance industry that the number of uninsured would skyrocket if businesses could not deduct health insurance premiums. Labor and management would warn that without allowing businesses to deduct their half of payroll taxes, wages would be reduced and unemployment would rise. Charities would trot out studies by leading economists to prove that charitable giving would decline by $100 billion or more without the charitable deduction.[37] States that depend heavily on income taxes would send delegations to Capitol Hill asking that these taxes remain deductible or that the deduction continue for at least a number of years to give state legislatures time to adjust. Local governments across the country, heavily dependent on taxes assessed against private residences, would plead with Congress to retain the real estate tax deduction; without it, localities would be under pressure to lower tax rates, which could jeopardize crucial

> *"Any tax system that exists in the real world has survived efforts to patch loopholes, efforts to impose fairness and social policy, and changes made for political reasons." (William Gale and Kevin Hassett)*

public services. Finally, low-income working households and their advocates would plead for the earned-income tax credit, which for so many households makes living conditions tolerable.

Flat tax supporters discount most of these fears, citing economic studies to substantiate their views.[38] Indeed, I have argued throughout this book that eliminating or substantially restricting most tax preferences and lowering all tax rates would make the income tax laws fairer, simpler, and economically sounder, though I have added always that reasonable transition provisions would be necessary to cushion certain adverse effects of the new laws. But I know, and readers know, that we cannot expect purity in either the income tax or a consumption tax.

Let us posit that Congress retains only four special provisions as it contemplates a flat tax: personal deductions for mortgage interest and charitable gifts, and business deductions for health insurance premiums and payroll taxes. Applying such provisions would raise the revenue-neutral rate by 5 percentage points from about 21 percent to about 26 percent, according to Eugene Steuerle.[39] The earned-income tax credit (EITC), possibly the hardest for Congress to resist, would cost about another half percentage point. Retaining deductions for state and local income and property taxes would add about another 1.5 percentage points. We have not yet accounted for grandfathering old capital, which could add in the range of 2.5 to 4.0 percentage points. At this point, the revenue-neutral flat rate would be around or well above 30 percent,[40] far in excess of what Armey and Shelby have in mind or what the public would tolerate.

In choosing between a flat tax or the income tax, we need to compare the flat tax that Congress might enact after all political concessions have been made with the income tax we might have were Congress again to become serious about real tax reform.

We now understand why Armey-Shelby contains no transition provisions. This cold-turkey approach recognizes that any concession likely would breed another, and then another, progressively undermining the flat-tax cause. We also see why we must compare the flat tax that Congress might enact after all political concessions have been made with the income tax we might have were Congress again, as in 1985 and 1986, to become serious about real tax reform.

A Better Alternative: Reforming the Income Tax

For individuals, a pure flat tax differs from a pure income tax only in the treatment of income from savings and investments. That difference matters greatly. I believe that income from savings and investments belongs in the tax base, subject to limitations mentioned elsewhere in this book. To exempt all dividends, interest, and capital gains of our richest citizens would make our tax system less fair and is unnecessary to achieve desirable rates of economic growth. Although taxing capital income adds significant complexity to the tax laws—we must have rules that measure capital income, which means worrying about inflation and depreciation deductions, and we must have rules determining when capital gains are to be taxed—the advantages of counting capital income have overriding value.

Achieving a far simpler tax system by eliminating most tax preferences, a principal goal of flat tax supporters, is equally appropriate for the income tax. This alternative for the income tax is explored at length in Chapter 14. If, however, Congress would not accept such comprehensive reforms for the income tax, we could not expect anything different were Congress to contemplate a flat tax. We have also seen that the economic goals of the flat tax likely would flounder without something close to a pure flat tax. If the tax is sufficiently impure, we should expect, as Hall and Rabushka admitted from the outset, that it would lighten the tax burdens of high-income households at the expense of all other households.

By contrast, incremental base broadening of the income tax, done wisely, should advance the economic efficiency and the fairness of the income tax. Comprehensively reforming the income tax and substantially reducing all tax rates remains the single best idea for achieving a just and economically sound tax system; fixing the income tax incrementally, also explored in Chapter 14, would be next best.

14

Conclusions and Recommendations

Specific Recommendations * Final Observation

This book addresses a central question for our nation: Is the federal individual income tax so flawed that it ought to be replaced by a consumption tax, such as a flat tax, or should Congress repair the income tax? The flaws are massive, but they exist because Congress has refused to restrict the income tax to its original calling—to serve as a fair, reliable, and sensible source of federal revenue. Instead, for most of the twentieth century, Congress tried to force the income tax to be something it cannot successfully be—a vehicle for effectively conducting unlimited social and economic programs. Such ambitions have left us with a body of laws sufficiently daunting to intimidate even the finest tax experts; worse, too little of that complexity serves the cause of tax justice or economic growth.

The solution, however, is not to discard the income tax for a consumption tax on the misguided premise that a Congress so willing to politicize the income tax would resist corrupting a new consumption-based system. America's best hope for a tax system that meets our commonly shared goals of fairness, simplicity, and economic growth is to repair the income tax.

Let us begin with fairness. A fair tax system generally taxes households equally that have equal abilities to pay and exacts appropriately more from households that have greater abilities to pay. Consumption, measured over our lifetime, theoretically could provide as fair a basis as the income tax for judging our ability to pay. But in any particular year, a consumption tax can be unusually harsh or mild. It will typically claim a high percentage of our income when we are young and building a family or old and in retirement because our consumption needs tend to be large during these years relative to our income. A consumption tax will claim a modest percentage of our income during those middle years when our income and our ability to save are highest. By contrast, an income tax, if correctly constructed, ebbs and flows with the level of our current income and thus with our current ability to pay. Precisely our current ability to pay should be the keystone of our tax system rather than speculations about our lifetime ability to pay. A flat tax, because of its personal allowances, can temper extremes of other consumption taxes, but the prominent flat tax proposals ignore all unearned income. In any year, therefore, they are likely to overstate the ability to pay of households with little or no unearned income and understate the ability to pay of households with substantial unearned income.

A sound tax system should not unnecessarily interfere with economic growth. A reformed income tax can satisfy this goal through base-broadening reforms and lower tax rates that would minimize distortions of our economic choices. A sound tax system also should be reasonably simple. Then, taxpayers can understand it, need spend only a minimum of time and money to comply with it, and, provided that it also is fair, can have confidence that others are paying their share. A reasonably simple tax system also is much easier to administer by the IRS and offers much greater assurance that all taxpayers are treated evenhandedly. A reformed income tax can be reasonably simple.

Congress could effectively reform the income tax by proceeding in either of two ways. Approach 1 would be fundamental, Approach 2 incremental. Approach 1 would extend initiatives outlined in Treasury I—*Tax Reform for Fairness, Simplicity, and Economic Growth*—the 1984 report of the secretary of the Treasury to Ronald Reagan, who sought "a sweeping and comprehensive reform of the entire tax code."[1] Treasury I called upon Congress to vastly simplify the tax system, define real taxable income comprehensively, sharply lower all tax rates, and tax capital gains and ordinary income at the same tax rates. Approach 1 would borrow heavily from the principal flat tax proposals that tax nearly all fringe benefits and eliminate itemized deductions. Unlike these flat tax proposals, Approach 1 would tax interest, dividends, capital gains, and other "unearned income" because, simply, they are income. It also would retain progressive tax rates for high-income households because they have a disproportionate ability to pay taxes out of their discretionary income; all remaining households would pay a flat rate.

Fundamental tax reform largely would preempt Congress from manipulating the income tax laws for political gains. It would be good for the economy because, by placing most investments on the same level playing field and lowering all tax rates, it would emphasize each investment's potential for income and appreciation. It would provide the greatest assurance that all households' abilities to pay would be judged by the same standards, thus increasing the likelihood that households with equal abilities to pay would be taxed equally and that households with greater abilities to pay would pay appropriately more.

Yes, fundamental reform would mean eliminating most tax preferences. With rare exception, income would be counted regardless of who paid it, how it was paid, or how it was used. The few surviving tax preferences would have cleared two tall hurdles: First, each preference must advance a highly compelling social or economic goal that could not be achieved satisfactorily through direct government subsidies; second, the preference must have overriding importance to the goals of maximizing the income tax base and minimizing tax rates.

By eliminating most tax preferences and substantially lowering all tax rates, fundamental tax reform would minimize incentives to cheat and the loss of tax revenues from cheating. Most tax returns would be simple to prepare. In fact, if family circumstances do not change from one year to the next—for example, if you remain married and have no additional children—you may not have to prepare a tax return because the IRS may have sufficient data from W-2 and 1099 forms.

Although fundamental reform would be best for our nation in the long run, it would be very difficult to achieve politically. Congress would be reluctant to relinquish one of its favorite tools for appealing to voters. Households that benefit most from tax preferences also could be expected to pressure Congress to resist fundamental reform. Finally, many households who benefit little today from tax preferences but expect or hope to benefit from them in the future may also resist reform because they are uncertain about what it would achieve.

We should remember, however, the enormous momentum in favor of Treasury I leading up to the Tax Reform Act of 1986. Heavily compromised in the end, the act nevertheless achieved major tax reform. The lessons of 1986 teach that fundamental income tax reform would be possible upon the concurrence of two developments: when a majority of voters are sufficiently informed about tax policy to realize that reform is in their best interest, and when they elect a president and congressional leaders who believe in fundamental reform and have the courage and skill to mobilize a majority of both houses of Congress to vote for it.

Approach 2 would move incrementally in the direction of these reforms and thus would meet less political resistance. It would eliminate fewer tax preferences. But it would narrow their excesses and would focus tax relief more on those who need it most. All tax rates on ordinary income would diminish on a revenue-neutral basis; but rate reductions would be decidedly less because the tax base would expand decidedly less. Under these circumstances, we could expect Congress to retain a special tax rate for capital gains. Overall, the tax laws would be fairer, simpler, and more accommodating to economic growth than are current laws. They would be less so, however, than if Congress adopted fundamental reforms.

Specific Recommendations

Approach 1: Fundamental Reform

Space does not permit a list of all reforms that would be included in Approach 1, but I will mention major changes. All reforms assume that Congress would adopt transition rules that would allow an orderly adjustment to the new system.

Gross Income.   Like Armey-Shelby, Approach 1 counts all fringe benefits in the tax base other than pension-plan contributions and accumulations. It does so by adding them to gross income because they are economic income and because their inclusion is necessary to help determine each household's ability to pay. As discussed shortly, Approach 1 makes room for refundable tax credits for employer-paid health insurance premiums and for child care; no other fringe benefits currently excluded permanently from income clear the high hurdles for special tax treatment.

Employer-sponsored pension plans would continue to receive favorable treatment granted under existing laws because of the plans' potential to increase saving rates of a significant percentage of ordinary workers. But the rules would be reformed to increase participation and protections for ordinary workers and to decrease benefits for high-income employees, as discussed in Chapter 11.

All interest income would be taxable. No longer would distinctions be made between interest on savings accounts, corporate bonds, and U.S. bonds and notes, currently taxable, and interest on state and local bonds, currently (with limited exceptions) tax exempt. The exemption for interest on state and local bonds unjustifiably favors jurisdictions that combine the strongest credit rating, and thus the greatest capacity to borrow, with a concentration of wealthy citizens who can lend the most and benefit most from the exemption.

Incentive stock options, increasingly a form of compensation for highly valued employees, unfairly allow these employees to convert ordinary income into capital gains and to postpone recognizing their gains until they dispose of the stock. Approach 1 would impose the same rules for taxing incentive stock options that currently apply to other forms of stock options. These rules treat the employees' gains as ordinary income and usually tax employees on their gains long before they sell their stock.

Stockholders no longer would be entitled to defer their gains when they swap their appreciated stock for an acquiring corporation's stock, and real estate owners no longer would be entitled to defer their gains when they swap their real estate for other real estate. These deferrals have been an exception to the general rule that capital gains become taxable when realized through a sale or an exchange, they have unfairly favored particular stockholders and real estate owners, and they cannot be justified on economic grounds. Once the new rules apply, merger and acquisition negotiations will take into account the tax to be paid by stockholders whose company might be acquired; and real estate owners contemplating a real estate swap will consider the tax they will owe when judging whether to receive at least some cash in the transaction.

Approach 1 would make inflation adjustments for tax brackets and basic relief provisions discussed further on. Because of administrative difficulties, inflation adjustments would not be made across the board for income and deductions. If administrative issues can be resolved, Approach 1 would include a lifetime exemption, as discussed in Chapter 12, for a modest amount of capital gains because most if not all capital gains of ordinary taxpayers are attributable to inflation.

Because inflation is such a major component of the gain realized by homeowners when they sell their principal residence and because a principal residence is the major asset of most Americans, Approach 1 generally would exempt ordinary homeowners from tax on their gain. Owners of expensive principal residences typically would owe tax on part of their gain, all in accordance with rules set forth in Chapter 10.

Approach 1 would continue to experiment with a special, low tax rate for capital gains from certain investments in new enterprises. Current evidence is unconvincing that the special tax treatment has significantly stimulated growth of new, worthy enterprises, but we have too little evidence to warrant abandoning the experiment at this time.

Eliminating the double taxation of corporate income should strengthen the economy if the amount of the forgone tax is raised in a revenue-neutral way. The solutions are complicated. For example, because many stockholders are exempt from the individual income tax on dividends and capital gains, eliminating the corporate tax would mean that a great deal of corporate income would not be taxed even once. A sensible initial step would be to grant taxpayers who are subject to U.S. income taxes a tax credit for the corporate tax attributable to dividends on their stock. Approach 1, however, would be conditioned on Congress recovering the lost revenue by raising ordinary tax rates applicable primarily to higher-income taxpayers, who would benefit primarily from the tax credit.

The step-up-in-basis rule, which provides a windfall to heirs, would be eliminated except for modest amounts of assets, as delineated in Chapter 7. Owners of inherited assets who later sell the assets would receive a tax credit for any estate tax paid with respect to those assets, to assure heirs that the value of those assets at the date of death is not subject to double taxation.

All unearned income of dependent children, which in most cases is attributable to gifts from parents, would be taxed under rules applicable today to the unearned income of children who are under the age of 14. This means, for the most part, that the children's capital gains, dividends, interest, and other unearned income would be taxed at the parents' highest marginal tax rate. Approach 1 thereby eliminates a significant manipulation of the tax laws primarily by higher-income families who have been shifting wealth to their dependent children to obtain lower tax rates (once the children are 14 or older) on funds typically used for camp, travel, college, or other expenses that otherwise would have been paid by the parents.

Deductions and Credits.   A charitable deduction would be retained because its elimination might have serious adverse consequences for many charities. All taxpayers would be eligible for the deduction. To minimize oversight concerns of the IRS and to give tax relief only for gifts beyond the ordinary level we might expect from any taxpayer, the deduction should be available only for cumulative gifts that exceed a specified dollar amount and a percentage of a taxpayer's adjusted gross income, as discussed in Chapter 7.

A household tax credit, based on household size, would replace the standard deduction, itemized deductions, personal exemptions, the child credit, and all education credits. The new credit would protect sufficient income from tax to cover basic living expenses. The exact tax-free income thresholds are beyond the scope of these recommendations, but the thresholds should be elevated somewhat from today's thresholds to reflect standards appropriate for the most prosperous country in the world. Comparatively egalitarian entitlement of each same-sized household to the same credit is preferred over entitlement to the same personal exemptions and deductions, which provide greater relief for households in higher marginal tax brackets.

Because of the importance of health insurance, Approach 1 might include a refundable tax credit for employer-paid health insurance premiums, but employer plans must be adapted to the following rules: All employees who meet new eligibility rules prescribed for pension plans (see recommendations in Chapter 11) must benefit; the subsidized premium must be limited to basic individual or family coverage as determined from government guidelines; and all of an employer's eligible employees who are in the same family circumstances—such as all single individuals—must be entitled to the same policy. Unlike today's tax exclusion, the credit would help households that do not owe taxes and need assistance most.

The size of the maximum credit would require considerable study, as well as how much the credit should decline as incomes rise. The issues are extremely complicated. First, the credit must be large enough so that, when the premiums are paid by employers, workers can afford to pay the new taxes on them, a particular problem for lower-income workers. Second, when the premiums are paid by workers themselves either through salary reduction plans or independent of work, the credits should be large enough to make sure that substantial numbers of lower-income workers will opt to pay the premiums, in order to increase the number of insured workers. Third, the new credits, if large enough, likely would induce some employers to discontinue paying premiums because a number of employees might be better off, after taxes, having the amount added to their wages and paying the premiums themselves; in such cases, the government's costs would be higher than under the current rules that exclude the premiums from income. Further, some employees would elect not to be insured under salary-reduction plans if they were worse off under the new system than under the old.

In short, the consequences of moving entirely from the existing system—the exclusion for health insurance premiums paid through work and the itemized deduction for individually paid health insurance—to a system of tax credits, although appealing theoretically on equity and efficiency grounds, must be better understood before Congress proceeds. We must understand far better the government's costs and the impact on insurance coverage. In the interim, the existing exclusion should be limited to employer plans that satisfy the conditions set forth at the beginning of this discussion of tax credits; and a special refundable tax credit should be added for low-income households to help them pay the costs of health insurance they elect to acquire.

The earned-income tax credit, so vital to low-income working families, would be retained and extended to somewhat higher levels. The EITC also would be larger for married parents than for a single parent with the same number of children because married parents' costs of living are likely greater. These modifications to the EITC would reduce the marriage penalty when low-income single parents marry.

The dependent-care credit, also vital to low-income working families who owe taxes, would be retained and expanded because of the rising costs of child care. The credit also would be refundable in order to help working parents who need subsidies most to meet child-care costs. Amounts paid by an employer for child care, or the value of child care provided by an employer, would be included in the employee's income but would be counted as child-care expenses paid by the employee and thus would be eligible for the dependent-care credit.

Approach 1 also would add a low-income second-mortgage credit, described in Chapter 10, that would subsidize second-mortgage loans to help qualified low-income renters make the down payment on a modest home. This credit, far more than existing homeownership tax subsidies, could greatly expand the number of first-time homeowners and yield widespread advantages for the communities in which these new homeowners reside.

Approach 2: Incremental Reform

Incremental reform would move in the direction of the above reforms but would include other tax preferences that had strong voter support. These other tax preferences would be refined so that subsidies would provide greater relief to ordinary households and less relief to high-income households.

In each case, we would want Congress to ask questions noted in Chapter 1: What is the goal of the tax preference? Who ought to benefit primarily from it? Does it focus well on that goal? What is the anticipated revenue loss to the federal government? Does the goal justify the revenue loss and the likely need to raise tax rates to recover the revenue? How much will the tax preference alter the price of the activity being preferred—for example, how much more do health insurance companies charge for premiums because the premiums are tax subsidized—and do the advantages of the subsidy outweigh the additional price? To what extent does the tax preference justify other tax preferences? In other words, how does Congress answer the question posed by constituents: If you are going to extend relief there, why not here? Finally, the administrative issues: How difficult is the tax preference to understand? What will it cost taxpayers in time and money to claim it correctly? What is the government's cost for overseeing it?

My answers to these questions led to Approach 1, which finds justification for only a few tax preferences. Reforms more tolerant of tax preferences yet improving their focus can be seen by examining the mortgage-interest deduction, the most popular and expensive of all itemized deductions and one that is eliminated by Approach 1. In Approach 2, Congress might confine the deduction to mortgages on a principal residence, believing that the deduction for second-home mortgages excessively rewards taxpayers who do not need such subsidies. To focus the deduction on ownership of basic homes, Congress could reduce the loan ceiling far below $1.1 million. Congress also would eliminate the preferential deduction for interest on home equity loans, which allows only homeowners to deduct interest on consumer loans. A more extreme reform would be to convert the deduction, which subsidizes high-income households most, into a tax credit, such as a credit equal to 15 percent of interest paid on loans up to the specified ceiling. In this way, Congress would reduce the subsidy for high-income households and would provide an identical tax subsidy among all households whose eligible interest payments were identical.

Depending on the choices made, Congress could drastically reduce, without eliminating, the cost of subsidizing home-mortgage interest payments. Through similar reasoning, it also could drastically reduce the cost of more than 100 other individual income tax preferences, and correspondingly reduce tax rates.

Final Observation

I wrote at the outset that because the tax system never has been adequately explained to the public, politicians never have known what tax system the public actually would prefer. I promised to help fill this void. If I have been successful, readers should feel comfortable asking politicians questions about tax policy that generally are not asked. Readers also should feel comfortable making judgments about politicians' answers. These exchanges should elevate the national conversation about which tax polices would serve this nation best. A public informed about tax policies also offers the greatest hope for real reform.

Throughout this project I heard doubts about whether people who were not expert in tax policy or economics could understand the issues. I hope readers believe not only that the doubters were wrong but also that Louis Eisenstein was right. You may recall his observation quoted in the preface: The difficulty, he said, "is that they might understand too well." We will see.

Notes

Preface

1. Louis Eisenstein, *The Ideologies of Taxation* (New York: Ronald Press, 1961), 227.

Chapter 1

1. Glossary terms appear in bold at first use.

2. *New York Times,* January 8, 1862.

3. *Congressional Globe,* 38th Cong., 1st sess. (1864), 1876. See Sheldon D. Pollock, *The Failure of U.S. Tax Policy* (University Park: Pennsylvania State University Press, 1996), 43.

4. Cited in Sidney Ratner, *Taxation and Democracy in America* (New York: Octagon Books, 1980), 324.

5. Ibid., 13.

6. U.S. House, Rept. 5, 63rd Cong., 1st sess. (1913), reprinted in *U.S. Bureau of Internal Revenue Bulletin, Cumulative Bulletin 1939–1,* pt. 2 (January-June 1939), 3.

7. Franklin D. Roosevelt, Campaign Address, October 21, 1936, Worcester, Massachusetts, "In 1776 the Fight Was for Democracy in Taxation. In 1936 That Is Still the Fight," *The Public Papers and Addresses of Franklin Roosevelt,* vol. 5, *The People Approve, 1936* (New York: Random House, 1938), 270–77.

8. Randolph E. Paul, *Taxation for Prosperity* (Indianapolis: Bobbs-Merrill, 1947), 96–97.

9. Ratner, *Taxation and Democracy in America,* 496.

10. See Charles Murray, "Americans Remain Wary of Washington, *Wall Street Journal,* December 23, 1997, citing American Enterprise Institute/Roper Center data.

11. In 1993, average tax collections of OECD countries were 38.7 percent of their GDPs. See Joel Slemrod and Jon Bakija, *Taxing Ourselves,* 2nd ed. (Cambridge: MIT, 2000), 19–21.

12. Advisory Commission on Intergovernmental Relations, "Changing Public Attitudes on Governments and Taxes" (Washington, D.C., 1993), 1.

13. Rhoda T. Tripp, comp., *International Thesaurus of Quotations* (Thomas Crowell, 1970), 628.

14. Slemrod and Bakija, *Taxing Ourselves,* 2–3.

15. See Joseph J. Minarik, *Making Tax Choices* (Washington, D.C.: Urban Institute Press, 1985), 4–6.

16. See *San Jose Mercury News,* September 13, 1992, citing a Gallup Poll conducted August 31–September 2, 1991, for Knight-Ridder Newspapers and Cable News Network.

17. Minarik, *Making Tax Choices,* 7.

18. See J. Lav, "Taxes on Middle-Income Families Are Declining," Center on Budget and Policy Priorities, revised April 19, 2000, 1.

19. Internal Revenue Service, *Income Tax Compliance Research: Net Tax Gap and Remittance Gap Estimates,* Publication 1415 (4–90) *(supplement to Publication 7285)* (Washington, D.C.: IRS), 2, table 1.

20. Michael J. Boskin, ed., *Frontiers of Tax Reform* (Stanford: Hoover Institution Press, 1996), xi.

21. Slemrod and Bakija, *Taxing Ourselves,* 103, figure 4.3.

22. Ibid., 101.

23. Sheldon D. Pollock, *The Failure of U.S. Tax Policy,* (University Park: Pennsylvania State University Press, 1996), 5.

24. Philip M. Stern, *The Rape of the Taxpayer* (New York: Random House, 1973); John F. Witte, *The Politics and Development of the Federal Income Tax* (Madison: University of Wisconsin Press, 1985); Jeffrey H. Birnbaum and Alan S. Murray, *Showdown at Gucci Gulch* (New York: Random House, 1987); Donald L. Bartlett and James B. Steele, *America: Who Really Pays the Taxes?* (New York: Simon & Schuster, 1994); Pollock, *The Failure of U.S. Tax Policy.*

Chapter 2

1. Since the Sixteenth Amendment, Congress assumed it had the power to tax virtually any form of income realized by taxpayers. Decisions by the U.S. Supreme Court over the years confirmed this view. For example, in *Commissioner v. Glenshaw Glass Co.,* 348 U.S. 426, 431 (1955), the Supreme Court held that the Sixteenth Amendment allowed Congress to tax all "accessions to wealth, clearly realized, and over which the taxpayers have complete dominion."

2. David F. Bradford, *Untangling the Income Tax* (Cambridge: Harvard University Press, 1986), 7.

3. Much has been written about the definition of income for tax purposes. Some of the best discussions are by Richard Goode, "The Economic Definition of Income," in *Comprehensive Income Taxation,* ed. Joseph A. Pechman (Washington, D.C.: Brookings Institution, 1977), chapter 1; and by Bradford, *Untangling the Income Tax.* For economic theories of income different from Haig-Simons, see Goode, 1–7.

4. Robert M. Haig, *The Federal Income Tax* (New York: Columbia University Press, 1921); Henry C. Simons, *Personal Income Taxation: The Definition of Income as a Problem of Fiscal Policy* (Chicago: University of Chicago Press, 1938).

5. Richard A. Musgrave, "In Defense of an Income Concept," *Harvard Law Review* 81 (1967–1968): 44. For the view that the income concept of Haig-Simons may have value as an analytic tool but not for guiding income tax policy, see Boris I. Bittker, "A 'Comprehensive Tax Base' as a Goal of Income Tax Reform," *Harvard Law Review* 80 (1967): 925–85; and Boris I. Bittker, "Comprehensive Income Taxation: A Response," *Harvard Law Review* 81 (1968): 1032–43. For rebuttals of Bittker's argument, see Joseph A. Pechman, "Comprehensive Income Taxation: A Comment," *Harvard Law Review* 81 (1967–1968): 63–67; and Charles O. Galvin, "More on Boris Bittker and the Comprehensive Tax Base: The Practicality of Tax Reform and the ABA's CSTR," *Harvard Law Review* 81 (1968): 1016–31. For the view that "the problem of defining

individual income, quite apart from any problem of measurement, appears in principle insoluble," see Nicholas Kaldor, *An Expenditure Tax* (London: Allen and Unwin, 1955), 70.

6. *New York Times*, December 1, 1996.

Chapter 3

1. Jeffrey Birnbaum and Alan S. Murray, *Showdown at Gucci Gulch* (New York: Vintage Books, 1988), 5.

2. See, for example, W. Elliott Brownlee, *Federal Taxation in America: A Short History* (Cambridge: Cambridge University Press, 1996); John F. Witte, *The Politics and Development of the Federal Income Tax* (Madison: University of Wisconsin Press, 1985).

3. Two cases actually were involved: *Hyde v. Continental Trust Company* and *Pollock v. Farmers' Loan and Trust Company*, 157 U.S. 429 (1895), rehearing 158 U.S. 601 (1895).

4. Cited in Sidney Ratner, *Taxation and Democracy in America* (New York: Octagon Books, 1980), 331.

5. Andrew Mellon, *Taxation: The People's Business* (New York: Macmillan, 1924), 15.

6. Ibid., 13

7. Ibid., 138.

8. See Jonathan Hughes, *American Economic History* (Glenview, Ill.: Scott, Foresman, 1983), 469.

9. See Mark H. Leff, *The Limits of Symbolic Reform: The New Deal and Taxation, 1933–1939* (Cambridge: Cambridge University Press, 1984), 106.

10. John F. Kennedy, "Special Message to the Congress on Tax Reduction and Reform," January 24, 1963.

11. C. Eugene Steuerle, *The Tax Decade* (Washington, D.C.: Urban Institute Press, 1992), table 2.1, 19.

12. Ibid., figure 2.2, 20.

13. See Alexander Hamilton, *The Founding of the Nation*, ed. Richard B. Morris (New York: Dial, 1957), 322, citing Hamilton's final, or second, *Report on the Public Credit to the U.S. Senate*, American State Papers 5, January 16,1795, 329–38.

14. David S. Broder, "Forgotten but Not Paid," *Washington Post National Weekly Edition*, January 12, 1998, 4.

15. Carolyn Webber and Aaron Wildavsky, *A History of Taxation and Expenditure in the Western World* (New York: Simon & Schuster, 1986), 534.

Chapter 4

1. Only the first two pages plus schedules A–D of the Clintons' tax return are included here.

2. Teresa Tritch, "Your Taxes," *Money* magazine, March 1997, 81–86.

3. I have assumed that Beverly's pension benefits are not forfeitable. See Chapter 11.

4. Beginning in 1985, Congress indexed all tax brackets annually for inflation. Indexation eliminated **bracket creep**—the taxation of a taxpayer's income at a higher tax bracket because of an increase in her income attributable to inflation. Thus, if inflation rose 3 percent last year, all brackets will increase this year by 3 percent.

5. Note that the Antons did not lose the benefit of the 15 percent tax rate on most of their taxable income even though some of their taxable income reached the 28 percent bracket. Each tax bracket applies solely to certain taxable income. In fact, taxpayers with more than $271,050 of taxable income in 1997 were subject to all five tax brackets on portions of their income.

Chapter 5

1. Joint Committee on Taxation, *Estimates of Federal Tax Expenditures for Fiscal Years 2000–2004* (Washington, D.C.: Government Printing Office [GPO], 1999), JCS-13-99, 17.

2. This is one of the few definitions of tax preferences on which the Joint Committee and the Office of Management and Budget (OMB) disagree. In recent years, OMB has not treated the maximum capital gains rate as a tax preference.

3. Ibid., 3.

4. The actual amount of personal deductions claimed on all 1997 returns was $1.69 trillion, or $150 billion more than appears in column A; but $150 billion was unused by taxpayers because their deductions exceeded their AGI. Because the NTL substantially increases the gross income even of low-income taxpayers, I have assumed, for the sake of simplicity, that all personal exemptions and standard deductions would be claimed under the NTL, though some statistically insignificant amount would not.

5. Joint Committee, *Estimates*, 2.

6. Ibid.

7. Congressional Budget Office, *Budget of the United States Government Fiscal Year 1992*, part 3 (Washington, D.C.: GPO, 1992), 19.

8. Congressional Budget Office, *Maintaining Budget Discipline: Spending and Revenue Options* (Washington, D.C.: GPO, 1999), 238.

9. For these purposes, AGI is increased for certain other items otherwise excluded from income, such as foreign earned income and housing costs. Relatively few taxpayers are affected.

10. William D. Andrews, "Personal Deductions in an Ideal Income Tax," *Harvard Law Review* 86(1972): 309–85.

11. Boris I. Bittker, "A 'Comprehensive Tax Base' as a Goal of Income Tax Reform," *Harvard Law Review* 80 (1967). Bittker also detected an air of moral superiority in some adversaries about their "purer" approach to tax policy, what other law professors have characterized in recent years as a "tone of moral absolutism." Pechman agreed with Bittker that "emotion-packed terms" such as "loophole" should be eschewed when referring to exceptions to Haig-Simons principles; "preference," he believed, was an appropriate neutral choice. Joseph A. Pechman, "Comprehensive Income Taxation: A Comment," *Harvard Law Review* 81 (1967): 66–7.

12. Pechman, "Comprehensive Income Taxation," 66.

13. Richard A. Musgrave, "In Defense of an Income Concept," *Harvard Law Review* 81 (1967–1968): 44.

14. Charles O. Galvin, "More on Boris Bittker and the Comprehensive Tax Base: The Practicality of Tax Reform and the ABA's CSTR," *Harvard Law Review* 81 (1968): 1019.

15. The $16.8 trillion estimate for 2000 to 2004 reflects an increase in NTL income of 8 percent per year from the $6.27 trillion estimated for 1997. According to annual income tax reports of the IRS, the annual increase in AGI from 1994 through 1997 slightly exceeded 8 percent.

Chapter 6

1. C. Eugene Steuerle, *The Tax Decade* (Washington, D.C.: Urban Institute Press, 1992), 5.

2. Thomas B. Edsall, *The New Politics of Inequality* (New York: W. W. Norton, 1984), 203.

3. Samuel P. Huntington, *American Politics: The Promise of Disharmony* (Cambridge: Harvard University Press, 1981), 4.

4. Ibid., 33.

5. Adam Smith, *The Wealth of Nations*, ed. Edward Cannan (New York: Modern Library, 1937), 423.

6. Ben Wattenberg, "An Interview with Barber Conable and Joseph Pechman," *Public Opinion* (February/March 1985): 2.

7. James Madison, "The Federalist No. 10," in *The Federalist*, ed. Jacob E. Cooke (Middletown: Wesleyan University, 1961), 61. In the same essay, Madison also wrote, "The apportionment of taxes on the various descriptions of property, is an act which seems to require the most exact impartiality; yet, there is perhaps no legislative act in which greater opportunity and temptation are given to a predominant party, to trample on the rules of justice" (60).

8. U.S. Department of the Treasury, *Tax Reform for Fairness, Simplicity, and Economic Growth*, vol. 1 (Washington, D.C.: Treasury Department, November 1984), iii.

9. Ibid., 11.

10. C. Eugene Steuerle, "The Conservative Case for Progressive Taxation," *Tax Notes* 52, no. 2 (July 15, 1991): 359.

11. John Rawls, *A Theory of Justice* (Cambridge: Harvard University Press, 1971), 100.

12. Arthur M. Okun, *Equality and Efficiency* (Washington, D.C.: Brookings Institution, 1975), 119.

13. U.S. House Committee on Ways and Means, prepared by staff, *Background Materials on Federal Budget and Tax Policy for Fiscal Year 1991 and Beyond* (Washington, D.C: GPO, February 1990), tables 3, 16.

14. Arthur Okun has written that "capitalism and democracy are really a most improbable mixture. Maybe that is why they need each other—to put some rationality into equality and some humanity into efficiency." Okun, *Equality and Efficiency*, 120.

15. Michael Walzer, "In Defense of Equality," in *The New Conservative: A Critique from the Left*, ed. Louis Coser and Irving Howe (New York: Quadrangle, 1973), 107–23.

16. Richard A. Musgrave and Peggy B. Musgrave, *Public Finance in Theory and Practice*, 4th ed. (New York: McGraw-Hill, 1984), 232; Joseph E. Stiglitz, *Economics of the Public Sector*, 2nd ed. (New York: W. W. Norton, 1988), 399. For a critique of many popular justifications for horizontal equity, see Louis Kaplow, "Horizontal Eq-

uity: Measures in Search of a Principle," *National Tax Journal* 42, no. 2 (June 1989): 139–54.

17. Richard Goode, *The Individual Income Tax* (Washington, D.C.: Brookings Institution, 1976), 17.

18. Joseph Pechman, *Federal Tax Policy*, 5th ed. (Washington, D.C.: Brookings Institution, 1987), 63.

19. See David F. Bradford, *Untangling the Income Tax* (Cambridge: Harvard University Press, 1986) 8.

20. For these reasons, Louis Kaplow of Harvard Law School has maintained that horizontal equity has no significance apart from vertical equity. According to Kaplow, if the tax laws produce vertical equity, they necessarily will produce horizontal equity. Kaplow, "Horizontal Equity," 39. For the view that horizontal equity has its own normative value, see Richard A. Musgrave, "Horizontal Equity, Once More," *National Tax Journal* 43, no. 2 (1990): 113. For an analysis of the Kaplow-Musgrave debate, see Paul R. McDaniel and James R. Repetti, "Horizontal and Vertical Equity: The Musgrave/Kaplow Exchange," *Florida Tax Review* 1, no. 10 (1993): 607.

21. Bill Bradley, *The Fair Tax* (New York: Pocket Books, 1984), 13.

22. For 1992, the Internal Revenue Service estimated that the net tax gap—the net revenue loss after future efforts to collect—from the failure of people to pay their individual income taxes would be in the range of $110 billion to $127 billion. Assuming that these sums reflect average tax payments of 20 percent on the missing income, over $500 billion of income escaped tax that year. Internal Revenue Service, *Income Tax Compliance Research: Net Tax Gap and Remittance Gap Estimates* Publication 1415 (4–90)(supplement to publication 7285), (Washington, D.C.: IRS), 2, table 1.

23. Joe Spellman, "On the Road Again, Goldberg Pushes His Simplification Plan," *Tax Notes* 48, no. 10 (September 3, 1990): 1214.

24. *New York Times*, June 23, 1989.

25. Mortimer Caplin, ". . . And Drop Investment Tax Credits," *Wall Street Journal*, March 29, 1993.

26. Rudolph G. Penner, "The Future of Tax Reform," in *National Tax Association—Tax Institute of America: Proceedings of the Eighty-second Annual Conference* (Columbus, Ohio: National Tax Association, 1989), 3.

27. The Revenue Reconciliation Act of 1990 discourages the introduction of tax-relief measures because they now must be paid for by reducing other domestic programs or by increasing taxes elsewhere.

28. Joseph Kraft, "Power to Destroy," *Washington Post*, December 7, 1969.

29. Michael J. Graetz, *The Decline [and Fall?] of the Income Tax* (New York: W. W. Norton, 1997), 116.

30. Milton Friedman, *Capitalism and Freedom* (Chicago: University of Chicago Press, 1982), 173.

31. Milton Friedman, *Wall Street Journal*, February 22, 1996.

32. Joseph Pechman, *Tax Reform, The Rich and the Poor*, 2nd ed. (Washington, D.C.: Brookings Institution, 1989), 5.

33. Steuerle, *The Tax Decade*, 27.

Chapter 7

1. U. S. Senate Committee on the Budget, *Tax Expenditures: Relationship to Spending Programs and Background Material on Individual Provisions* (Washington, D.C.: GPO, June 1986), 290.

2. 2. See Congressional Budget Office, *The Tax Treatment of Employment-Based Health Insurance* (Washington, D.C.: GPO, March 1994), 30, table 4.

3. U.S. House Report accompanying Taxpayer Relief Act of 1997. See *RIA's Complete Analysis of the Taxpayer Relief Act of 1997* (New York: Research Institute of America, 1997), 2, 136–37.

4. If our investment is a depreciable asset, such as an office building, then our tax basis declines by the amount of each year's depreciation.

5. Alternatively, some experts propose to treat bequests as taxable transactions to the testator. In such cases, the final income tax return of a decedent would include his unrealized gains, as if he had sold his investments the moment before he died; and the resulting income tax liability would be subtracted from the value of his estate, just as it would have been had he actually sold his investments the moment before he died.

6. John F. Kennedy, "Special Message to the Congress on Tax Reduction and Reform," January 24, 1963.

7. *Giving USA 1999* (New York: AAFRC Trust for Philanthropy, 1999), 26.

8. Charles T. Clotfelder and Richard L. Schmalbeck, "The Impact of Fundamental Tax Reform on Nonprofit Organizations," in *Economic Effects of Fundamental Tax Reform*, ed. Henry J. Aaron and William G. Gale (Washington, D.C.: Brookings Institution, 1996), 220.

9. See Robert E. Hall and Alvin Rabushka, *The Flat Tax*, 2nd ed. (Stanford: Hoover Institution, 1995), 99; chapter 13.

10. *Giving USA Update #2* (New York: AAFRC Trust for Philanthropy, 1995), 5.

11. Jeffrey L. Yablon, "As Certain as Death—Quotations About Taxes," *Tax Notes* 77, no. 13 (December 29, 1997): 1490.

Chapter 8

1. Theodore Roosevelt, "Man with the Muckrake," address at Washington, D.C., April 14, 1906, in *The Writings of Theodore Roosevelt*, ed. William H. Harbaugh (Indianapolis: Bobbs-Merrill, 1967), 300.

2. James MacGregor Burns, *The American Experiment, Volume II: The Workshop of Democracy* (New York: Alfred A. Knopf, 1985), 157.

3. Russell Conwell, *Acres of Diamonds* (Old Tappan, N.J.: Pyramid, 1960), 20, 23.

4. Roosevelt, "Man with the Muckrake."

5. *Brushaber v. Union Pacific*, 240 U.S. 1, 25 (1916).

6. Sheldon D. Pollack, *The Failure of U.S. Tax Policy* (University Park: Pennsylvania State University Press, 1996), 212–13.

7. Michael J. Graetz, a leading professor of taxation, recently suggested excluding the first $75,000 or even $100,000 of income from tax, applying a flat 20 percent rate to the balance, and making up for the lost revenue through a value-added tax.

Under Graetz's scheme, the great majority of households with the capacity to pay some income tax would pay none. Instead, the income tax would again become a class tax, and the mass of taxpayers would be subjected to a large consumption tax. *The Decline [and Fall?] of the Income Tax* (New York: W. W. Norton, 1997), 265–66.

8. Edward N. Wolff, "Who Are the Rich? A Demographic Profile of High-Income and High-Wealth Americans," Working paper series 98-6, Office of Tax Policy Research, University of Michigan Business School, September 1997, 5, 31, 40. Wolff defined net worth as "the current value of all marketable or fungible assets less the current value of debts," and he included in this definition "the cash-surrender value of pension plans, including IRAs and Keogh plans" (3–4), which often are excluded from net worth computations.

9. Wolff, "Who Are the Rich?" table 1, 36; Wolff's computations were based on Federal Reserve Board data.

10. Franklin D. Roosevelt, *The Public Papers and Addresses of Franklin D. Roosevelt*, vol. 4, *The Court Disapproves 1935* (New York: Random House, 1938), 270.

11. Robert J. Shapiro, *Why Fairness Matters: Progressive Versus Flat Taxes* (Washington, D.C.: Progressive Foundation, 1996), 10, 9.

12. Center on Budget and Policy Priorities, "Top One Percent of Population Received as Much After-Tax Income in 1994 as the Bottom 35 Percent, Analysis Finds," study released August 14, 1997.

13. Quoted in Peter Passell, "Economic Scene," *New York Times*, March 28, 1996.

14. Moshe Buchinsky and Jennifer Hunt, "Wage Mobility in the United States," working paper 5455, National Bureau of Economic Research, Cambridge, Mass., February 1996.

15. Adam Smith, *An Inquiry into the Nature and Causes of the Wealth of Nations*, vol. 2, ed. R. H. Campbell and A. S. Skinner (Indianapolis: Liberty Classics, 1981), 842. Earlier in his treatise, Smith stated, presumably for people who are not rich, that the "subjects of every state ought to contribute towards the support of the government, as nearly as possible, in proportion to their respective abilities; that is, in proportion to the revenue which they respectively enjoy under the protection of the state" (825).

16. U.S. Department of the Treasury, Office of Tax Analysis, "Distributional Effects of Recent Tax Reform Proposals," report prepared by Julie-Anne Cronin, James Nunns, and Eric Toder, November 1996, distributed on request.

17. John Rawls, *A Theory of Justice* (Cambridge: Harvard University Press, 1971), 14–15. For a general discussion of theories of distributive justice under the income tax laws, see Richard A. Musgrave and Peggy B. Musgrave, *Public Finance in Theory and Practice*, 4th ed. (New York: McGraw-Hill, 1984), 82–101.

18. Dwight D. Eisenhower, radio and television address to the nation on the subject of taxes, *U.S. Code Congressional and Administrative News*, 83rd Cong., 2d. sess., vol. 1 (1954), 1669.

19. Joseph A. Pechman, *Tax Reform: The Rich and the Poor*, 2nd ed. (Washington, D.C.: Brookings Institution, 1989), 42.

20. Irving Kristol, "About Inequality," *Commentary* 57 (1957): 42.

21. The quotation of nineteenth-century commentator James McCullough appears in Lindsey, who found it cited in James T. Smith, *Federal Tax Reform* (New York: McGraw-Hill, 1961), 16. Lawrence B. Lindsey, *The Growth Experiment* (New York: Basic Books, 1990), 166.

22. Lindsey, *The Growth Experiment,* 164–65.

23. Gregory Fossedal, "The American Dream," *Wall Street Journal,* February 14, 1997.

24. Kristol, "About Inequality," 43.

25. See Joseph Bankman and Thomas Griffith, "Social Welfare and the Rate Structure: A New Look at Progressive Taxation," *California Law Review* 75, no. 6 (1987): 1910–11.

26. Robert E. Hall and Alvin Rabushka, *Low Tax, Simple Tax, Flat Tax* (New York: McGraw-Hill, 1983), 22.

27. U.S. Department of the Treasury, Office of Tax Analysis, "Assessing Marriage Penalties and Bonuses," report prepared by Nicholas Bull, Janet Holtzblatt, James R. Nunns, and Robert Rebelein for the National Tax Association Proceedings, Ninety-first Annual Conference on Taxation, Austin, Tex., November 8–10, 1998, 327–40.

28. See Daniel N. Shaviro, "Effective Marginal Tax Rates on Low-Income Households," *Tax Notes* 84, no. 7 (August 23, 1999): 1191–1201.

29. For the seminal work that questions progressive tax rates, see Walter J. Blum and Harry Kalven Jr., "The Uneasy Case for Progressive Taxation," *University of Chicago Law Review* 19, no. 3 (1952): 417–520.

Chapter 9

1. Richard A. Musgrave and Peggy B. Musgrave, *Public Finance in Theory and Practice,* 4th ed. (New York: McGraw-Hill, 1984), 291.

2. We are examining here only the efficiency of the federal income tax. A truly efficient federal tax structure, covering all taxes, would have three components: taxes that correct for market failures, such as energy and pollution taxes that can improve economic efficiency; taxes that charge for uses of federal property, such as federal highways and waterways, and that have no effect on economic efficiency; and a broad-based, largely neutral tax on incomes or consumption.

3. Joel B. Slemrod and Jon Bakija, *Taxing Ourselves,* 2nd ed. (Cambridge: MIT, 2000), 104.

4. Dale W. Jorgenson, "The Economic Impact of Fundamental Tax Reform," in *Frontiers of Tax Reform,* ed. Michael Boskin (Stanford: Hoover Institute, 1996), 194.

5. Joel B. Slemrod, "Income Creation or Income Shifting? Behavioral Responses to the Tax Reform Act of 1986," *American Economic Review* 85, no. 2 (May 1995): 175–80.

6. Dr. Belkor's corporation, which filed income taxes based on the calendar year, paid taxes on the $200,000 of profits in 1986 and 1987. These taxes, however, were recovered by his corporation in 1988: the additional $400,000 of salary paid to him that year created $400,000 of losses for his corporation, and these losses could be applied to offset the $400,000 of profits in the earlier years. The tax savings for Dr. Belkor were reduced somewhat by the loss of earnings on the $400,000 of tax payments before they were recovered.

7. Robert K. Triest, "The Efficiency Cost of Increased Progressivity," in *Progressivity and Income Inequality*, ed. Joel B. Slemrod (New York: Cambridge University Press, 1994), 137.

8. Slemrod and Bakija, *Taxing Ourselves*, 111.

9. Patric Henderschott, comments in *Do Taxes Matter? The Impact of the Tax Reform Act of 1986*, ed. Joel B. Slemrod (Cambridge: MIT Press, 1990), 80.

10. Lawrence B. Lindsey, *The Growth Experiment* (New York: Basic Books, 1990), 58–59. Lindsey, along with most mainstream economists but few other supply-siders, believes that when tax rates are lowered in times of recession, the supply-side effect typically is preceded by a temporary **demand-side effect**: with more after-tax income to spend, consumers would demand more goods, at least in the short run, thereby jump-starting the economy. Most supply-siders view demand-side effects as small or nonexistent.

11. *Economic Report of the President* (Washington, D.C.: GPO, 1993), 471, table B-108.

12. Lindsey, *The Growth Experiment*, 76.

13. C. Eugene Steuerle, *The Tax Decade* (Washington, D.C.: Urban Institute Press, 1992), 186–87, table 12.1; Steuerle cited *Budget of the U.S Government 1990* (Washington, D.C.: GPO, 1989), 4–18.

14. Marginal federal tax rates fell far less than would have been the case had many of the advantages of ERTA not been cut back by legislation in 1982 and 1984 and had Social Security taxes not been substantially increased in 1984.

15. See Jerry A. Hausman, "Labor Supply," in *How Taxes Affect Economic Behavior*, ed. Henry J. Aaron and Joseph A. Pechman (Washington, D.C.: Brookings Institution, 1981), 27–83.

16. See Gary Burtless and Barry Bosworth, "Effects of Tax Reform on Labor Supply, Investment, and Savings," *Journal of Economic Perspectives* 6, no. 1 (winter 1992): 3–25.

17. Congressional Budget Office, "Effects of the 1981 Tax Act on the Distribution of Income and Taxes Paid," staff working paper (Washington, D.C.: GPO, 1986), iv, 50–53. See also Gary Burtless, "The Supply-Side Legacy of the Reagan Years: Response of Labor Supply," a paper for the conference The Economic Legacy of the Reagan Years: Euphoria or Chaos? Oakland University, June 30–July 1, 1989; Joel Slemrod and Alan J. Auerbach, "The Economic Effects of the Tax Reform Act of 1986," *Journal of Economic Literature* 35 (June 1997): 589–632. For an earlier study that suggests more dynamic effects of the act on labor supply, see Martin Feldstein, "Behavioral Response to Tax Rates: Evidence from the Tax Reform Act of 1986," *American Economic Review* 85, no. 2 (May 1995): 170–74.

18. Triest, "The Efficiency Cost," 141; see also Enrique G. Mendoza, Assaf Razin, and Linda L. Tesar, "Effective Tax Rates in Macroeconomics: Cross-Country Estimates of Tax Rates on Factor Incomes and Consumption," *Journal of Monetary Economics* 34, no. 2 (December 1994): 297–324; and Thomas MaCurdy, David Green, and Harry Paarsch, "Assessing Empirical Approaches for Analyzing Taxes and Labor Supply," *Journal of Human Resources* 25 (1990): 415–90. Economist Robert Frank argues that if supply-siders were right, "the cumulative effect of the last century's dramatic rise in real wages should have been a significant increase in hours worked. In fact, however, the length of the work week is significantly lower now than in

1900." "Progressive Taxation and the Incentive Problem," working paper series 98-4, Office of Tax Policy Research, Ann Arbor, Mich., February 1998, 4.

19. Triest, "The Efficiency Cost," 142–43.

20. Nada Eissa, "Taxation and Labor Supply of Married Women: The Tax Reform Act of 1986 as a Natural Experiment," working paper 5023, National Bureau of Economic Research, February 1995.

21. For 1977 statistics, see U.S. Department of Labor, U.S. Bureau of Labor Statistics, *Handbook of Labor Statistics*, Bulletin 2340, August 1989; for 1997 statistics, see U.S. Bureau of Labor Statistics, "Current Population Survey," unpublished report, March 1997.

22. See Thomas Mroz, "The Sensitivity of an Empirical Model of Married Women's Hours of Work to Economic and Statistical Assumptions," *Econometrica* 55 (1987): 765–800.

23. Martin Feldstein, "How Big Should Government Be?" *National Tax Journal* 50 (June 1997): 209.

24. See Dale W. Jorgenson and Kun-Young Yun, "The Excess Burden of Taxation in the United States," *Journal of Accounting, Auditing & Finance* 6, no. 4 (fall 1991): 487–509; Charles L. Ballard, "Marginal Efficiency Cost Calculations for Different Types of Government Expenditure: A Review," paper presented at the Australian Conference in Applied General Equilibrium, Melbourne, Australia, May 27–28, 1991.

25. Laurence J. Kotlikoff finds that "properly designed fiscal policy can have clear and powerful savings affects in most neoclassical models." He also notes that there "is as yet no convincing empirical evidence and certainly no professional consensus that households make saving decisions in accordance with the dictates of neoclassical organization." *What Determines Saving?* (Cambridge: MIT, 1989), 229, 30. In short, the data do not yet confirm what the economic models predict.

26. Eric M. Engen and William G. Gale, "The Effects of Fundamental Tax Reform on Saving," in *Economic Effects of Fundamental Tax Reform*, ed. Henry J. Aaron and William G. Gale (Washington, D.C.: Brookings Institution, 1996), 96.

27. Robert E. Hall, "Intertemporal Substitution in Consumption," *Journal of Political Economy* 96, no. 2 (1988): 339–40.

28. *Economic Report of the President* (Washington, D.C.: GPO, 1994), 300, table B-27.

29. To appreciate the controversy among leading economists on the subject of IRAs and other tax-deferred plans generally, see the following three articles in *Journal of Economic Perspectives* 10, no. 4 (fall 1996): Glenn R. Hubbard and Jonathan S Skinner, "Assessing the Effectiveness of Saving Incentives," 73–90; James M. Poterba, Steven F. Venti, and David A. Wise, "How Retirement Saving Programs Increase Saving," 91–112; and Eric M. Engen, William G. Gale, and John Karl Scholz, "The Illusory Effects of Saving Incentives on Saving," 113–38.

30. Data compiled from Bureau of Economic Analysis, Department of Commerce, http://www.bea.doc.gov/bea/dn/saverate.htm, April 2000.

31. B. Douglas Bernheim, commenting on Eric M. Engen and William G. Gale, "The Effects of Fundamental Tax Reform on Saving," in *Economic Effects of Fundamental Tax Reform*, ed. Henry J. Aaron and William G. Gale (Washington, D.C.: Brookings Institution, 1996), 113.

32. Congressional Budget Office, *Assessing the Decline in the National Saving Rate* (Washington, D.C.: GPO, 1993), 32.

33. Laurence J. Kotlikoff, "Saving and Consumption Taxation: The Federal Retail Sales Tax Example," in *Frontiers of Tax Reform*, ed. Michael J. Boskin (Stanford: Hoover Institution Press, 1996), 165.

34. Kevin Phillips, *The Politics of Rich and Poor* (New York: Random House, 1990), 62.

35. George Gilder, *Wealth and Poverty* (New York: Basic Books, 1981), 188, 245.

36. Cited in Robert Lenzner and Stephen S. Johnson, "Seeing Things as They Really Are," *Forbes*, March 10, 1997, 122–28.

37. Lindsey, *The Growth Experiment*, 81–102.

38. Congressional Budget Office, "Effects of the 1981 Tax Act on the Distribution of Income and Taxes Paid," staff working paper (Washington, D.C.: GPO, 1986), section II.23.

39. Joel Slemrod, "On the High-Income Laffer Curve," in *Tax Progressivity and Income Inequality*, ed. Joel Slemrod (New York: Cambridge University Press, 1994), 208. Eugene Steuerle thought Slemrod's research was "right on the mark," adding that if the Laffer curve (supporting supply-side theory) had any life left, it would likely be at rates far higher than those of the 1990s. Steuerle also rejected Lindsey's view that increases during the 1980s in the relative income of the very highest paid workers were attributable to changes in their work habits. If so, he said, "then I should probably be able to prove it by surveys on hours worked or evidence that American executives work much harder than some of their more poorly paid international counterparts, as in Japan. No such evidence, as far as I know, has ever been produced." Slemrod, *Tax Progressivity and Income Inequality*, 215.

40. Daniel Feenberg and James Poterba, "Income Inequality and the Incomes of Very High Income Taxpayers," in *Tax Policy and the Economy* 7, ed. James Poterba (Cambridge: MIT, 1993), 145–77.

41. Eissa, "Taxation and Labor Supply of Married Women."

42. Martin Feldstein and Daniel Feenberg, "Higher Tax Rates with Little Revenue Gain: An Empirical Analysis of the Clinton Plan," *Tax Notes* 58, no. 12 (March 22, 1993): 1653–57. Robert J. Barro, a colleague of Feldstein's at Harvard, expected that the receipts from the rate increases "probably will be close to zero and may actually be negative." "Higher Taxes, Lower Revenues," *Wall Street Journal*, July 9, 1993.

43. Jane G. Gravelle, "Behavioral Responses to Proposed High-Income Tax Rate Increases: An Evaluation of the Feldstein-Feenberg Study," *Tax Notes* 59, no. 8 (May 24, 1993): 1097–1102.

44. U.S. Treasury Department, Office of Tax Analysis, "Income Shifting in Response to Higher Tax Rates: The Effects of OBRA 93," report prepared by Ann D. Parcell for Allied Social Science Associations Meetings, San Francisco, Calif., January 5–7, 1995.

45. Internal Revenue Service, *Statistics of Income—1995, Individual Income Tax Returns*, Washington, D.C. 1997, 23; Internal Revenue Service, *Statistics of Income—1997, Individual Income Tax Returns* (Washington, D.C.: IRS, 2000), 23.

46. U.S. Department of the Treasury, Office of Tax Analysis, "The Effect of Income Taxes on Household Behavior," report prepared by Gerald Auten and Robert Carroll, released April 1997.

47. Ben Wattenberg, "Tax Philosophy: An Interview with Barber Conable and Joseph Pechman," *Public Opinion* 8, no. 1 (February/March 1985): 5.

48. Henry J. Aaron, "Lessons for Tax Reform," in *Do Taxes Matter? The Impact of the Tax Reform Act of 1986,* ed. Joel B. Slemrod (Cambridge: MIT Press, 1990), 330.

Chapter 10

1. U.S. Department of Housing and Urban Development, *HUD Budget: FY 2001* (Washington, D.C: GPO, 2000), 53–57.

2. See Senate Budget Committee, Tax Expenditures: Relationships to Spending Programs and Background Material on Individual Provisions, 99th Cong., 2d sess., S. Prt. 99–159, June 1986, 155–61. When they appeared in the original 1913 legislation, deductions for mortgage interest and real estate taxes were viewed not as housing policy but as appropriate to measure one's ability to pay (and to promote fiscal federalism, in the case of the real estate tax deduction).

3. Jason DeParle, "Slamming the Door," *New York Times Magazine,* October 20, 1996, 53.

4. Dumas Malone, *Jefferson the Virginian* (Boston: Little, Brown, 1948), 238; Joint Center for Housing Studies, *The State of the Nation's Housing 1997* (Cambridge: Harvard University Press, 1997) 17, 27.

5. Cited in Joint Center for Housing Studies, *The State of the Nation's Housing 1997,* 8.

6. Andrew S. Berky and James P. Shenton, eds., *The "Historians" History of the United States,* vol. 1 (New York: G. P. Putnam's Sons, 1966), 186–87.

7. See Richard K. Green and Michelle J. White, "Measuring the Benefits of Homeowning: Effects on Children," Chicago: Center for the Study of the Economy and the State, 1994, mimeo; Denise DiPasquale and Edward L. Glaeser, "Incentives and Social Capital: Are Home Owners Better Citizens?" working paper series W97-3, *Joint Center for Housing Studies,* Cambridge, Harvard University, 1997; and William M. Rohe and Michael A. Stegman, "The Impact of Homeownership on the Social and Political Involvement of Low-Income People," *Urban Affairs Quarterly* 30, no. 1 (September 1994): 152–72.

8. National Housing Task Force, *A Decent Place to Live* (Washington, D.C.: NHTF, March 1988), 8.

9. Joint Center for Housing Studies, *The State of the Nation's Housing 1997,* 20.

10. Ibid., 20, 22, 35.

11. Center on Budget and Policy Priorities, *In Search of Shelter: The Growing Shortage of Affordable Rental Housing,* study prepared by Jennifer Daskal, release June 1998, 1. This study noted that over half of all poor renter families with children have one or more working members (27).

12. "The Unsheltered Life," *U.S. News & World Report,* November 11, 1996, 29.

13. Joint Center for Housing Studies, *The State of the Nation's Housing 1995* (Cambridge: Harvard University Press, 1995), 18.

14. Currently, a Mortgage Credit Certificate program provides a limited nonrefundable tax credit to first-time home buyers for their mortgage-interest payments. The program is of little benefit to low-income households primarily because most of them do not owe taxes after applying other tax credits. Households also are entitled to relief

from penalties for early withdrawals of taxable IRAs and relief from income tax for early withdrawals from Roth IRAs for withdrawals of up to $10,000 for first-home purchases; these relief provisions have little value to low-income renters because few can afford to have IRAs, and those who do have modest accounts.

15. See National Association of Home Builders, Economics, Mortgage Finance and Housing Policy Division, *The Impacts of the Tax Reform Act of 1986: An Overview* (Washington, D.C.: NAHB, September 10, 1986).

16. Congressional Budget Office, *Reducing the Deficit: Spending and Revenue Options* (Washington, D.C.: GPO, March 1997), 338, Rev–04.

17. U.S. Census Bureau, "Who Can Afford to Buy a House in 1993?" report prepared by Howard Savage, *Current Housing Report Series* H121/97–1, 1997, 3.

18. Haig-Simons would tax all interest received, subject to cost-of-living adjustments. Under our tax laws, however, a great deal of interest on state and local bonds is tax exempt, which greatly complicates the rules that should apply to interest payments. Our laws prohibit deductions for interest payments on loans used to acquire tax-exempt bonds.

19. Consider, for example, a $400,000 house in Washington, D.C. That house might rent for about $2,500 per month or $30,000 per year, plus utilities. Real estate taxes, insurance, and maintenance costs might amount to $12,000, leaving a profit of $18,000 before mortgage-interest payments and income taxes. If the mortgage balance were 60 percent of the house value (we will assume that the typical mortgage has aged somewhat), the mortgage would be $240,000; and if the interest rate were 8 percent, the interest payments would be $19,200.

20. Glenn B. Canner, Thomas A. Durkin, and Charles A. Luckett, "Recent Developments in Home Equity Lending," *Federal Reserve Bulletin* (April 1998): 244.

21. Ronald Reagan, *The President's Tax Proposals to the Congress for Fairness, Growth, and Simplicity* (Washington, D.C: GPO, May 1985), 62–64.

22. Ibid., 63.

23. See Congressional Research Service, *Limiting State-Local Tax Deductibility in Exchange for Increased General Revenue Sharing: An Analysis of the Economic Effects*, S. Prt. 98–77, August 1983. Reagan's *Proposals* went so far as to conclude, with respect to all then-remaining deductions for state and local taxes, that, "on average, state and local governments gain less than fifty cents for every dollar of Federal revenue lost because of the deduction." *Proposals*, 64.

24. Richard A. Musgrave, *The Theory of Public Finance* (New York: McGraw Hill, 1959), ch. 1.

25. In 1993, only 11.6 percent of the gain protected by the tax-free rollover rule belonged to the bottom half of all taxpayers; about 65 percent of the gain belonged to the top 19 percent of all taxpayers. Data computed by Internal Revenue Service from Form 2119, Sale of Your Home, attached to Form 1040 for income tax returns filed for 1993; data was faxed to author by the Statistical Information Services Office of the Internal Revenue Service.

26. See endnote 19.

27. Of 3 million sales and $50.5 billion of gains reported for 1993, only 148,000 taxpayers reported a taxable gain, on which they paid a mere $300 million of taxes. See Leonard Burman, Sally Wallace, and David Weiner, *How Capital Gains Taxes Distort Homeowners' Decisions*, National Tax Association Proceedings, Eighty-ninth

Annual Conference, Boston, Mass., 1996 (Washington, D.C.: National Tax Association, Tax Institute of America, 1997), 382–90.

28. Computation of this fraction has since been modified by 1998 legislation.

29. Congressional Committee Reports Accompanying the Taxpayer Relief Act of 1997, H.R. 2014, Section 312.

30. Internal Revenue Service, Statistical Information Service Office, Project 11013, 149–50.

31. See Henry Aaron, *Shelter and Subsidies* (Washington, D.C.: Brookings Institution, 1972); Martin Feldstein, "Inflation, Tax Rules and the Accumulation of Residential and Nonresidential Capital," working paper 753, National Bureau of Economic Research, Cambridge, Mass., September 1981; Patric Hendershott, "Government Policies and the Allocation of Capital Between Residential and Industrial Uses," working paper 1036, National Bureau of Economic Research, Cambridge, Mass., December 1982.

32. David Laidler, "Income Tax Incentives for Owner-Occupied Housing," in *The Taxation of Income from Capital,* ed. Arnold Harberger and Martin J. Bailey (Washington, D.C.: Brookings Institution, 1969).

33. Committee for Economic Development, Research and Policy Committee, *Restoring Prosperity: Budget Choices for Economic Growth* (New York and Washington, D.C: Committee for Economic Development, 1992), 33. The committee relied on research by Edwin S. Mills in "Social Returns to Housing and Other Fixed Capital," *AREUEA Journal* 17, no. 2 (1989): 197–211. According to Mills, "the government data show that returns to housing have been no more than 37% as great as returns to non-housing capital during the 1929–1986 period" (207). Patric Hendershott found Mills's estimates greatly overstated and concluded that based on 1985 law, overinvestment in housing might be only 10 percent compared with optimal conditions. Hendershott, "Comments on Social Returns to Housing and Other Fixed Capital," *AREUEA Journal* 17, no. 2 (1989): 213. Nevertheless, even a 10 percent overinvestment in housing can significantly affect national economic growth.

34. Jonathan Skinner, "The Dynamic Efficiency Cost of Not Taxing Housing," *Journal of Public Economics* 59 (1996): 414, 397.

35. Ibid., 414.

36. Dale W. Jorgenson, "Reconstructing the Agenda for U.S. Tax Reform," paper presented to the House Republican Conference, Washington, D.C., August 11, 1993.

37. Congressional Budget Office, *The Tax Treatment of Homeownership: Issues and Options,* September 1981, 32.

38. U.S. Census Bureau, "Housing Affordability 1993," September 9, 1997, tables 5–4 and 5–2, www.census.gov.

39. J. Michael Collins, Eric S. Belsky, and Nicolas P. Retsinas, "Towards a Targeted Homeownership Tax Credit," Joint Center for Housing Studies, Harvard University, W98–5, November 1998.

40. The $6,000 inflation adjustment prior to 2000 is generous for lower-cost houses and would continue to be generous for such houses acquired in the future. Nonetheless, using a uniform figure for all houses makes administrative sense because of its simplicity and because a lower adjustment would not raise much revenue compared with the administrative costs to homeowners and to the IRS.

Chapter 11

1. Eugene Steuerle, "Tax Reform and Private Pensions," *Tax Notes* 70, no. 13 (March 18, 1996): 1694.

2. Employee Benefit Research Institute, "Americans Say They Are Saving for Retirement, but They May Be Falsely Confident About Their Preparations," *EBRI News* (October 31, 1995).

3. B. Douglas Bernheim, *The Merrill Lynch Baby Boom Retirement Index: Update 1997* (Princeton: Merrill Lynch, May 1997), 18, 19. See also B. Douglas Bernheim, *Is the Baby Boom Generation Preparing Adequately for Retirement? Summary Report* (Princeton: Merrill Lynch, 1993).

4. U.S. Census Bureau, *Asset Ownership of Households: 1993*, report by T. J. Eller and Wallace Fraser, Current Population Reports P70–47, August 1995. See also Congressional Budget Office, *Baby Boomers in Retirement: An Early Perspective* (Washington, D.C.: GPO, September 1993).

5. Arthur B. Kennickell, Martha Starr-McCluer, and Annika E. Sunden, "Family Finances in the U.S.: Recent Evidence from the Survey of Consumer Finances," *Federal Reserve Bulletin* (January 1997): 6.

6. Jonathan Clements, *Wall Street Journal*, January 10, 1994. The study assumes 9 percent annual investment gains prior to retirement, 8 percent annual gains after retirement, 3 percent inflation, and a need for retirement income for 30 years, at which time your savings are depleted. T. Rowe Price's figures assume that Joseph will run out of money at age 95.

7. Social Security Administration, *Income of the Population 55 or Older, 1996*, April 1996, SSA publication 13–11871, April 1998, tables v.A.4 and vii.5.

8. Competitiveness Policy Council, *Saving More and Investing Better: A Strategy for Security Prosperity,* Fourth report to the president and Congress, September 1995, 30.

9. Joint Committee on Taxation, *Estimates of Federal Tax Expenditures for Fiscal Years 2000–2004* (Washington, D.C.: GPO, 1999), JCS–13–99, 23.

10. The loss of Social Security taxes was about $39 billion in 1992, as reported by Alicia Munnell, then senior vice president of the Federal Reserve Bank of Boston. Alicia H. Munnell, "Current Taxation of Qualified Pension Plans: Has the Time Come?" *New England Economic Review* (March/April 1992): 15. The figure for 2000 ought to be closer to $50 billion and for five years is likely to exceed $250 billion.

11. Employee Benefit Research Institute, "Estimated Total Pension Assets in the U.S., 1985–present," EBRI unpublished report, December 1999.

12. According to a survey by the National Federation of Independent Business, 23 percent of private employers with under 100 employees in 1985 offered pension plans. See Employee Benefit Research Institute, *EBRI Databook on Employee Benefits* (Washington, D.C.: EBRI, 1990), 80, table 4-3. In 1985, about 98 percent of all employers employed fewer than 100 employees. See *EBRI Issue Brief* (April 1996) for figures in 1987, which approximate those for 1985.

13. U.S. Department of Labor, Social Security Administration, U.S. Small Business Administration, Pension Benefit Guaranty Corporation, *Pension and Health Benefits of American Workers: New Findings from the April 1993 Current Population Survey* (Washington, D.C.: GPO, May 1994), 12.

14. U.S. Department of Labor, Pension and Welfare Benefits Administration, "Pension Availability and Coverage in Small and Large Firms," report prepared by Jules H. Lichtenstein, in *Trends in Pensions 1992*, ed. John A. Turner and Daniel J. Beller (Washington, D.C.: GPO, 1992), 99.

15. Spencer Rich, "Caught in the Pinch of a Pension Predicament," *Washington Post*, November 25, 1996.

16. U.S. Department of Labor et al., *Pension and Health Benefits of American Workers*, tables B1, B-1.

17. Dallas L. Salisbury and Nora Super Jones, eds., *Pension Funding & Taxation: Implications for Tomorrow* (Washington, D.C.: Employee Benefit Research Institute, 1994), 108. See also David E. Bloom and Richard B. Freeman, *The Fall in Private Pension Coverage in the U.S.* (Cambridge: National Bureau of Economic Research, 1992).

18. William E. Even and David Macpherson, *Trends in Individual and Household Pension Coverage*, report submitted to the Department of Labor, contract no. 41USC252C3, February 1995.

19. U.S. Department of Labor, *Retirement Benefits of American Workers: New Findings from the September 1994 Current Population Survey*, 1995, table B17, 72.

20. Ibid, 12.

21. Social Security Administration, *Income of the Population 55 or Older, 1996*, SSA publication 13–11871, April 1998, table V.C.2, 78–9.

22. Department of Labor, Bureau of Labor Statistics, *Employer Costs for Employee Compensation, 1986–97*, Bulletin 2505, August 1998, tables 5 and 137.

23. The last serious proposal to require most employers to adopt a pension plan, made in 1981 by the Commission on Pension Policy appointed by President Reagan, got nowhere.

24. The favorable tax treatment of pension plans initially was prompted primarily by accounting concerns. Employees could forfeit their entire pensions either because employers could revoke the plan or because creditors of employers could attach the assets; thus it did not make sense to tax participants until they actually received benefits. Nancy J. Altman, "Rethinking Retirement Income Policies: Nondiscrimination, Integration, and the Quest for Worker Security," *Tax Law Review* 42, no. 3 (1987): 446, 450.

25. Nonunion plans may exclude members of collective bargaining units, but this rule merely accommodates the separate treatment of plans for union members.

26. Jane G. Gravelle, *The Economic Effects of Taxing Capital Income* (Cambridge: MIT, 1994), 188–89.

27. To be deductible, contributions to a defined contribution profit-sharing plan, which allows employers to decide each year how much they wish to contribute, may not exceed 15 percent of the compensation of all participants for that year; this limitation typically means that annual additions to a participant's account will not exceed 15 percent of his compensation. In contrast, contributions to a defined contribution pension plan, to which contributions by employers are mandatory each year, may be as high as 25 percent of a participant's compensation (not to exceed $30,000). ("Compensation" that is taken into account for these purposes cannot exceed the maximum level for the year.) If an employer operates both profit-sharing and pension plans, the maximum contribution for a participant under the combined plans cannot exceed the lesser of 25 percent of the participant's compensation or $30,000.

28. My computation ignores Medicare taxes on the $30,000 as well as any state income taxes on the $30,000 and its earnings. If they were taken into account, Carol's investment account would be considerably smaller.

29. National Taxpayers Union Foundation, *Capital Ideas* 6, no. 1 (March/April 1998): 1.

30. Employers with 100 or fewer employees may also adopt a SIMPLE plan, which also is far simpler than a regular pension plan.

31. See Stuart Dorsey, Christopher Cornwell, David Macpherson, *Pensions and Productivity* (Kalamazoo, Mich.: W. E. Upjohn Institute for Employment Research, 1998).

32. Alicia H. Munnell, "Current Taxation of Qualified Pension Plans: Has the Time Come?" *New England Economic Review* (March/April 1992): 17–18.

33. Gravelle, *The Economic Effects of Taxing Capital Income,* 190–3. For the view that the evidence is inconclusive as to whether pension plans increase personal saving, see Congressional Budget Office, *Tax Policy for Pensions and Other Retirement Saving* (Washington, D.C.:, GPO, 1987), 80.

34. William G. Gale, "The Effects of Pensions on Household Wealth: A Reevaluation of Theory and Evidence," *Journal of Political Economy* 106, no. 4 (1998): 706–23.

35. Leaders of the movement to broaden the federal income tax base have long been critical of the tax relief for pension plans. See Stanley S. Surrey and Paul R. McDaniel, *Tax Expenditures* (Cambridge: Harvard University Press, 1985), 82–89; Richard Goode, *The Individual Income Tax* (Washington, D.C.: Brookings Institution, 1976), 111–12; Emil M. Sunley Jr., "Employee Benefits and Transfer Payments," in *Comprehensive Income Taxation,* ed. Joseph A. Pechman (Washington, D.C.: Brookings Institution, 1977), 75–114; Daniel Halperin, "Interest in Disguise: Taxing the 'Time Value of Money,'" *Yale Law Journal* 95 (1986): 506; and Michael J. Graetz, "The Troubled Marriage of Retirement Security and Tax Policies," *University of Pennsylvania Law Review* 135 (1987): 851.

36. Louis Kaplow, "Comments," in William D. Andrews and David F. Bradford, "Savings Incentives in a Hybrid Income Tax," in *Uneasy Compromise: Problems of a Hybrid Income-Consumption Tax,* ed. Henry J. Aaron, Harvey Galper, and Joseph A. Pechman (Washington, D.C.: Brookings Institution, 1988), 308.

37. See Federal Income Tax Regulations, para. 1.105–11(c)(3)(i).

Chapter 12

1. See James R. Repetti, "The Use of Tax Law to Stabilize the Stock Market: The Efficacy of Holding Period Requirements," *Virginia Tax Review* 8, no.3 (winter 1989): 591–637, which argues that "the use of holding periods to curb speculation is inappropriate and decreases societal welfare."

2. Leonard E. Burman, *The Labyrinth of Capital Gains Tax Policy* (Washington, D.C.: Brookings Institution Press, 1999), 29. When compared with 24 industrialized *and* developing countries, our capital gains tax rates appear to be higher than most, according to a 1998 survey (Arthur Andersen LLP, as reported by Mark Bloomfeld and Margo Thorning, "Tax Policy for Competitiveness, Growth, and Retirement Security," *Tax Notes* 82, no. 11 [March 15, 1999]: 1689).

3. "Fact Sheet: Why 'Jenkins-Archer' Without Amendment" (September 9, 1989) was released under a cover letter dated September 22, 1989, and was signed by Representatives Jenkins, J. J. Pickle, Beryl Anthony, Ronnie G. Flippo, Andrew Jacobs Jr., and Michael Andrews.

4. Internal Revenue Service, *Statistics of Income—1997, Individual Income Tax Returns* (Washington, D.C.: IRS, 1999), 36.

5. Congressional Budget Office, *Perspectives on the Ownership of Capital Assets and the Realization of Capital Gains* (Washington, D.C.: GPO, May 2, 1997), 2.

6. A separate policy consideration is whether tax relief should be offered in cases where taxing income bunched into a single year, such as from the sale of a family business, creates an unusual hardship for a household.

7. Walter J. Blum, "A Handy Summary of the Capital Gains Arguments," reprinted from *Tax Notes* 44, no. 10 (September 1989): 1145, in *The Capital Gains Controversy: A Tax Analyst's Reader,* ed. J. Andrew Hoerner (Arlington, Va.: Tax Analysts, 1992), 34. Blum's summary originally was published in two articles in the 1950s. He considered 25 arguments that have been made for not taxing capital gains.

8. Today's 20 percent rate, established in 1997, restored the rate that had existed from 1981 to 1986. The 1986 Reform Act raised the rate to 28 percent in what Ronald Reagan described as the act's "great compromise." In return, Congress reduced the top tax rate on salaries, dividends, and other ordinary income from 50 percent to 28 percent for high-income taxpayers. A higher capital gains rate, however, never set well with Republicans such as George Bush. In language representative of the first school, Bush as president insisted in 1989 that "nothing can make America more competitive than restoring the [capital gains tax] differential," the difference between the top rate on ordinary income and on capital gains. See "Remarks at the Presentation Ceremony for the Minority Enterprise Development Week Awards, October 4, 1989," *Weekly Compilation of Presidential Documents* 25, no. 40 (October 9, 1989): 1503. Jude Wanniski, who is not an economist but an outspoken opponent of all capital gains taxes, in 1993 took Bush's case a step further: "The principal source of our country's difficulties is the capital gains tax." See the *Wall Street Journal,* May 11, 1993. The bitterness of that political debate can be seen from remarks of Congressman Richard Gephardt: "The President has named a lot of his friends to be ambassadors; I guess this . . . proposal is to take care of those who didn't get named. . . . The limousines are circling the White House."

9. The additional realizations will move some taxpayers into higher tax brackets and may also reduce their personal exemptions and itemized deductions, which could reduce the static loss slightly below $10 billion.

10. See Jane G. Gravelle, *Can a Capital Gains Tax Cut Pay for Itself?* Congressional Research Service, Library of Congress, Report for Congress, March 23, 1990; Henry J. Aaron, "The Capital Gains Mystery," *Tax Notes* 54, no. 10 (March 9, 1992): 1269–75; and Alan J. Auerbach, "Capital Gains Taxation and Tax Reform," *National Tax Journal* 42, no. 3 (September 1989): 391–401. In 1990, the Congressional Budget Office suggested that the revenue-maximizing rate was between 26 and 32 percent; the Joint Committee on Taxation suggested a rate of 28.5 percent. U.S. Congress, Joint Committee on Taxation, *Explanation of Methodology Used to Es-*

timate Proposals Affecting the Taxation of Income from Capital Gains, JCT-12-90 (Washington, D.C.: GPO, March 27, 1990), 41.

11. Auerbach, "Capital Gains Taxation and Tax Reform," 392.

12. Burman, *The Labyrinth of Capital Gains Tax Policy* , 146.

13. Martin Feldstein, Joel Slemrod, and Shlomo Yitzhaki, "The Effects of Taxation on the Selling of Corporate Stock and the Realization of Capital Gains," *Quarterly Journal of Economics* 94, no. 4 (June 1980): 777–91; and Lawrence B. Lindsey, "Capital Gains Rates, Revenues, and Realizations," in *Taxes and Capital Formation,* ed. Martin Feldstein (Boston: National Bureau of Economic Research, 1987), 17–25.

14. Lindsey, "Capital Gains Rates, Revenues, and Realizations," 23.

15. For an excellent review of the literature and issues, see George R. Zodrow, "Economic Analyses of Capital Gains Taxation: Realizations, Revenues, Efficiency and Equity," *Tax Law Review* 48, no. 3 (1993): 422–527. See also Gerald Auten, "Do Capital Gains Tax Rates Affect Revenues?" unpublished study, 1995.

16. Burman, *The Labyrinth of Capital Gains Tax Policy,* 146.

17. Standard & Poor's DRI, "Capital Gains Taxes and the Economy: A Retrospective Look," paper prepared for American Council for Capital Formation, Center for Policy Research, Washington, D.C., July 1999, 4. This 14 percent rate is far higher than in the past mainly because of much larger holdings today by mutual funds, which have a high turnover rate. See Jane G. Gravelle and Lawrence B. Lindsey, "Capital Gains," special report, *Tax Notes* 38, no. 4 (January 25, 1988): 397–405, reproduced in J. Andrew Hoerner, ed., *The Capital Gains Controversy: A Tax Analyst's Reader* (Arlington, Va.: 1992).

18. Auerbach wrote in 1989 that the average holding period for capital assets is about four years, but he was counting gains and losses. "Capital Gains Taxation and Tax Reform," 3. When only gains are taken into account, the average holding period is closer to seven years.

19. Michael Kinsley, "Angel of Death Loophole" *New Republic* (July 13, 1997), 4.

20. Congressional Budget Office, *CBO Memorandum: An Analysis of the Potential Macroeconomic Effects of the Economic Growth Act of 1998,* 2.

21. See Martin Feldstein et al., "The Effects of Taxation."

22. Cited in footnote 1 of Kenneth W. Gideon, assistant secretary (tax policy), Department of the Treasury, statement before the U. S. Senate Committee on Finance, March 6, 1990, regarding the proposed reduction in capital gains taxes contained in President Bush's proposed budget for the fiscal year 1991.

23. U.S. Department of the Treasury, Office of Tax Analysis, "Estimation and Interpretation of Capital Gains Realization Behavior: Evidence from Panel Data," report prepared by Gerald E. Auten, Leonard E. Burman, and William C. Randolph, OTA paper 67, May 1989, 22. Taxpayer behavior also will be influenced by the extent to which a change in rates is considered temporary or permanent, whether a reduction in rates occurs soon after taxpayers have sold off lots of assets, and such other factors as income levels and consumption needs.

24. Joseph A. Stiglitz, *Economics of the Public Sector,* 2nd ed. (New York: W. W. Norton, 1988), 243.

25. Michael J. Boskin, testimony before the Senate Finance Committee, March 28, 1990, as reported in Hoerner, *The Capital Gains Controversy,* 185–88. See also

testimony of Allen Sinai before the Senate Small Business Committee, October 2, 1990, as reported in Hoerner, *The Capital Gains Controversy*, 227–34.

26. See statement of Mark Bloomfeld, president, American Council for Capital Formation, before the Committee on Ways and Means of the U.S. House of Representatives, June 23, 1999, quoting studies of David Wyss.

27. Aaron, "The Capital Gains Tax Cut Mystery," 1270. Aaron wrote, "[If we assume that] that the average annual rate of return to capital is 10 percent, that one-third of this return accrues in the form of capital gains, and that the effective rate of tax on these capital gains is the maximum statutory rate of 30 percent, a reduction of the capital gains tax rate by one-half (about what President Bush is seeking for assets held three years or more) would increase the rate of return by 7 percent, which would boost private saving by just under 3 percent. If these crude assumptions were valid, given the current U.S. net private saving rate of under 5 percent of gross domestic product, the capital gains cut would boost saving by 0.15 percent of gross domestic product. Given standard economic models, such an increase in saving would raise growth of national income by no more than two one-hundredths of 1 percent of gross domestic product."

28. Eugene Steuerle, "The New Tax Cut Debate: Second of Two Parts: Economic Effects," *Tax Notes* 53, no. 11 (December 16, 1991): 1313–14. Jane Gravelle sounded a graver note. She believed that the lower tax would cause such an increase in government deficits that "taking into account feedback effects in the economy will merely increase the projected negative effect [of a lower capital gains tax] on the deficit." See Gravelle, *Can a Capital Gains Tax Cut Pay for Itself?* For an excellent discussion of the Boskin-Gravelle debate, see J. Andrew Hoerner, "Tax Incentives for Capital and Economic Growth: A Critique," *Tax Notes* 48, no. 7 (August, 13, 1990): 813–21.

29. CBO, in its analysis of a 1998 proposal to reduce the maximum capital gains rate to 15 percent, believed that increasing the after-tax rate of return for capital gains would induce more private saving but with little economic impact. "Even if revenue remained unchanged and private savings rose by an amount that is generally regarded as optimistic, private saving would rise by only *0.3 percent,* adding only *0.06 percent* to the nation's capital stock after 10 years." See CBO, *CBO Memorandum: An Analysis of the Potential Macroeconomic Effects of the Economic Growth Act of 1998,* 4.

30. Ibid., 15–16.

31. See Barry Bosworth, "Comments," in *Uneasy Compromise: Problems of a Hybrid Income-Consumption Tax,* ed. Henry J. Aaron, Harvey Galper, and Joseph A. Pechman (Washington, D.C.: Brookings Institution, 1988), 266. See Ralph B. Bristol Jr., J. Andrew Hoerner, and Cathy Hubbard, "Tax Association Conferees Cite Many Reasons (but Few Solutions) for Dismal U.S. Savings Rate," *Tax Notes* 47, no. 10 (June 4, 1990): 1163–67, which reviewed Kotlikoff's presentation at the National Tax Association/Tax Institute of America's May 21–22 symposium, entitled "Tax and Budget Policies in the 1990s: Illusions and Realities."

32. They pay U.S. capital gains taxes only in limited situations, such as from investments in U.S. real estate or from the sale of a U.S.-based business that they own.

33. The American Center for Capital Formation assures us that "the success of the one [new firm] will more than offset the failure of the two losers." American Council

for Capital Formation, *Special Report: Capital Gains Taxes and U.S. Economic Growth: A Retrospective Look*, July 1999, 4.

34. Gravelle and Lindsey, "Capital Gains," 397.

35. Arnold C. Cooper, William C. Dunkelberg, Carolyn Y. Woo, William J. Dennis Jr., *New Business in America: Their Owners* (Washington, D.C.: NFIB Foundation, 1990): 6–7. See Jane G. Gravelle, *CRS Report for Congress: Capital Gains Taxes, Innovation and Growth* (28 January 1999): 2, footnote 3, for reference to a 1997 Moneytree Survey Report that noted that formal venture capital accounted for only $11.5 billion (slightly less than 1 percent) of investment out of total investments of $1,173.0 billion in our economy.

36. CBO, *CBO Memorandum: An Analysis of the Potential Macroeconomic Effects of the Economic Growth Act of 1998*, 7.

37. The relative unimportance of capital gains taxes is suggested in a 1988 study by the Small Business Administration that found that outside investors in these companies seek very high annual rates of return and reject opportunities to invest if they lack faith in the talent of management or if the equity is overpriced. See Robert J. Gaston and Sharon Bell, *The Informal Supply of Capital*, a report submitted to the U.S. Small Business Administration Office of Advocacy, January 29, 1988. For another aspect of the issue, see Yolanda K. Henderson's argument that the capital gains tax rate significantly influenced the cost of capital to emerging corporations: "Capital Gains Taxation and the Cost of Capital for Mature and Emerging Corporations," paper prepared for the American Council for Capital Formation Conference on Saving—The Challenge for the U.S. Economy, October 11–13, 1989.

38. Heidi Glenn, "CBO Under Fire—The Politics and Economics of Capital Gains," *Tax Notes* 80, no. 7 (August 17, 1998): 758. CBO's study concluded: "No research . . . has estimated the amount by which start-up investment responds to a lower tax rate on capital gains." See CBO, *CBO Memorandum: An Analysis of the Potential Macroeconomic Effects of the Economic Growth Act of 1998*, 5.

39. Glenn, "CBO Under Fire—The Politics and Economics of Capital Gains," 758.

40. Standard & Poor's DRI, "Capital Gains Taxes and the Economy: A Retrospective Look," 8. For a different view, see M. Kevin McGee, who recently wrote: "I find . . . that a reduction in the capital gains tax consistently increases investment proportionately more in *old* firms than it does in new firms." See "Capital Gains Taxation and New Firm Investment," *National Tax Journal* 51, no. 4 (December 1998): 654.

41. Jane G. Gravelle, *CRS Report for Congress: Capital Gains Taxes, Innovation and Growth*, January 28, 1999, 6.

42. James M. Poterba, "Capital Gains Tax Policy Toward Entrepreneurship," *National Tax Journal* 42, no. 3 (September 1989): 375, 384. Even advocates of lower capital gains taxes may view today's capital gains rate as less of a deterrent to start-up investments than is the limitation on the right to deduct capital losses. Capital losses always offset capital gains. If, however, capital losses exceed capital gains, only $3,000 of the excess may be deducted each year against wages, interest, and other ordinary income. The remainder may be carried forward to subsequent years, when the same rules apply: the losses offset capital gains; any excess of losses can offset up to $3,000 of ordinary income. This limited ability of capital losses to reduce ordinary income means that an investor who loses several hundred thousand dollars in a start-up company and who does not have large offsetting gains gets little tax relief from the loss that year or

perhaps in succeeding years. Congress has imposed the $3,000 limitation for good reason. It prevents investors from gaming the system by realizing capital losses and capital gains in alternate years. For example, an investor who has a $100,000 capital loss and a $100,000 capital gain knows that if he realizes both this year (Case A), his loss saves him *$20,000*—the 20 percent tax on his $100,000 gain. In the absence of the $3,000 limitation, he might elect to realize his $100,000 loss this year (Case B) to offset $100,000 of ordinary income taxed at 39.6 percent, which would save him *$39,600* in taxes. He then could realize his $100,000 gain next year, paying *$20,000* in taxes, for a net advantage of *$19,600* over Case A. Such manipulations would be very costly to the government.

43. Although certain corporations do not qualify as small businesses, such as those engaged in professional services like law and medicine, most businesses for which outside capital is sought do qualify. The law, however, is unlikely to affect significantly the investment behavior of high-income people who pay the alternative minimum tax (see Chapter 4). This is so because the 50 percent capital gains tax exclusion is considered a preference that can be subject to the alternative minimum tax.

44. IRS, *Statistics of Income—1997,* 36.

45. See U.S. Congress, Joint Committee on Taxation, *Explanation of Methodology Used to Estimate Proposals Affecting the Taxation of Income from Capital Gains,* 48–49; John Lee, "Capital Gains Myths," *Tax Notes* 67, no. 6 (May 8, 1995): 818; CBO, *Distributional Effects of the Administration's Capital Gains Proposal,* (Washington, D.C.: GPO, March 5, 1990).

46. According to data compiled by the Congressional Budget Office for the years 1979 to 1985, "When families' incomes and gains are averaged over a seven-year period, families with incomes of $100,000 or more account for about 70 percent of all realized gains"; during any one of those years, these families accounted for 75 percent to 87 percent of the gains. CBO, *Perspectives on the Ownership of Capital Assets and the Realization of Capital Gains,* 2.

47. CBO, *Perspectives on the Ownership of Capital Assets and the Realization of Capital Gains,* 12, table 3. All figures were based on 1993 dollars.

48. See, for example, Arthur B. Kennickell, Douglas A. McManus, and R. Louise Woodburn, "Weighting Design for the 1992 Survey of Consumer Finances," a study released by them on March 11, 1996. At the time, Kennickell was employed by the Board of Governors of the Federal Reserve System, McManus by Freddie Mac, and Woodburn by the Internal Revenue Service.

49. Citizens for Tax Justice, "Proposed GOP Captial Gains Tax Cut Means More Money for the Rich, Crumbs for the Rest," news release, July 7, 1999.

50. Because inflation adjustments also would increase the number and size of capital losses, Treasury has, in the past, been concerned that an inflation adjustment would lose more tax revenues than would a reduction in the capital gains tax. According to the Congressional Budget Office, "Inflation typically makes up a larger percentage of capital gains than the percentage that would be excluded under a fixed exclusion. The second fact is that, by converting many nominal gains into losses, indexing would make it possible for tax-conscious investors to shelter most of their capital gains income from tax." CBO, *Indexing Capital Gains* (Washington, D.C.: GPO, August 1990), 27.

51. If interest accrued on unrealized gains, the lock-in effect would be exacerbated unless unrealized gains were taxed at death.

52. John F. Kennedy, Special Message to the Congress on Tax Reduction and Reform, January 24, 1963. Kennedy noted exceptions for the transfer of household and personal effects, assets transferred to a surviving spouse, a certain minimum amount of property in every case, and transfers of appreciated property to charity.

53. C. Eugene Steuerle, "The Capital Gains Debate That Wasn't," *Tax Notes* 70, no. 5 (January 29, 1996): 603.

54. Ibid.

55. Ibid.

56. Gravelle and Lindsey, "Capital Gains," 18.

57. Auerbach, "Capital Gains Taxation and Tax Reform," 398.

58. New York State Bar Association, Tax Section, Tax Report #662, June 27, 1990, with cover letter dated June 28, 1990 from Arthur A. Feder, chair.

59. See Leonard E. Burman and Peter D. Ricoy, "Capital Gains and the People Who Realize Them," *National Tax Journal* 50, no. 3 (September 1997): 428.

60. Martin Feldstein, "Why Capital Gains Taxes Are Unfair," *Wall Street Journal*, November 21, 1994.

61. For example, from 1982 through 1985, 10 of the largest corporations in the United States—AT&T, DuPont, Boeing, General Dynamics, Pepsico, General Mills, Transamerica, Texaco, International Paper, Greyhound, and IC Industries—had no overall income tax liability, though each company had substantial economic profits. Stockholders who bought and sold their stocks during these years at a profit did not suffer a double tax on their gains. See Citizens for Tax Justice, *130 Reasons Why We Need Tax Reform* (Washington, D.C., 1996), 3.

62. Joel Slemrod and Jon Bakija, *Taxing Ourselves* (Cambridge: MIT, 1996), 66–67.

63. As explained in Chapter 8, this carryover-basis rule should not pose major administrative problems today, particularly with the allowance of a modest step-up in basis as recommended.

64. One possibility would be for Congress to make the alternative minimum tax inapplicable to these gains.

65. See James R. Repetti, "Management Incentives, Needless Tax Complexity, and Capital Gains," *Tax Notes* 75, no. 7 (May 19, 1997): 981–91.

Chapter 13

1. Steve Forbes, "Steve Forbes on the Flat Tax and How Much Your Family Saves," http://sun.kent.wednet.edu/ksd/dr/socialstudies/Forbes/issues/sfflattax.html.

2. The value of Gates's Microsoft stock would suffer a one-time loss at the time the flat tax is adopted unless the flat tax contained transition rules covering deductions for depreciation and for interest on pre-flat-tax debts, as explained later in this chapter.

3. Patrick J. Buchanan, "A Flawed Flat Tax and the Way Out," *New York Times*, January 17, 1996.

4. Lawrence H. Summers, "An Evaluation of the Flat Tax," speech delivered by then deputy secretary of the Treasury Summers at the Brookings Institution, Washington, D.C., February 16, 1996; reprinted in *Tax Notes* 70, no. 12 (March 11, 1996): 1555–58.

5. Robert E. Hall and Alvin Rabushka, *Low Tax, Simple Tax, Flat Tax* (New York: McGraw-Hill, 1983). See also Robert E. Hall and Alvin Rabushka, *The Flat Tax,* 2nd ed. (Stanford: Hoover Institution Press, 1995).

6. Their flat tax was introduced in the 104th Congress on July 19, 1995. It appeared in H.R. 2060 in the House of Representatives and in S. 1050 in the Senate.

7. Leslie Wayne, "Flat Tax Goes from 'Snake Oil' to G.O.P. Tonic," *New York Times,* November 14, 1999. Readers who turned to page 23 of the article would have learned that flat-tax proposals would change the tax base as well.

8. David F. Bradford, *Blueprints for Basic Tax Reform,* 2nd ed. (Arlington, Va.: Tax Analysts, 1984), 37.

9. Joel Slemrod and Jon Bakija, *Taxing Ourselves,* 2nd ed. (Cambridge: MIT, 2000), 172.

10. Congressman Dick Armey and Senator Richard Shelby, "Summary: The Freedom and Fairness Restoration Act," a release from their offices dated March 9, 1999, 4.

11. The 22 percent rate calculated by Hall and Rabushka is referred to in William G. Gale, "Building a Better Tax System: Can a Consumption Tax Deliver the Goods?" *Tax Notes* 69, 6 (November 6, 1995): 783. See also C. Eugene Steuerle, "The Simple Arithmetic of Flat Taxes," *Tax Notes* 70, no. 8 (February 19, 1996): 1041; Steuerle stated that at the higher level of personal exemption or standard deduction proposed by many flat-tax proponents, "a tax rate of approximately 21 percent is required to maintain current federal income taxes." His figure is consistent with conclusions of the Treasury Department in 1996. See U.S. Treasury Department, Office of Tax Analysis, "'New' Armey-Shelby Flat Tax Would Still Lose Money, Treasury Finds," *Tax Notes* 70, no. 4 (January 22, 1996): 451–61.

12. Special rules apply for income of a corporate subsidiary and for certain dividends received by corporations.

13. Gross active income includes income from the export of property or services from the United States but excludes income from the import of property or services from outside of the United States. The latter provision is highly controversial.

14. A national sales tax, or VAT, in its pure form, would operate regressively because lower-income households consume a disproportionately high percentage of their income. Exempting certain staples from tax, such as food and clothing, could cushion its regressivity but would create administrative and other problems. Some advocates of a national sales tax or VAT believe that they can achieve the same degree of progressivity as the flat tax by including a government rebate for households based on household size and income. See Lawrence Zelenak, "Flat Tax vs. VAT: Progressivity and Family Allowances," *Tax Notes* 69, no. 9 (November 27, 1995): 1129–34.

15. Not deducting investment costs but exempting their return, and deducting investment costs but paying tax on their return, generally produce equivalent after-tax results under a flat-tax rate, as can be seen from the following example. Assume that you earn $100,000 this year and want to invest it for one year, then cash it in. Assume further that the return will be 10 percent, or $10,000, and that the tax rate is 20 percent. If your investment is not deductible but your income from it is tax exempt, you will have $80,000 to invest after taxes, earn $8,000 that is tax exempt, and have a total of $88,000 after taxes at the end of the year. Alternatively, if you were entitled to deduct the $100,000 investment but were taxed on the income, you would invest $100,000, earn $10,000, and have $110,000 before taxes. If you then

sold the investment and paid a 20 percent tax on $110,000, you also would have $88,000 left after taxes.

16. Richard Musgrave explains that deducting fully the cost of property in the year it is acquired "exempts the normal return to capital from taxation. By allowing immediate deduction of the investment cost against other income, the government in effect renders an interest-free loan to the investor. In the course of continuous reinvestment, this loan will generate an income stream the present value of which, after tax, equals the tax on the normal return on the initial investment. The only returns that remain in the [business] tax base are rent, monopoly profits, compensation for risk, and reward for superior entrepreneurial effort. . . . Once the correct income concept is applied, the claim that all income is treated equally becomes invalid. . . . As viewed from the sources side, income taxation under the flat tax should be described as a tax on wages, with capital income largely exempted and the two sources treated quite unequally." Richard A. Musgrave, "Clarifying Tax Reform," *Tax Notes* 70, no. 6 (February 5, 1996): 735.

17. Hall and Rabushka, *Low Tax,* 125.

18. The pure income tax, as defined here, would ignore imputed income and would tax people on their capital gains only when the gains are realized, not when they accrue.

19. William G. Gale and Kevin A. Hassett, "A Framework for Evaluating the Flat Tax," March 3, 1998, 4, mimeo.

20. Summers, "An Evaluation of the Flat Tax," 1558.

21. U.S. Department of the Treasury, Office of Tax Analysis, "'New' Armey-Shelby Flat Tax Would Still Lose Money, Treasury Finds," Tax Notes 70, no. 4 (January 22, 1996): 451–61. A part of their tax savings would stem from the elimination of estate and gift taxes.

22. See William G. Gale, Scott Houser, and John Karl Scholz, "Distributional Effects of Fundamental Tax Reform," in *Economic Effects of Fundamental Tax Reform,* ed. Henry J. Aaron and William G. Gale (Washington, D.C.: Brookings Institution, 1996), 283, 305. For the proposition that middle- and high-income wage earners would tend to lose under a flat tax, see Amy Dunbar and Thomas Pogue, "Sources of Gains and Losses from Switching to a Flat Tax," *Tax Notes* 80, no. 9 (August 31, 1998): 1065–72.

23. Ibid., see examples 2 and 3, 459–60.

24. Henry J. Aaron and William G. Gale, eds., *Economic Effects of Fundamental Tax Reform* (Washington, D.C.: Brookings Institution, 1996), 1.

25. Hall and Rabushka, *Low Tax,* 53.

26. Gale, "Building a Better Tax System," 784.

27. Representatives Dick Armey and Senator Richard Shelby, "Summary: The Freedom and Fairness Restoration Act," release of March 9, 1999, obtained from the Internet: http://flattax.gov/proposal/flat-sum.asp, 4, 31 August 1999.

28. Reported in Louis Lyons, "Consumption Tax Would Spur Growth, Witnesses Tell Ways and Means," *Tax Notes* 71, no. 1 (April 1, 1996): 14.

29. To understand why economists reach such different conclusions about the consequences of fundamental tax reform, we must understand differences in the economic models they use. On this subject, see Eric Engen, Jane Gravelle, and Kent Smetters, "Dynamic Tax Models: Why They Do the Things They Do," paper presented at the National Tax Association Symposium, The Post-Election Agenda: Implementation or

Confrontation? Arlington, Va., *National Tax Journal* 50, no. 3 (May 19–20, 1997): 657–82; see also Joint Committee on Taxation, *Tax Modeling Project and 1997 Symposium Papers*, JCS–21–97 (Washington, D.C.: GPO, November 20, 1997).

30. Aaron and Gale, *Economic Effects of Fundamental Tax Reform,* 1. In fact, saving through pension plans and IRAs might even decline because of competition from other forms of savings that would receive comparable tax advantages. Although contributions to pension plans and IRAs would be deductible, distributions from pension plans and IRAs would be taxable. A comparable after-tax effect would be achieved from the same investments if made in one's personal, nonretirement account: the contribution would not be deductible, but distributions of the original amount plus its earnings would be tax exempt.

31. Ibid., 15. See also William G. Gale, "The Kemp Commission and the Future of Tax Reform," *Tax Notes* 70, no. 6 (February 5, 1996): 723.

32. Alan J. Auerbach, "Tax Reform, Capital Allocation, Efficiency, and Growth," in *Economic Effects of Fundamental Tax Reform*, ed. Aaron and Gale, 29–82.

33. Ibid., 61.

34. Ibid., 80.

35. Gale and Hassett, "A Framework for Evaluating the Flat Tax," 8.

36. See Peter Passell, "The Tax Code Heads into the Operating Room," *New York Times,* September 3, 1999.

37. See Price Waterhouse and Caplin & Drysdale, *Impact of Tax Restructuring on Tax-Exempt Organizations* (Washington, D.C.: 1997), 3. For criticism of the report, see "Republic of Taxes: When Uncle Sam Takes, Do Americans Give?" *Philanthropy* 11, no. 2 (spring 1997): 12–15.

38. For different views of economists on the impact of a flat tax on housing prices, see, for example, Dennis R. Capozza, Richard K. Green, and Patric Henderschott, "Tax Reform and House Prices: Large or Small Effect," paper presented at the Ninety-first National Tax Association Annual Conference on Taxation, Austin, Tex., November 8–10, 1998. For the view that a flat tax would not significantly deflate housing values, see Jane G. Gravelle, *Effects of Flat Taxes and Other Proposals on Housing: Full Report* (Washington, D.C.: Congressional Research Service, 1996); see also Bruce R. Bartlett, "Will the Flat Tax KO Housing?" *Wall Street Journal,* August 2, 1995. For different views of economists on the impact on charitable giving from eliminating the charitable deduction, see Fred Stokeld, "Charities Fear Loss of Deduction Under Flat Tax Proposals," *Tax Notes* 70, no. 8 (February 19, 1996): 935–38. For the view that charitable giving would not change substantially without a charitable deduction, see Robert J. Breshock, "Would A Flat Tax Flatten Philanthropy?" Philanthropy (spring 1996), 14–5, 34.

39. C. Eugene Steuerle, "The Simple Arithmetic of Flat Taxes," *Tax Notes* 70, no. 8 (February 19, 1996): 1041.

40. See Gale, "The Kemp Commission," 721.

Chapter 14

1. U.S. Department of the Treasury, *Tax Reform for Fairness, Simplicity, and Economic Growth,* vol. 1 (Washington, D.C.: Treasury Department, November 1984), iii.

Glossary

Accelerated depreciation See depreciation deductions.

Acquisition indebtedness Indebtedness that qualifies for the home-mortgage interest deduction and is incurred for the purchase, construction, or substantial improvement of a principal or secondary residence.

Adjusted gross income (AGI) Gross income minus specified adjustments (distinguished from personal exemptions, standard deductions, and itemized deductions) on the individual income tax return, such as for IRA contributions, moving expenses, alimony payments, and self-employed health insurance premiums.

Alternative minimum tax (AMT) An alternative to the regular income tax that must be paid if it is higher than the regular tax. The AMT typically is owed by certain individual taxpayers who make extensive use of tax preferences.

Average tax rate The tax rate determined by dividing a taxpayer's total tax by the total taxable amount.

Benefit theory A theory for distributing tax burdens in ratio to the benefits each taxpayer receives from actions of the federal government.

Bracket creep An increase in the tax bracket applicable to a taxpayer's taxable income because his or her income has risen with inflation.

Broad-base low-rate system A system that subjects most income to tax (the broad base) at low tax rates. Contrast a narrow-base high-rate system, in which tax rates must be considerably higher to raise the same tax revenue because the tax base has been reduced by large numbers of exclusions, deferrals, deductions, and credits.

Cafeteria plan A plan adopted by an employer that allows employees to take reduced salaries in exchange for their employers' paying certain personal expenses of employees, tax-free.

Capital gain (loss) An increase (decrease) in the value of an asset held for investment purposes.

Compound interest Earning interest on interest.

Consumption expense A personal expense, to be distinguished from an expense incurred for the production of income.

Consumption tax A tax on what is consumed but not saved or invested.

Cost-benefit analysis Analysis of the relationship between the cost of a public expenditure and its anticipated benefits.

Cost of capital What businesses must pay to lenders to borrow and to investors to attract their investments.

Couples neutrality Identical treatment of couples whether or not they are married.

Deadweight loss See economic efficiency of the tax laws.

Demand-side effect An increase in consumer demand, and thus economic activity generally, attributable to a reduction in taxes.

Depreciation deductions Deductions spread over the useful life of an asset to reflect its assumed decline in value. Accelerated depreciation allows for larger depreciation deductions during the early years of an asset's useful life and smaller deductions during later years.

Diminishing marginal utility of income See marginal utility of income.

Discretionary spending programs Programs whose funding levels are determined and controlled in annual appropriation acts. Contrast entitlement programs.

Disposable income Income received by individuals, including transfer payments, minus personal taxes and fees paid to the government.

Double taxation Taxing corporate income twice; for example, first taxing the corporation and again taxing shareholders when the income is distributed to them as a dividend.

Earned income Income from personal services, such as wages and salaries.

Earned-income tax credit (EITC) A refundable tax credit for certain low-income individuals.

Economic distortions from tax policies Inefficient economic decisions of taxpayers in response to the tax laws, such as decisions to save or work less because of an increase in tax rates, that slow economic growth.

Economic efficiency of the tax laws A measure of the extent to which tax laws are capable of raising revenue without reducing economically productive activities. Efficient tax laws allow government to raise revenue with minimal economic distortions. Economists refer to economic losses from economic distortions as economic costs, deadweight losses, or excess burdens.

Economic income Income measured pursuant to economic theory.

Efficiency cost See economic efficiency of the tax laws.

Elasticity (of demand or supply) The percentage change in the quantity of a good consumed (or supplied) as a result of a percentage change in its price. The more elastic the demand or supply, the more the market will respond to a change in price.

Entitlement programs Programs that create a legal obligation of the federal government, such as Social Security and Medicare, to make payments to beneficiaries year after year.

Equal proportional sacrifice A theory that the hardship or sacrifice from paying taxes can be equal for two individuals when the government imposes a higher tax rate on the last dollar of income of a high-income taxpayer than on the last dollar of income of a low-income taxpayer. For analogous theory, see marginal utility of income.

Estate tax A tax levied on the value of the estate of a decedent.

Excise tax A tax on the manufacture, sale, or use of goods, on the carrying on of an occupation or profession, or on the transfer of property.

Externality Also known as a spillover effect. An activity of A that affects the welfare of B in a way that is outside the direct market of A's activity. Externalities may be positive or negative. For example, Mount Holyoke College, whose market is its students, staff, and faculty, strengthens the economy (a positive externality) of

South Hadley, where it is located. By contrast, air and water pollution by coal-mining companies produce negative externalities for neighboring communities.

Feedback effect See revenue feedback effect.

FICA Federal Insurance Contributions Act, which covers Social Security and Medicare taxes. See social insurance taxes.

Flat tax A term commonly used today to refer to a consumption tax that includes a single, or flat, tax rate.

Flat (or proportional) tax rate The same tax rate for all taxpayers.

401(k) plan A tax-favored employer-based retirement plan that allows participants to make tax-deductible contributions from their wages.

Gross domestic product (GDP) The sum of all income earned in the production of goods and services within the United States.

Gross income Income potentially subject to tax that must be reported on annual federal individual income tax returns.

Haig-Simons A widely accepted definition of income developed by economists Robert M. Haig and Henry C. Simons.

Home equity loan A loan to a homeowner of up to $100,000 that is secured by his or her principal or secondary residence and qualifies for the home-mortgage inter-est deduction even if the funds are not used for purposes relating to the residence.

Horizontal equity Equal taxation of equals, often interpreted to require equal taxa-tion of people who have equal abilities to pay.

Imputed rental income The net value to owners from the use of consumer durables, such as personal residences, measured by the fair rental value of such durables minus the cost (including depreciation deductions) of owning and main-taining them.

Income effect The tendency to acquire less of good A and more of good B because good A has become relatively cheaper, such as the tendency to save less and con-sume more when the tax on saving is reduced. Contrast substitution effect.

Inflation adjustments in the tax laws Adjustments such as in the size of personal exemptions, standard deductions, and tax brackets to reflect the impact of changes in the general price level of goods and services.

In-kind benefits Benefits paid in forms other than cash, such as Medicare and Med-icaid assistance.

Itemized deductions A specified number of deductions from AGI, for purposes of calculating taxable income, that may be claimed by any taxpayer; the deductions require substantiating evidence. Compare standard deduction.

Keogh plan A tax-favored retirement plan created by the self-employed.

Labor productivity Average real output per hour of labor.

Laffer curve A graph of the relationship between tax rates and tax revenue devel-oped by Arthur Laffer; he believed it showed that raising tax rates above certain thresholds would reduce tax revenue. See supply-side economics.

Lock-in effect The disincentive of a capital gains tax on one's decision to realize gains on appreciated assets.

Marginal tax rate The tax rate that applies to the next dollar of income or deduction.

Marginal utility of income The benefit derived from an extra dollar of income. Ad-vocates of progressive tax rates believe that the utility of income declines (the de-clining marginal utility of income) as income rises above certain thresholds.

Marriage bonus Paying less in taxes on the same amount of income if married rather than single.

Marriage neutrality Tax laws that burden married people identically regardless of the state in which they reside or the allocation between them of their taxable income.

Marriage penalty Paying more taxes on the same amount of income if married.

Median tax return The tax return that lies at the exact middle—an equal number of returns lies above and below—of all tax returns under consideration.

National savings The sum of government and private savings.

Net income The excess of gross income over the costs of producing it.

Net worth The value of all assets minus all debts and liabilities.

Nominal capital gains Gains on the sale or exchange of capital assets without adjustment for inflation.

Normal income tax law (NTL) The hypothetical income tax law developed by the Joint Committee on Taxation that eliminates tax preferences.

Ordinary income All taxable income except capital gains.

Passive income Income from savings and investments.

Personal deductions Deductions unrelated to the production of income, such as standard deductions and deductions for charitable gifts and state and local taxes.

Personal exemption An amount per family member that can be subtracted from adjusted gross income in calculating taxable income.

Personal saving Saving by households.

Private saving Saving by households and businesses.

Productivity Average real output per unit of input.

Progressive tax burdens Tax liabilities increase disproportionately as the taxable amount increases. Progressive tax burdens can be achieved without progressive tax rates, such as in the case of a flat tax rate combined with thresholds that protect a basic amount of income from tax.

Progressive tax rates Tax rates that increase as the taxable amount increases.

Proportional tax rate See flat tax rate.

Realized capital gain A capital gain resulting from the sale or exchange of an appreciated asset.

Refundable tax credit A credit that first offsets a taxpayer's tax liability, with any unused portion paid to the taxpayer by the government.

Regressive tax rate A tax rate that declines as the taxable amount increases.

Revenue feedback effect The production of additional tax revenue from favorable developments in the tax laws that, in turn, generate favorable economic behavior by taxpayers.

Revenue-neutral tax reforms Reforms of the tax system that do not alter the amount of tax revenue that is to be collected.

Salary-reduction plan See cafeteria plan.

Social insurance taxes Social Security and Medicare taxes (see FICA).

Standard deduction A deduction from AGI, for purposes of calculating taxable income, that may be claimed by any taxpayer without proof of actual expenses. Compare itemized deductions.

Static revenue loss The loss of tax revenue from taxing the same amount of income at a lower tax rate.

Step-up-in-basis rule A rule that allows most assets of a decedent to obtain a new tax basis in the hands of heirs equal to the fair market value of the assets at the date of the decedent's death.

Substitution effect The tendency to acquire more of good A and less of good B because good A has become relatively cheaper, such as the tendency to save more and consume less when the tax on saving is reduced. Contrast income effect.

Supply-side economics An economic theory that reducing tax rates from certain levels will increase tax revenues. See Laffer curve.

Taxable income The income that is subject to tax after subtracting all adjustments and deductions.

Tax avoidance Legal behavior to reduce tax liabilities.

Tax base The total of all taxable income on all tax returns.

Tax basis The cost of an investment, less any depreciation, for determining gain or loss.

Tax credit An offset of the actual tax owed, such as a child care credit.

Tax evasion Illegal behavior to avoid paying taxes due.

Tax expenditures The federal government's loss of tax revenue from tax preferences.

Tax gap The gap between the amount of taxes that are owed and the amount of taxes that actually are collected.

Tax incidence A term used to identify who bears the ultimate burden of a tax, as distinguished from the payer of the tax. For example, although employers and employees each pay half of all Social Security taxes, most or all of the employer's share ultimately is borne by workers through a reduction in their wages.

Tax neutrality A principle that the tax system should produce identical after-tax results for economic activities that produce the same economic results.

Tax preferences Provisions of the income tax laws that, according to the Joint Committee on Taxation, depart from an economic definition of income and offer tax savings to particular taxpayers.

Unearned income Income, such as dividends and interest, from the investment of capital rather than from labor.

Utility of income See marginal utility of income.

Vertical equity Appropriate differences in tax burdens that reflect differences among taxpayers in their abilities to pay.

Bibliography

Aaron, Henry. *Shelter and Subsidies.* Washington, D.C.: Brookings Institution, 1972.
_____. "Lessons for Tax Reform." In *Do Taxes Matter? The Impact of the Tax Reform Act of 1986,* edited by Joel B. Slemrod. Cambridge: MIT, 1990.
_____. "The Capital Gains Mystery." *Tax Notes* 54, no. 10 (March 9, 1992): 1269–75.
Aaron, Henry J., and William G. Gale, eds. "Introduction." In *Economic Effects of Fundamental Tax Reform.* Washington, D.C.: Brookings Institution, 1996.
Advisory Commission on Intergovernmental Relations. "Changing Public Attitudes on Governments and Taxes." Washington, D.C.: ACIR, 1993.
Alesina, A., and D. Roderick. "Distribution, Political Conflict, and Economic Growth." In *Political Economy, Growth, and Business Cycles,* edited by A. Cuckierman, Z. Hercowitz, and L. Leiderman. Cambridge: MIT, 1992.
Altman, Nancy J. "Rethinking Retirement Income Policies: Nondiscrimination, Integration, and the Quest for Worker Security." *Tax Law Review* 42, no. 3 (1987): 433–508.
American Council for Capital Formation. *Special Report: Capital Gains Taxes and U.S. Economic Growth: A Retrospective Look.* Washington, D.C.: July 1999.
Andrews, William D. "Personal Deductions in an Ideal Income Tax." *Harvard Law Review* 86 (1972): 309–85.
Armey, Dick, Representative, and Senator Richard Shelby, "Summary: The Freedom and Fairness Restoration Act." News release, March 9, 1999. http://flattax.gov/proposal/flat-sum.asp, 4, August 31, 1999.
Auerbach, Alan J. "Capital Gains Taxation and Tax Reform." *National Tax Journal* 42, no. 3 (September 1989): 391–401.
_____. "Tax Reform, Capital Allocation, Efficiency, and Growth." In *Economic Effects of Fundamental Tax Reform,* edited by Henry J. Aaron and William G. Gale. Washington, D.C.: Brookings Institution, 1996.
Auten, Gerald. "Do Capital Gains Tax Rates Affect Revenues?" Unpublished study, 1995.
Ballard, Charles L. "Marginal Efficiency Cost Calculations for Different Types of Government Expenditure: A Review." Paper presented at the Australian Conference in Applied General Equilibrium, Melbourne, Australia, May 27–28, 1991.
Bankman, Joseph, and Thomas Griffith. "Social Welfare and the Rate Structure: A New Look at Progressive Taxation." *California Law Review* 75, no. 6 (1987): 1905–67.
Barro, Robert J. "Higher Taxes, Lower Revenues." *Wall Street Journal,* July 9, 1993.
_____. "Bob Dole, Supply-Sider." *Wall Street Journal,* August 29, 1996.

Bartlett, Bruce R. "Will the Flat Tax KO Housing?" *Wall Street Journal*, August 2, 1995.

Bartlett, Donald L., and James B. Steele. *America: Who Really Pays the Taxes?* New York: Simon & Schuster, 1994.

Berky, Andrew S., and James P. Shenton, eds. *The "Historians" History of the United States.* Vol. 1. New York: G. P. Putnam's Sons, 1966.

Bernheim, B. Douglas. *Is the Baby Boom Generation Preparing Adequately for Retirement? Summary Report.* Princeton: Merrill Lynch, 1993.

_____. *The Merrill Lynch Baby Boom Retirement Index: Update 1997.* Princeton: Merrill Lynch, May 1997.

Birnbaum, Jeffrey H., and Alan S. Murray. *Showdown at Gucci Gulch.* New York: Random House, 1987.

Bittker, Boris I. "A 'Comprehensive Tax Base' as a Goal of Income Tax Return." *Harvard Law Review* 80 (1967): 925–85.

_____. "Comprehensive Income Taxation: A Response," *Harvard Law Review* 81 (1968): 1032–43.

Bloom, David E., and Richard B. Freeman. *The Fall in Private Pension Coverage in the U.S.* Cambridge: National Bureau of Economic Research, 1992.

Bloomfield, Mark. Statement Before Committee on Ways and Means of the U.S. House of Representatives, June 23, 1999.

Bloomfield, Mark, and Margo Thorning. "Tax Policy for Competitiveness, Growth, and Retirement Security." *Tax Notes* 82, no. 11 (March 15, 1999): 1686–93.

Blum, Walter J. "A Handy Summary of the Capital Gains Arguments." *Tax Notes* 44, no. 10 (September 4, 1989): 1145–59. Reprinted in *The Capital Gains Controversy: A Tax Analyst's Reader,* edited by J. Andrew Hoerner. Arlington, Va.: Tax Analysts, 1992, 31–44.

Blum, Walter J., and Harry Kalven Jr. "The Uneasy Case for Progressive Taxation." *University of Chicago Law Review* 19, no. 3 (1952): 417–520.

Boskin, Michael J. Testimony Before the Senate Finance Committee, March 28, 1990. Reprinted in *The Capital Gains Controversy: A Tax Analyst's Reader,* edited by J. Andrew Hoerner. Arlington, Va.: Tax Analysts, 1992, 185–88.

_____, ed. *Frontiers of Tax Reform.* Stanford: Hoover Institution Press, 1996.

Bosworth, Barry. "Comments." In *Uneasy Compromise: Problems of a Hybrid Income-Consumption Tax,* edited by Henry J. Aaron, Harvey Galper, and Joseph A. Pechman. Washington, D.C.: Brookings Institution, 1988, 266.

Bradford, David F. *Untangling the Income Tax.* Cambridge: Harvard University Press, 1986.

Bradley, Bill. *The Fair Tax.* New York: Pocket Books, 1984.

Breshock, Robert J. "Would a Flat Tax Flatten Philanthropy?" *Philanthropy* (spring 1996): 14–15, 38.

Bristol, Ralph B., Jr., J. Andrew Hoerner, and Cathy Hubbard. "Tax Association Conferees Cite Many Reasons (but Few Solutions) for Dismal U.S. Savings Rate." *Tax Notes* 47, no. 10 (June, 4, 1990): 1163–67.

Broder, David S. "Forgotten but Not Paid." *Washington Post National Weekly Edition,* January 12, 1998.

Brownlee, W. Elliott. *Federal Taxation in America: A Short History.* Cambridge: Cambridge University Press, 1996.

Brushaber v. Union Pacific, 240 U.S. 1, 25 (1916).

Buchinsky, Moshe, and Jennifer Hunt. "Wage Mobility in the United States." Working paper 5455, National Bureau of Economic Research, Cambridge, Mass., February 1996.

Budget of the U.S Government 1990. Washington, D.C.: GPO, 1989.

Burman, Leonard E. *The Labyrinth of Capital Gains Tax Policy.* Washington, D.C.: Brookings Institution, 1999.

Burman, Leonard E., and Peter D. Ricoy. "Capital Gains and the People Who Realize Them." *National Tax Journal* 50, no. 3 (September 1997): 427–51.

Burman, Leonard, Sally Wallace, and David Weiner. *How Capital Gains Taxes Distort Homeowners' Decisions.* National Tax Association Proceedings, Eighty-ninth Annual Conference, Boston, Mass., 1996. Washington, D.C.: National Tax Association, Tax Institute of America, 1997, 382–90.

Burns, James MacGregor. *The American Experiment, Volume II: The Workshop of Democracy.* New York: Alfred A. Knopf, 1985.

Burtless, Gary. "The Supply-Side Legacy of the Reagan Years: Response of Labor Supply." Paper presented at the conference The Economic Legacy of the Reagan Years: Euphoria or Chaos? Oakland University, June 30–July 1, 1989.

Burtless, Gary, and Barry Bosworth. "Effects of Tax Reform on Labor Supply, Investment, and Savings." *Journal of Economic Perspectives* 6, no. 1 (winter 1992): 3–25.

Canner, Glenn B., Thomas A. Durkin, and Charles A. Luckett. "Recent Developments in Home Equity Lending." *Federal Reserve Bulletin* (April 1998): 241–51.

Caplin, Mortimer. ". . . And Drop Investment Tax Credits." *Wall Street Journal,* March 29, 1993.

Capozza, Dennis R., Richard K. Green, and Patric Henderschott. "Tax Reform and House Prices: Large or Small Effect?" Paper presented at the Ninety-first National Tax Association Annual Conference on Taxation, Austin, Tex., November 8–10, 1998.

Center on Budget and Policy Priorities. "Top One Percent of Population Received as Much After-Tax Income in 1994 as the Bottom 35 Percent, Analysis Finds." Study released August 14, 1997.

————. "In Search of Shelter: The Growing Shortage of Affordable Rental Housing." Study by Jennifer Daskal, released June 1998.

Citizens for Tax Justice. *130 Reasons Why We Need Tax Reform.* Washington, D.C.: 1996.

Clements, Jonathan. "Figuring Needs for Your Retirement Can Become a Job in Itself." *Wall Street Journal,* January 10, 1994.

Clotfelder, Charles T., and Richard L. Schmalbeck. "The Impact of Fundamental Tax Reform on Nonprofit Organizations." In *Economic Effects of Fundamental Tax Reform,* edited by Henry J. Aaron and William G. Gale. Washington, D.C.: Brookings Institution, 1996.

Collins, J. Michael, Eric S. Belsky, and Nicolas P. Retsinas. "Towards a Targeted Homeownership Tax Credit." Joint Center for Housing Studies, Harvard University, W98–5, November 1998.

Commissioner v. Glenshaw Glass Co., 348 U.S. 426, 431 (1955).

Committee for Economic Development, Research and Policy Committee. *Restoring Prosperity: Budget Choices for Economic Growth.* New York and Washington, D.C: Committee for Economic Development, 1992.

Competitiveness Policy Council. *Saving More and Investing Better: A Strategy for Security Prosperity.* Fourth report to the president and Congress, September 1995, 30.

Congressional Budget Office. *The Tax Treatment of Homeownership: Issues and Options.* Washington, D.C.: Government Printing Office (GPO), September 1981.

_____. *Limiting State-Local Tax Deductibility in Exchange for Increased General Revenue Sharing: An Analysis of the Economic Effects.* Washington, D.C.: GPO, August 1983.

_____. "Effects of the 1981 Tax Act on the Distribution of Income and Taxes Paid." Staff working paper. Washington, D.C.: GPO, 1986.

_____. *Tax Policy for Pensions and Other Retirement Saving.* Washington, D.C.: GPO, 1987.

_____. *Distributional Effects of the Administration's Capital Gains Proposal.* Washington, D.C.: GPO, March 5, 1990.

_____. *Indexing Capital Gains.* Washington, D.C.: GPO, August 1990.

_____. *Budget of the United States Government Fiscal Year 1992.* Part 3. Washington, D.C.: GPO, 1992.

_____. *Assessing the Decline in the National Saving Rate.* Washington, D.C.: GPO, 1993.

_____. *Baby Boomers in Retirement: An Early Perspective.* Washington, D.C.: GPO, September 1993.

_____. *The Tax Treatment of Employment-Based Health Insurance.* Washington, D.C.: GPO, March 1994.

_____. *Reducing the Deficit: Spending and Revenue Options.* Washington, D.C.: GPO, March 1997.

_____. Tax Analysis Division. "Recent Evidence on Taxpayers' Response to the Rate Increases in the 1990s." Report by Frank Sammartino and David Weiner. Washington, D.C.: GPO, May 1997.

_____. *Perspectives on the Ownership of Capital Assets and the Realization of Capital Gains.* Washington, D.C.: GPO, May 2, 1997.

_____. *CBO Memorandum: An Analysis of the Potential Macroeconomic Effects of the Economic Growth Act of 1998.* Washington, D.C.: GPO, August 1998.

_____. *Maintaining Budget Discipline: Spending and Revenue Options.* Washington, D.C.: GPO, 1999.

Congressional Committee Reports Accompanying the Taxpayer Relief Act of 1997. H.R. 2014, Section 312.

Congressional Globe, 38th Cong., 1st sess. (1864), 1876.

Congressional Research Service, Library of Congress. *Can a Capital Gains Tax Cut Pay for Itself?* Report by Jane G. Gravelle for Congress. Washington, D.C., March 23, 1990.

Conwell, Russell. *Acres of Diamonds.* Old Tappan, N.J.: Pyramid, 1960.

Cooper, Arnold C., William C. Dunkelberg, Carolyn Y. Woo, and William J. Dennis Jr. *New Business in America: Their Owners.* Washington, D.C.: NFIB Foundation, 1990.

DeParle, Jason. "Slamming the Door." *New York Times Magazine*, October 20, 1996, 53.

DiPasquale, Denise, and Edward L. Glaeser. "Incentives and Social Capital: Are Home Owners Better Citizens?" Working paper series W97-3, Harvard University Joint Center for Housing Studies, Cambridge, Mass., 1997.

Dorsey Stuart, Christopher Cornwell, and David Macpherson. *Pensions and Productivity.* Kalamazoo, Mich.: W. E. Upjohn Institute for Employment Research, 1998.

Dunbar, Amy, and Thomas Pogue. "Sources of Gains and Losses from Switching to a Flat Tax." *Tax Notes* 80, no. 9 (August 31, 1998): 1065-72.

Economic Report of the President. Washington, D.C.: GPO, 1993.

Economic Report of the President. Washington, D.C.: GPO, 1994, table B-27.

Edsall, Thomas B. *The New Politics of Inequality.* New York: W. W. Norton, 1984.

Eisenhower, Dwight D. Radio and television address to the nation on the subject of taxes. *U.S. Code Congressional and Administrative News,* 83rd Cong., 2d. sess., vol. 1 (1954), 1669.

Eissa, Nada. "Taxation and Labor Supply of Married Women: The Tax Reform Act of 1986 as a Natural Experiment." Working paper 5023, *National Bureau of Economic Research,* Cambridge, Mass., February 1995, 1-36.

Employee Benefit Research Institute. *EBRI Databook on Employee Benefits.* Washington, D.C.: EBRI, 1990.

_____. *Pension Tax Expenditures: Are They Worth the Cost? EBRI Issue Brief* 124 (February 1993).

_____. "Americans Say They Are Saving for Retirement, but They May Be Falsely Confident About Their Preparations." *EBRI News* (October 31, 1995): 1-2.

_____. *EBRI Issue Brief,* (April 1996).

_____. "Estimated Total Pension Assets in the U.S., 1985-Present." *Pension Investment Report* (October 26, 1998).

Engen, Eric, Jane Gravelle, and Kent Smetters. "Dynamic Tax Models: Why They Do the Things They Do." Paper presented at the National Tax Association symposium, The Post-Election Agenda: Implementation or Confrontation? Arlington, Va. *National Tax Journal* 50, no. 3 (May 19-20, 1997): 657-82.

Engen, Eric M., and William G. Gale. "The Effects of Fundamental Tax Reform on Saving." In *Economic Effects of Fundamental Tax Reform,* edited by Henry J. Aaron and William G. Gale. Washington, D.C.: Brookings Institution, 1996.

Engen, Eric M., William G. Gale, and John Karl Scholz, "Do Saving Incentives Work?" *Brookings Papers on Economic Activity* 1 (1994): 85-180.

_____. "The Illusory Effects of Saving Incentives on Saving." *Journal of Economic Perspectives* 10, no. 4 (fall 1996): 113-38.

Even, William E., and David Macpherson. "Trends in Individual and Household Pension Coverage." Report submitted to the Department of Labor, contract no. 41USC252C3, February 1995.

Feenberg, Daniel, and James Poterba. "Income Inequality and the Incomes of Very High Income Taxpayers." In *Tax Policy and the Economy* 7, edited by James Poterba. Cambridge: MIT, 1993.

Feldstein, Martin. "Inflation, Tax Rules and the Accumulation of Residential and Nonresidential Capital." Working paper 753, National Bureau of Economic Research, Cambridge, Mass., September 1981.

_____. "Why Capital Gains Taxes Are Unfair." *Wall Street Journal,* November 21, 1994.

_____. "Behavioral Response to Tax Rates: Evidence from the Tax Reform Act of 1986." *American Economic Review* 85, no. 2 (May 1995): 170–74.

_____. "How Big Should Government Be?" *National Tax Journal* 50, no. 2 (June 1997): 197–213.

Feldstein, Martin, and Daniel Feenberg. "Higher Tax Rates with Little Revenue Gain: An Empirical Analysis of the Clinton Plan." *Tax Notes* 58, no. 12 (March 22, 1993): 1653–57.

Feldstein Martin, Joel Slemrod, and Shlomo Yitzhaki. "The Effects of Taxation on the Selling of Corporate Stock and the Realization of Capital Gains." *Quarterly Journal of Economics* 94, no. 4 (June 1980): 777–91.

"The Flat Tax: 'Nutty' It's Not." *Wall Street Journal,* February 22, 1996.

Fossedal, Gregory. "The American Dream." *Wall Street Journal,* February 14, 1997.

Frank, Robert. "Progressive Taxation and the Incentive Problem." Working paper series 98-4, Office of Tax Policy Research, Ann Arbor, Mich., February 1998, 4.

Friedman, Milton. *Capitalism and Freedom.* Chicago: University of Chicago Press, 1982 .

Gale, William G. "Building a Better Tax System: Can a Consumption Tax Deliver the Goods?" *Tax Notes* 69, no. 6 (November 6, 1995): 781–86.

_____. "The Kemp Commission and the Future of Tax Reform." *Tax Notes* 70, no. 6 (February 5, 1996): 717–29.

_____. "Will Tax Cuts Generate Much Economic Growth?" *Tax Notes* 72, no. 2 (July 8, 1996): 239.

_____. "The Effects of Pensions on Household Wealth: A Reevaluation of Theory and Evidence." *Journal of Political Economy* 106, no. 4 (1998): 706–23.

Gale, William G., and Kevin A. Hassett. "A Framework for Evaluating the Flat Tax." March 3, 1998. Mimeo.

Gale, William G., Scott Houser, and John Karl Scholz. "Distributional Effects of Fundamental Tax Reform." In *Economic Effects of Fundamental Tax Reform,* edited by Henry J. Aaron and William G. Gale. Washington, D.C.: Brookings Institution, 1996, 281–320.

Galvin, Charles O. "More on Boris Bittker and the Comprehensive Tax Base: The Practicality of Tax Reform and the ABA's CSTR." *Harvard Law Review* 81 (1968): 1016–31.

Gaston, Robert J., and Sharon Bell. *The Informal Supply of Capital.* Report submitted to the U.S. Small Business Administration Office of Advocacy, January 29, 1988.

Gideon, Kenneth W. Statement of assistant secretary (tax policy), Department of the Treasury, before the U. S. Senate Committee on Finance, March 6, 1990.

Gilder, George. *Wealth and Poverty.* New York: Basic Books, 1981.

Giving USA 1999. New York: AAFRC Trust for Philanthropy, 1999

Giving USA Update #2. New York: AAFRC Trust for Philanthropy, 1995.

Glenn, Heidi. "CBO Under Fire—The Politics and Economics of Capital Gains." *Tax Notes* 80, no. 7 (August 17, 1998): 757–59.

Goode, Richard. *The Individual Income Tax.* Washington, D.C.: Brookings Institution, 1976.

_____. "The Economic Definition of Income." In *Comprehensive Income Taxation*, edited by Joseph A. Pechman. Washington, D.C.: Brookings Institution, 1977, ch. 1.

Graetz, Michael J. "The Troubled Marriage of Retirement Security and Tax Policies." *University of Pennsylvania Law Review* 135 (1987): 851–908.

_____. *The Decline [and Fall?] of the Income Tax.* New York: W. W. Norton, 1997.

Gravelle, Jane G. *Can a Capital Gains Tax Cut Pay for Itself?* Congressional Research Service, Library of Congress, Report for Congress, March 23, 1990.

_____. "Behavioral Responses to Proposed High-Income Tax Rate Increases: An Evaluation of the Feldstein-Feenberg Study." *Tax Notes* 59, no. 8 (May 24, 1993): 1097–1102.

_____. *The Economic Effects of Taxing Capital Income.* Cambridge: MIT, 1994.

_____. *Effects of Flat Taxes and Other Proposals on Housing: Full Report.* Washington, D.C.: Congressional Research Service, 1996.

_____. *CRS Report for Congress: Capital Gains Taxes, Innovation and Growth.* January 28, 1999.

Gravelle, Jane G., and Lawrence B. Lindsey. "Capital Gains." Special report. *Tax Notes* 38, no. 4 (January 25, 1988): 397–405. Reproduced in *The Capital Gains Controversy: A Tax Analyst's Reader,* edited by J. Andrew Hoerner. Arlington, Va.: Tax Analysts, 1992, 17–24.

Green, Richard K., and Michelle J. White. "Measuring the Benefits of Homeowning: Effects on Children." Chicago: Center for the Study of the Economy and the State, 1994. Mimeo.

Haig, Robert M. *The Federal Income Tax.* New York: Columbia University Press, 1921.

Hall, Robert E. "Intertemporal Substitution in Consumption." *Journal of Political Economy* 96, no. 2 (1988): 339–57.

Hall, Robert E., and Alvin Rabushka. *Low Tax, Simple Tax, Flat Tax.* New York: McGraw-Hill, 1983.

_____. *The Flat Tax.* 2nd ed. Stanford: Hoover Institution Press, 1995.

Halperin, Daniel. "Interest in Disguise: Taxing the 'Time Value of Money.'" *Yale Law Journal* 95 (1986): 506–52.

Hamilton, Alexander. *The Founding of the Nation,* edited by Richard B. Morris. New York: Dial, 1957.

Harbaugh, William H., ed. *The Writings of Theodore Roosevelt.* Indianapolis: Bobbs-Merrill, 1967.

Harberger, Arnold C. "The Incidence of the Corporation Income Tax." *Journal of Political Economy* 70 (1962): 215–40.

Hendershott, Patric. "Government Policies and the Allocation of Capital Between Residential and Industrial Uses." Working paper 1036, National Bureau of Economic Research, Cambridge, Mass., December 1982.

_____. "Comments on Social Returns to Housing and Other Fixed Capital." *AREUEA Journal* 17, no. 2 (1989): 213–17.

Henderson, Yolanda K. "Capital Gains Taxation and the Cost of Capital for Mature and Emerging Corporations." Paper prepared for the American Council for Capital Formation Conference on Saving—The Challenge for the U.S. Economy, October 11–13, 1989.

Hoerner, J. Andrew. "Tax Incentives for Capital and Economic Growth: A Critique." *Tax Notes* 48, no. 7 (August 13, 1990): 813–21.

Hoerner, J. Andrew, ed. *The Capital Gains Controversy: A Tax Analyst's Reader.* Arlington, Va.: Tax Analysts, 1992.

Holik, Dan, Susan Hostetter, and John Labate. "1985 Sales of Capital Assets." Paper presented at the 150th Annual Meeting of the American Statistical Association, Washington, D.C., August 6–10, 1989.

Hubbard, Glenn R., and Jonathan S. Skinner. "Assessing the Effectiveness of Saving Incentives." *Journal of Economic Perspectives* 10, no. 4 (fall 1996): 73–90.

Hughes, Jonathan. *American Economic History.* Glenview, Ill.: Scott, Foresman, 1983.

Huntington, Samuel P. *American Politics: The Promise of Disharmony.* Cambridge: Harvard University Press 1981.

Hyde v. Continental Trust Company 157 U.S. 429 (1895), rehearing 158 U.S. 601 (1895).

Internal Revenue Service. *Income Tax Compliance Research: Net Tax Gap and Remittance Tax Gap Estimates.* Publication 1415 (4–90)(supplement to publication 7285). Washington, D.C.: IRS, April 1990, table 1.

_____. *Statistics of Income—1977: Individual Income Tax Returns.* Washington, D.C.: IRS, 1980.

_____. *Statistics of Income—1997: Individual Income Tax Returns.* Washington, D.C.: IRS, 1999.

Jenkins, J., J. Pickle, Beryl Anthony, Ronnie G. Flippo, Andrew Jacobs Jr., and Michael Andrews, representatives. "Fact Sheet: Why 'Jenkins-Archer' Without Amendment." Report of September 9, 1989, released under cover letter dated September 22, 1989.

Jerry A. Hausman. "Labor Supply." In *How Taxes Affect Economic Behavior,* edited by Henry J. Aaron and Joseph A. Pechman. Washington, D.C.: Brookings Institution, 1981.

Joint Center for Housing Studies. *The State of the Nation's Housing 1995.* Cambridge: Harvard University Press, 1995.

_____. *The State of the Nation's Housing 1997.* Cambridge: Harvard University Press, 1997.

Joint Committee on Taxation. *Explanation of Methodology Used to Estimate Proposals Affecting the Taxation of Income from Capital Gains.* JCT–12–90. Washington, D.C.: GPO, March, 27, 1990.

_____. *Tax Modeling Project and 1997 Symposium Papers.* JCS–21–97. Washington, D.C.: GPO, November 20, 1997.

_____. *Estimates of Federal Tax Expenditures for Fiscal Years 2000–2004.* JCS–13–99. Washington, D.C.: GPO, 1999.

Jorgenson, Dale W. "Reconstructing the Agenda for U.S. Tax Reform." Paper prepared for the House Republican Conference, Washington, D.C., August 11, 1993.

_____. "The Economic Impact of Fundamental Tax Reform." In *Frontiers of Tax Reform,* edited by Michael Boskin. Stanford: Hoover Institute, 1996.

Jorgenson, Dale W., and Kun-Young Yun. "The Excess Burden of Taxation in the United States." *Journal of Accounting, Auditing & Finance* 6, no. 4 (fall 1991): 487–509.

Kaldor, Nicholas. *An Expenditure Tax*. London: Allen and Unwin, 1955, 70.

Kaplow, Louis. "Comments." In William D. Andrews and David F. Bradford, "Savings Incentives in a Hybrid Income Tax." In *Uneasy Compromise: Problems of a Hybrid Income-Consumption Tax*, edited by Henry J. Aaron, Harvey Galper, and Joseph A. Pechman. Washington, D.C.: Brookings Institution, 1988, 300–08.

_____. "Horizontal Equity: Measures in Search of a Principle." *National Tax Journal* 42, no. 2 (June 1989): 139–54.

Kennedy, John F. "Special Message to the Congress on Tax Reduction and Reform." January 24, 1963.

Kennickell, Arthur B., Douglas A. McManus, and R. Louise Woodburn. "Weighting Design for the 1992 Survey of Consumer Finances." Study released March 11, 1996.

Kennickell, Arthur B., Martha Starr-McCluer, and Annika E. Sunden. "Family Finances in the U.S.: Recent Evidence from the Survey of Consumer Finances." *Federal Reserve Bulletin* (January 1997): 1–24.

Killingsworth, Mark. *Labor Supply*. Cambridge: Cambridge University Press, 1983.

Kinsley, Michael. "Angel of Death Loophole." *New Republic* (July 13, 1997): 4.

Kotlikoff, Lawrence J. *What Determines Saving?* Cambridge: MIT, 1989.

_____. "The Crisis in U.S. Saving and Proposals to Address the Crisis." *National Tax Journal* 43, no. 3 (September 1990): 223–46.

_____. "Saving and Consumption Taxation: The Federal Retail Sales Tax Example." In *Frontiers of Tax Reform*, edited by Michael J. Boskin. Stanford: Hoover Institution, 1996.

Kraft, Joseph. "Power to Destroy." *Washington Post*, December 7, 1969.

Kristol, Irving. "About Inequality." *Commentary* 57 (1957): 41–47.

Laidler, David. "Income Tax Incentives for Owner-Occupied Housing." In *The Taxation of Income from Capital*, edited by Arnold Harberger and Martin J. Bailey. Washington, D.C.: Brookings Institution, 1969, 51–76.

Lee, John. "Capital Gains Myths." *Tax Notes* 67, no. 6 (May 8, 1995): 809–20.

Leff, Mark H. *The Limits of Symbolic Reform: The New Deal and Taxation, 1933–1939*. Cambridge: Cambridge University Press, 1984.

Lenzner, Robert, and Stephen S. Johnson. "Seeing Things as They Really Are." *Forbes* 10 (March 1997): 122–28.

Lindsey, Lawrence B. "Capital Gains Rates, Revenues, and Realizations." In *Taxes and Capital Formation*, edited by Martin Feldstein. Boston: National Bureau of Economic Research, 1987.

_____. *The Growth Experiment*. New York: Basic Books, 1990.

Lyons, Louis. "Consumption Tax Would Spur Growth, Witnesses Tell Ways and Means." *Tax Notes* 71, no. 1 (April 1, 1996): 14–16.

MaCurdy, Thomas, David Green, and Harry Paarsch. "Assessing Empirical Approaches for Analyzing Taxes and Labor Supply." *Journal of Human Resources* 25 (1990): 415–90.

Madison, James. "The Federalist No. 10." In *The Federalist*, edited by Jacob E. Cooke. Middletown: Wesleyan University, 1961.

Malone, Dumas. *Jefferson the Virginian*. Boston: Little, Brown, 1948.

Manvel, Allen D. "Another Look at Tax Preference Costs." *Tax Notes* 59, no. 5 (May 3, 1993): 705–7.

McDaniel, Paul R., and James R. Repetti. "Horizontal and Vertical Equity: The Musgrave/Kaplow Exchange." *Florida Tax Review* 1, no. 10 (1993): 607–22.

McGee, M. Kevin. "Capital Gains Taxation and New Firm Investment." *National Tax Journal* 51, no. 4 (December 1998): 653–73.

McIntyre, Robert S. Citizens for Tax Justice director's Testimony before the House Ways and Means Committee, January 25, 1995, 5.

Mellon, Andrew. *Taxation: The People's Business.* New York: Macmillan, 1924.

Mendoza, Enrique G., Assaf Razin, and Linda L. Tesar. "Effective Tax Rates in Macroeconomics: Cross-Country Estimates of Tax Rates on Factor Incomes and Consumption." *Journal of Monetary Economics* 34, no. 2 (December 1994): 297–324.

Merrill, Peter, Ken Wertz, and Svetank Shah. "Corporate Tax Liability Under the USA and Flat Taxes." *Tax Notes* 68, no. 6 (August 7, 1995): 741–45.

Mills, Edwin S. "Social Returns to Housing and Other Fixed Capital." *AREUEA Journal* 17, no. 2 (1989): 197–211.

Minarik, Joseph J. *Making Tax Choices.* Washington, D.C.: Urban Institute Press, 1985.

Mroz, Thomas. "The Sensitivity of an Empirical Model of Married Women's Hours of Work to Economic and Statistical Assumptions." *Econometrica* 55 (1987): 765–800.

Munnell, Alicia H. "Current Taxation of Qualified Pension Plans: Has the Time Come?" *New England Economic Review* (March/April 1992): 12–24.

Murray, Charles. "Americans Remain Wary of Washington." *Wall Street Journal,* December 23, 1997.

Musgrave, Richard A. *The Theory of Public Finance.* New York: McGraw Hill, 1959, ch. 1.

_____. "In Defense of an Income Concept." *Harvard Law Review* 81 (1967–1968): 44–62.

_____. "Horizontal Equity, Once More." *National Tax Journal* 43, no. 2 (1990): 113–22.

_____. "Clarifying Tax Reform." *Tax Notes* 70, no. 6 (February 5, 1996): 731–36.

Musgrave Richard A., and Peggy B. Musgrave. *Public Finance in Theory and Practice.* 4th ed. New York: McGraw-Hill, 1984.

National Association of Home Builders, Economics, Mortgage Finance and Housing Policy Division. *The Impacts of the Tax Reform Act of 1986: An Overview.* Washington, D.C.: NAHB, September 10, 1986.

National Housing Task Force. *A Decent Place to Live.* Washington, D.C.: NHTF, March 1988, 1–64.

National Taxpayers Union Foundation. *Capital Ideas* 6, no. 1 (March/April 1998): 1–2.

New York State Bar Association, Tax Section. Tax Report #662, June 27, 1990, with cover letter dated June 28, 1990, from Arthur A. Feder.

Okun, Arthur M. *Equality and Efficiency.* Washington, D.C.: Brookings Institution, 1975.

Passell, Peter. "Economic Scene." *New York Times,* March 28, 1996.

_____. "The Tax Code Heads into the Operating Room." *New York Times,* September 3, 1999.

Paul, Randolph E. *Taxation for Prosperity.* Indianapolis: Bobbs-Merrill, 1947.

Pechman, Joseph A. "Comprehensive Income Taxation: A Comment." *Harvard Law Review* 81 (1967–1968): 63–67.

_____. *Federal Tax Policy*. 5th ed. Washington, D.C.: Brookings Institution, 1987.

_____. *Tax Reform: The Rich and the Poor*. 2nd ed. Washington, D.C.: Brookings Institution, 1989.

Penner, Rudolph G. "The Future of Tax Reform." In *National Tax Association—Tax Institute of America: Proceedings of the Eighty-second Annual Conference*. Columbus, Ohio: National Tax Association, 1989.

Phillips, Kevin. *The Politics of Rich and Poor*. New York: Random House, 1990.

Pollock, Sheldon D. *The Failure of U.S. Tax Policy*. University Park: Pennsylvania State University Press, 1996.

Pollock v. Farmers' Loan and Trust Company. 157 U.S. 429 (1895), rehearing 158 U.S. 601 (1895).

Poterba, James M. "Capital Gains Tax Policy Toward Entrepreneurship." *National Tax Journal* 42, no. 3 (September 1989): 375–89.

Poterba, James M., Steven F. Venti, and David A. Wise. "How Retirement Saving Programs Increase Saving." *Journal of Economic Perspectives* 10, no. 4 (fall 1996): 91–112.

"Presentation Ceremony for the Minority Enterprise Development Week Awards, October 4, 1989." *Weekly Compilation of Presidential Documents* 25, no. 40 (October 9, 1989): 1503.

Price Waterhouse and Caplin & Drysdale. *Impact of Tax Restructuring on Tax-Exempt Organizations*. Washington, D.C.: 1997.

Ratner, Sidney. *Taxation and Democracy in America*. New York: Octagon Books, 1980.

Rawls, John. *A Theory of Justice*. Cambridge: Harvard University Press, 1971.

Reagan, Ronald. *The President's Tax Proposals to the Congress for Fairness, Growth, and Simplicity*. Washington, D.C: GPO, May 1985.

Repetti, James R. "The Use of Tax Law to Stabilize the Stock Market: The Efficacy of Holding Period Requirements." *Virginia Tax Review* 8, no. 3 (winter 1989): 591–637.

_____. "Management Incentives, Needless Tax Complexity, and Capital Gains." *Tax Notes* 75, no. 7 (May 19, 1997): 981–91.

"Republic of Taxes: When Uncle Sam Takes, Do Americans Give?" *Philanthropy* 11, no. 2 (spring 1997): 12–15.

Research Institute of America. "RIA's Analysis of Federal Taxes: Income." *Weekly Alert*, June 10, 1993.

Rich, Spencer. "Caught in the Pinch of a Pension Predicament." *Washington Post*, November 25, 1996.

Rohe, William M., and Michael A. Stegman. "The Impact of Homeownership on the Social and Political Involvement of Low-Income People." *Urban Affairs Quarterly* 30, no. 1 (September 1994): 152–72.

Roosevelt, Franklin D. "A Message to the Congress on Tax Revision." In *The Public Papers and Addresses of Franklin D. Roosevelt*, vol. 4, *The Court Disapproves, 1935*. New York: Random House, 1938, 270–77.

_____. "In 1776 the Fight Was for Democracy in Taxation. In 1936 That Is Still the Fight." In *The Public Papers and Addresses of Franklin D. Roosevelt*, vol. 5, *The People Approve, 1936*. New York: Random House, 1938, 522–29.

Salisbury, Dallas L., and Nora Super Jones, eds. *Pension Funding & Taxation: Implications for Tomorrow.* Washington, D.C.: Employee Benefit Research Institute, 1994.

San Jose Mercury News. September 13, 1992.

Senate Budget Committee. *Tax Expenditures: Relationships to Spending Programs and Background Material on Individual Provisions.* 99th Cong., 2d sess., S. Prt. 99–159, June 1986, 155–61.

Shapiro, Robert J. *Why Fairness Matters: Progressive Versus Flat Taxes.* Washington, D.C.: Progressive Foundation, 1996.

Shaviro, Daniel N. "Effective Marginal Tax Rates on Low-Income Households." *Tax Notes* 84, no. 7 (August 23, 1999): 1191–1201.

Simons, Henry C. *Personal Income Taxation: The Definition of Income as a Problem of Fiscal Policy.* Chicago: University of Chicago Press, 1938.

Sinai, Alle. Testimony presented to the Senate Small Business Committee, October 2, 1990. Reprinted in *The Capital Gains Controversy: A Tax Analysts Reader,* edited by J. Andrew Hoerner. Arlington, Va.: Tax Analysts, 1992, 227–34.

Skinner, Jonathan. "The Dynamic Efficiency Cost of Not Taxing Housing." *Journal of Public Economics* 59 (1996): 397–415.

Slemrod, Joel B. "On the High-Income Laffer Curve." In *Tax Progressivity and Income Inequality,* edited by Joel Slemrod. New York: Cambridge University Press, 1994.

_____. "Income Creation or Income Shifting? Behavioral Responses to the Tax Reform Act of 1986." *American Economic Review* 85, no. 2 (May 1995): 175–80.

Slemrod, Joel B., ed. *Do Taxes Matter? The Impact of the Tax Reform Act of 1986.* Cambridge: MIT, 1990.

_____. *Tax Progressivity and Income Inequality.* Cambridge: Cambridge University Press 1994.

Slemrod, Joel, and Alan J. Auerbach. "The Economic Effects of the Tax Reform Act of 1986." *Journal of Economic Literature* 35 (June 1997): 589–632.

Slemrod, Joel B., and Jon Bakija. *Taxing Ourselves.* 2nd ed. Cambridge: MIT, 2000.

Smith, Adam. *The Wealth of Nations,* edited by Edward Cannan. New York: Modern Library, 1937.

_____. *An Inquiry into the Nature and Causes of the Wealth of Nations.* Vol. 2, edited by R. H. Campbell and A. S. Skinner. Indianapolis: Liberty Classics, 1981.

Smith, James T. *Federal Tax Reform.* New York: McGraw Hill, 1961.

Social Security Administration. *Income of the Population 55 or Older, 1996.* SSA publication 13–11871, April 1998, tables V.C.2, v.A.4, and vii.5.

Standard & Poor's DRI. "Capital Gains Taxes and the Economy: A Retrospective Look." Paper prepared for the American Council for Capital Formation, Center for Policy Research, Washington, D.C., July 1999.

Stern, Philip M. *The Rape of the Taxpayer.* New York: Random House, 1973.

Steuerle, C. Eugene. "The Conservative Case for Progressive Taxation." *Tax Notes* 52, no. 2 (July 15, 1991): 359–60.

_____. "The New Tax Cut Debate: Second of Two Parts: Economic Effects." *Tax Notes* 53, no. 11 (December 16, 1991): 1313–14.

_____. *The Tax Decade.* Washington, D.C.: Urban Institute Press, 1992.

_____. "The Capital Gains Debate That Wasn't." *Tax Notes* 70, no. 5 (January 29, 1996): 603–04.

_____. "The Simple Arithmetic of Flat Taxes." *Tax Notes* 70, no. 8 (February 19, 1996): 1041–42.

_____. "Tax Reform and Private Pensions." *Tax Notes* 70, no. 13 (March 18, 1996): 1693–94.

Stiglitz, Joseph E. *Economics of the Public Sector.* 2nd ed. New York: W. W. Norton, 1988.

Stokeld, Fred. "Charities Fear Loss of Deduction Under Flat Tax Proposals." *Tax Notes* 70, no. 8 (February 19, 1996): 935–38.

Summers, Lawrence H. "An Evaluation of the Flat Tax." Speech delivered by Deputy Secretary of the Treasury Summers at the Brookings Institution, Washington, D.C., February 16, 1996. Reprinted in *Tax Notes* 70, no. 12 (March 11, 1996): 1555–60.

Sunley, Emil M., Jr. "Employee Benefits and Transfer Payments." In *Comprehensive Income Taxation,* edited by Joseph A. Pechman. Washington, D.C.: Brookings Institution, 1977, 75–114.

Surrey, Stanley S., and Paul R. McDaniel. *Tax Expenditures.* Cambridge: Harvard University Press, 1985.

Taylor, John B. "Supply Side: The Whole Story." *New York Times,* October 15, 1996.

Triest, Robert K. "The Efficiency Cost of Increased Progressivity." In *Tax Progressivity and Income Inequality,* edited by Joel B. Slemrod. Cambridge: Cambridge University Press, 1994, 137–69.

Tritch, Teresa. "Your Taxes." *Money Magazine,* March 1997, 81–6.

"The Unsheltered Life." *U.S. News & World Report,* November 11, 1996, 29–33.

U.S. Census Bureau. *Asset Ownership of Households: 1993.* Report by T. J. Eller and Wallace Fraser. Current Population Reports P70-47, August 1995.

_____. "Who Can Afford to Buy a House in 1993?" Report by Howard Savage. *Current Housing Report Series* H121/97-1, 1997.

U.S. Congress, Joint Committee on Taxation. *Explanation of Methodology Used to Estimate Proposals Affecting the Taxation of Income from Capital Gains.* Washington, D. C.: Government Printing Office, March 27, 1990.

U.S. Department of Commerce, Bureau of Economic Analysis. *Personal Saving Rate.* http://www.bea.doc.gov/bea/dn/saverate.htm, February 17, 2000.

U.S. Department of Labor. *Retirement Benefits of American Workers: New Findings from the September 1994 Current Population Survey.* Washington, D.C.: GPO, 1995.

U.S. Department of Labor, Bureau of Labor Statistics. *Handbook of Labor Statistics.* Bulletin 2340, August 1989.

_____. "Current Population Survey." Unpublished report, March 1997.

_____. *Employer Costs for Employee Compensation, 1986–97.* Bulletin 2505, August 1998, tables 5 and 137.

U.S. Department of Labor, Pension and Welfare Benefits Administration. "Pension Availability and Coverage in Small and Large Firms." Report by Jules H. Lichtenstein. In *Trends in Pensions 1992,* edited by John A. Turner and Daniel J. Beller. Washington, D.C.: GPO, 1992, 97–117.

U.S. Department of Labor, Social Security Administration, U.S. Small Business Administration, and Pension Benefit Guaranty Corporation. *Pension and Health Ben-*

efits of American Workers: New Findings from the April 1993 Current Population Survey. Washington, D.C.: GPO, May 1994.

U.S. Department of the Treasury. *Tax Reform for Fairness, Simplicity, and Economic Growth.* Vol. 1. Washington, D.C.: Treasury Department, November 1984.

U.S. Department of the Treasury, Office of Tax Analysis. "Estimation and Interpretation of Capital Gains Realization Behavior: Evidence from Panel Data." Report by Gerald E. Auten, Leonard E. Burman, and William C. Randolph. OTA Paper 67, May 1989.

_____. "Income Shifting in Response to Higher Tax Rates: The Effects of OBRA 93." Report by Ann D. Parcell for Allied Social Science Associations Meetings, San Francisco, Calif., January 5–7, 1995.

_____. "'New' Armey-Shelby Flat Tax Would Still Lose Money, Treasury Finds." *Tax Notes* 70, no. 4 (January 22, 1996): 451–61.

_____. "Distributional Effects of Recent Tax Reform Proposals." Report by Julie-Anne Cronin, James Nunns, and Eric Toder, November 1996. Distributed on request.

_____. "The Effect of Income Taxes on Household Behavior." Report by Gerald Auten and Robert Carroll, April 1997.

_____. "Assessing Marriage Penalties and Bonuses." Report by Nicholas Bull, Janet Holtzblatt, James R. Nunns, and Robert Rebelein for the National Tax Association Proceedings, Ninety-first Annual Conference on Taxation, Austin, Tex., November 8–10, 1998, 327–40.

U.S. House, Rept. 5, 63 Cong., 1st sess., 1913. Reprinted in *U.S. Bureau of Internal Revenue Bulletin, Cumulative Bulletin 1939–1* pt. 2, January-June 1939.

U.S. House Committee on Ways and Means. *Background Materials on Federal Budget and Tax Policy for Fiscal Year 1991 and Beyond.* Report by staff. Washington, D.C.: GPO, February 1990.

U.S. House Report accompanying Taxpayer Relief Act of 1997. See *RIA's Complete Analysis of the Taxpayer Relief Act of 1997.* New York: Research Institute of America, 1997.

U.S. Senate Committee on the Budget. *Tax Expenditures: Relationship to Spending Programs and Background Material on Individual Provisions.* Washington, D.C.: GPO, June 1986.

Walzer, Michael. "In Defense of Equality." In *The New Conservative: A Critique from the Left,* edited by Louis Coser and Irving Howe. New York: Quadrangle, 1973, 107–23.

Wanniski, Jude. "The principal source of our country's difficulties." *Wall Street Journal,* May 11, 1993.

Wattenberg, Ben. "Tax Philosophy: An Interview with Barber Conable and Joseph Pechman." *Public Opinion* 8, no. 1 (February/March 1985): 2–7, 59–60.

Wayne, Leslie. "Flat Tax Goes from 'Snake Oil' to G.O.P. Tonic." *New York Times,* November 1999, 14, 23.

Webber, Carolyn, and Aaron Wildavsky. *A History of Taxation and Expenditure in the Western World.* New York: Simon & Schuster, 1986.

Witte, John F. *The Politics and Development of the Federal Income Tax.* Madison: University of Wisconsin Press, 1985.

Wolff, Edward N. "Who Are the Rich? A Demographic Profile of High-Income and High-Wealth Americans." Working paper series 98-6, Office of Tax Policy Research, University of Michigan Business School, September 1997.

Zelenak, Lawrence. "Flat Tax vs. VAT: Progressivity and Family Allowances." *Tax Notes* 69, no. 9 (November 27, 1995): 1129-34.

Zodrow, George R. "Economic Analyses of Capital Gains Taxation: Realizations, Revenues, Efficiency and Equity." *Tax Law Review* 48, no. 3 (1993): 422-527.

Index